PORTUGUESE SYNTAX

OXFORD STUDIES IN COMPARATIVE SYNTAX
Richard Kayne, General Editor

Principles and Parameters of Syntactic Saturation
Gert Webelhuth

Verb Movement and Expletive Subjects in the Germanic Languages
Sten Vikner

Parameters and Functional Heads: Essays in Comparative Syntax
Edited by Adriana Belletti and Luigi Rizzi

Discourse Configurational Languages
Edited by Katalin E. Kiss

Clause Structure and Language Change
Edited by Adrian Battye and Ian Roberts

Dialect Variation and Parameter Setting: A Study of Belfast English and Standard English
Alison Henry

Parameters of Slavic Morphosyntax
Steven Franks

Particles: On the Syntax of Verb-Particle, Triadic, and Causative Constructions
Marcel den Dikken

The Polysynthesis Parameter
Mark C. Baker

The Role of Inflection in Scandinavian Syntax
Anders Holmberg and Christer Platzack

Clause Structure and Word Order in Hebrew and Arabic: An Essay in Comparative Semitic Syntax
Ur Shlonsky

Negation and Clausal Structure: A Comparative Study of Romance Languages
Raffaella Zanuttini

Tense and Aspect: From Semantics to Morphosyntax
Alessandra Giorgi and Fabio Pianesi

Coordination
Janne Bondi Johannessen

Adverbs and Functional Heads: A Cross-Linguistic Perspective
Guglielmo Cinque

A Handbook of Slavic Clitics
Steven Franks and Tracy Holloway King

XP-Adjunction in Universal Grammar: Scrambling and Binding in Hindi-Urdu
Ayesha Kidwai

Multiple Feature Checking and Grammatical Functions in Universal Grammar
Hiroyuki Ura

Portuguese Syntax: New Comparative Studies
Edited by João Costa

Portuguese Syntax

New Comparative Studies

Edited by
João Costa

OXFORD
UNIVERSITY PRESS

2000

OXFORD

UNIVERSITY PRESS

Oxford   New York
Athens   Auckland   Bangkok   Bogotá   Buenos Aires   Calcutta
Capte Town   Chennai   Dar es Salaam   Delhi   Florence   Hong Kong   Istanbul
Karachi   Kuala Lumpur   Madrid   Melbourne   Mexico City   Mumbai
Nairobi   Paris   São Paulo   Shanghai   Singapore   Taipei   Tokyo   Toronto   Warsaw

and associated companies in
Berlin   Ibadan

Copyright © 2000 by Oxford University Press, Inc.

Published by Oxford University Press, Inc.
198 Madison Avenue, New York, New York 10016

Oxford is a registered trademark of Oxford University Press

Library of Congress Cataloging-in-Publication Data
Portuguese syntax : new comparative studies / Edited by João Costa.
p. cm.— (Oxford studies in comparative syntax)
Includes bibliographical references and index.
ISBN 0-19-512575-4—ISBN 0-19-512576-2
(pbk.)
1. Portuguese language—Syntax. I. Costa, João, 1972–
II. Series.
PC5201.P67   1999
469.5—dc21   99-28002

1 3 5 7 9 8 6 4 2

Printed in the United States of America
on acid-free paper

CONTENTS

PORTUGUESE SYNTAX

Introduction

This collection of essays brings together a number of studies dealing with aspects of Portuguese syntax within the Principles and Parameters framework (Chomsky and Lasnik 1993) and its extension known as the Minimalist Program (Chomsky 1995). According to this framework, explanatory adequacy in the description of languages may be attained by determining the universal language-independent principles that govern the shape of natural languages rather than by postulating language-specific and construction-specific rules for describing isolated phenomena. Language variation is explained by a minimal set of parameters, with different values specified for different languages. Under the Minimalist Program, it is explicitly proposed that language-specific variation may be a consequence of morphological variation reflected in the syntax.[1]

Most chapters in this volume address theoretical issues raised by this line of inquiry: the authors seek an explanation for specific constructions of Portuguese, which both follows from universal principles made available by the theory and shows why the same options are not employed in other languages. By compiling these studies in one volume, we want to present a systematic overview of different scholars' ideas on related topics on the syntax of Portuguese. We also hope to enlarge the empirical scope of modern comparative syntax by showing the specificity of Portuguese for crucial issues in language variation research, such as V-movement, richness of inflection, and functional clausal structure. In this introduction, I present a brief summary of each chapter, emphasizing where they differ and how they relate to each other.

The exceptional properties of Portuguese clitic placement have long been a puzzle to Romance linguistics. It is therefore not surprising that five of the nine chapters are about clitics. The specificity of Portuguese with respect to clitic placement has to do with the fact that Portuguese (together with Galician; see Uriagereka 1995) clitics may appear in enclitic position in finite tensed clauses:

Portuguese:
(1)   A Maria viu-o.
      the Maria saw him(ACC)
      'Maria saw him.'

In this respect, Portuguese (and Western Romance) differs from other Romance languages, such as French (cf. (2)) or Spanish (cf. (3)):

French:
(2)   Marie l'a vu.
      Marie him(ACC) has seen
      'Marie saw him.'

Spanish:
(3)   Maria lo vio.
      Maria him(ACC) saw
      'Maria saw him.'

Concerning the right analysis of clitic placement, all authors in this volume share the assumption in (4):[2]

(4)   The distribution of clitics may not be explained by morphophonology alone. Syntax is relevant for explaining the distribution of clitics.

No author proposes ignoring the morphophonological factors involved in the behavior of clitics (we will see that Barbosa and Duarte and Matos incorporate some of these aspects in their analysis). The main insight of (4) is the observation that clitics move in a way parallel to head movement in general (Baker 1988; Kayne 1991), obeying syntactic constraints on movement. For proving this hypothesis true, several questions must be answered; some of them are listed in (5):

(5)   a. If syntax is the key factor in the distribution of clitics, how does clitic placement relate to other syntactic phenomena?

      b. If clitics move, where do they move to? Do they adjoin to a functional projection, or do they adjoin to the lexical verb?

      c. If clitics move, what is the trigger for their movement? Does it correlate with specificity (Corver and Delfitto 1993; Uriagereka 1995)? If so, can we conclude anything concerning configurational meaning?

      d. If they adjoin to an inflectional head, how does that correlate with richness of inflection?

      e. What can the syntax of clitic placement tell us about the clausal structure of the language?

f. How are clitics syntactically different from other pronominal elements?

g. Portuguese allows proclisis and enclisis: is one syntactically derived from the other? If so, which is the basic one?

h. What do we learn about the interface morphophonology/syntax from the behavior of clitics?

Crucially, even those chapters that are not about clitics make claims with consequences for the analyses proposed by the several authors.

Following Kayne (1991), several authors argue for a correlation between clitic placement and V-movement: under this type of analysis, cliticization occurs at the inflectional level, either as adjunction to a functional projection, as in the oversimplified representation in (6), or as a consequence of the verb moving to a functional projection past a clitic (enclisis, schematically represented in (7a)) or not moving to a functional projection higher than the clitic (resulting in proclisis, as in (7b)):

(6)

$$
\begin{array}{c}
FP \\
\diagup\diagdown \\
F' \\
\diagup\diagdown \\
F \quad \dots \\
\diagup\diagdown \quad t_{Cl} \\
Cl \quad F
\end{array}
$$

(7)

a
$$
\begin{array}{c}
F' \\
\diagup\diagdown \\
F \quad XP \\
\diagup\diagdown \quad \diagup\diagdown \\
V \quad F \quad Cl \dots
\end{array}
$$

b
$$
\begin{array}{c}
F' \\
\diagup\diagdown \\
F \quad XP \\
\diagup\diagdown \\
Cl \quad \dots \\
\quad V
\end{array}
$$

The first type of analysis is advocated by Raposo, who proposes that cliticization comes about via left-adjunction of the clitic to a functional head (the head of FP). Raposo further proposes that the verb in Portuguese is always at the same projection independently of enclisis or proclisis. He derives the difference between enclisis and proclisis in terms of whether the verb moves to the head position or to the specifier of the functional projection. This chapter makes the interesting theoretical contribution of extending the main ideas of Chomsky (1994) concerning phrase structure theory. Raposo points out that moving heads to specifiers is a structure-preserving transformation, provided that a null form *pro* occupies this position. The specificity of *pro* as a host for adjoined clitics follows from its properties as both minimal and maximal category: as a maximal category, it may be generated in the specifier position of the functional head; as a minimal category, it may head-adjoin.

Raposo argues for his analysis on the basis of the distribution of finite verbal forms with different types of subjects. From an examination of the readings permitted by SE (reciprocal versus nonreciprocal), he concludes that some postverbal subjects must be analyzed as sitting in Spec, IP, which implies that finite verbal forms are in a higher functional projection.

Raposo's chapter raises the question of why the verb must move to the specifier of the functional projection only when this position is occupied by an empty pronominal. Raposo proposes that this is a consequence of F having to be licensed by overt material in its specifier. This kind of principle is reminiscent of the type of phonological constraint used by Barbosa to derive enclisis.

Barbosa's chapter shares with Raposo's the observation that the syntax of subjects and the syntax of clitics are related to each other. However, these authors' conclusions differ: Barbosa proposes that subjects in Portuguese are never in Spec, IP. Instead, they are left-dislocated, being adjoined to CP. In favor of this analysis, she observes that proclisis triggers are elements that in languages like Italian must be independently analyzed as left-dislocated, hence adjoined to CP. Further, she notes that proclisis triggers may not undergo such an analysis even in Italian, where it is easy to correlate movement versus base-generation in CP-adjunction with the obligatoriness of clitic doubling. Her observation is that Italian left-dislocated elements, which following Cinque (1990) she analyses as base adjoined in adjunction to CP, are those elements that in Portuguese appear in enclisis context. On the other hand, elements that in Italian undergo what Cinque calls *Focus-movement* and display *wh*-movement properties are those that trigger proclisis in Portuguese. This observation leads Barbosa to suggest that patterns of cliticization are closely related to the Null Subject Parameter: enclisis is triggered by a prosodic constraint preventing clitics from appearing at the onset of an Intonational Phrase. Assuming a prosody/syntax mapping telling that elements adjoined to CP are not to be included in the same Intonational Phrase, all sequences Cl-V will be barred at the phonological component if the clitic is initial. In cases of movement to Spec, CP, the clitic in Cl-V order will not be the initial element; hence, this construction is not barred at PF. The relation between this analysis and the Null Subject Parameter is important: if Spec, IP needed to be filled in, in sequences of the type *Subject-Cl-V*, the subject would be the initial overt material in the Intonational Phrase. When Spec, IP is occupied by *pro*, the clitic has to follow the verb.

From a comparative perspective, Barbosa shows that the hypothesis that preverbal subjects in Null Subject Languages are left-dislocated or A-bar moved has explanatory force beyond the cliticization facts of European Portuguese. She shows that the same hypothesis may account for apparently unrelated phenomena, such as the distribution of subject clitics in Nothern Italian dialects, *en/ne*-cliticization in French, Italian, and Catalan, and restrictions on bound variable interpretation of overt elements.

Barbosa's contribution is important for the light it sheds on several of the questions raised in (5): it shows the correlation between cliticization and other syntactic phenomena, it relates richness of inflection (strength of inflectional features as far as the Extended Projection Principle is concerned) with cliticization, and it makes an explicit proposal for the way syntax and phonology interact in the distribution of clitics.

Barbosa criticizes an alternative view on the distribution of subjects that relates several A-positions with different discourse functions. This is the position defended in my contribution. I investigate possible word orders and distribution of arguments in Portuguese and show that Portuguese qualifies as a discourse-configurational language. As far as subjects are concerned, I argue that there are three positions for subjects in Portuguese: Spec, VP when the subjects are focused, Spec, IP, for unfocused definite subjects, and left-dislocated position for unfocused indefinite subjects. My argument for these positions is based on the distribution of adverbs, on asymmetries with respect to extraction of *wh*-elements across different types of subjects, on co-occurrence of postverbal subjects and overt pronouns, and on position of subjects with respect to complements. Although it is not fully compatible with the claims put forward in Barbosa's chapter, this discussion of subjects makes it possible to think of a way of making Barbosa's and Raposo's observations on subjects compatible, since under this description both Spec, IP and the left-dislocated position are available, though for different types of subjects.

I also look at the distribution of objects, concluding that objects scramble in Portuguese, as in Germanic languages for defocusing purposes. My contribution is influenced by the works of Zubizarreta (1994) and Reinhart (1995), who claim that syntactic operations may be prosodically motivated. Following their suggestions, I suggest that for analyzing the pattern I describe, a theory of markedness is necessary. Such a theory must determine unmarked specifications for subject and object concerning values for definiteness and information structure, so the other values may be derived from this one, yielding marked syntactic configurations. Under such a theory, it is predicted that arguments appear in their canonical position when the unmarked values for definiteness and information structure are met.

My chapter contributes to the overall discussion in this volume concerning the syntax of subjects and the relevance of discourse configurationality for Portuguese syntax. In Portuguese, discourse functions are encoded in different word orders, a fact that has to be captured by the grammar. The chapter argues for the codification in prosodic terms, while Raposo claims that functional projections may be related to given discourse functions. This chapter also takes a position on the notion of markedness, which is shared by Duarte and Matos: knowing the unmarked specification of the elements involved in a word order (in the latter chapter, the unmarked specification for clitic placement) is an important starting point for the analysis of syntactic phenomena.

Duarte and Matos make a very interesting contribution to the discussion of enclisis and proclisis: they show on the basis of acquisition data and teenager and adult mistakes that enclisis is the basic order in European Portuguese, and that clitics in Portuguese are not true clitics but are undergoing a change into affix-like elements. They argue that this particular status of clitics may explain enclisis without resorting to movement of the verb to a functional projection higher than IP (i.e., avoiding postulation of functional projections). Instead, they propose a minimalist analysis of this pattern, under which strong feature checking between heads takes place under immediate adjunction. In all Romance languages, cliticization involves checking of strong features; hence, according to their proposal, a clitic head must be immediately adjoined to the head where its strong features are checked.

Duarte and Matos argue on the basis of data with adverbials and inversion in *wh*-questions that cliticization takes place earlier in the derivation, low in the syntactic tree, more specifically at the AgrOP node. Since object DPs do not move overtly to Spec, AgrOP, the clitic must check its features by head-adjunction rather than under Spec-head agreement. Under this analysis, a configuration in which both the clitic and the verb must check strong formal features against the AgrO head, there is a conflict in the sense that if the clitic is immediately adjoined to AgrO, it will intervene between the V and AgrO, preventing the former from checking its features. If the V is immediately adjoined to AgrO, it is the clitic that may not check its strong features. At this stage, Duarte and Matos's observations concerning the morphological status of clitics become relevant. They propose that, because of their affixal nature, clitics are not true syntactic heads in Portuguese; hence, they do not count as interveners for strong checking purposes. In the other Romance languages, on the contrary, they do count, and hence enclisis does not emerge. The only way for a clitic to check its strong features in AgrO is by movement of the whole DP to Spec, AgrOP.

Although Duarte and Matos's contribution reflects a different perspective from that in the other chapters on cliticization, it nevertheless sheds new light on the nature of the syntax-morphology interface. Empirically, it shows that enclisis is the default pattern. Theoretically, it strengthens the minimalist claim that cross-linguistic variation should be explained in terms of the richness of inflection and strength of morphological/categorial features (Chomsky 1995).

At first sight, Martins's analysis defends the opposite approach to cliticization, that it takes place high in the clause. However, her analysis of clitic climbing shares two important features with that of Duarte and Matos: the relevance of Agreement projections for cliticization and the idea that the core IP heads (those identified in Pollock 1989's work: AgrS and TP) may be the crucial ones to determine clitic placement.

Martins, tackling the question of why clitics move, claims that specificity is a morphologically encoded feature. This feature is hosted by the head AgrS, where clitics have to move to. Martins follows the tradition initiated by Postal (1969) and Raposo (1973), analyzing clitics as Determiners, a category that, according to most analyses, may encode specificity (Enç 1991; Longobardi 1994, among many others). According to this analysis, and following the minimalist assumption that morphology drives movement, Martins proposes that the licensing of the specificity feature contained in the clitic D-head is done by moving it to the AgrS head.

Based on these assumptions, Martins proposes that clitic climbing in Romance in general, and Portuguese in particular, may be explained in minimalist terms without facing the problem of optionality. She proposes a unification of ECM and Control constructions, under which in both cases the selected infinitival complement is not a CP but an IP. Martins argues for such an analysis, elaborating on a combination of the Case-based approach to the distribution of PRO of Chomsky and Lasnik (1993) with an implementation of economy of projection. The basic idea is that if two structures serve the same function (i.e., if they both satisfy the lexical selectional requirements of a matrix verb), the one containing fewer functional projections is selected as grammatical. Building on a comparison between Portuguese and Icelandic, Martins concludes that the categorial status of ECM and Control infinitival complements is TP.

The conclusion that these infinitival complements are TPs together with the independently motivated assumption that AgrS is the head hosting clitics makes the interesting prediction that clitic climbing is just a regular case of clitics checking their specificity feature against an AgrS head. The only difference between contexts of clitic climbing and contexts not allowing clitic climbing is that in the former the only accessible AgrS head for clitics to check off their specificity feature is the one associated with the matrix verb.

Martins's argument has important consequences for the questions raised in (5): it provides an interesting empirical extension of one of the two main hypotheses concerning the locus of cliticization; by locating it at the AgrS level, Martins provides a simple explanation for clitic climbing. From a comparative perspective, it brings together interesting data from several Romance languages and Icelandic, showing the relevance of clitic placement to determine the actual clausal structure to be assumed for different constructions. It takes a strong position with respect to the trigger for cliticization: the checking of a specificity-related feature.

The assumption that specificity and other semantic information is encoded in the syntactic structure and that different functional domains correlate with different semantic readings is also expressed in Postma's chapter. Postma looks at the properties of the distributive universal quantifiers *todo* 'every' and *cada* 'each' in Brazilian Portuguese, concluding that the set of properties associated with them is a consequence of the syntactic environment where they are found. This observation on the relation between structure and meaning independently strengthens the point made by several other authors in this volume concerning the motivation for clitic movement: creating a configuration where some semantic value of the displaced element is encoded.

Postma shows that in spite of the surface differences between *todo* and *cada*, both of these quantifiers are bidistributive. This means that both quantifiers must bind two open variables: the only difference is that *cada* must bind an argumental variable in its nuclear scope, while *todo* looks for an open variable either in plurality or in the aspectual specification of some tenses. Postma provides evidence that imperfect tenses behave as indefinites in the sense that they need to be bound by a quantificational expression. The specificity of *cada* in requiring an open variable in an argumental position follows, according to Postma, from the fact that binding of this variable is to be established under connectedness. Since *cada*, unlike *todo*, does not display agreement morphology, and hence may not be assumed to be in a Spec-head relationship with a D-head, there will be a connectedness problem if the variable to be bound is not in a right branch with respect to the position of the quantifier *cada*. Excluding the relevance of this difference between the two quantifiers, by virtue of it being a side effect of the morphosyntactic properties of *cada*, Postma reaches a unification of the two quantifiers, establishing that universal quantification is bidistributive.

Postma's contribution is important, since it shows the specificity of Brazilian Portuguese with respect to the type of contrasts it lexicalizes. It also makes specific claims on how semantic aspects are encoded and derivable from the syntax, and how morphological properties determine syntactic behavior. It thus provides some answers to the questions listed in (5), since it argues that morphological properties of specific lexical items (in this case, the possibility of agreement or not) have direct influence on the syntactic structure. This claim is also defended for clitics in the chapters by Raposo, Duarte and Matos, and Barbosa). Furthermore, it shows that different meanings follow from different syntactic structures, as argued in Martins's chapter for the motivation of clitics.

Postma's hypothesis that morphological specification of forms is to be related with different syntactic configurations may be found again in the chapter by Galves, who proposes an analysis of the change from Classical Portuguese into Brazilian Portuguese and European Portuguese in terms of the status of agreement in these three languages. According to Galves, who develops Chomsky's (1995) idea that Agreement is not necessary as an independent functional head, Agreement is instantiated in different languages, by being associated to different types of heads: Agr may or may not be associated with Infl or with Comp (as also proposed in Rizzi 1990). Elaborating on this theory, Galves proposes that clitics are formal ϕ-features, which need to be licensed in a local relation to the head Agreement is associated with.

Galves's proposal concerning the difference between enclisis and proclisis is very similar to that of Duarte and Matos: she proposes that enclisis and proclisis are not to be considered equivalent, since the status of enclitics is the same as other inflectional morphemes. According to this set of assumptions, Galves proposes that discourse-configurationality in Classical, Brazilian, and European Portuguese is the consequence of the existence of an Agr feature independent of Tense. This interpretation extends the classification made in my chapter. In Galves's chapter, the description is mainly about the preverbal material and the possibility of licensing sentence-external topics. The main difference between Classical Portuguese, on the one hand, and Brazilian and European Portuguese, on the other, is the availability of Verb Second only in the latter, which under Galves's analysis is interpreted with the Agr feature not being licensed via verb movement to C. In European Portuguese, Agr is still associated with C, but it is checked via movement of the quantified subjects (in the case of proclisis) to Spec, CP. Brazilian Portuguese shows an additional step in the evolution of the language: not only Agr is not licensed via verb movement to C, but also C is no longer the host for the Agreement feature. Galves claims that Agreement in Brazilian Portuguese hosts an independent head and the verb moves only up to T, not to Agr, explaining the impoverished inflectional paradigm. As in European Portuguese, different types of subjects surface in different positions (a fact also discussed in the chapters by Barbosa, Raposo, and me), although the clausal structure is different from the one proposed for Brazilian Portuguese.

Galves's contribution is important for the light it sheds on the importance of comparing closely related languages for investigating parametric variation, and for its theoretical claims concerning Portuguese: it relates discourse-configurationality with the nature of inflectional features and makes specific proposals regarding the clausal structure of the language and the relation between cliticization and the location of agreement features.

The issue of the nature of agreement morphology is also tackled by Menuzzi. He looks at alternations between anaphors and pronouns in contexts of binding by an NP like *a gente* lit. 'the people', meaning: 'we', which is semantically specified as first person plural pronoun, although morphologically it is specified as third person singular. Although verbal morphology always surfaces as third person singular, in some contexts the semantic and morphological properties of the NP *a gente* cause a conflict, namely, for the choice of the appropriate pronominal form in binding contexts. Menuzzi shows that the best way to solve the conflict is to have a pronominal form that is underspecified for number. The only form in the pronominal paradigm meeting this requirement is *si* (SE-anaphor), which may have as antecedent both plural and singular NPs. However, this form is supposed to be excluded in nonlocal environments, given its regular behavior as an anaphor. Menuzzi shows quite convincingly that there is a correlation between locality and number specification in the sense that the more local the relation between antecedent and pronominal form, the more *si* is favored. Likewise, the less local the relation antecedent–pronominal form, the more the first person plural pronoun is favored. Menuzzi concludes from this pattern that conditions on binding may not be taken to be absolute and that they are best understood as violable constraints in a sense reminiscent of the use of violability in the work in Optimality Theory, first proposed by Prince and Smolensky (1993). According to this view, locality and number specification conflict, and the more one is satisfied, the less the other is satisfied. Choice of pronominal forms is in this sense a consequence of evaluation by constraints with respect to relative rather than absolute well-formedness.

Menuzzi's contribution relates to the other chapters in the sense that it clearly proposes how the morphological shape of pronominal forms (or choice of specific pronominal forms) interacts with syntactic constraints. Moreover, it shows how the meaning of a form (in this case first person plural interpretation of the form *a gente*) may influence sentence grammar, independently of this feature specification being morphologically represented. This issue correlates with how syntax encodes aspects of what at first sight appears to be a property of discourse rather than strict syntax, an issue also discussed by Barbosa, Galves, Raposo, and me.

The discussion of how syntax encodes meaning is also discussed by Ambar. She looks at the difference between participial clauses in Portuguese and in other Romance languages, showing that they pattern differently for the following set of proprieties: (a) the iterative versus single event reading reflected in the incompatibility versus compatibility with adverbs like *yesterday*; (b) no object agreement versus object agreement; (c) availability of causative/resultative constructions (e.g., John has Bill examined) versus unavailability; (d) in the context of inversion, in Portuguese, the order Have-Subject-Past Participle is available, whereas in the other languages it is not.

Ambar relates these properties to a further difference between participial clauses and infinitival clauses, namely, the possibility of hosting negation and clitics, which is only available for the latter type of clause. She suggests that these properties may be derived, once we assume that there are two temporal domains in the sentence structure, which she expresses in terms of two T-functional projections. The first domain is associated with the subject, while the second is associated with the object. Ambar proposes that for a sentence to be grammatical, at least one of the tenses must be active (though both require licensing). Furthermore, she suggests that the eventive versus stative reading associated with different lexical items in infinitival clauses and the lack of such a semantic distinction in participials follows from the fact that only in the former are the two tense heads active, though weak. She further assumes that eventive readings are associated with a strong intrinsic tense feature of the verb, while generic readings derive from a weak intrinsic tense feature of the verb. This predicts that the only verbs that may undergo lexical movement are statives, since only in this case are the weak features of the verb and those of the functional category compatible. The feature strength profile of the participial clauses is quite different, predicting no differences between different types of verbs.

Ambar's analysis provides an interesting alternative to the analysis of participial clauses made in Kayne (1989), dispensing with Agreement projections, a goal outlined in Chomsky (1995). Her contribution is of great relevance for the general discussion underlying the other chapters here, since it illustrates how to implement the general idea that meaning is encoded in the syntax. She does so by resorting to a system of feature checking and by explicitly establishing links between feature values and semantic notions, a strategy also employed in Martins's discussion. However, unlike Martins, Ambar may not accept the idea that Agreement projections are the hosts for clitics. In this sense, Ambar's argument resembles Barbosa's in the sense that both provide new views on Portuguese clausal structure and its relevance for cliticization. From a comparative perspective, Ambar's chapter shows that Portuguese participial constructions differ from other Romance languages, and surprisingly pattern like English.

It is hoped that the facts and analyses discussed in this volume and their relevance for theoretical issues will contribute to the wider research program of comparative syntax in the Principles and Parameters framework. A key idea in this model is that cross-linguistic variation is related to specification of different functional heads and to the different settings of universal parameters (see Belletti and Rizzi 1996 for discussion). Most chapters here make explicit claims with respect to the correct representation of the functional clause structure of Portuguese and the setting of parameters for this language (feature strength, targets of V-movement, role of agreement). In this respect, we hope that the analyses of Portuguese proposed here may further clarify the range and limits of potential cross-linguistic variation, and the exact formulation of the principles that are part of Universal Grammar.

Notes

1. For detailed outlines of the Principles and Parameters framework, see Freidin (1991), Chomsky and Lasnik (1993). For a precise introduction to the Minimalist Program, see Zwart (1993), Epstein et al. (1996).

2. See also Uriagereka (1995).

References

Baker, Mark. 1988. *Incorporation*. Chicago: University of Chicago Press.

Belletti, Adriana, and Luigi Rizzi. 1996. *Parameters and Functional Heads*. New York: Oxford University Press.

Chomsky, Noam. 1994. "Bare Phrase Structure." *MIT Occasional Papers in Linguistics*. Department of Linguistics and Philosophy, MIT.

———. 1995. *The Minimalist Program*. Cambridge, Mass.: MIT Press.

Chomsky, Noam, and Howard Lasnik. 1993. "Principles and Parameters Theory." In Joachim Jacobs et al. (eds.) *Syntax: An International Handbook of Contemporary Research*. Berlin: Mouton de Gruyter.

Cinque, Guglielmo. 1990. *Types of A-Bar Dependencies*. Cambridge, Mass.: MIT Press.

Corver, Norbert, and Denis Delfitto. 1993. "Feature Asymmetry and the Nature of Pronoun Movement." Paper presented at the GLOW Colloquium, University of Lund, April 1993.

Enç, Murvet. 1991. "The Semantics of Specificity." *Linguistic Inquiry* 22: 1–26.

Epstein, Samuel, Höskuldur Thráinsson, and Jan-Wouter Zwart. 1996. Introduction. In Werner Abraham et al. (eds.) *Minimal Ideas*. Amsterdam: John Benjamins.

Freidin, Robert. 1991. Introduction. In Robert Freidin (ed.) *Principles and Parameters in Comparative Grammar*. Cambridge, Mass.: MIT Press.

Kayne, Richard. 1989. "Facets of Romance Past Participle Agreement." In Paola Benincá (ed.) *Dialect Variation and the Theory of Grammar*. Dordrecht: Foris.

————. 1991. "Romance Clitics, Verb Movement and PRO." *Linguistic Inquiry* 22: 647–686

Longobardi, Giuseppe. 1994. "Reference and Proper Names: A Theory of N-Movement in Syntax and Logical Form." *Linguistic Inquiry* 25: 609–665.

Pollock, Jean-Yves. 1989. "Verb Movement, Universal Grammar and the Structure of IP." *Linguistic Inquiry* 20: 365–424.

Postal, Paul. 1969. "On So-called 'Pronouns' in English." In David Reibel and Sanford Schane (eds.) *Modern Studies in English*. Englewood Cliffs, N.J.: Prentice-Hall.

Prince, Alan, and Paul Smolensky. 1993. *Optimality Theory: Constraint Interaction in Generative Grammar*. Forthcoming, MIT Press.

Raposo, Eduardo. 1973. "Sobre a forma *o* em Português." *Boletim de Filologia XXII*: 364–415.

Reinhart, Tanya. 1995. *Interface Strategies*. Forthcoming, MIT Press.

Rizzi, Luigi. 1990. *Relativized Minimality*. Cambridge, Mass.: MIT Press.

Uriagereka, Juan. 1995. "Aspects of the Syntax of Clitic Placement in Western Romance." *Linguistic Inquiry* 26: 79–123.

Zubizarreta, Maria Luisa. 1994. "Word Order, Prosody and Focus." Ms., University of Southern California.

Zwart, Jan-Wouter. 1993. "Dutch Syntax: A Minimalist Approach." Ph.D. dissertation, University of Groningen.

1

MANUELA AMBAR

Infinitives versus Participles

Assuming that both infinitival and participial structures do have Tense—as proposed in my earlier work (1988, 1993, 1994) and, with independent motivation by Kayne (1993), Déchaine, Hoekstra and Rooryck (1994), Giorgi and Pianesi (1992) and Peres (1992); see also Hernanz (1991) and De Miguel (1992) for a proposal considering the existence of an Aspect node in the same type of structures[1]—we still have to say why these two structures have different behaviors concerning at least the following phenomena: the value of their tenses (generic versus single event reading), agreement, Case, word order, passive voice, negation, and cliticization.

This work aims to shed some light on these questions and is organized as follows: first, I will consider what constitutes the crucial motivation for considering two tenses in sentence structure: the generic versus the single event reading in infinitives versus participles, respectively, through the observation of lexical restrictions on verb movement in both type of constructions.[2] Second, I will see how my proposal can be conciliated with the following facts: subject agreement versus object agreement, nominative Case versus accusative Case (in infinitives versus absolute participial constructions versus have+past participle constructions), cliticization, passive voice, and word order. I will then conclude with some conjectures on passives and on certain differences between Old and Modern Portuguese.

1.1 Basic proposal

I will assume that in sentence structure two tenses[3] can be projected—a higher tense, traditionally associated with nominative Case, and a lower tense, dominating the VP,[4] plausibly responsible for accusative Case. Each one can be overt or empty and have strong or weak features; for the determination of "strong" versus "weak," besides empirical evidence, I will consider the notion of paradigm ("richness" versus "poverty" of specification).

Sentences would then have two zones, one belonging to the subject and the other to the object. Depending on the strong versus weak status of their tenses and on the relation they establish with heads immediately dominating them (by necessity of feature checking, e.g., Focus, Case, clitic movement), both can be active or one active and the other inert (nonactivity of both would lead to a nonsentence), this recalling Chomsky's (1992), Bobaljik's (1992), and Laka's (1993) suggestions about the activity of Case.

Both tenses must be identified. I will assume that at LF they must be linked to another tense or operator in the spirit of Guéron and Hoekstra (1988). An independent tense is identified in its local domain, this correlating with independent or nonindependent clauses. The c-commanding tense (once identified) is the anchoring Tense of the sentence. It is why negation and cliticization are related to it (cf. Kayne 1975, 1989; Zanuttini 1994).

1.2 Infinitives versus participles: Genericity versus single event reading

To understand how infinitives differ from participles, I will consider some crucial aspects of each one in turn.

1.2.1 Inflected infinitives: Genericity

Since Raposos's (1987) analysis, the distribution of inflected infinitives is well known.[5] Here I will only be concerned with the occurrence of inflected infinitive as complement of epistemic verbs.

The contrast in (1) is crucial for Raposo's proposal (1987):

(1)   a. * Penso os deputados terem votado a proposta.
          think +1ps the deputies have +3pspl voted the proposal

      b. Penso terem os deputados votado a proposta.

In his terms, Agr has to be Case marked. In finites, it is Case marked by Tense; in the absence of Tense—as with inflected infinitives—it has to look for another Case assigner. In sentential complements of epistemic and declarative verbs, Agr raises to Comp to be assigned Case by the main verb; once marked with Case, it can assign nominative Case to its subject. The contrast in (1) follows: (1a) is ungrammatical because Agr cannot be Case marked in situ, due the presence of two X^{max} (CP and IP); (1b) is well formed, since Agr in Comp can be Case marked by the main verb.

If we adopt Raposo's analysis, the contrast in (2) suggests that some other phenomenon is involved:

(2)   a. Penso terem eles comprado o livro.
          think+1ps have+3pspl they bought the book

      b. *Penso comprarem eles o livro.

In fact the ungrammaticality of (2b) is unexpected. Given the presence of inversion, Agr is in Comp where it is Case marked by the main verb. Then Agr is licensed and the sentence should be grammatical.

Contrasts of the same type were pointed out by Rizzi (1982) with the observation that the so-called Aux-to-Comp rule gives acceptable results when the verb is an auxiliary or copula, but not when it is not. Pollock (1989) also captured the similarity between the lexical restrictions on Aux-to-Comp in Italian and Portuguese infinitives and those holding on Verb Movement to (Agr to) [-finite] Tense in French. According to his proposal, only movement of auxiliary verbs would not induce a violation of the θ-Criterion, these verbs being not θ-role assigners. However, Pollock (1989) observed that the domain of application of the so-called Aux-to-Comp, at least in Portuguese, was larger than the one traditionally assumed, since unaccusative verbs could raise, as illustrated by examples like (3), taken from Perlmutter (1976):

(3)   a.   Ele disse acontecerem coisas como essas só nos Balcãs.
           he said happen+agr things like these in the Balkans

Considering that all verbs in (3) were unaccusatives, Pollock suggested that Portuguese could be added to the list of languages whose lexical restrictions on verb movement were accounted for by this theory, once assuming that unaccusatives were verbs failing to be θ-role assigners.

However, verb movement is possible not only with auxiliary and unaccusative verbs, as observed by Pollock, but also with lexical verbs of the type *comer/comprar* 'to eat, to buy', which in some environments produce ungrammatical sentences (cf. (2b)) but in others produce well-formed ones, as exemplified in the following:

(4)   a.   Penso comerem as crianças demasiados chocolates.
           think+1ps buy+3ppl children too many chocolates

           'I think children eat too many chocolates.'

      b.   O João afirmou comprarem eles o jornal todas as sextas-feiras.
           John declared buy+agr they the newspaper every Friday

           'John declared they buy the newspaper every Friday.'

If we compare the sentences in (4) with the one in (3), some common behavior is apparent. In both paradigms, independently of the type of verbs, all sentences have a stative status. For some reason the basic aktionsart value of the eventive verb shifts into an arguably stative one. I (1993) related this phenomenon to a requirement of genericity in the inflected infinitival complements of epistemic verbs and verbs of saying, as stated in (5):

(5)   In the ungrammatical sentences the temporal interpretation is the one associated with a definite reference to a single event, with "comprar" ("to buy") showing its intrinsic properties of eventive verb. In the well-formed sentences, on the contrary, a habitual/generic reading is available. Instead of a single event reading, we get a stative one.

The occurrence of past participle in these constructions constitutes an exception to the preceding generalization. Consider the following sentences:

(6) a. Penso terem os deputados votado a proposta.
   think+ps have+3pspl the deputies voted the proposal

   b. Penso ter a Joana comido a sopa.
   think+1ps have Joana eaten the soup

In (6), no habitual/generic reading is available. On the contrary, the temporal interpretation of the sentence is the one related with the single event reading, which is normally associated with the basic aktionsart value of the eventive verb.

This exception is still more interesting when we observe that in finites of indicative present where *have+past participle* occurs, the single event interpretation is not possible, as attested by the ungrammaticality induced by the occurrence of the definite article *o* (the) or of the adverb *yesterday* in (7):

(7) a. O Pedro disse que eles têm comprado *o livro/(muitos) livros.
   Peter said that they have bought *the book/many books

   b. O Pedro disse que eles têm comprado muitos livros *ontem/ultimamente.
   Peter said that they have bought many books *yesterday/lately.

But whenever *have* is in the subjunctive, in the infinitive, or in another nonfinite tense,[6] the single event reading becomes possible:

(8) a. Não penso que eles tenham comprado o livro ontem.
   I don't think they have+subj bought the book yesterday

   b. O Pedro disse terem eles comprado o livro/muitos livros.
   Peter said to have they bought the book/many books

If in inflected infinitival complements of epistemic verbs there is a general requirement of genericity, this requirement might be respected also in infinitives where *have+past participle* occurs. I have suggested (initially in Ambar 1988) that these facts should be added to the empirical motivation for the proposal that past participles have tense. My proposal is that in these structures the auxiliary *have*—a stative verb (cf. Kayne 1993, where *have* is BE with a preposition incorporated)—falls under generalization (5) and that the Past Tense effect of these constructions, to which the single event reading is related, is provided by the Participle.[7] I am then suggesting that, in sentences like (8), the participle behaves like a clause embedded to *have*, which in turn is embedded to the epistemic verb. In order to understand this compatibility between Participle and single event reading, I will look at the behavior of participles in other contexts.

1.2.2 Past participle and single event

Unlike inflected infinitives, in Absolute Participial Clauses a single event reading is available, but a stative one is not, as shown in (9) and (10), respectively:

(9) a. Votada a proposta, os deputados abandonaram a assembleia.
         voted the proposal, the deputies left the assembly

     b. Comprados os livros, os estudantes sairam da livraria.
         bought the books, the students left the library

(10) a. *Estado feliz, o Pedro iniciou a nova vida.
          been happy, Peter started a new life

      b. *Tido o livro, o Pedro abandonou a biblioteca.
          had the book, Peter left the library

      c. *Comidos demasiados chocolates, as crianças ficaram doentes.
          eaten too many chocolates, the children stay sick

The perfective value of the past participle is a well-known fact. I will assume that this perfective value is a manifestation of tense in relation to lexical properties of the verb (morphological features in the sense of DiSciullo 1996). In fact a perfective is always past.[8]

If one considers that the crucial difference between infinitives and participles has to be found in the opposite behavior of their tenses, which entails different behaviors concerning the acktionsart, then a logical program of research is to relate this main difference with other properties that differ from one construction to another. Namely, one expects that the facts distinguishing infinitives from participles—for example, Case, cliticization, word order, passive and negation—are somehow related to the main contrast concerning tense described in the previous sections.

1.3 The analysis

I will assume that sentences have the representation proposed by Chomsky (1992, 1995) following the split Inlf hypothesis of Pollock (1989) and the c-commanding AgrS view of Belletti (1990) with one more projection: TPO. The existence of this projection was motivated by the description of facts presented in the preceding section. Crucially, the factors interact: different behavior of *have+past participle* according to the different inflectional morphology on *have* (cf. (7) versus (8)), the contrast between the ungrammaticality of inflected infinitives according to the eventive versus stative status of the verb and to the type of determination on the object. These factors lead to the conclusion that the temporal interpretation in each case is the result of an interaction between inflection (mainly tense), tense and aktionsart, determination/quantification of the complement. These aspects are responsible for the distinction between stative and eventive verbs.

I will now investigate what the representation of sentence structure for an inflected infinitive embedded to an epistemic verb should be:

(11)

```
                        VP
                       /\
                      V   CP
                  pensar  /\
                         C'
                        /\
                       C ... TPS
                      +T   /\
                        Spec  T'
                             /\
                            T  ...
                           TPO
                          /\
                      Spec  T'O
                           /\
                         TO   VP
                        +gen /\
                          Spec  V'
                               /\
                              V   NP
                          comprar +gen
                             buy
```

I will assume that the lower tense has to raise to the c-commanding tense[9] and, further, that an independent nonspecified tense is a generic. In (11) the presence of $[+T(ense)]$[10] in Comp makes the morphological tense of the sentence (T^S) an independent tense. Once this independent tense is not specified, it is generic. Then the lower Tense (T^O) has to be a generic tense too (also weak in terms of specification); if not, with incompatible features, both tenses would conflict and the structure would crash. TP^S represents the morphological tense of the sentence related with the subject, whereas TP^O is the tense related with the object. The relevant tense for infinitives is TP^S; for participles it is TP^O. I will now consider the analysis of each construction in turn.[11]

1.3.1 Infinitives

Recall the first main contrast concerning infinitives given in (2b) versus (4a) repeated here as (12):

(12) a * Penso comer a Joana a sopa.

　　　 b. Penso comerem as crianças demasiados chocolates.

Clearly, what is responsible for this contrast is the different determination of the object in each sentence. Assuming the representation (11), we see that in (12) both tenses—TS and TO—are nonspecified and that the verb raised to a position above the subject before the Spell-Out—(12b) without subject-verb inversion is ruled out, as observed by Raposo (1987). With this in mind, let us assume the following hypothesis: the verb raises to T^S in order to check its features—although, being nonspecified, T^S is strong in this construction due to the tense feature in Comp. Then, keeping Raposo's idea, the verb (more precisely, T^S) goes to Comp[12] to check the [+T] feature. As for subject, for my purposes it suffices to assume that it raises at least to Spec of T^{S13} to check nominative Case. What is relevant here is that the verb has passed through TO and TS. Since these tenses are nonspecified, the tense feature of the verb (lexically determined) has to be nonspecified too. If not, when the verb passes through TO, this feature will conflict with the nonspecified status of TO. This is the picture when the verb is stative—its tense feature being nonspecified, there is no conflict and the sentences are well formed; if, on the contrary, we have an eventive verb, its tense feature being [+ specified] (+strong), there would be a conflict and the structure would crash. We would then expect sentences in (12) to be excluded. However, as we saw, they are possible whenever the determination on the NP object is of the type [+generic] (-specified).

I will assume, then, that an eventive verb, in order to have its lexical tense feature specified, has to have it linked to a [+specific] feature (existing on the morphological tense or in any other category—DP, for instance); if not, its feature will go on open or nonspecific.[14] The difference between eventive and stative verbs would be the existence of this potential strong feature in eventive verbs (which would become a specified feature when related with another specified feature) versus its absence in stative verbs—which, having no such feature, would be inert with respect to other features.

Suppose now that if a DP object that is not a generic (if it is a DP [+specific])[15] also has to have its [+specific] feature linked to another [+specific] feature.[16] It is why the [+specific] feature of the DP has to be in Spec of T^O at least at LF.[17] This is the case of sentence (12a), where there is a specific determination on the object. Then the [+specific] feature has to raise to spec of TPO; by Spec-head agreement, TO receives the [+specific] feature of the object. Once the verb is in TO, its potential [+specified] feature is activated, the result being that we have a real eventive verb with a specified tense that will conflict with the nonspecific T^S to which it has to raise for morphological checking necessity—the ungrammaticality of sentences like (12a) is predicted. Stative verbs do not have this potential feature therefore they are immune to the presence of such a feature in Spec of TPO. The structure will crash only in the presence of an eventive verb whose complement has a specific determination. Since stative verbs do not have such a feature, they cannot check the specified tense of participles—there would be a conflict, and structures like the ones in (10) would crash. I predict all the contrasts presented here. I will now turn to participles.

1.3.2 Participles

I will analyze participles that enter into two constructions: the so-called Absolute Participial Clause (APC) and *have + past participle* structures. I will assume that both constructions have the same basic underlying structure as all the other sentences, infinitives included. The question is why they differ in several aspects.

I propose that participles are the structures that activate the TO area. In other words, TPO is the specified tense and is stronger than T^S. T^S will be activated only if necessary, depending on the structure and correlating with the contrasts found in these constructions.

Crucial for my analysis in these structures are the Case opposition (nominative versus accusative) and the agreement facts. In APC nouns are always possible; however, nouns do not have visible Case:

(13) Chegada a Maria a casa, o Pedro saiu.
      Tenho encontrado a Maria no cinema.

The relevant behavior has to be observed in pronouns where Case is overt. In APC only nominative pronouns are available, whereas in *have+past participle* constructions accusative ones are the choice, as exemplified by (14) and (15), respectively:

(14) a. Chegada *ela* a casa, o Pedro saiu.
         arrived+fem she at home, Peter left

      b. * Chegada-*a* a casa, . . .
         arrived+fem, 3ps her (accusative), . . .

(15) a. * O João tem encontrado *eles* no cinema.
         John has met they in the cinema

      b. O João tem-*nos* encontrado no cinema.
         John has met them in the cinema

Portuguese behaves like Italian with respect to ergative verbs, in which context nominative Case is assigned to the participle subject, but they differ in the context of transitive verbs, where accusative Case is allowed in Italian as described by Belletti (1981, 1990, 1993) but not in Portuguese:

(16) a. *Conosciuta io

      b. Conosciutame

      c. Arrivata io / tu, . . .

      d. * Arrivata me, . . . (Belletti 1990)

(17) a. Conhecida eu, . . .

      b. *Conhecida me, . . .

      c. Chegada eu, . . .

      d. * Chegada me

I will first concentrate on the Portuguese contrast exemplified by (17). Suppose that for a clause to exist as clause it must have TO linked to another tense—T^S. Two possibilities are then available: either TO is directly linked to TS or TO is linked to a higher TO, which in turn ends up linked to TS. If the tense that immediately c-commands TS is TS, the TS zone of the participle is activated; if it is TO, the TO zone is activated, this suggesting that, besides the Spec-head relation, in grammar the head-

head relation plays an important role, as observed by Chomsky (1986).[18] The first situation is realized in APC, the second one in *have+past participle* structures.

Assuming that APCs are clauses adjoined to IP, as proposed by Belletti (1990), Hernanz (1991), Vinet (1989), and myself (Ambar 1988), TS of the matrix clause c-commands the participal clause—the zone that is activated is then TS.[19] And if the TS zone is activated, nominative Case is available. It is not clear, however, why an object has to be marked nominative instead of accusative. Further explanation is needed.

In Portuguese the agreement marker of past participle is *o(s) / a(s)* for masculine/feminine singular (plural) (or *o* for the default case, where there is no agreement). Curiously, these forms coincide with accusative pronouns of third person singular (plural). One natural assumption is to consider that, just like pronouns, the agreement markers of the participle have to be assigned accusative Case. But if Case is checked by the agreement marker of the participle, the object cannot check its Case feature in TO; rather, it has to look for another Case position. Since the TS zone can be activated due to the presence of the c-commanding TS of the matrix clause, that position is Spec of TS. I predict that, independently of the ergative or unergative status of the verb,[20] nominative Case is assigned in these constructions and clitics are not possible because the head T^O, responsible for accusative Case, is already filled by the participle marker *o(s) / a(s)*—see the ungrammaticality of (17b) and of (18):[21]

(18)   *Comprado(s)-o(s), a Maria saiu.
        bought-them, Mary left

Once, in order to check Case, the object goes through spec, TO (and Spec, Agr^O).[22] By spec-head relation, it agrees with the verb. Agreement is induced in this case by necessity of Case checking but is dissociated of it. The NP can raise for other reasons, and agreement will still be induced. I am suggesting that whenever there is overt object agreement, the object has passed in Spec of TO (AgrO), in the spirit of Kayne (1989); consequently, no overt agreement indicates that the object has not raised. This is the case of nouns in *have+past participle* constructions in Portuguese:

(19)   Tenho guardado as tuas cartas.
        I have kept your letters

A natural assumption is that nouns in Portuguese have weak accusative Case features, whereas pronouns have strong ones; then nouns raise to check Case at LF and pronouns raise before the Spell-Out. In Old Portuguese, however, there was overt agreement, suggesting that for some reason the NP object had to raise:

(20)   E porque, como vistes, tem passados.
        Na viagem tão ásperos perigos . . .
        and because, as you have seen, has passed+agr
        in the trip so hard dangers (Camões)

One possibility is that accusative Case was stronger and had to be checked before the Spell-Out. However, if in Modern Portuguese nouns check accusative Case at

LF, in (13) the NP *a Maria* did not raise for Case reasons. I assume that it raises to check a Focus feature, but see (26). Modern Portuguese still has constructions in the context of *have+past participle* where there is agreement:

(21) Tenho as tuas cartas guardadas.
      I have your letters kept+acc.fem.sing

In (21) the temporal interpretation of present perfect is lost; instead, we have a resultative value. Comparing (19) and (21), we see that the difference lies in the position of the object—following the verb in (19), preceding it in (21). It is possible to conclude that the NP object has raised, but that raising in this case was not once more induced by Case checking necessity (cf. (26)).

As for Italian, one possibility is to assume that the agreement elements of the participle do not require Case checking. Then the object can check its Case in TO, the result being the occurrence of accusative pronouns in this context. On the other hand, cliticization is also possible—since TO is not filled by case-marked forms, it behaves like other normal inflectional heads and, consequently, can receive clitics. The TS zone is not necessary and is not activated, the result being that, in Italian, accusative clitics appear in APC and nominative pronouns are not possible.[23]

With ergative verbs, however, Spec of VP is empty; the object has to pass there, the result being that it no longer can go to Spec of TO (subjects do not have accusative Case).[24] Then the NP object has to check its Case features in another head; the only possibility is to raise and to activate the TS zone. This is possible because of the presence of the c-commanding matrix Ts. Nominative is then assigned.[25]

I will now address *have+past participle* constructions in more detail. Why is nominative never possible there? My earlier remarks concerning the status of participle agreement elements with respect to Case also hold for these constructions, the difference being that now the matrix c-commanding tense is not T^S but T^O. Compare the two structures in (22) and (23) representing, respectively, ASC and Have+Past Participle (T^S and T^O and the corresponding heads they activate in each case are in italic):

(22) [TPS[CP[C'[C *chegados* $_k$ [TPS *eles*$_i$ [TS' *TS*$_k$ [TPO eles$_i$ [TO, t$_k$ [VP t$_i$ [V' t$_k$ [NP t$_i$]]]]]]]]]]] [TPS ... *TS* ...]]

(23) ... [TP^O [T$^{O'}$ *TO* [VP [V' ter (have) [TP^O ... *To* ... [VP ...

Then, in (23), the T^S zone cannot be activated, and nominative Case is not available. However, the accusative pronoun can check its Case in Spec of the higher T^O (belonging to *have*), where there is no Inflection of past participle to check Case. The result are sentences like (24):

(24) Tenho-as escrito.
      I have them written

Another issue is now at stake. My generalization states that whenever the NP object raises, there is visible agreement. However, in (24) no agreement shows up; raising of clitics contrasts, then, with raising of nouns, which induce agreement as shown by sentence (21).

Assuming that, in order to have overt agreement, the NP with which the head agrees has to be in Spec and that clitics can be heads (cf. Kayne 1991, among others), the contrast between (21) and (24) follows: the clitic moves directly to the matrix T^O; because it does not pass through Spec, there is no Spec-head agreement. On the contrary, NPs whose heads are nouns have to go to Spec, then agreement is induced. The behavior of clitics, however, is more complex. In apparent contradiction with what I have just said are sentences such as the following:

(25)   Tenho-as guardadas
        I have them ranged+agr

where an accusative clitic is combined with agreement. Example (25) has the same reading as (21).

Recalling that in (13) and (21) the DP object has not raised for Case reasons, it is necessary to find another motivation for the DP movement in this structure. As said earlier, *a Maria* in (13) and *as cartas* in (21) raise to check a feature [+focus] in a focus projection (FP). Examples (13) through (21) would have the following structure:

(26)   [TPS[TS' tenho$_i$ [TPO as cartas$_k$ [TO' t$_i$[VP[V' t$_i$ [FP t$_k$ [F' F [TPO t$_k$ [TO' guardadas$_j$ [VP [V' t$_j$ t$_k$]]]]]]]]]]]]^{26}

If clitics are heads with strong features to check in a head position, we would expect the clitic in (25) to behave like the ones in (24), that is, without agreement. Thus, if agreement is available, one possible explanation is that clitics have a mixed status, behaving either like heads or like maximal projections. Then, as a projection, the clitic can go to a Spec position. Since it has a Focus feature to check, just like nouns, it has to go to Spec of Focus Phrase after it raises to Spec of the matrix T^O to check accusative Case. Assuming the proposal made earlier for the Italian (and Portuguese) requirement of nominative with ergative verbs in APC, we still account for the impossibility of sentences like (27) in Modern Portuguese:[27]

(27)   *Tenho a morte chegada.
        I have the death arrived

Only T^O can be activated in the participle because it is c-commanded by T^O of *have*. As in (26), the NP would raise to the Focus position and then, in order to have its Case checked, it would raise to Spec of matrix T^O. However, this is an improper movement for the reasons already presented: a NP in Spec of VP—a subject position—cannot raise to an object position (spec of the matrix T^O), as observed earlier.[28] Neither nominative nor accusative is then allowed, as confirmed by the ungrammaticality of (28) and (29), respectively:

(28)   *Tenho-a chegada.
        I have her arrived

(29)   *Tenho ela chegada.
       I have she arrived.

The contrasts presented are then predicted. Finally, I will briefly refer some remarks on passives.[29] Until now I have not addressed the deep subject position of the participle, in spec of VP. APCs behave like passives: the object goes to a nominative position, and the NP, which is assigned a θ-role agent, stays in situ in Spec of VP. The only way to have the Case features checked is by means of a preposition: *por*. I predict the well-formedness of sentences like (30):

(30)   Saudado pelos deputados, o presidente abandonou a asembleia.
       'Welcome by the deputies, the president left the assembly.'

However, in participial constructions of the type (31), no agent of passive is allowed:

(31)   *Ele tem guardado os livros pela Joana.
       'He has ranged the books by Joana.'

But focused structures of the preceding type are well-formed:

(32)   Ainda tenho os livros guardados por ele.
       'I still have the books ranged by him.'

The simplest way to derive the difference between these structures would be to consider that in each construction *have* is a different verb. In (31)—the case of the complex tense—*have* would be a raising verb, which does not assign a θ-role to its subject, whereas in (32) *have* would be a verb assigning a θ-role to its subject. Then in the first case we would not have any phonetically realized NP in Spec of the more embedded VP, since it would be occupied by a trace; in the second case, Spec of VP of *have* would be a θ-position, and just like in APC the NP would be licensed if a preposition is inserted. However, I prefer an analysis in which only one verb *have* would be considered. The different temporal interpretation of each construction is certainly an important element for a deeper understanding of this issue.

1.4 Conclusions

Departing from the study of lexical restrictions on verb movement in Portuguese inflected infinitival complements of epistemic verbs, and assuming that temporal and aspectual relations are the result of an interaction between different factors—morphological tense, determination/quantification of the object, allowed by some few mechanisms of grammar, for example, morphological features checking, along the lines of Chomsky (1992, 1995), Spec-head and head-head relations (cf. Chomsky 1986, 1995)—I have proposed an analysis that attempts to account for some crucial differences between infinitives and participles.

Under the proposal that two tenses—T^S and T^O—are necessary in sentence structure in order to relate properties of the subject with properties of the object, my analysis made predictions on agreement, Case, tense value (generic versus single event reading, correlating with stative versus eventive verbs, respectively). If this analysis proves to be adequate, further research will be needed to understand the behavior of infinitives and participles with respect to other phenomena, such as negation, and to see the predictions it makes for other structures to which Tense is related. Namely, I hope that further research on this topic will lead to a more accurate understanding and a more precise definition of concepts like [+ or − finite].

Notes

The presentation of this paper at the Linguistic Symposium of Romance Languages was partially subsidized by the University of Lisbon. I thank Itziar Laka and João Peres for relevant discussion.

1. The motivation underlying these works is, however, quite different. Even my first proposal (cf. Ambar 1988) for the existence of Tense (and Comp) in participle constructions was built on another type of argumentation. What is interesting is that, departing from different data in different languages and making use of different tools, the works referred to in the text arrived at the same conclusion. This is still more interesting when authors also are working in different areas, such as Peres (1992), whose work is in the field of formal semantics.

2. For a development of this issue see Ambar (1992, 1993). The analysis of infinitives presented here is based on this last work.

3. Conceptually, these two tenses do not coincide with those proposed by Giorgi and Pianesi (1992), but the main idea underlying my claim has some similarity with their hypothesis. However, in my proposal there is no V projection between these two tenses; they are always present in sentence structure and are only partially concerned with temporal interpretation (in fact, I think this is accomplished by the interaction with other factors (very plausibly semantic or pragmatic ones). For space reasons and because this work, like the ones by Hernanz (1991) and De Miguel (1992), came to my attention after the presentation of this paper at the University of Mexico, I will not discuss them here in detail.

4. In a sense corresponding to what has been called verbal aspect. But see n. 8.

5. A discussion of this analysis is presented in Ambar (1988, 1992). This does not concern us here.

6. The exact definition of finite and nonfinite is another interesting topic that will not be dealt with here.

7. The question now is how the single event reading compatible with the participle is projected in all the embedded sentences. I will not deal with this question here. Ambar (paper presented at Grammar and Variation, McGill University, 1996; published 1998) attempts to understand this fact in comparison with English, Spanish, Italian, and French, since finites in these last three languages behave like infinitives in Portuguese and English w.r.t. have+participle.

8. The distinction between *perfective* and *imperfective* and the exact definition of these terms is a polemic issue. Aristotle made the distinction, relating it with tense here. I will not go through the discussion of concepts like Tense, Aspect, Mood, and Aktionsart. I am convinced that crucially we have tense features lexically determined in the verb (as stated by Di Sciullo 1996): aktionsart, checked in TO, which in relation with morphological TS and with object determination or quantification (very plausibly of the subject too), gives as a result all the temporal and so-called aspectual specifications. Aspect would then be an epiphenomenon.

From this perspective, however, it is necessary to have a general view of the puzzling effects and relations of Tense in other constructions.

9. This goes in the direction of work by Guéron and Hoekstra (1988) and Laka (1990), among others. In a previous work on Focus (Paris International Workshop on the Grammar of Focus, 1996), I proposed that TO must always raise in order to link the event to the focus position under a condition that was called Tense Matching Condition. The landing site and the level of this movement seem to vary with the structure and with the language.

10. This tense occurs only in complements of epistemic verbs. Motivation for the presence of such a feature (operator in Raposo's 1987 terms) was presented in Meireles and Raposo (1983), Jakubowicz (1985), Raposo (1987), and Ambar (1988, 1992).

11. In work in progress the analysis proposed here for participles and infinitives is being extended to other tenses (moods) in other constructions.

12. In Raposo's term, Agr must raise to Comp in order to be Case marked by the matrix verb; in the minimalist view, Case is not assigned via government. We could then keep Raposo's idea that the verb goes to Comp and say that it goes there to check its Tense feature. However, it is not clear that the verb goes to Comp. In focus constructions some facts suggest that it does not. I do not pursue this question here but am developing it in another work.

13. It is not clear that Agr is necessary; it seems that it can be dispensed with, confirming Chomsky's (1995) hypothesis. If AgrS is not present in sentence structure, we have to assume either that the verb raises to Comp (but then we would have the problem pointed out in n. 12) or that it goes to a projection above TS but below Comp. This could be a Focus Phrase or a Sigma Phrase in the spirit of Uriagereka (1992) and Rouveret (1992), and Laka (1990), respectively.

14. When there is overt morphological T^S on the verb, this tense will link the tense feature of the verb, without conflict. Further research is needed on Tense in other structures.

15. This goes in the direction of work by Diesing (1992) and Martins (1995), where [+specific] DPs have to go out of the VP or of T^O (TS in my terms), respectively. As for the terminology used here, I am following work by Enç (1991) and Diesing (1992). As observed by Enç, the presence or absence of the accusative marker in Turkish produces corresponding alternations in the semantic interpretation—when the object NP is marked accusative, it has a "specific" reading. For Enç (1997), "NPs that are marked [+specific] must satisfy a Familiarity Condition, which basically requires that there be a discourse referent corresponding to the [+specific] reading (the Familiarity Condition is based on ideas in Heim (1982, p. 7))."

16. Or potentially specified feature—the case of the eventive verb, where no morphological tense is present to link that feature. Very plausibly the c-commanding Tense of the sentence is the one to which all the [+specific] elements end up linked. This area needs further research.

17. These restrictions on the verb movement seem to belong to the semantic field, as we can see for the oddity of interpretation. Plausibly, the level where this is accomplished will vary across languages.

18. Other facts, which I cannot deal with here, suggest this claim.

19. Plausibly verb+tense raises to Comp position to be linked to the matrix TS. Note that I am not assuming with Kayne (1989) and Belletti (1990) that the participle raises in order to assign Case to the participle subject. For an analysis in the sense of the one defended here, see Ambar (1988); for analyses discussing and arguing against a Comp position, see, respectively, Hernanz (1991) and DeMiguel (1992). Space limitations preclude my discussing this issue here.

20. Although only nominative Case is possible in Portuguese in these constructions, some fine contrasts must be pointed out: (i) in first and third person singular the occurrence of a pronoun gives good results, but the occurrence of a pronoun in second person singular is

odd; (ii) the occurrence of these nominative pronouns is worse in the context of transitive verbs than in the context of ergative ones. Note that agreement of the subject zone is specified for person and number, whereas agreement of the object zone is specified for gender and number. It is then natural that the conflict be more sensitive to person and gender, which do not belong to the intersection of both sets of features. First and third person singular give better results because the subject agreement markers for these persons are weaker (cf., for instance, inflected infinitive, where they are phonetically empty). These facts suggest that person and number (probably also gender) "trigger different types of relation between a subject and a verb," as observed by Rigau (1991). Ergatives give better results because the nominative pronoun has passed through Spec, VP, a "deeper" subject position.

21. I am deriving an old stipulation of generative grammar: past participles absorb accusative Case (Chomsky 1981).

22. See n. 13.

23. Belletti (1993), following a proposal by Friedman and Siloni (1993), distinguishes AgrO from AgrPstPrt and attributes the occurrence of clitics in Italian versus nonoccurrence in other Romance languages to a plausible nonexistence of AgrO in these languages. Portuguese facts seem to suggest that this idiosyncratic projection for participles is not necessary. One could wonder why other structures (e.g., subjunctive, indicative, gerundive) would not behave similarly. As for the impossibility of clitics in past participles that enter into complex tense structures, the reason has to be independent of the properties of the participle. It probably is related to the impossibility of agreement in Portuguese in these structures. In complex tense structures the participle must be in a given relation with *have*.

24. The reason that subjects cannot raise to T^O or Agr^O in these constructions is mysterious to me, but this is a more general question, which also implies the study of Exceptional Case Marking constructions. I do not have a principled answer to this question; I simply adopt Chomsky's (1992) presupposition that a subject, Spec of VP can go to Spec of T^S (a nominative position) but not to T^O (AgrO).

25. Note that I am predicting that in Italian as in Portuguese structures like *Tenho a morte chegada* 'I have the death arrived' are excluded, since the subject of the ergative verb once in Spec of VP can no longer go to the object position—Spec of T^O.

26. I am abstracting from the following aspects: presence of Agr, which category fills Spec, VP, and discussion on the final landing site of the participle—TO or Focus positions.

27. Sentences like (27) were possible in Old Portuguese (as shown in work in progress). The difference w.r.t. Modern Portuguese has to be found in the behavior of the ergative verb. My analysis, combined with Kayne's (1994) noun raising hypothesis for relatives, is also supposed to make some predictions on participle agreement in relatives in Old Portuguese, which behaves differently from Modern Portuguese but similarly to Modern French and Italian. Space reasons preclude my discussing this topic here.

28. In Exceptional Case Marking structures the subject of an embedded clause has accusative Case, then plausibly it has raised to Spec TO (Agr^O) to check Case. Apparently this constitutes evidence against my hypothesis. Note, however, that in the case of ECM the NP goes to Spec of the matrix T^O from the embedded Spec, T^S and not from Spec, VP. What seems to be forbidden by grammar is raising of a NP in Spec of VP to a Spec of T^O (or AgrO).

29. This analysis is developed in work in progress where it is applied to negation.

References

Ambar, M. 1988. *Para uma Sintaxe da Inversão Sujeito Verbo em Português*. Lisbon: Edições Colibri, 1992

———. 1992. "Temps et Structure de la Phrase." In H.-G. Obenauer and A. Zribi-Hertz (ed.)

Structure de la Phrase et Theorie du Liage. Paris: Sciences du Langage, Presses Universitaires de Vincennes.

———. 1993. "Aux-to-Comp and Lexical Restrictions on Verb Movement." In G. Cinque, J. Koster, J.-Y. Pollock, L. Rizzi, and R. Zanuttini (eds.) *In Paths Towards Universal Grammar: Studies in Honour of Richard Kayne*. Washington, D.C.: Georgetown University Press.

———. 1994. "The Tense of Past Participles." Paper presented at Langues et Grammaire I, University of Paris VIII.

———. 1996. "Inflected Infinitives Revisited—Genericity and Single Event." Presented at Grammaire et Variation, ACFAS 1996, McGill University. Published in *Canadian Journal of Linguistics* 43(1): 5–36, 1998.

Belletti, A. 1981. "Frasi ridotte absolute." *Rivista di Grammatica Generativa* 6: 3–32.

———. 1990. *Generalized Verb Movement*. Turin: Rosenberg and Sellier.

———. 1993. "Case Checking and Clitic Placement." *GenGenP, vol. 1, n.2*. University of Geneva.

Bobaljik, Jonathan, 1992. "Ergativity and ergative unergatives." In C. Phillips (ed.) *Papers on Case and Agreement II*, MIT Working Papers in Linguistics, 45–88.

Chomsky, N. 1981. *Lectures on Government and Binding*. Dordrecht: Foris.

———. 1986. *Barriers*. Cambridge, Mass.: MIT Press.

———. 1992. "A Minimalist Program for Linguist Theory." Ms., MIT.

———. 1995. *The Minimalist Program*. Cambridge, Mass.: MIT Press.

Déchaine, T. Hoekstra, and J. Rooryck. 1994. "Augmented and Non-augmented HAVE." Ms., University of Leiden.

De Miguel, E. 1992. *El Aspect en la Sintaxis del Espanol: Perfectividad e Impersonalidad*. Madrid: Ediciones de la Universidad de Madrid.

Diesing, M. 1992. *Indefinites*. Cambridge, Mass.: MIT Press.

Di Sciullo, A. M. 1996. "Romance Verbs and Variation." Paper presented at the Linguistic Symposium on Romance Languages 1996, Mexico.

Enç, M. 1991. "The Semantics of Specificity." *Linguistic Inquiry* 22: 1–26.

Friedman, M.A., and T. Siloni 1993. "Agr/Object Is Not Agr/Participle." Ms., University of Geneva.

Giorgi, A., and F. Pianesi. 1992. "For a Syntax of Tense." Ms., University of Catania and IRST, Povo (Trento).

Guéron, J., and T. Hoekstra. 1988. "T-Chains and the Constituent Structure of Auxiliaries." In *Constituent Structure: Papers from the 1987 Glow Conference*. Dordrecht: Foris.

Heim, I. 1982. "The Semantics of Definite and Indefinite Noun Phrases." Ph.D. dissertation, University of Massachusetts.

Hernanz, M. L. 1991. "Spanish Absolute Constructions and Aspect." *Catalan Working Papers in Linguistics* 1991. Barcelona: University Autonoma of Barcelona.

Jakubowicz, C. 1985. "Do Binding Principles Apply to Infl?" *Proceedings of NELS 15*, 188–206.

Jonas, D., and J. Bobaljik. 1993. "Specs for Subjects: The Role of TP in Icelandic." In J. D. Bolaljik and C. Philips (eds.) *MIT Working Papers in Linguistics 18: Papers on Case and Agreement I*. Department of Linguistics and Philosophy, MIT.

Kayne, R. 1975. *French Syntax: The Transformational Cycle*. Cambridge, Mass.: MIT Press.

———. 1989. "Facets of Romance Past Participle Agreement." In P. Beninca (ed.) *Dialect Variation and the Theory of Grammar*, 85–103. Dordrecht: Foris.

———. 1991. "Romance Clitics, Verb Movement, and PRO." *Linguistic Inquiry* 22: 647–686.

———. 1993. "Toward a Modular Theory of Auxiliary Selection." *Studia Linguistica* 47: 3–31.

———. 1994. *The Antisymmetry of Syntax.* Cambridge, Mass.: MIT Press.

Laka, I. 1990. *"Negation in Syntax: On the Nature of Functional Categories and Projections."* Ph.D. dissertation, MIT.

———. 1993. "Unergatives That Assign Ergative, Unaccusatives That Assign Accusative." In J. D. Bobaljik and C. Philips (eds.) *MIT Working Papers in Linguistics 18: Papers on Case and AgreementI,* 149–172. Department of Linguistic and Philosophy, MIT.

Martins, A. M. 1995. *"Clíticos na História do Português."* Ph.D. dissertation, University of Lisbon.

Meireles, J., and E. Raposo. 1983. "Subjunctives and Disjoint Reference in Portuguese: Some Implications for the Binding Theory." Ms., University of Lisbon.

Peres, J. 1992. Toward an Integrated View of the Expression of Time in Portuguese. In *Cadernos de Semântica.* Lisboa: University of Lisbon.

Perlmutter, D. 1976. "Evidence for Subject Downgrading in Portuguese." In J. Schmidt-Radefeldt (ed.) *Readings in Portuguese Linguistics.* North-Holland: Schmidt and Radefeldt.

Pollock, J.-Y. 1989. "Verb Movement, Universal Grammar and the Structure of IP." *Linguistic Inquiry* 20: 365–424.

Raposo, E. 1987. "Case Theory and Infl-to-Comp: The Inflected Infinitive." *Linguistic Inquiry* 18: 85–109.

Rigau, G. 1991. "On the Functional Properties of Agreement." In *Catalan Working Papers in Linguistics 1991.* Barcelona: University Autonoma of Barcelona.

Rizzi, L. 1982. *Issues in Italian Syntax.* Dordrecht: Foris.

Rouveret, A. 1992. "Clitics, Morphological Checking, and the Wackernagel Position in European Portuguese." Ms., University of Paris VIII.

Uriagereka, J. 1992. "An F-Position in Western Romance." Ms., University of Maryland.

Vinet, M-T. 1989. "Des petites propositions à valeur aspectuelle." *Canadian Journal of Linguistics,* 342: 171–192.

Zanuttini, R. 1994. "Re-examining Negative Clauses." In G. Cinque, J. Koster, J-Y Pollock, L. Rizzi, and R. Zanuttini (eds.) *Paths Towards Universal Grammar: Studies in Honor of Richard Kayne.* Washington, D.C.: Georgetown University Press.

2

PILAR BARBOSA

Clitics

A Window into the Null Subject Property

The Null Subject Languages (henceforth NSLs) have been shown to display the following cluster of properties (Rizzi 1982; Jaeggli 1984; Burzio 1986; Kenstowicz 1987):

(1) a. phonologically null subjects

   b. SV, VS order alternations (so-called free-inversion)

   c. lack of *that*-trace effects: extraction is from postverbal position (see also Campos 1997)

Property (1b) is illustrated by the following two Italian sentences:

(2) a. Gianni telefona.
     Gianni calls

   b. Telefona Gianni.
     calls Gianni

The following contrasts between English and Spanish illustrate property (1c):

(3) a. *Who did you say that bought a computer?

   b. Quién dices que compró un ordenador?
     who say-2sg that bought a computer
     'Who did you say bought a computer?'

The lack of *that*-trace effects exhibited in (3b) generalizes to all of the Romance NSLs. Rizzi (1982) and Jaeggli (1984) pursue an account of this contrast based on the claim that the subject in the NSLs is extracted not from the preverbal but from the postverbal position. Burzio (1986:165) notes that subjects in Italian are *never* extracted from the preverbal position. Consider the following Italian sentences:

(4) a. *(Ne₁)sono cadute [tre—₁]
         NE are fallen three

     b. Tre (*ne) sono cadute.
         'Three of them have fallen.'

(5) Quante—₁ *(ne₁) sono cadute?
     how many NE are fallen

     'How many of them have fallen?'

Example (4b) shows that *ne*-cliticization is not compatible with a preverbal subject in Italian. The fact that only the inverted form (4a) has a *wh*-moved counterpart shows that the subject *cannot be* extracted from the preverbal position. This conclusion reinforces Jaeggli's (1984) and Rizzi's (1982) hypotheses and raises the question of why this peculiar property should cluster together with the Null Subject property.

According to most analyses, (Rizzi 1982, 1990; Burzio 1986; Belletti 1990, among many others) the preverbal subject in (2a) has been A-moved to Spec, IP. It has been often noted (Brito and Duarte 1983; Brito 1984; Ambar 1988; Calabrese 1990; Saccon 1993; Pinto 1994, among many others) that the preverbal subject in (2a) has different discourse properties from the postverbal subject in (2b): preverbal subjects are topics, whereas postverbal subjects are foci. Based on this observation, Saccon (1993), Pinto (1994), Adger (1996), Grimshaw and Samek-Lodovici (1994), and Costa (1996) proposed that overt movement to Spec, IP in the NSLs is triggered by some "topic" feature. Under this approach, the NSLs differ from the non-NSLs in the possibility of leaving foci subjects in situ, but, from a strictly *configurational* point of view, subject initial constructions in the NSLs do not differ substantially from subject initial constructions in the non-NSLs: in both cases the subject is raised to Spec, IP, an A-position.

In this chapter, I will challenge the claim that subjects in the NSLs are ever raised to a preverbal A-position. I will argue that, in spite of appearances, there are significant structural differences between constructions with preverbal subjects in Italian/Catalan/Portuguese as opposed to French or English. I will claim that these contrasts can be accounted for only if we assume that the real A-position for lexical subjects in the NSLs is the postverbal position. Overt subject initial constructions in these languages are instances of either Clitic Left Dislocation (CLLD) (see Cinque 1990 for a thorough discussion of this construction) or of A'-movement of the subject. Thus, in (2b) the DP *Gianni* is the argumental subject, whereas in (2a) it is not. Example (2b) is derived via verb raising past the VP to a higher functional head. The subject remains inside the VP at Spell-Out (see Ordónez 1998 and Costa 1996, among many others, for arguments that the subject stays inside the VP in postverbal subject constructions):

(6)   [IP [I' telefona [VP Gianni t]]]
         |_____|

Example (2a) should be analyzed as illustrated in (7). In (7) the DP *Gianni* is Clitic Left Dislocated (i.e., *base-generated* in an adjoined position and doubled by *pro*, the real subject argument):

(7)   [IP Giannii [IP telefona *pro* i . . .]]

In (7) the DP *Gianni* is licensed by "rules of predication," in the sense of Chomsky (1977). IP contains an "open" position (*pro*, a pronominal category without independent reference) satisfied by the entity referred to by the dislocated DP (see Iatridou 1991 for the suggestion that CLLD constructions are licensed by predication, and Raposo 1996 for a somewhat similar analysis of topicalization in Portuguese and English). In (7) the CLLDed DP is adjoined to IP, but it can also be adjoined to the projection that is the landing site for *wh*-movement, subject to language-particular restrictions (see Rizzi 1997 for an overview of the relative positioning of CLLDed phrases and *wh*/Focus-movement in Italian; Solà 1992 and Vallduvi (1992) for Catalan; Zubizarreta 1998 for Spanish; and Duarte 1987 for Portuguese).

In addition to (8), SVO order can also be derived by extracting the subject directly from the postverbal position via A'-movement, as illustrated in (8):

(8)   [Focused/QP Subject . . . [I' [I V] [VP t]]
                               |_____|

I will argue that the subset of QPs that cannot be discourse topics, such as bare QPs, nonspecific indefinite QPs, and affective operators in the sense of Klima (1964), are extracted by A'-movement whenever they precede the verb. In most of the Romance NSLs (with the exclusion of Portuguese), definite DPs can also be directly extracted by A'-movement, in which case they must be stressed and bear contrastive focus, yielding the construction known as Focus movement, illustrated in the following for Italian (see Torrego 1984 for Spanish; Bonet 1990, Vallduví 1992, and Sola 1992 for Catalan; Dobrovie-Sorin 1994 for Romanian; Cinque 1990 and Rizzi 1997 for Italian):[1]

(9)   GIANNI telefona (non Carlo)
         Gianni (focus) calls (not C.)

Raposo 1994 and Rizzi (1997) propose that Focus movement and *wh*-movement have the same landing site in Italian: the specifier position of a Focus Phrase, lower than embedded complementizers but higher than IP. Linguists working on Spanish (Uribe-Etxebarria 1991; Zubizarreta 1995), Catalan (Bonet 1990; Vallduví 1992; Sola 1992), and Romanian (Dobrovie-Sorin 1994) have argued that Focus movement and *wh*-movement target Spec, IP in these languages. In line with Vallduví (1992) and Sola (1992), I will suggest that, since Spec, IP is free, given that it is not the landing site for A-movement in the NSLs, it is available as a landing site for A'-movement. In addition, I will propose that the Romance NSLs vary as to the structure of the left periphery. An intermediate projection between embedded complementizers and IP is available in Italian and Portuguese (see also Culicover 1992; Martins 1994; Uriagereka 1995a,b, Raposo 1994, 1997; Ambar 1998) but apparently is unavailable in Catalan and Spanish, as argued in the sources cited. In the case of Portuguese, both Spec, IP and the specifier of this intermediate position (FP) are available as possible landing sites for quantificational operator movement. Topics may be adjoined to IP or FP.

Even though (7) and (8) may look superficially similar, particularly in the case of bare or negative QPs, which do not need to bear contrastive focus when they are moved to the front of the clause, they are radically different structures, with different properties. Whereas in (8) the subject has A'-properties, in (7) it does not, since, as will be discussed later, CLLD does not display any of the familiar A'-properties: it does not display weak crossover effects (Duarte 1987; Rizzi 1997; Raposo 1996); it does not license parasitic gaps (Duarte 1987; Raposo 1996); it does not obey subjacency; and it does not reconstruct for the purposes of proper binding of the trace of cliticized *ne* (Cinque 1990). Another property of (7) that distinguishes it from (8) and from preverbal subject constructions in the non-NSLs is that the dislocated DP must be a discourse topic. Topichood follows straightforwardly from general properties of left-dislocation.

Under this approach, properties (1b) and (1c) of the cluster of features associated with the Null Subject property are side effects of the same phenomenon. Since the real A-position for subjects is the postverbal position, *wh*-movement is expected to take place from this position and no other; as for the SV/VS alternation, it results from the CLLD option, which is independently available. This enables us to pose new questions regarding the Null Subject property, namely, why the NSLs should be verb initial. I will not attempt to answer this question here (but see Barbosa 1995).

This overall analysis has much in common with previous proposals by Rigau (1987), Contreras (1991), Bonet (1990), Vallduví (1990, 1992), Solà (1992), Alexiadou and Anagnostopoulou (1998), and, more recently, Pollock (1997).

I will examine the patterns of clitic placement in European Portuguese (henceforth EP) and will argue that the alternations between cl-V and V-cl order in subject initial constructions can only be accounted for once the analysis just sketched is assumed. In so doing, I will be introducing data from Catalan and Romanian that reinforce this analysis. Then I will discuss certain restrictions on the distribution of preverbal subjects in inflected infinitival complements of epistemic and declarative verbs and in indirect commands in EP. I will argue that these facts constitute independent evidence for the claim that preverbal subjects do not raise to an A-position in EP. Finally, I will discuss certain asymmetries regarding adnominal *en/ne*-cliticization from subjects in French and in Italian/Catalan. I will claim that these can only be explained once the analysis developed for EP is extended to all of the Romance NSLs.

2.1 Clitic placement in European Portuguese

In most Romance languages, pronominal clitics immediately precede the verb in finite clauses. In EP, however, a structure equivalent to the Spanish example in (10) (with clitic-verb order) is ruled out:[2]

(10)   *Lo* vio Juan.   (Spanish)
'Juan saw him.'

(11)   a. *O* viu o João.   (Portuguese)
HIM saw the J.
'John saw him.'

b. Viu-o o João.

In EP the position of the clitic with respect to the verb varies according to context. Thus, enclisis is obligatory with most preverbal subjects (cf. (12)). When the subject belongs to a subset of quantified expressions, such as bare or negative quantifiers, proclisis is required:

(12)   A Maria viu-o / * *o* viu.
the Maria saw-HIM / *HIM* saw
'Maria saw him.'

(13)   Nenhum aluno / alguém o viu
no student someone saw *HIM*
'No student / someone saw him.'

The following is an overview of the different patterns found.[3]

2.1.1 Overview of clitic placement in European Portuguese

2.1.1.1 Contexts of enclisis

Verb initial utterances:
(14)   *O* viu / viu-o o João.
HIM saw the J.
'John saw him.'

Preverbal subjects with the exclusion of certain QPs to be mentioned later:
(15)   a. O Pedro viu-o / *o viu
the Pedro saw-him / him saw

b. Um aluno viu-a / *a viu
a student saw-HER / her saw

Topics:
(16)   Esses livros, dei-os / *os dei à Maria.
those books, I-gave-them / *them I-gave to Maria
'Those books, I gave them to Maria.'

Sentential adverbs:

(17)   Geralmente vejo-a / *a vejo de manhâ
       generally see-1–SGher / *her see-1-SG the morning

       'Usually, I see her in the morning.'

2.1.1.2 Contexts of proclisis

Embedded clauses:

(18)   Eu duvido que ele a visse.
       I doubt that he her see-Past-Subj

Whenever the following elements precede *the verb*:

(19)   *Bare QPs:*
       Ninguém / alguém o viu.
       no one / someone him saw

       'No one/someone saw him.'

Nonspecific indefinite QPs:

(20)   Algum aluno se esqueceu do livro.
       some student SE forgot of-the book

       'Some student forgot the book.'

Affective operators in the sense of Klima (1964):

(21)   a. *Negative QPs:*
          Nenhum aluno se esqueceu do livro.
          no student SE forgot of-the book

          'No student forgot the book.'

       b. *DPs modified by a Focus particle:*
          Só o Pedro *o* viu.
          only the Peter him saw

          'Only Peter saw him.'

Wh-*phrases:*

(22)   Quem *o* viu?
       who him saw

       'Who saw him?'

Sentential negation and aspectual adverbs in preverbal position:

(23)   a. O João não a viu.
          the John not her see/*see her

          'John didn´t see her.'

       b. O Pedro já / nunca o viu.
          the Peter already/ never him saw

          'Peter already/never saw him.'

This pattern of clitic placement has many properties in common with that observed in different varieties of medieval Romance (see Martins 1994 and Barbosa 1996a for extensive discussion). The restrictions on clitic placement in medieval Romance have been argued to fall under the larger phenomenon of "directional clitics," which also includes "second position" (2P) clitics, widely attested cross-linguistically (Halpern 1992a; Halpern and Fontana 1992; Benincà 1991; Fontana 1996; Barbosa 1996; Hock 1996). In the next section I will give a brief overview of some recent studies of this class of clitics.

2.1.2 The ban against first position clitics

As noted by Adolf Tobler (1875), atonic pronouns never stood in initial position in Old French: if the group of verb and pronoun object began a sentence, the pronoun always followed the verb and was enclitic. The following are examples taken from Old French, but the same is true of other early Romance dialects, such as Provençal, Italian, Romanian, Spanish, and Portuguese.

(24)   a. Li reis *me* veit.   (Old French: Ramsden, 1963)
           the kings me see

       b. Veit *me* li reis.

       c. *_me_ veit li reis

There are no instances of clitic-first in OR, a phenomenon that has been known in the literature as the Tobler-Mussafia Law (see Ramsden 1963; Lema and Rivero 1990; Rivero 1986; Benincà 1991, Cardinaletti and Roberts 1991; Halpern 1992a; Halpern and Fontana 1992; Fontana 1996). In modern EP the same generalization applies, although the situation is slightly different: only quantified subjects trigger cl-V order.

Halpern (1992a), Halpern and Fontana (1992), Fontana (1996), Barbosa (1996a) and Hock (1996) suggested that the alternations in clitic placement in Old Romance are related to a larger phenomenon that also includes 2P clitics—elements that tend to appear in second position in the clause. This is illustrated in the Serbo-Croatian examples in (25). Serbo-Croatian allows essentially free ordering of the major constituents of a clause, but the sentential clitics always come second.

(25)   a. covek = je voleo Mariju
           man AUX loved Mary

       b. Voleo = je Mariju covek

       c. covek = je Mariju voleo
           'The man loved Mary.'   (Halpern 1992a:1)

Second position clitics are observed in a number of languages throughout the world (see Halpern and Zwicky 1996 and the references cited there for extensive discussion). An increasing body of literature shows that the placement of 2P clitics cannot be explained entirely in syntactic terms, but that prosodic facts need to be considered as well (see Tegey 1977; Inkelas and Zec 1990; Zec and Inkelas 1990; Halpern 1992; Hock 1992, 1996; Percus 1993; Schutze 1994). Halpern (1992a, b; see also Halpern and Fontana 1992) argues that what Old Romance has in common with languages with 2P clitics is a constraint operating in Prosodic structure (P-structure) that bars a clitic from being the first element within a defined prosodic domain. Schematically:

(26)   * [Y cl W] where Y ranges over a particular prosodic domain

When the syntax places some constituent in front of the clitic (within this domain), nothing happens. When no element with a phonetic matrix precedes the clitic, the derivation is barred in P-structure and the clitic is forced to surface in a position other than that assigned to it by the syntax, namely, to the right of the adjacent word.[4] The process that positions the clitic after the first prosodic word in the string takes place at an intermediate level between syntax and PF and is labeled by Halpern as Prosodic Inversion (but see Sadock 1991 and Marantz 1988 for different ways of implementing this):

(27)   clitic$*$X$*$Y $\Rightarrow$ X$*$clitic$*$Y

To illustrate how Halpern's analysis works for the Old French examples given earlier, I assume that, in the syntax, verbal clitics are left adjacent to finite V:

(28)   a. Li reis *me* veit.
            the kings me see
            'The kings see me.'

        b. *Me veit li reis.

When P-structure is built, (28b) is ruled out in violation of (26). Prosodic inversion then applies as a Last Resort operation, yielding (29):

(29)   Veit *me* lei reis.

Lema and Rivero (1989, 1990), Benincà (1991), and Cardinaletti and Roberts (1991) propose instead that enclisis is derived via verb movement in the syntax.

In Barbosa (1993, 1996), I defended the view that a prosodic constraint along the lines of (26) is also operative in Modern Portuguese. In Barbosa (1996a), however, I argued against the idea that enclisis is derived from an underlyingly proclitic structure via Last Resort movement (in P-structure or in the syntax), but is rather an alternative derivation altogether that is chosen when proclisis crashes at the PF-interface. In the next section, I will briefly review some arguments in support of the claim that prosody is the key to understanding the distribution of EP clitics.

2.1.3 Arguments for a prosodic account of the alternations between enclisis and proclisis

Most researchers working on modern EP have proposed a purely syntactic account of clitic placement (Madeira 1992; Rouveret 1992; Martins 1994; Uriagereka 1995a, b; Duarte and Matos, chapter 4, this volume). In fact, the relation between enclisis and prosody in EP is not quite transparent: examples such as (24) are bad in EP and require enclisis. However, it is very hard to pinpoint a single syntactic generalization that might be driving these alternations. One might attempt to define the contexts of proclisis in terms of the notion "operator," given that negation, aspectual adverbs, and certain QPs trigger proclisis. However, prepositional complementizers also trigger proclisis, and they are not operators. On the other hand, null operators are not proclisis triggers. A case in point is provided by yes/no questions. In yes/no questions in Germanic a null operator counts as a first position for V-second, that is, empty operators matter as much as phrases with a phonological matrix. This is not so in the case of clitic placement in EP, where yes/no questions trigger V-cl order, thus behaving as if null operators were irrelevant:

(30)   Viste-a / * a viste?
        saw-her

        'Did you see her?'

Thus, what appears to be relevant here is whether *material with a phonological matrix* precedes the cl/V complex, which suggests that the constraint is phonological.

The relevance of a prosodic condition on clitic placement is also defended in Frota and Vigário (1996). Working within the framework of Prosodic Phonology, these authors note that it is sometimes possible to have enclisis in embedded contexts as long as there is an Intonational Phrase (IntP) boundary between what they take to be the "trigger" of proclisis and the clitic.

In Barbosa (1996a), I provide cross-linguistic evidence that indirectly supports the adequacy of Halpern's prosodic hypothesis when applied to EP. As mentioned there, Halpern's constraint predicts the possibility of the existence of a language where violations of (26) might be "fixed" in some way other than by switching to enclisis. For instance, in the case of a language that has two clitic forms with the same syntax but a different phonetic shape, one reduced and prosodically constrained and the other not so constrained, one would predict the reduced form to be barred in just those environments where V-cl order occurs in EP. In Barbosa (1996a), I claim that Megleno-Romance, a Balkan language spoken in some villages northwest of Thessaloniki in Greece, studied by Campos (1994), is such a language. In what follows I will briefly review Campos's data, since they will prove to be essential to a proper understanding of clitic placement in EP.

As reported in Campos (1994), some pronominal clitics in Megleno-Romance have full and reduced forms:

(31)   Direct Objects

	Full	Reduced
1sg	mi	
2sg	ti	
3sg M	la	
F	au	-u
1pl	na	
2pl	va	
3pl M	va	
F	li	

(32)   Indirect Objects

	Full	Reduced
1sg	ã	-ñ
2sg	ats	-ts
3sg M	ai	-i
F	ai	-i
1pl	na	
2pl	va	
3pl M	la	
F	fla	

The reduced forms -*u* 'her, it-fem' and -*i* 'to him/her' are never found in sentence initial position. Instead, the full clitics *au* and *ai* appear:

(33)   *Ai/*i* zízi la bábâ . . .
       her told to grandmother
       'He told his grandmother.'   (Campos 1994: 3)

The full forms *au* 'her, it-fem' and *ai* 'him/her-indirect-object' are used:

At the beginning of an utterance or after a pause:

(34)   *Au* lov mullárea, *au* anvii an ruguzinâ.
       her took woman-the her wrapped in rug
       'He took the woman (and) wrapped her with a rug.'   (Campos 1994: 8)

After the subject:

(35)   Túntsea ampirátu *au* sculasi ctíia di tâtun.
       Then king-the it-fem took box-the of tobacco
       'Then the king took the tobacco box.'   (Campos 1994: 8)

After a dislocated element:

(36)   a. Iuâ Lámña *au* flai . . .
           I monster-the her found
           'I found the monster.'

       b. . . . si la niviâstâ *ai* fuzí búlu din cap.
           and to bride her took-out veil-the from head
           '. . . He removed the bride's veil.'   (Campos 1994: 8)

The reduced clitics appear in environments that are very reminiscent of those in which we find proclisis in EP:

After the complementizer ca *'that' and the relative complementizer* tsi*':*

(37)   a. Fiâsi ca *u* grisó.
           made that her forgot
           'He faked that he did not remember her.'   (Campos 1994: 5)

b. Ma fichúru tsi *u* talchó . . .
but boy-the that her killed . . .
'But the boy who killed her . . .'   (Campos 1994: 5)

After the subjunctive marker si:
(38) Ram kinisíts s-*u* lom niviâsta Si
had left SUBJ her take bride-the and . . .
'We had left to take the bride and . . .'   (Campos 1994: 4)

After the conditional ácu *'if'*:
(39) Acu *u* liâu fiâta . . .
if her take girl-the
'If I take the girl . . . '   (Campos 1994: 5)

After the adverb con *'when'*:
(40) Con *u* dâzvii, flo un niniâl.
when it-fem unfolded, found a ring
'When she unfolded it, she found a ring.'   (Campos 1994: 6)

After the conjunction câ *'because'*:
(41) . . . câ *u* prisâri cúla mai depârti . . .
. . . because it-fem jumped castle-the more far
'. . . because he jumped further than the castle . . .'   (Campos 1994: 6)

After the negative nu *'not'*:
(42) Tsîsta uom âri una fiâtâ tsi an lúmi nu u lasâ s-iasâ
This man has a daughter who to world not her lets SUBJ-go out   (Campos 1994: 6)

After an emphatic *subject:*
(43) Rápu zísi ca: "Iuâ u talchoi Lámña!"
Arab-the said that: I her killed ogre-the
'The Arab said: "I killed the ogre."'   (Campos 1994: 6)

A purely syntactic account of the alternations between the weak and strong forms of the pronoun in Megleno-Romance is very hard to maintain: in the direct object paradigm, for instance, there is one weak form for the feminine singular and no weak form for the masculine. Thus, the restrictions on the distribution of the weak/strong alternates can only be accounted for in the prosody, and Halpern's constraint in (26) yields the right results when applied to the reduced forms.

What is relevant for the present purposes is to note that the environments that condition the distribution of the different clitic forms in Megleno-Romance are remarkably similar to those that condition the proclisis/enclisis alternations in EP. Since, in order to account for Megleno-Romance, some PF interface constraint akin to Halpern's (26), is necessary, and the facts discussed earlier also suggest that prosody appears to be relevant in EP, it is very tempting to assume that in EP, too, a similar constraint is at work. By hypothesis, enclisis would be EP's "answer" to violations of (26); Megleno-Romance, by contrast, would have the option of realizing the strong form in that context.

In earlier work, I have proposed that the following prosodic constraint is operative in EP:

(44)   *[IntP cl V . . .] IntP = Intonational Phrase

According to the theory of prosodic domains developed in work by Selkirk 1984, 1986, 1993), Nespor and Vogel (1986), among others, the output of the syntactic component is submitted to a set of phonological phrasing rules, which rebracket and relabel the structure to form a purely phonological bracketing. P-structure is hierarchically organized in categories of different types: syllable, prosodic word, phonological phrase, intonational phrase, utterance. In this vein, (44) says that the clitic is barred from appearing at the left edge of the prosodic constituent that immediately dominates the Prosodic Phrase (ϕ), the Intonational Phrase domain.

Inkelas (1989) and Halpern (1992) proposed that 2P clitics are directional clitics in the sense that they must adjoin to a Prosodic Word to their left. In Barbosa (1996a) I discussed some arguments against the enclitic nature of EP clitics and argued for the weaker version stated in (44), which simply says that EP clitics cannot be initial in the IntP. This claim presupposes that, in EP, the IntP initial position is prosodically constrained: particular requirements are imposed on prosodic words that sit at the right edge of the IntP boundary. In effect, there is independent evidence that suggests that this is indeed the case.

Frota (personal communication) observes that certain function words in EP have two different realizations depending on whether they are right-adjacent to an IntP boundary. Consider the example in (45) and the two different P-structures that may be assigned to it:

(45)   As angolanas ofereceram especiarias ao jornalista.
       the girls from Angola offered spices to-the journalist

(46)   a. [[As angolanas]ϕ [ofereceram especiarias] ϕ [ao jornalista]ϕ]$_I$

       b. [[As angolanas]ϕ [ofereceram especiarias]ϕ] [[ao jornalista]ϕ]$_I$

In (46b), where the function word ao is immediately to the right of an IntP boundary, it is pronounced as [aw], the form that corresponds to the pronunciation of the word in isolation. In (46a) it is pronounced as [o]. This observation has led Frota to suggest that there is a correlation between the strong form and right-adjacency to an IntP boundary. Thus, it appears that the IntP-initial position is some sort of "strong" position in EP.

The [aw]/[o] alternation noted by Frota is similar to the alternations between the reduced and strong forms of Megleno-Romance clitics. Since, as noted, the environments that block the weak form are roughly the same as those that block the proclitic form in EP, and there is independent evidence that the IntP initial positive is a "strong" position, I conclude that (44) is rather plausible. Clitics are nonstressed items, so it is not surprising that they should be banned from occurring at the right edge of an IntP boundary if this position is "strong."[5]

The Megleno-Romance facts also bear on a long-standing issue in the literature on clitic placement in EP, namely, the question of whether proclisis is "triggered" by context, enclisis being the "basic" option. Thus, both Frota and Vigário (1996) and Duarte and Matos (chapter 4, this volume) propose that enclisis is "undone" in the context of a trigger that consists of a class of items that includes "operator-like" elements, according to the latter, or "function words which have the phonological status of prosodic words," according to the former. If the distribution of the Megleno-Romance reduced form is to be put in parallel with the distribution of proclisis in EP, as I think it should in view of the similarity of the environments in which both occur, then the environments in question have no "undoing" effect on a basic enclitic form. In Megleno-Romance both clitic forms are proclitics. When the right environment is not met, the nonreduced form is chosen. Likewise, in standard EP, enclisis emerges when the derivation with proclisis crashes in the PF-interface. This approach has the added advantage of being in line with the extensive body of literature on 2P clitics. Assuming that proclisis in EP is derived from enclisis would set EP clitics apart from the bulk of languages that display similar alternations. In the next section I will show how these leading ideas can be implemented in a more precise way.

2.1.4 The analysis

In the syntax, proclitics are placed in the checking domain of the inflectional head to which the verb raises.

(47)   cl ... [Infl V] ...]

In Barbosa (1996a), I argue that proclitics do not adjoin to the head containing the verb, but rather are adjoined to IP. Since the arguments that led to that proposal are complex and not directly relevant to my main purposes here, I will simply assume that the clitic is adjoined to the Infl head that contains the clitic.

Constraint (44), repeated here as (48), stars every P-structure in which no phonetic material precedes the clitic within the IntP domain containing it:

(48)   *[IntP cl V ...] IntP = Intonational Phrase

This accounts for the impossibility of (49a) in opposition to (49b):

(49)   a. *O viu o João.
        HIM saw the J.
        'John saw him.'

       b. Quem o viu?
        who HIM saw
        'Who saw him?'

Example (49b) has the following (partial) P-structure, where the constraint in (48) is not violated:

(50)   [IntP quem o viu]

The representation in (50) converges at the PF-interface. Example (49a), by contrast, is assigned a P-structure in which (48) is violated:

(51)   * [IntP o viu]

By (48), (51) is not a well-formed P-structure, so the derivation "crashes" at the PF interface. An alternative derivation is then chosen in which the clitic, rather than being positioned in the checking domain of Infl, directly moves from its base position inside the VP shell to an intermediate functional head through which the verb raises on its way to Infl (AgrO or Asp); see Barbosa 1996a for discussion, and Barbosa 1996b for the idea that right adjunction for head movement is allowed in the grammar, contrary to Kayne 1994; see also Duarte and Matos 1995 for the idea that enclisis is derived low in the structure). This yields (52b):

(52)   a. [IP . . . [ASP [Asp viu] o] [VP o João . . . t . . .]]

        b. Viu-o.

When mapped into prosodic structure, (52) will not violate the filter in (48). Now consider P-structures of derivations containing sentential negation:

(53)   a. Não a vi.
           not her see-1SG
           'I didn't see her.'

        b. P-structure: [Int P não a vi]

In constructions with sentential negation the proclitic does not find itself in initial position within the IntP, so the derivation converges, barring the Last Resort option that would yield enclisis.

Now I turn to the question of why CLLD should require enclisis:

(54)   *Esse livro o dei ao Pedro.
          that book it gave to-the P.

A number of researchers working in Prosodic Phonology have argued that topics are mapped into Intonational Phrases of their own (Nespor and Vogel 1986; Kanerva 1990; Halpern 1992a, b). Thus, (55) has the P-structure in (55):

(55)   [IntP Esses livros] [IntP os dei à Maria.]

Representation (55) crashes, since it violates the constraint in (48). An alternative derivation is then chosen, with enclisis.

2.1.5 Subject initial constructions

In subject initial constructions the position of the clitic varies according to the nature of the subject. If the subject is a bare quantifier, the universal quantifier, a negative QP, or a DP modified by a focus operator, proclisis emerges; enclisis is obligatorily found in all other cases. I will be adopting the term *quantificational operator* to refer to this rather heterogeneous set of QPs. This term is borrowed from Vallduví (1992) for reasons that will become clear later.

The similarities between the distribution of the strong form in Megleno-Romance and enclisis in EP are particularly striking in the case of subjects. Although Campos does not discuss quantified subjects, he observes that there is a contrast between emphatic and nonemphatic subjects. The reduced form is possible *only when the subject is emphatic.* Continuing to establish a correlation between proclisis in EP and choice of the reduced form in Megleno-Romance, I note that emphatic subjects in Megleno-Romance pattern with the restricted group of quantified expressions that trigger proclisis in EP. In addition, the following generalization emerges: the pattern of cliticization found with CLLDed objects is the pattern observed with neutral (nonquantificational) subjects in preverbal subject position.

Yet another significant observation is that in EP CLLD is barred with the set of expressions that require proclisis in EP: bare quantifiers, negative quantifiers, nonspecific indefinite QPs, and DPs modified by focus operators cannot be doubled by a resumptive clitic, as shown in the following.

(56) a. *Nada posso dar-to/ to dar.
        nothing I can give-it-to-you

      b. *Alguém posso vê-lo/ o ver amanhã.
        someone I-can see him tomorrow

      c. *Nenhuns alunos, vi-os/ os vi ontem.
        no students I-saw-them/ them saw yesterday

      d. *Até o Pedro, vi-o/ o vi ontem.
        even Peter I-saw-him yesterday

      e. *Algum aluno, devo-o/ o devo ter prejudicado, mas não sei qual.
        some student I-must have damaged but I don´t know which one

Note that although the QPs in (56) cannot be doubled by a clitic, they can be fronted leaving a gap in their base position. In this case proclisis is the only option.

(57) a. Nada$_i$ te posso dar e$_i$.
        nothing$_i$ you I-can give e$_i$
        'I can give you nothing.'

b. Alguém$_i$ / algum aluno ela viu e$_i$, mas não sei quem.

someone$_i$ some student she saw e$_i$ but not I-know who

'She saw someone/some student, but I don't know who.'

c. Nenhuma resposta$_i$ me deram e$_i$ até hoje.

no answer e$_i$ to me they-gave e$_i$ until today

d. Até com o Pedro ela se zangou e$_i$.

even with the Peter e$_i$ she SE argued e$_i$

'She argued even with Peter.'

I thus arrive at the following generalizations:

(58) a. CLLD requires enclisis in opposition to quantificational operator-fronting, which requires proclisis.

b. The set of expressions that "trigger" proclisis (independently of their status of subjects or objects) coincides with the set of expressions that cannot be CLLDed.

Before I elaborate on the consequences of (58b) for a theory of subject positions, I will concentrate on (58a). I will briefly review the properties that distinguish CLLD from Focus-movement and quantificational operator movement in most of Romance. These are well documented for Italian (Cinque 1990; Rizzi 1997), Spanish (Torrego 1984; Laka 1990; Contreras 1991; Zubizarreta 1998), and Catalan (Vallduví 1992; Sola 1992; Bonet 1990). Then I will discuss the implications of these analyses for Portuguese, a language that displays yet another kind of constituent fronting, more akin to English topicalization (Duarte 1987; Martins 1994; Raposo 1994, 1996). Finally, I will show how the results of this investigation combine with my theory of clitic placement in EP to yield the different patterns of clitic placement observed with constituent fronting.

2.1.5.1 CLLD, Focus-movement and quantificational operator movement

The topic comment articulation in Romance is commonly expressed by the construction that Cinque (1990) has labeled CLLD. In this construction, the topic constituent is placed in the front of the clause and is resumed by a clitic coreferential with it. Cinque (1990), argued that CLLD involves *base-generation* of the dislocated topic in an adjoined position wherefrom it is linked to the clitic pronoun inside the clause. The basis of his argumentation is a systematic comparison with another Italian construction that I will label Focus-movement (after Uriagereka 1995a,b; Rizzi 1997; Raposo 1996). In Italian, Focus-movement expresses the focus-presupposition articulation and consists in preposing the focal element and assigning it special stress:

(59) IL TUO LIBRO ho letto (, non il suo).

'Your book (focus) I have read (not his).' (Rizzi 1997)

According to Rizzi (1997), this option is restricted to contrastive focus. Other Romance languages that have been described as having equivalents to (59) are Romanian (Dobrovie-Sorin 1994), Spanish (Torrego 1984; Laka 1990, Contreras 1991; Uribe-Etxebarria 1991; Zubizarreta 1998), and Catalan (Vallduví 1992; Sola 1992; Bonet 1990).

A number of properties distinguish CLLD from Focus. As discussed in Cinque 1990, all of them point to the conclusion that Focus involves *wh*-movement, whereas CLLD does not. The main superficial difference is that a "resumptive" clitic is impossible with a focalized object but is obligatory with a CLLD object. Second, CLLD does not give rise to weak crossover effects, even though such effects are detectable with Focus (Rizzi's 1997 judgments):

(60)   a. Gianni$_1$, sua$_1$ madre lo$_1$ ha sempre apprezzato.
           'Gianni, his mother always appreciated him.'

       b. ??GIANNI$_1$ sua$_1$ madre ha sempre apprezzato t$_1$ (non Piero).
           'Gianni his mother always appreciated (not Peter).'

Another piece of evidence that led Cinque to the conclusion that CLLD should not be analyzed as involving *wh*-movement is provided by another diagnostic for *wh*-movement in Italian, *ne*-cliticization. As discussed in Belletti and Rizzi (1981) and Rizzi (1982), partitive *ne* is obligatory when the QP it is associated with is in object position:

(61)   *(Ne$_{i)}$ ho smarrite [quattro e$_i$] (di quelle lettere)   (Cinque 1990: 69)
       of-them (I) lost four (of those letters)

Whenever the QP is in preverbal subject position or CLLDed, *ne* is obligatorily absent:

(62)   a. [Quattro t$_i$] (*ne$_i$) sono andate smarrite.
           four NE are gone lost

       b. [Quattro]$_i$ credo che [le$_i$ abbiano smarrite].
           four I-think that them they-have lost   (Cinque 1990: 70)

By contrast, the obligatoriness of *ne* is preserved under *wh*-movement and Focus-movement:

(63)   a. Quante pietre hai preso?
           how many stones have-you taken

       b. *Quante hai preso?
           how many have-you taken
           (Cf. *Ho preso tre 'I have taken three.')

       c. Quante *ne* hai prese?
           how many of-them have-you taken
           (Cf. Ne ho prese tre 'I have taken three of them.')   (Cinque 1990: 69)

(64)   a. *Ne* ha invitati molti.
          of-them has invited many

       b. MOLTI, *ne* ha invitati.
          many of them has invited

       c. *MOLTI, ha invitato/ invitati.
          many has invited

The fact that Focus-movement patterns with *wh*-movement with respect to the obligatoriness of *ne* suggests that it involves A'-movement. Assuming that the trace of *ne* needs to be properly bound, it is bound under reconstruction. Example (63b) shows that CLLD is incompatible with *ne*. This can be explained if CLLD does not involve movement, but rather base-generation of the topic in front of the clause and some rule of construal between it and the resumptive clitic. In this configuration there is no source for *ne*:

(65)   [Quattro]ᵢ [credo che [leᵢ abbiano smarrite]]
       four I-think that them they-have lost

Duarte (1987) and Raposo (1996) discuss other properties that conspire against a movement analysis of CLLD: CLLD does not obey subjacency and does not license parasitic gaps. I will not review these facts here, but I refer the reader to the sources cited for illustration.[6]

Regarding Focus-movement, I will follow Raposo (1994), Raposo and Uriageraka (1996), and Rizzi (1997) in assuming that Focus involves A'-movement to Spec, FP, where FP is a head located between C and IP:

(66)   [FP GIANNI [F' ho visto t]]
       ↑_____|

       Gianni (focus) I have seen

In Italian CLLDed constituents may appear to the right or left of Focus. Iatridou (1991) and Raposo (1996) propose that the topic comment articulation is licensed by "rules of predication" (Chomksy 1977) that require that the topic be "base-generated" in a position of adjunction to the XP that is predicated of it. Rizzi (1997), by contrast, assumes that topics in general are introduced by a Topic Phrase headed by a Top head that "defines a kind of 'higher predication.'" I will return to this issue later, but a few words are in order here regarding Focus fronting and certain quantificational operators.

2.1.5.2 *Quantificational operators*

Cinque (1990) notes that when the fronted object is a bare quantifier (*qualcosa* 'something', *qualcuno* 'someone', etc.), though not if it is a quantified NP (*qualche* N'/*alcuni* N' 'some N'', *molti* N' 'many N''', etc.), the resumptive pronoun may be missing:

(67)   a. Qualcuno, (lo) troveremo.
        someone (him) we-will-find

        b. Qualcosa, di sicuro, io (la) farò.
        something for sure I it will-I-do

(68)   a. Qualche errore, Carlo *(lo) ha fatto.
        some error Carlo (it) has made

        b. Alcuni libri, *(li) ho comperati.
        some books (them) I-have bought

According to Cinque (1990), the presence or absence of the clitic in (67) and (68) is not optional and correlates with a difference in the interpretation of the quantifier. If the speaker has something or someone specific in mind, the clitic is required. If the interpretation is 'something or other' or 'someone unspecified', the clitic is *obligatorily absent*. Cinque proceeds to observe that constructions such as those in (68)—without a resumptive clitic—are subject to weak islands, contrary to CLLD constructions. This suggests that these constructions involve (successive cyclic) movement of the bare quantifier rather than base-generation; that is, they are instances of A'-movement. This analysis is illustrated in (69b) for the example (69a), where the bare QP is nonspecific:

(69)   a. Qualcuno, troveremo.
        someone we will find

        b. [FP Qualcuno [F' troveremo t]]
        |_____|

Example (69a) is just like (66) *without focal stress* on the moved constituent. According to Rizzi (1997), the QPs that are incompatible with a resumptive clitic can be focused. However, Cinque's description suggests that the QPs that are incompatible with a resumptive clitic behave differently from the other DPs in that *they do not necessarily need to bear contrastive focus* when extracted by A'-movement. I thus arrive at the following picture for Italian: there are in principle two ways of putting an object at the front of the clause—CLLD and Focus-movement. Focus-movement is an instance of A'-movement, but CLLD does not pass any of the diagnostics for movement: it does not display weak crossover effects, it does not license parasitic gaps, it does not obey subjacency, and it does not reconstruct for the purposes of the Proper Binding Condition. CLLD expresses the topic comment articulation. For this reason, CLLDed constituents must be capable of referring to some contextually salient object or set of objects. Thus it is not surprising that QPs that lack a lexical restriction, nonspecific indefinites, or negative QPs cannot be CLLDed. They can be fronted by A'-movement, though, but in this case they do not need to bear contrastive focus, unlike other nominal expressions.

Vallduví's (1992) work on Catalan reinforces the picture just described. In Catalan, negative quantifiers and certain other quantifiers that are roughly the same class that triggers proclisis in EP must be string adjacent to the verb when fronted. In this, they behave like fronted *wh*-phrases and differently from CLLDed phrases, which do not need to be string adjacent to V. Consider a typical CLLD construction in Catalan (Vallduví 1992:127):

(70)   [El sou]₁ [a la gent]₂ no l₁'hi₂ regalen.
       the pay to the people not it to-them give-3Pl
       'They don´t give the pay to people for free.'

The two fronted constituents can be freely switched around:

(71)   [a la gent]₂ [el sou]₁ no l₁'hi₂ regalen.

Vallduví shows that if one of the two left-hand phrases is a negative quantifier, the linear order among the phrases is not free any more (note that in Catalan a negative bare quantifier can be doubled by a clitic while still displaying this restriction):

(72)   a. El sou a ningú (no) l'hi regalen.
          'They don't give the pay to anyone for free.'

       b. *A ningú el sou (no) l'hi regalen.

Subject negative quantifiers behave alike, as shown by the comparison of examples (73) and (74). In (73), subject and object may be switched around freely:

(73)   a. Els dolents l'empresa no els vol.
          the bad-ones the company no them want
          'The company doesn't want the bad ones.'

       b. L' empresa els dolents no els vol.

When the subject is a negative quantifier, as in the following sentences, left-adjacency to the verbal string is required again:

(74)   a. Els dolents ningú (no) els vol.
          'No one wants the bad ones.'

       b. *Ningú els dolens (no) els vol.

Vallduví concludes the following: "It is clear, then, that these negative quantifiers do not appear in the typical IP-adjunction slot left-detached phrases appear in, but rather in a position within IP which is left-adjacent to the verbal string. The left-adjacency requirement for *ningú* in (15) [my (74)] has nothing to do with the grammatical status as a subject, as shown by the fact that it also applies in (14) [my (72)], where *ningú* is an indirect object. It is rather its status as a quantificational operator that appears to determine its inability to allow other left-hand phrases between itself and the verbal string" (Vallduví 1992:328). According to Vallduví, this adjacency requirement does not affect all QPs, but a subset of them that includes *poques* N' ("few N"), *alguna cosa* 'something', *tothom* 'everyone', among others. These latter QPs do not bind a clitic within IP, unlike *ningú*.

Vallduví further observes that fronted *wh*-phrases are subject to the same adjacency restriction, which applies in matrix as well as embedded questions. In addition, the QPs in question are in complementary distribution with a preverbal *wh*-phrase:

(75) a. Què₁ no regalen t₁ a ningú?
          what not give 3PL to no one
          'What don't they give to anyone for free?'

      b. *Què a ningú (no) li regalen?

      c. *A ningú què (no) li regalen?

(76) a. Qui farà poques coses?
          who do-FUT-3SG few things
          'Who'll do few things?'

      b. *Qui poques coses farà?

      c. *Poques coses qui farà?

It is clear that these QPs and *wh*-phrases occupy the same position. In view of the fact that this position must be string adjacent to the verb, but lower than complementizers, Vallduví suggests that it is Spec, IP. Schematically:

(77) [CP C [IP XP [IPwh\ +Op QP [I' [I V] . . . t]]]]

XP stands for left-adjoined topics, and Spec, IP is filled by either a fronted *wh*-phrase or a fronted quantificational operator, regardless of its status as subject or object. Vallduví follows previous proposals according to which Catalan's basic order is VOS (Bonet 1990; Contreras 1991), so Spec, IP is empty and available for this role as a quantifier-related position.

Thus, there is a subset of quantificational expressions that are fronted by A'-movement without requiring contrastive Focus. Vallduví refers to these QPs as "quantificational operators" and describes them as being incapable of functioning as "links." A "link phrase" "points to the file card that it denotes in the file-structured knowledge-store of the hearer and selects it among the sentence participants as the sole point of information entry" (Vallduví 1992b:335). The expressions that cannot serve as link phrases range over QPs without a lexical restriction, nonspecific indefinites, and +affective operators.

To sum up, I conclude that both Focus fronting and fronting of quantificational operators involve A'-movement. For Italian, I follow Rizzi (1997) in assuming that Focus-movement targets Spec, FP, since topics may appear to the right of Focus:

(78)   A Gianni, QUESTO, domani, gli dovrete dire.
'To Gianni, THIS, tomorrow, you should tell him.'

Regarding Spanish and Catalan, the strict adjacency that is required between a focused constituent and the inflected verb (see Laka 1990, Bonet 1990; Uribe-Etxebarria 1991; Contreras 1991; and Zubizarreta 1998) suggests that Focus targets Spec, IP, like *wh*-movement and movement of quantificational operators. Vallduví (1990, 1992) argues that focus-preposed focus constituents are syntactically distinct from preposed quantificational operators (including *wh*-operators) despite the apparent similarity. I will not go into that issue here. As will be noted later, Portuguese lacks the former kind of constituent fronting, even though it has the latter (Duarte 1987; Raposo 1996), a fact that indirectly confirms Vallduví´s suggestion that the two kinds of movement should be distinguished. Before I turn to Portuguese, however, I will address the issue of whether CLLD involves adjunction to XP or rather recursive Topic Phrases.

2.1.5.3 Base-generated adjunction or recursive Topic Phrases?

As mentioned earlier, Iatridou (1991) and Raposo (1996) propose that the topic comment articulation is licensed by "rules of predication" (Chomksy 1977) that require that the topic be "base-generated" in a position of adjunction to the XP that is predicated of it. In the spirit of Kayne (1994), Rizzi (1997) assumes that topics in general (CLLDed topics included) are introduced by the usual X-bar schema: a Topic Phrase headed by a Top head that "defines a kind of 'higher predication.'" Raposo (1996) makes the more radical proposal that the topic and its associated clause are not merged by the core syntactic principles but by rules of predication that belong to the domain of discourse. In this way, Raposo can still maintain Kayne's restrictive X-bar schema while allowing for base-generated adjunction of topics.

In what follows, I will introduce data from Romanian discussed in Dobrovie-Sorin (1994) that might be taken as evidence that the configuration of adjunction is indeed required in the case of dislocated topics. The same data suggest that Romanian fits rather well into the clause structure suggested by Vallduví for Catalan in (77).

2.1.5.3.1 ROMANIAN SUBJUNCTIVE COMPLEMENTS   Romanian subjunctives are introduced by a particle, *să*, as illustrated in (80):

(79)   a. Vreau să vina Ion mîine.
[I] want să come John tomorrow

b. Vreau să -l examineze Popescu pe Ion.
[I] want să -him examine Popescu to John

'I want that Popescu examine him, John.'

This particle has been the topic of much debate in the literature (see Dobrovie-Sorin 1994; Terzi 1992; Rivero 1987), since it appears to have some of the properties of a complementizer, as well as some of the properties of an Infl head. Thus, it can co-occur with the complementizer *ca,* as shown in the following:

(80) a. Vreau *ca* mîine să vina Ion.
       [I] want that tomorrow să come John.
       'I want John to come tomorrow.'

  b. Doresc *ca* pe Ion să -l examineze Popescu.
     [I] wish that *pe* Ion să -him examine Popescu

Moreover, a subject cannot appear to its immediate right:

(81) *Vreau *ca* mîine să Ion vina.

What is of interest here is the distribution of the complementizer *ca.* In the absence of any material in the front of *să, ca* is preferably absent:

(82) ?? aș vrea *ca să* -l examineze Popescu pe Ion.
       [I] would like that *să* him examine P. *pe* Ion
       'I would like that P. examine John.'

Ca becomes obligatory in case there is a topic in the front of *să*: a sentential adverb (cf. (80a) with (83a)) or a dislocated object (cf. (80b) with (83b)).

(83) a. *Vreau mîine să vină Ion.
       [I] want tomorrow să come John.
       'I want John to come tomorrow.'

  b. *Doresc pe Ion să -l examineze Popescu.
     [I] wish pe Ion să -him examine Popescu

Interestingly, *ca* is also obligatory with a preverbal subject:

(84) a. Vreau *ca* Ion să vină.
       [I] want that John să come

  b. *Vreau Ion să vină.

Thus, I observe that preverbal subjects pattern with dislocated elements and sentential adverbs. Interestingly, when the fronted constituent is focused, *ca* is not required. Consider the following examples (from Manuela Ungureanu, personal communication):

(85) a. Aș vrea (*ca*) numai Ion să vină la petrecere.
       [I] want that only Ion să come to the party
       'I want only John to come to the party.'

(86) a. Vreau (*ca*) MÎINE să vină Ion.
      [I] want that tomorrow (focus) să come Ion.
      'It is tomorrow that I want John to come.'

      b. Vreau (*ca*) ION să vină.
      'It is John that I want to come.'

Moreover, with *wh*-extraction, *ca* is also absent (in fact, its presence results in unacceptability):

(87) a. Nu stia (*ca) unde să plece.
      not know-3SG that where să go
      'He doesn't know where to go.'

Assuming that Focus fronting involves movement (as argued earlier for Focus-movement in Italian), it is not surprising that it patterns with *wh*-movement in dispensing with the presence of *ca*.

Here I will pursue an account of the contrast between Topic and Focus with respect to the distribution of the complementizer *ca* that relies on the distinction between adjuncts and specifiers and hence runs counter to Kayne's (1994) antisymmetry hypothesis, as well as Rizzi's (1997) extension of it to the analysis of dislocated topics in Italian. I will take the difference between Topic and Focus to correlate with exactly this distinction. CLLDed topics as well as sentential adverbs are base-generated in an adjoined position, whereas fronted Focus involves A'-movement to the specifier of the XP projected by the subjunctive particle (recall that *wh*-movement in Romanian can target the specifier position of the head containing *sa*, so it is plausible to assume that this position is an A'-position).

It has often been proposed that adjunction to an argument is not allowed (Chomsky 1986; McCloskey 1996; Boskovič 1996). Boskovič (1996) argued that the restrictions on the occurrence of *ca* in Romanian subjunctives can be explained along those lines. Here I will simply adopt his approach. I start by noting that, when CP is embedded, topics cannot intervene between the verb and the indicative complementizer:

(88) *Stiu ieri că a plecat mama.
      know-1SG yesterday that came mother
      'I know that mother came yesterday.'

By hypothesis, (88) is ruled out by the ban on adjunction to an argument. Now reconsider the following examples:

(89) a. Vreau *ca* mîine să vina Ion.
      [I] want that tomorrow să come John
      'I want John to come tomorrow.'

      b. *Vreau mîine să vina Ion.
      [I] want tomorrow să come John
      'I want John to come tomorrow.'

(90)   Vreau MÎINE să vina Ion.
       [I] want tomorrow să come John
       'I want John to come tomorrow.'

In (90a) the complementizer *ca* is followed by the particle *să*. I will follow Terzi (1992) in assuming that *să* is a Mood head. In addition, I will assume, with Boskovič (1996) and Dobrovie-Sorin (1994), that the adverb as well as dislocated DPs are in a position of adjunction. Example (89a) would be analyzed as follows:

(91)   Vreau [CP*ca* [MP mîine [MP să vina Ion]]]

Since MP is not an argument in (91), adjunction is possible. Boskovič proposes that the absence of *ca* reflects the absence of a CP projection. Adopting this suggestion, (89b) will be analyzed as in (92):

(92)   *Vreau [MP mîine [MP să vina Ion]]

In (92) the adverb *mîine* is adjoined to the argument of the verb *vreau*, in violation of the ban against adjunction to arguments. Now take example (92), which contains a focused adverbial. As suggested above, fronted Focused elements occupy the specifier position of the MP, the projection headed by *sa'*. Assuming that when *ca* is absent no CP is projected, we get (93) as the structure assigned to (92):

(93)   Vreau [MP MÎINE [M' să vina Ion]]

Example (93) does not involve adjunction to MP, the argument of the verb *vrea*, so it does not violate the ban on adjunction to an argument. The difference in status between (92) and (93) thus crucially depends on a distinction between adjunct and specifier, which is formulated in X-bar theoretic terms.

Now I turn to subjects. As noted previously, preverbal nonfocused subjects require the presence of *ca* (cf. the contrast between (84a) and (84b)). Focused subjects can dispense with *ca* (cf. (86b)). I repeat the relevant paradigm as (94):

(94)   a. Vreau ca Ion să vină.
          [I] want that Ion *să* come
          'I want Ion to came.'

       b. *Vreau Ion să vina.
          [I] want John să come
          'I want Ion to come.'

       c. Vreau ION să vina.
          'It is Ion that I want to come.'

This paradigm shows that preverbal (neutral) subjects pattern with object CLLD and with sentential adverbs. The analysis developed by Vallduví for Catalan extends rather naturally to this paradigm. Recall that Vallduví adopted the VOS hypothesis for Catalan and argued that preverbal neutral subjects in Catalan were "left-detached," just like other "left-detached" objects. The Spec, IP position was the landing site for *wh*-movement and quantificational operators. Extending Vallduví's proposal to Romanian, we have the following structure for (95a), where Ion is a left dislocated topic doubled by resumptive *pro*:

(97)   *Vreau [MP Ion₁ [MoodP să vina *pro* ₁]]

Example (94b), by contrast, is analyzed as an instance of Focus-movement, where the subject is moved to Spec, MP.

(98)   Vreau [MP ION₁ [M' să vină t₁]]

Example (95) violates the ban against adjunction to an argument, but (96) does not. This extension of Vallduví's analysis of Catalan to Romanian entails that the A-position for subjects in Romanian is to the right of the verb. Unlike Catalan, however, Romanian allows for VSO order, as shown in the following:

(97)   Vreau ca pîna mîine *să* termine Ion cartea asta.
       [I] want that until tomorrow *sa* finish John this book

It is a well-known fact that the Romance languages vary with respect to the position of postverbal subjects relative to other arguments. This variation is not directly relevant, though. What matters for now is to show that in Romanian as well as in Catalan there is a subject position to the right of the verb. In the case of Romanian, VSO order is possible. Catalan has only VOS order. In both cases, the preverbal field can be further divided in two cases: the position that is adjacent to the verbal string, which is an A'-position, and the recursive position for topics. Since the dichotomy adjunct versus specifier appears to be able to handle the distribution of the complementizer in Romanian, I will conclude that dislocated topics are adjoined to the XP that is predicated of them as long as it is not to an argument. Frame adverbs belong to the class of elements that are so adjoined.

Now that I have clearly distinguished CLLD from Focus-movement and quantificational operator movement, I can turn to the complex matter of constituent fronting in EP.

2.1.5.4 Constituent fronting in EP: CLLD, topicalization, and quantificational operator movement

Unlike most Romance languages, Portuguese has a construction where a definite object DP topic corresponds to a clause internal direct object gap (the following example is adapted from Raposo 1996):

(98)   A garrafa de whisky vou comprar ec de certeza.
       the bottle of whisky will-1stSG buy ec for sure

Equivalents to (98), without focal stress on the fronted constituent, are out in the Romance languages discussed. Duarte (1987) and Raposo (1996) observe that topicalization in EP has different properties from Focus and is closer to English topicalization. In the first place, (98) expresses the topic-comment articulation: the DP *essa garrafa de whisky* stands for a discourse referent, and the clause is understood as asserting something about it. Moreover, (98) can be felicitously uttered in answer to the question "What will you buy?" without an exclusive focus reading. It asserts that "as far as the bottle of whisky is concerned, I will buy it for sure" and is entirely compatible with my buying things other than the bottle of whisky.

Raposo (1996) notes that (98) and its CLLD counterpart in (99) are equivalent, semantically and discourse-wise:

(99)   A garrafa de whisky vou comprá-la de certeza.
        the bottle of whisky will-1stSG buy it for sure

        'The bottle of whisky, I will buy it for sure'

In both, the initial DP sets a "point of reference" for the predication conveyed by "the associated clause." However, both Raposo (1996) and Duarte (1987) note that topicalization in EP has properties that set it apart from CLLD. Unlike CLLD, topicalization displays island effects, licenses parasitic gaps, and shows weak crossover effects. For all these reasons, these authors conclude that topicalization involves movement. Duarte proposes that topics directly move to a position of adjunction to CP or IP. Raposo (1996) and I (Barbosa 1996a) suggest that topicalization does not involve movement of the topic from a position within the clause. Raposo (1996), in particular, proposes that what moves is an empty operator, the trace of which serves as an open position whose reference is fixed by the topic. The following facts support his proposal.

In the first place, Portuguese has definite null objects, as illustrated in the following (see Raposo 1986 and Duarte 1987):

(100)   Viste o Carlos?
        saw the Carlos

        'Did you see Carlos?

        Vi ec na televisão.
        saw ec on TV

        'I saw him on TV.'

Null object constructions are fine in EP as long as a salient object or a set of objects is made available either from previous discourse or by the pragmatic context of the utterance that may recover the content of the gap. Raposo (1986) has argued that these constructions have all the diagnostic properties of *wh*-movement, thus being best analyzed as involving movement of a null operator to Spec, CP:

(101)   [CP OP [vi t na televisão]]

Raposo (1996) observes that the various subcases of topicalization all have a corresponding null object sentence, which suggests the representation of the topicalized counterpart to (100)

(102)   O Carlos vi na televisão
        'Carlos, I saw on TV.'

includes (101) plus a base-generated topic:

(103)   [$_{CP}$ O Carlos [$_{CP}$ OP [vi t na televisão]]]

The other argument for analyzing (102) as in (103) with the topic base-generated in the front of the clause rather than directly moved from a position from within the clause comes from a comparison with superficially similar constructions that involve fronted quantificational operators. I have noted earlier that affective operators, nonspecific indefinites, and QPs without lexical restrictions cannot serve as discourse links. Thus, the analysis of topicalization in (103) predicts that the following sentences

(104)   a. Nada$_1$ posso fazer ec$_1$ por ti.
           nothing can-1SG do ec for you
           'There is nothing I can do for you.'

        b. [A ninguém]$_1$ daria esse livro ec$_1$.
           to noone would-give-1SG that book ec

should have different properties from (102), since the only possible derivation for them is one in which the QP directly moves to an A'-position from within the sentence.

This prediction is in effect fulfilled. Raposo (1994, 1996) notes that (102) has a different intonational contour from the sentences in (103): in (102) the topic can be set out from the rest of the sentence by a pause, whereas this is not possible in (104a, b). Besides this prosodic difference, there is also evidence that topics and fronted quantificational operators occupy different syntactic positions. In the first place, while topicalized constituents can precede a fronted *wh*-word, quantificational operators strongly resist occupying that position:

(105)   Esse livro, quem vai comprar ec?
        'That book, who is going to buy?'

(106)   a. *Nada quem vai comprar ec?
           nothing who is-going to buy ec

        b. *Só a um advogado que amigo teu entregou o caso?
           only to one lawyer what friend of-yours delivered the case

           'Which friend of yours handed in the case to only one lawyer?'   (from Raposo 1994)

Examples (106) may be fine as echo-questions, but they sound terrible as real questions. The contrast between (105) and (106) reinforces the view that topics are adjoined to CP, whereas fronted quantificational operators must occupy a position within CP.

A further argument that topics and quantificational operators fill a different position comes from the phenomenon of "recomplementation," discussed in Uriagereka (1988) and in Raposo (1994, 1996). In EP it is possible to have a topic sandwiched between two complementizers:

(107) a. Acho que esse livro que já (o) li.
           think-1SG that that book that already (it) read-1SG   (from Raposo 1994, parentheses mine)

       b. Acho que amanhã que vai haver reunião.
           'I think that tomorrow that there will be a meeting.'

When the fronted constituent is a quantificational operator, however, "recomplementation" is impossible:

(108) a. Disseram-me que a poucas pessoas (*que) foi entregue um convite.
           they-told-me that to few people that was delivered an invitation

       b. Disseram-me que nada (*que) vão poder fazer.
           they-told-me that nothing that they-will be able to do

These facts suggest that fronted quantificational operators occupy a position that is different from topics. Topics can be outside CP, but quantificational operators cannot. This contrast can be explained after adopting Raposo's (1996) proposal according to which topics are not moved from a position within CP but are base-generated in a position of adjunction to the XP that is predicated of them, which contains an open position made available by a null operator. The expressions that cannot act as discourse links, by contrast, must be moved when fronted. Raposo (1994) proposes that *wh*-words and quantificational operators move to the specifier of an intermediate position between IP and CP, namely, FocusP. Topics can adjoin to this projection. Thus, (108b) would be analyzed as in (109):

(109) Disseram-me [$_{CP}$ que [$_{FP}$ nada$_1$ [$_{IP}$ vão poder fazer t$_1$]]]
           they-told-me that nothing they-will be-able to-do t

To sum up the results of this section, I have noted that the topic-comment articulation in Portuguese can be expressed by means of CLLD or topicalization. CLLD does not pass any of the diagnostics for movement; topicalization has movement properties. CLLDed and topicalized constituents must be capable of referring to an object or set of objects in the domain of discourse. In both cases, the topic is in a position of adjunction to the XP that is predicated of it. In CLLD, XP contains a resumptive clitic whose reference is fixed by the topic. In topicalization, a null operator provides the open position required for predication. The QPs that cannot refer to an object or set of objects in the domain, such as affective operators, nonspecific indefinites, or QPs lacking a lexical restriction, must move when fronted. By hypothesis, they move to Spec, FP (I will return to this later).

In the next section I will focus on the implications of these conclusions for my analysis of clitic placement in EP.

2.1.5.5 Consequences for cliticization

Recall that I proposed that clitics in EP are subject to the prosodic constraint in (48), repeated here as (110):

(110)   *[IntP cl V . . .] IntP = Intonational Phrase

Now consider the different patterns of clitic placement in sentences with a fronted constituent. Topicalization requires enclisis, regardless of whether the topic is contrastive focus:

(111)   a. Esse livro, dou-lhe /*lhe dou.
            'That book I will give him.'

        b. Esse livro dou-lhe, mas este não.
            'That book I will give him, but not this one.'

Quantificational operator movement requires proclisis:

(112)   [Nenhuma resposta]$_i$ me deram e$_i$ até hoje.
        no answer to me they-gave e$_i$ until today

Example (112) contains a fronted object that is a negative QP. In the preceding section, I proposed to analyze this kind of construction as an instance of A'-movement. Thus, (112) is analyzed as in (113). As before, I assume that the clitic is placed in the checking domain of Infl:

(113)   [FP [nenhuma resposta]$_1$ [F' [IP me deram t$_1$ até hoje]]

With regard to cliticization, (113) falls under the *wh*-movement cases discussed earlier. In the mapping to PF, (113) is assigned the following P-structure:

(114)   [IntP nenhuma resposta me deram até hoje]

In (114) the clitic is not the first element in the IntP, so the derivation proceeds to PF.

Now I turn to topicalization. Consider the syntactic representation of (111a) with proclisis:

(115)   *Esse livro [OP$_1$ [lhe dou t$_1$]]
        that book to-him I-give

Even though (115) differs from its CLLD equivalent with respect to operator movement inside the clause, it is entirely equivalent to CLLD for the purposes of P-structure building. As noted earlier, topics (regardless of whether they are doubled by a clitic) are mapped into Intonational Phrases of their own (Nespor and Vogel 1986; Kanerva 1990; Halpern 1992; Frota 1995a, b). Thus, the syntactic representation in (115) will be mapped as in (116):

(116)   [Esse livro]$_{IntP}$[te dou]$_{IntP}$

Example (116) crashes, since it violates the constraint in (110).

The claim that topics form their own IntPs in EP is in conformity with Frota's (1994, 1995a,b, 1996a,b) work on Portuguese prosody. However, she notes that contrastive topics such as (111b) tend to be phrased together with the rest of the clause. I will return to this problem in a later section. For the moment, I ask the reader to keep this problem in the back of his or her mind, while I turn to adverbs.

The analysis of clitic placement proposed for topicalization and CLLD can be straightforwardly extended to sentential adverbs. Sentential adverbs contrast with aspectual adverbs with respect to clitic placement:

(117)   b. Amanhã vejo-a/ * a vejo.
           'Tomorrow I see her.'

        a. Nunca\já a vi / *vi-a
           never /already her saw
           'I never/already saw her.'

Earlier I observed that sentential adverbs can appear in recomplementation constructions:

(118)   Acho que amanhã que vai haver reunião.
        'I think that tomorrow that there will be a meeting.'

Aspectual adverbs, by contrast, cannot precede complementizers:

(119)   *Acho que nunca\já que a vi.
        think-1SG that never/already that her saw-1SG

Following much of the literature on the topic-comment articulation (Raposo 1996; Rizzi 1997), I assume that frame adverbs are topics in the sense that they introduce a point of reference with respect to which the whole clause is predicated. Aspectual adverbs, by contrast, are somewhere within IP/FP (as in effect is argued by Belletti 1990). Thus, (120a and b) are assigned the following syntactic representations in (121a and b), respectively:

(120)   a. *Amanhã a vejo.
           tomorrow her see

        b. Nunca a vi.

(121)   a. [Amanhã] [$_{IP}$ a vejo]

     b. [$_{FP}$ Nunca a vi]

Once again, assuming that clausal adjuncts are mapped into an IntP distinct from the IntP into which the clause is mapped, the syntactic representations in (121a and b) will correspond to distinct P-structures. Example (121b) will be mapped into a single IntP:

(122)   [Nunca a vi]$_{IntP}$

Example (122) does not violate (112), so the derivation proceeds, with proclisis. Example (121a), however, will be mapped into (123), where an IntP boundary is placed to the right of the topic adverb:

(123)   Amanhã]$_{IntP}$ a vejo]$_{IntP}$

Since (123) violates (110), the derivation crashes.

2.1.5.6 Subjects

Finally, I am in a position to consider the consequences of this analysis for constructions with preverbal subjects. Recall that proclisis is required when the preverbal subject is a quantificational operator. Enclisis is obligatory in all other cases. In Megleno-Romance, emphatic subjects require the reduced form of the clitic, whereas regular subjects require the nonreduced one. Recall in addition that the set of quantificational operators that triggers proclisis (independently of their status as subjects or objects) is best characterized as the set of expressions that cannot function as "links" (in the sense of Vallduví 1990, 1992). These two observations suggest that, *with respect to clitic placement*, preverbal subjects behave just like preverbal objects in both languages. In other words, the pattern of clitic placement varies according to whether the DP in question belongs to the class of QPs that can or cannot be discourse topics, and this behavior does not distinguish objects from subjects. This casts doubt on the idea that there is an extra position for subjects that is unavailable to objects, namely, A-movement to Spec, IP. If there were such an option, we would expect subjects to have a different behavior from other fronted DPs. Moreover, the fact that the set of quantified subjects that trigger proclisis coincides with the set of QPs that cannot be discourse topics would remain unaccounted for.

For this reason, in Barbosa (1993, 1996a) I proposed to analyze (124a) as an instance of subject CLLD. The DP *a Maria* is base-generated in the front of the clause, *not moved from argument position*, and is licensed by predication via an open position inside the clause, supplied by *pro*, which bears the theta-role assigned by V:

(124)   a. A Maria telefonou.

      the M. called

     b. [[A Maria$_i$] [$_{IP}$ telefonou pro$_i$]]

In (124a), *pro* is, by hypothesis, occupying the position occupied by postverbal subjects. Note that, alongside (124a), we can have (125):

(125)   Telefonou a Maria.
         called the Maria

I propose that the real L-related position for subjects is to the right of the raised verb:

(126) $[_{IP} [_I V_1] [S \ldots t_1 \ldots]]$

SV constructions can be derived by CLLD, with *pro* serving as the resumptive element (as illustrated in (124b)). When the subject belongs to the set of expressions that cannot serve as discourse topics, it can only be fronted by A'-movement, as happens with object quantificational operators. Once again, I observe that quantificational operator subjects may occupy the pre- or postverbal position:

(127)   a. Ninguém telefonou.
            'No one called."

         b. Não telefonou ninguém.
            not called no one
            'No one called.'

Example (127a) is analyzed as involving A'-movement of the postverbal subject to preverbal position:

(128) $[_{FP} Ninguém [_F telefonou t]]$

It is worth noting that, according to the analysis I proposed earlier (Barbosa 1996a), preverbal nonquantificational operator subject constructions in EP are *unambiguously* analyzed as CLLD constructions, with the DP topic construed with a null pronoun in subject position; they are *not* analyzed as instances of topicalization of the subject (with the DP topic construed with a null operator inside the clause). Indeed, there is evidence that subjects resist topicalization in EP.

Recall that in EP topics can appear between two complementizers (with or without a doubling clitic). Here I repeat the relevant examples for convenience:

(129)   Dizem que esses panfletos que o partido (os) distribuiu a todos os militantes.
         they-say that those pamphlets that the party them distributed to all the militants
         (Raposo 1996)

Subjects can also appear in recomplementation constructions:

(130)   Dizem que o partido que distribuiu esses panfletos a todos os militantes.
         they-say that the party that distributed those pamphlets to all the militants

Since it is not possible to claim that the DP *o partido* in (130) is sitting in Spec, IP, it must be either topicalized or CLLDed (with *pro* serving as the resumptive pronoun). In effect, quantificational operator subjects cannot appear in recomplementation constructions:

(131)   *Disseram-me que ninguém que apareceu ontem à noite.
        they-told-me that nobody that showed up yesterday at night

Interestingly, it can be shown that (130) is unambiguously analyzed as an instance of CLLD. Duarte (1987) and Raposo (1997) observe that bare NPs can be topicalized in EP. The following example is taken from Raposo (1997):

(132)   Livros do Tintim, li ec ontem antes de adormecer.
        books of-the Tintin I-read ec yesterday before falling asleep

        'Tintin comics, I read yesterday night before falling asleep.'

Solà (1992) and Raposo (1997), among others, have observed that bare DPs cannot be CLLDed. Thus, (132) minimally contrasts with (133):

(133)   *Livros do Tintim, li-os ontem antes de adormecer.
        books of-the Tintin I-read-then yesterday before falling asleep

These minimal pairs provide a test for topicalization versus CLLD. Applying this test to "subjects" in recomplementation constructions, it is apparent that bare DP topics construed with subjects are excluded:

(134)   a. *Disseram-me que *livros do Tintim* que andam baratos.
          they-told-me that books of-the T. that are cheap

        b. Disseram-me que *os livros do Tintim* que andam muito baratos.

Thus, I conclude that topics construed with subjects are unambiguously analyzed as instances of CLLD (not topicalization), with the topic base-generated in the front of the clause and doubled by *pro* in subject position:

(135) $[DP]_1 [_{IP} V \dots pro_1 \dots]$

Summing up the results of this section so far, I have argued that the patterns of clitic placement in EP suggest that subjects do not raise to an A-position to the left of the Infl head containing the verb. The real A-position for subjects is to the right of the raised verb. Contrary to appearances, "preverbal" subjects are topics construed with a *pro* subject. The expressions that cannot act as discourse links raise to an A'-position in the preverbal field.

My conclusions are thus very similar to those of Vallduví (1992) for Catalan. Recall that Vallduví argues that Spec, IP is an A'-position in Catalan. This position hosts *wh*-words and quantificational operators. Nominal preverbal expressions are "left-detached," that is, dislocated topics. Vallduví adopts previous proposals according to which Catalan is VOS. The subject is licensed for Case in postverbal position, and thus Spec, IP is not an L-related position, being free to be the landing site for *wh*-words and quantificational operators. Here I am claiming that the facts regarding clitic placement in EP also suggest that the preverbal field does not contain an A-position for subjects. Since postverbal subjects are licensed for Case, economy considerations bar movement of the subject to preverbal position. The preverbal field is thus the locus for A'-movement and topics (which do not involve movement, as argued).

Portuguese, however, is slightly different from Catalan, Spanish, and Romanian in that there is no strict adjacency requirement between *wh*-words and the verbal cluster in indirect questions. Recall from Vallduví´s discussion that, in Catalan, nothing can intervene between a *wh*-word and the verb. This adjacency requirement holds in matrix as well as embedded clauses:

Catalan:
(136)   a. ¿Què (*en Joan) farà (en Joan)?
            what (the Joan) will-do (the Joan)

            'What will J. do?'

         b. ¿No sé què (*en Joan) farà (en Joan).
            not know what (the Joan) will-do (the Joan)

            'I don't know what J. will do.'

In EP, however, adjacency between a *wh*-word and the verb is only required in matrix questions (see Ambar 1988):

Portuguese:
(137)   a. *Quando (*a Maria) veio (a Maria)?
            when (the Maria) came (the Maria)

         b. Não sei quando (a Maria) vem (a Maria).
            not know (I) when the Maria comes

As noted by Solà (1992) and Uribe-Etxebarria (1991), it is not just subjects that cannot intervene between a *wh*-word and the verb in embedded questions in Catalan and Spanish. Nothing, including adverbs, can intervene:

Spanish:
(138)   *¿ No se *con quien* mañana *hablare*.
            not know-1SG with whom tomorrow to-speak

In Portuguese, by contrast, an adverb may intervene between the verb and a *wh*-word in embedded clauses:

(139)   Não sei com quem amanhã deverei falar.
            not know-1SG with whom tomorrow should-1SG talk

I contend that the difference between Catalan/Spanish and Portuguese is the following. Catalan and Spanish have only one landing site for A'-movement, namely, Spec, IP. As Vallduví notes, this would explain why, when complementizers co-occur with *wh*-words in indirect *wh*-questions, the complementizer always appears to the left of the *wh*-word:

(140) a. Pregunten *que* el gavinet *on* el ficaràs.
           ask-3PL that the knife where it put-FUT-2SG
           'They are asking where you'll put the knife.'

       b. *Pregunten el gavinet *que on* el ficaràs.

Vallduví takes (140a) as showing that in *wh*-questions *wh*-phrases do not occupy the specifier position of CP but rather a slot below C. "Left-detached" phrases are adjoined to IP. Schematically:

(141) Pregunten [$_C$ que [$_{IP}$ el gavinet [$_{IP}$ on [$_{I'}$ el ficaràs]]]]

Portuguese, by contrast, has Spec, IP plus Spec, CP. In embedded questions, *wh*-phrases are in Spec, CP, and topics may appear to the left of the *wh*-phrase:

(142) a. Sabes *quando*, ao Pedro, mais lhe convém que
           know-2SG when, to-the P. more to-him is convenient that
           marquemos a reunião?
           schedule-1PL the meeting
           'Do you know when, to P., it is more convenient that we schedule the meeting?

       b. Ès capaz de me dizer *quem*, ao novo presidente, devemos apresentar primeiro?
           'Can you tell me who, to the new president, we should introduce first?'

In (142a) the *wh*-word is in Spec, CP, and the topic is adjoined to IP:

(143) Sabes[$_{CP}$*quando* [$_{C'}$[$_{IP}$ ao Pedro [$_{IP}$ mais lhe convém que . . .]]?]]

A similar analysis applies in those cases where an adverb or preverbal "subject" intervenes between a *wh*-word and the verb:

(144) a. Não sei ainda com quem amanhã de manhã deverei falar primeiro.
           'I don't know yet to whom tomorrow morning I should talk first.'

       b. Não sei ainda [$_{CP}$[*com quem*]$_1$ [$_{C'}$ [$_C$ +wh][$_{IP}$ amanhã[$_{IP}$deverei falar t $_1$]]]]

(145) a. Não sei o que o João fará.
           'I don't know what J. will do.'

       b. Não sei [$_{CP}$ [*o que*]$_1$ [$_{C'}$[$_C$ +wh][$_{IP}$[o João]$_2$[$_{IP}$fará *pro* $_2$ t$_1$]]]]

In (145b) the DP *o João* is a dislocated topic, adjoined to IP. Now note that if indeed Spec, IP can host quantificational operators in EP, one would predict a quantificational operator to be able to appear to the right of the subject in a structure like (145) (depending on minimality considerations). That this is indeed the case is confirmed by the following sentence:

(146)   Não sabíamos ainda por que razão o João [pouca bagagem]$_1$ levara com ele t$_1$.
         not know-1PL yet for what reason the J. little bagage took with him t

The embedded clause in (146) is analyzed as in (147):

(147)   [$_{CP}$ por que razão [$_{C'}$ [$_C$ +Wh] [$_{IP}$ o João [$_{IP}$ [pouca bagagem]$_1$ [$_{I'}$ levara *pro* t$_1$ com ele]]]]]

A further difference between EP and Spanish that can be explained along these lines regards adjacency requirements between fronted quantificational operators and the verb. In Spanish, a fronted quantificational operator must be adjacent to the verb. In Portuguese, it need not be adjacent to the verb (examples from Raposo 1994):

(148)   Pocos coches (*Alain Prost) ha conducido (Alain Prost) este ano.
         few cars (A.P.) has driven (A.P.) this year

(149)   Poucos carros o Alain Prost conduziu este ano!
         few cars the A.P. drove this year

As before, I assume that quantificational operators are fronted to Spec, IP in Spanish. This is why nothing can intervene between the phrase *pocos coches* and the verb. In EP, Spec, CP is a potential landing site for quantificational operators. Thus (149) is analyzed as follows:

(150)   [$_{CP}$ Poucos carros [$_{C'}$[$_{IP}$ o Alain Prost [$_{IP}$ conduziu *pro* este ano]]]]

Note that other topics besides subjects can in effect intervene between a fronted affective phrase and the verb in EP. Consider the following sentence:

(151)   Pouco afecto, aos meus filhos, nunca darei!
         little affection, to my children never will-give
         'Little affection, to my children, I will never give.'

In (151) the quantificational operator is in Spec, CP, and the topic is adjoined to IP. The analysis in (151) predicts that a fronted quantificational operator may move to Spec, IP. The following sentence appears to confirm this prediction:

(152)   a. [Nem ao seu melhor amigo]$_1$ a Maria [alguma ajuda]$_2$ ofereceu t$_2$ t$_1$
            not even to her best friend the Maria some help offered

b. $[_{CP}$ [Nem ao seu melhor amigo]$_1[_{C'}$ [$_{IP}$ a M.$[_{IP}$ [alguma ajuda]$_2$
$[_{I'}$ ofereceu pro t$_1$ t$_2$]]]]]

In (152b) I have taken CP to be the projection immediately above IP. However, (152a) can be embedded under a complementizer, as shown in the following:

(153)   O Carlos disse que nem ao seu melhor amigo a Maria alguma ajuda ofereceu.
        the Carlos said that not even to her best friend the M. some help offered

As mentioned earlier, a number of authors have proposed that some languages have an intermediate projection between subordinator Cs and IP (Laka 1990; Culicover 1992; Uriagereka 1995a, b; Rizzi 1997; Raposo 1999). Earlier I labeled this phrase FP to distinguish it from the projection headed by subordinator Cs. In Portuguese, root clauses can project up to FP and embedded Cs select FP. Romanian, Catalan, and Spanish lack FP. In what follows, I will assume that CLLDed subjects or objects can adjoin to IP. In Portuguese, they can also adjoin to FP as evidenced by the possibility of (154) and (155):

(154)   a. A Maria [até ao Pedro]$_1$ [pouca ajuda]$_2$ ofereceu t$_2$ t$_1$
           the M. even to P. little help offered

        b. $[_{FP}$ [A Maria]$_3$ $[_{FP}$ [até ao Pedro]$_1$ $[_{IP}$ [pouca ajuda]$_2$ $[_{I'}$' ofereceu pro_3 t$_2$ t$_1$]]]]

(155)   a. Ao Pedro até a Maria pouca ajuda ofereceu.

        b. $[_{FP}$ [ao Pedro]$_3$ $[_{FP}$ [até a Maria]$_1$ $[_{IP}$ [pouca ajuda]$_2$ $[_{I'}$' ofereceu t$_1$ t$_2$ ec_3]]]]

Quantificational operators move to A'-positions. In Portuguese these are the specifier position of the head the verb raises to (namely, Spec, IP) and Spec, FP.

2.1.5.6.1 BACK TO CLITIC PLACEMENT   Now consider how the analysis of clitic placement developed so far would work for the following examples:

(156)   *A Maria o viu.
        the Maria him saw

(157)   Ninguém o viu.
        nobody him saw

Example (156) has the simplified structure in (158) (here I am ignoring FP, for ease of exposition):

(158)   [A Maria]$_1$ $[_{IP}$ o viu pro $_1$]

In the mapping between syntax and P-structure, an IntP boundary is placed to the right of the CLLDed subject:

(159)   a Maria]IntP o viu]IntP

By the constraint in (111), (159) is an ill-formed P-structure, so the derivation does not proceed to PF. The alternative derivation with enclisis is then chosen as a Last Resort option.

Now consider (157). This is an instance of A'-movement of the subject:

(160)   [FP Ninguém [o viu   t]]

In P-structure *ninguém* is mapped into the same IntP that contains the clitic:

(161)   [IntP Ninguém o viu]]

Example (161) does not violate the prosodic constraint (110), and so the derivation proceeds to PF, with proclisis.

The structure in (159) will immediately look suspicious in view of the fact that one does not perceive a significant intonational break between the preverbal subject and the rest of the sentence. Object CLLD, by contrast, is generally marked, and a pause is more clearly perceived. Before I proceed to a more technical discussion of prosodic phrasing in EP, I would like to point out a few contrasts that weaken the intonational break argument as a reliable test for dislocation. I will start by comparing constructions that unambiguously involve CLLDed subjects as well as topic adverbs, and compare them with constructions with CLLDed objects. Consider the following recomplementation examples:

(162)   a. Disseram-me que a Maria que *pro* falou com a professora ontem.
          they-told-me that the M. that talked with the teacher yesterday

        b. Disseram-me que amanhã que vai estar muito calor.
          they-told-me that tomorrow that it-will be very hot

        c. Disseram-me que, esse livro, que não o podem dar ao Pedro.
          they-told-me that that book that not it they-can give to the P.

All of the preceding examples above contain a topic sandwiched between two complementizers, and the embedded clauses are interpreted as assertions about that topic. In (162a) the topic is connected with the (null) subject of the embedded clause, in (162b) the topic is an adverb, and in (162c) the topic is construed with the object clitic. To my ear, (162c) requires a much heavier intonational break than (162b) or (162a). If I were to take the presence of an intonational break as evidence for dislocation, I would have to abandon a dislocation analysis for (162a) given that no clear intonational break is required in (162a) when compared with (162c). However, this would have the unwanted result of letting in A-movement out of a finite clause (but see Poletto 1997 for a proposal precisely along these lines). What this means, then, is that, even in clear cases of dislocation, there is an intonational difference between topics construed with subjects and topics construed with lower arguments. This observation is very important, since it neutralizes any argument against the subject dislocation hypothesis that is based solely on intuitions of "markedness." Moreover, it shows that, in order to detect subject dislocation in a null subject language, one has to look for subtler evidence.

Here I will not attempt to give a principled explanation for why object CLLD requires a heavier intonational break (but see Duarte 1987 for a discussion of the notion of "marked topic"). For my present purposes, it suffices to make a statement of fact: the intonational break clue *does not distinguish between dislocation versus A-movement* in the case of subjects. Interestingly, topic adverbs pattern with subject topics rather than with object topics: no parenthetical intonation is required. These facts open a series of interesting questions that go well beyond the scope of the present study. For the moment I am simply interested in showing that the intonational pattern of CLLDed objects is different from that of CLLDed subjects, or even adverbs.

At this point, it would seem that I have reached a contradiction. I have shown that object topics require a heavier intonational break than dislocated subjects or topic adverbs. However, my analysis of clitic placement is based on the presence of an IntP boundary between any topic and the rest of the clause. Does this lead to a contradiction? I will addresss this issue in the next section, where I will consider recent findings in prosodic phrasing in EP.

2.1.6 An excursus into prosodic phrasing in EP

Recent experimental research on prosodic phrasing in EP (Frota 1994, 1995a,b, 1996a,b) has uncovered segmental, intonational, and durational evidence for the IntP domain in EP: (i) the IntP is minimally characterized by a nuclear pitch accent and a final boundary tone; (ii) it is the domain of preboundary lengthening; (iii) it defines the location of pauses; and (iv) it bounds segmental rules. Frota's work also shows that there is a distinction between two types of boundaries that are both IntP-boundaries: under certain conditions, two IntP-phrases may be phrased into one IntP (I-max) and thus be dominated by a phrase of the same category. The IntP nature of the dominees is supported by (i) and (ii): they always define the domain of an intonational contour, and of preboundary lengthening. The dominant IntP (Imax) defines the domain of preboundary lengthening, the location of pauses, and the domain for certain sandhi rules. In what follows, I will briefly review Frota's arguments for the need to distinguish these two kinds of IntP. As will be apparent, sandhi rules in EP are only blocked by an Imax boundary, so they cannot be used as a test for the IntP boundary.

In EP, the word final /s/ becomes voiced when it is followed by a word initial vowel (underline indicates that Fricative Voicing has applied):

(163)   As alunas africanas ofereceram canetas aos amigos.
         the students african gave pens to-the friends

         'The African students offered pens to their friends.'

Fricative Voicing is blocked when a parenthetical "slices" the utterance into more than one IntP (capitalization indicates that the rule has not applied):

(164)   [As alunaS] [até onde sabemoS] [obtiveram boas avaliações]
         'The students, as far as we know, had good evaluations.'

Fricative Voicing may apply in (164), as illustrated in the following:

(165) a. A<u>s</u> aluna<u>s</u>, até onde sabemoS, obtiveram boa<u>s</u> avaliações.

   b. A<u>s</u> alunaS, até onde sabemo<u>s</u>, obtiveram boa<u>s</u> avaliações.

Frota observes that Fricative Voicing can apply at only one side of the paren-thetical. In spite of the fact that Fricative Voicing applies in (165a, b), Frota shows that the subject and the parenthetical still form two different Intonational Contours. For this reason, she proposes that two IntPs may be grouped into a larger domain, the Imax. Fricative Voicing applies within the domain of Imax, which is defined as the IP domain that is dominated by the prosodic category of the immediately higher level. Example (165a) would thus be parsed as in (166):

(166)

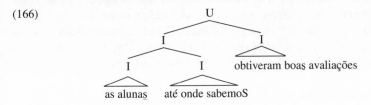

Factors such as length of the constituents and rate of speech may determine one of the three prosodic phrasings given in (167):

(167) a.   b.   c.

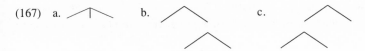

Example (164) is phrased as in (167a); (165b) is phrased as in (167b); and (165a) is phrased as in (167c).

According to the criteria mentioned, an SVO sentence such as (163) phrased as in (168) when it has a neutral or "broad focus" reading (i.e., when none of its con-stituents is particularly highlighted; see Frota 1994):

(168) [[as alunas africanas] $_\phi$ [ofereceram canetas] $_\phi$ [aos amigos] $_\phi$] $_{IntP}$

In (168), the subject does not define the domain of an intonational contour or of preboundary lengthening. These findings contradict the idea that preverbal (non-quantificational operator) subjects form a separate IntP, as my hypothesis would predict. However, IntP formation is subject to restructuring, and IntP restructuring is sensitive not only to the context of the utterance but also to purely prosodic con-siderations, such as the weight of the constituent, rate of speech, and style. For in-stance, Frota (1996a) observes that, when the subject is long, it is separated from the rest of the sentence by an Imax boundary. Here is the example she quotes:

(169) A<u>s</u> alunas do<u>s</u> AçoreS ofereceram caneta<u>s</u> aos amigos.
       'The students from the Azores offered pens to their friends.'

Fricative voicing is blocked in (169), which suggests that there is an Imax boundary after the subject.

According to Frota (1996a), the original IntP is broken into two IntPs because "the material dominated by the root sentence is long, and a break between subject and verb yields a sequence of two more or less equalized constituents. On the contrary, if the subject NP is a shorter constituent and a higher boundary between subject and verb will not have an equalizing effect, IP restructuring will be very unlikely and less acceptable." Thus, considerations of tree geometry play a role in determining IntP phrasing, in the case of subjects.

Even though Frota's experimental evidence shows that, in neutral utterances, short subjects tend to form an IntP with the verb, there are, here and there, references to the fact that the subject-verb boundary is special in the sense that it is prone to IP restructuring. In her discussion of another sandhi rule that is blocked by an Imax boundary, she mentions an example in which a *short* subject forms a separate Imax. In a sequence of two words, if w_1 has a word final [å] and w_2 has an identical word initial vowel, the two vowels are changed into the low vowel [a]. Imax is the appropriate domain for this rule. Frota quotes the following examples:

(170)   a. [[*A aluna*] $_\phi$ [*aceitou o emprego*]$_\phi$ [*no restaurante*] $_\phi$]$_{\text{IntP}}$

b. [[*A alunA*]$_{\text{IntP}}$ [*Aceitou o emprego no restaurante*]$_{\text{IntP}}$]$_U$
'The student accepted the job at the restaurant.'

In (170a) Vowel Merger applies, but in (170b) it is blocked. According to Frota, this is due to IP restructuring, so this is an example of IP restructuring with a short subject.

In effect, elsewhere Frota notes that the NP-VP boundary is particularly prone to restructuring. In her study on clash resolution in EP, for instance, she found that when a phi-boundary intervenes between the two clashing syllables, there is shortening of the first vowel/syllable involved in the clash. Then she added: "The shortening result was found to be a consequence of the insertion of acoustic pauses. All the pauses found in the data were inserted after a phi-boundary, which is a predictable position for pause insertion as phi-boundaries may restructure and become I-boundaries (*particularly if the I-boundary coincides with the NP\VP boundary*)" (Frota 1994:6, my emphasis). It is worth noting that the examples in the sample that contained a phi-boundary between the two clashing syllables were examples in which the phi-boundary coincided with the NP-VP boundary.

Thus, I conclude that the NP-VP boundary may restructure and become an I-boundary. At this point, the following question arises: Does this observation hold of any subject-verb boundary, or is there a difference between quantificational operator subjects and other subjects?

Consider the following minimal pair:

(171)   a. Só o meu tio *me* ofereceu dez mil escudos.
         only the my oncle me offered ten thousand escudos
         'Only my uncle offered me ten thousand escudos.'

b. Só o meu tio ofereceu-*me* dez mil escudos.

only the my oncle offered-me ten thousand escudos

'My uncle alone offered me ten thousand escudos.'

Examples (171a and b) vary minimally. In (171a) the clitic precedes the verb; in (171b) it follows the verb. The position of the clitic correlates with different interpretations. Example (171a) has an exclusive focus reading: out of the possible alternatives of who could have given me ten thousand escudos, only one is true, namely, the one in which my uncle gave me that amount of money. Example (171b) asserts that, as far as my uncle is concerned, he alone gave me that amount of money, but it is compatible with a situation in which other people also gave me that amount. Thus, only in (171a) is the particle *só* a true Focus operator, triggering proclisis. Now consider what happens without a clitic:

(172)   Só o meu tio que veio dos Açores ofereceu dez mil escudos.

only the my uncle that came from-the Azores offered ten thousand escudos

'Only my uncle that come from the Azores offered ten thousand escudos to my sister.'

'My uncle that came from the Azores alone offered ten thousand escudos to my sister.'

Example (172) may have the exclusive focus reading or the nonexclusive focus reading. The two meanings can only be teased apart by intonation. The nonexclusive reading requires that the subject correspond to the domain of an intonational contour; Fricative Voicing is blocked:

(173)   [[Só o meu tio que veio dos AçoreS]$_{IntP}$ [ofereceu dez mil escudos à minha irmã]$_{IntP}$]$_U$

In the exclusive reading, the intonational pattern is different: the subject does not constitute the domain of an intonational contour; moreover, Fricative Voicing is not blocked. Even though this claim is not based on an experimental study, there is a clear contrast in the intonational contour of the utterances that correspond to each reading, and the intuitions are sharp.

This suggests that quantificational operator subjects, no matter how long, do not restructure and become IntP boundaries. In other words, there is no equalizing effect. Recall that Frota (1996a) attributed IntP restructuring in example (169) above as the result of an equalizing effect: when the subject is long, the IntP is partitioned in two. The question that now arises, then, is why there is no such partitioning with quantificational operators in subject position, at least not in those situations in which intonation is the only way of disambiguating a true quantificational operator subject from a nonquantificational operator subject.

To sum up the results of this section so far, I have concluded that neutral SVO utterances are most often parsed as a single IntP, according to the criteria for the IntP domain isolated in Frota (1994, 1995a,b, 1996a,b); under certain conditions, the phi-boundary that separates the subject from the verb may restructure and become an IntP boundary; quantificational operator subjects resist IntP restructuring (in the sense just described).

These results suggest that the boundary that separates the verb from a non-quantificational subject is rather unstable: whether it is a phi-boundary or an IntP boundary depends on considerations of length, rate of speech, and style. The boundary that separates a quantificational subject from the verb does not have this unstable quality: no matter how long, an Imax boundary does not separate a quantificational operator subject from the verb. Assuming that there is indeed a prosodic restriction on clitics in EP to the effect that they cannot be the first element in the IntP domain, these descriptive observations suffice to make it plausible that the clitic should not be allowed to be placed immediately to the right of a nonquantificational subject in the syntax. This is so because, depending on considerations of length, rate of speech, and style, the subject could be phrased as a separate IntP and the clitic would find itself as the first element of an IntP. With quantificational operators, by contrast, there is no such danger, since they do not ever constitute a separate IntP. But then again, one would like to know why there is this split in the phrasing of quantificational operators as opposed to other subjects.

My answer to this question will be to claim that this difference in P-phrasing is decided in the mapping between syntax and prosodic structure, an abstract level that constitutes the initial parse, and can only "see" structure. This abstract level constitutes the input to rules of prosodic readjustment that are sensitive to geometry effects, length of the constituents, rate of speech, or style. Moreover, it precedes melody association.

Much of the current work in Prosodic Phonology assumes that prosodic structures are derived from syntax by a mapping procedure, being then subject to rules of prosodic readjustment. Different mapping algorithms have been proposed in the literature. Nespor and Vogel (1986) propose the following:

(174) 1. Phonological Phrase (ϕ) formation:
   a. ϕ domain: a lexical head X and all elements on its nonrecursive side that are still within the maximal projection of X.

   b. ϕ-restructuring: optional, obligatory, or prohibited inclusion of a branching or nonbranching f which is the first complement of X into the f that contains X.

   2. Intonational Phrase (IntP) Formation:
   a. I domain: (i) all the ϕs in a string that is not structurally attached to the sentence tree (i.e., "parenthetical expressions, nonrestrictive relative clauses, tag questions, vocatives, expletives and certain other moved elements," p. 188); (ii) any remaining sequence of adjacent ϕs in a root sentence.

   b. IP restructuring: an IP may be variably broken down into smaller IPs as a function of length, rate of speech, style, and contrastive prominence.

Even though (174.2) is somewhat vague, it is meant to convey the idea that the I-domain corresponds to the Xmax that corresponds to the clausal projection. Note that the expression "certain other moved elements" denotes topics. I propose that the I-domain is defined as the domain that is delimited by CP (or FP, if root clauses are FP projections). Constituents adjoined to root FP are outside this domain:

(175) a. Syntax: [XP] [$_{FP}$ (YP) V]

b. Initial Parse: [XP] $_{IntP}$ [([YP]) V]$_{IntP}$
YP = QPs, aspectual adverbs, negation
XP = topics, including sentential adverbs

This constitutes the initial parse that serves as input to rules of prosodic readjustment, which depend on the context of utterance, tree geometry, rate of speech, and so forth.

Now consider Nespor and Vogel's restructuring rules. There is an asymmetry between IP restructuring and φ restructuring. Whereas a φ may be included in another φ, to form a larger φ, an IntP can only be broken into smaller IntPs. The possibility that two initially parsed IntPs may be merged into a single IntP is not considered, and it is not clear why not. In a similar vein, Frota proposes that, in EP, a single IntP can be partitioned into smaller IntPs when certain conditions are met, such as length of the subject constituent.

Dresher (1993), in a study of the Tiberian Hebrew system of accents, proposes that prosodic readjustments are of two types: DIVISION of phrases, whereby a two-word phrase is further divided; and its opposite, SIMPLIFICATION, in which a phrase boundary is removed to create a longer phrase.

Here I propose that simplification may apply to IntPs derived in the initial parse if certain prosodic and discourse conditions are met; length of the constituent, rate of speech, rhythm, and discourse prominence are some of the factors that play a role in IntP restructuring. This approach is the inverse of Frota's. Whereas Frota claims that an IntP may be broken into shorter IntPs when the subject is long, I claim that two initially parsed IntPs can be simplified when the topic is short and certain other conditions are met. Short topics that are construed with *pro* subjects in "neutral" (broad-focus) utterances, as well as short adverbials and contrastive topics, are most often incorporated in the IntP that contains the verb, "marked" topics and long topics construed with *pro* subjects are phrased separately, and so forth. This approach has the advantage of explaining why there is a difference between quantificational operator subjects and other subjects: in the initial parse, quantificational operators fall within the IntP that contains the verb; other "subjects," by contrast, fall outside this domain and are more likely to be affected by readjustments that depend on the length of the constituent.

I will now turn to the consequences of this proposal for cliticization. I assume that the prosodic restriction stated in (110) is formulated in terms of a filter:

(176)   * [CL X] $_{IntP}$

Assuming that the syntactic and phonological components are derivationally related, the syntax is no longer accessible at the level at which the rules of prosodic readjustment take place; conversely, considerations such as length of a constituent or rate of speech are irrelevant to syntax. Now consider what would happen if the filter in (176) did not apply at a level at which the syntax is still accessible, that is, in the mapping between syntax and PF. Suppose that the structure contains a topic pronoun construed with a null subject. Simplification would apply, the pronoun would be phrased in the same IntP as the clitic, and (176) would not be violated. Now suppose that the "subject" is long and ends up forming a separate IntP. Example (176) would be violated. However, by the time P-structure is constructed, the syntax is no longer accessible, so the result would be an ill-formed utterance. This is why *no* derivation containing a clitic at the left edge of the clause (FP or CP) is allowed to proceed to PF. Example (176) applies in the mapping between syntax and PF, and at that level a topic pronoun is not distinguished from a longer topic. This is why there is no contradiction between (176) and the observation that preverbal subject pronouns require enclisis even though they belong to the same IntP that contains the verb.

2.1.7 Enclisis

As mentioned in the previous section, I take enclisis in EP to be the "elsewhere" option, that is, the option chosen when proclisis fails due to the prosodic filter (176). Enclisis is derived quite low in the structure. In Barbosa (1996a) I propose that the clitic right adjoins to an Infl head the verb moves through as it raises up. Matos and Duarte (chapter 4, this volume) propose that enclitics skip the V head and left-adjoin to the first functional projection above VP, AgrOP. As mentioned, I depart from these authors in taking enclisis to be the option chosen when the derivation with proclisis does not converge at the PF-interface. Matos and Duarte, by contrast, argue that enclisis is less costly or more "basic" than proclisis on the basis of data from language acquisition and from younger generations, where enclisis often occurs in contexts of proclisis, as shown in the following:

(177)   não chama-se nada (M. 20 months)
        not calls-SE nothing   (Duarte and Matos, chapter 4, this volume: 14)

On the surface, these data appear to constitute a problem to the Last Resort approach to enclisis implied by the analysis I have sketched. However, this problem is only apparent. According to the analysis proposed here, there are two alternative derivations: proclisis, whereby the clitic is placed in the checking domain of Infl; and enclisis, which, by hypothesis, involves incorporation with V in a lower Infl head (AspP or AgrOP).

These two options are in principle both available: that is why enclisis kicks in when proclisis does not converge at the PF-interface. This is not problematic. What is problematic is why, when both options lead to convergence, proclisis should win over enclisis in the standard dialect. I have no explanation for why this occurs, given that enclisis apparently involves a "shorter" move. Interestingly, the subset of contexts in which both options converge (according to the theory proposed here) coincides with the contexts in which there is variation. Regarding the child acquisition data, it is not surprising that enclisis should correspond to the initial stage. As noted in Duarte and Matos (chapter 4, this volume), assuming that all functional heads become "active" bottom-up, I predict that the derivation that involves higher functional layers should be acquired at a later stage. The interesting case is the speech of young adults, which is clearly undergoing a process of change toward generalized enclisis. I interpret the young adult data as confirming the hypothesis that there are indeed two possible derivations at stake, and two grammars. In the standard grammar, proclisis wins over enclisis when both converge. The grammar of the new generations is undergoing a change: enclisis is becoming the favored option.

This change could be viewed as a consequence of a process of reanalysis of clitics as affix-like elements, as suggested in Duarte and Matos (chapter 4, this volume). In Barbosa (1996a) I argue that the proclitic does not incorporate with the verb and that it is best analyzed as an X-bar theoretical minimal/maximal category, which actually undergoes XP-movement. Since a careful discussion of the arguments presented there would take me too far afield, I have glossed over that issue. However, if this idea is on the right track, proclisis involves XP-movement of a hybrid category, whereas enclisis involves lexical incorporation. The young adult data could then be taken as indicating that the option in which the clitic does not form a morphological unit with the verb is becoming less favored. I have no clear answer to the question of why there is an inversion in the optimality metric of these two dialects. However, I take the fact that there is fluctuation in *exactly* the subset of cases where some indeterminacy is predicted by the theory to be an indirect argument for its adequacy.

This concludes my discussion of clitic placement in EP. One of the major consequences of this investigation is the claim that preverbal subjects in EP do not raise to an A-position in the syntax. However, for my proposal to be complete, I need to give independent evidence that this is indeed the case. This is the topic of the next section.

2.2 Independent evidence for the CLLD analysis of preverbal subjects in European Portuguese

That certain constructions in the NSLs can be analyzed only in terms of subject CLLD is widely acknowledged (see Belletti 1990 for Italian and Duarte 1987 for EP, among many others). However, it has always been assumed that this is a somewhat "marked option" that coexists with the "unmarked option" of subject raising to an A-position (whichever position that might be). The analysis of clitic placement proposed in the previous section makes the much stronger claim that preverbal subjects in EP do not raise to an A-position in the syntax. The question that now arises is whether there is any evidence, apart from clitic placement, that may confirm this hypothesis. In what follows I will introduce two sets of arguments in favor of this hypothesis.

2.2.1 Inflected infinitives embedded under epistemic verbs

Raposo (1987) observes that in inflected infinitival clauses embedded under epistemic and declarative predicates the order between the subject and the verb carrying the inflection is necessarily verb-subject. The following example, taken from Raposo (1987), illustrates this restriction:

(178)   a. *Penso [os deputados terem votado essa proposta].
              I-think the deputees to-have-3PL voted that proposal

b. Penso [terem os deputados votado essa proposta].

I-think to-have-3PL the deputees voted that proposal

Raposo (1987) interpreted this restriction as the result of obligatory Infl raising to Comp. As noted in Ambar (1988), Raposo's judgments differ from those of Mateus et al. (1989), who consider equivalents of (178a) to be milder violations (cf. ?? vs *). According to Ambar, (178a) is somewhat marginal though not completely out. In addition, she notes that when the subject is modified by a focus particle, (178a) becomes completely well-formed.

(179)   Disseram-me [só eles terem visto esse filme].

they-told-me only they to-have-3PL seen that movie

Raposo (1994:40) observes that "the possibility of material occurring before the inflected infinitive is much more general," adding that "the whole gamut of affective operators may occur there, and the phenomenon is not restricted to subjects." By "affective operators" he means the whole set of QPs that trigger proclisis. Here are some of the examples he mentions:

(180)   Disseram-me [muita gente ter visto esse filme].

they-told-me many people to-have seen that movie

(181)   a. Disseram-me [nada terem esses turistas visitado].

they-told-me nothing to-have-3PL those tourists visited

b. Disseram-me [so essa cidade terem os turistas visitado].

they-told-me only that dity to-have-3PL the tourists visited

This contrast between the by now familiar set of QPs that trigger proclisis and other DPs is exactly the kind of effect that is expected under the analysis proposed here. Assuming that, for some reason, CLLD is impossible with inflected infinitives embedded under epistemic or declarative verbs, the only option left to front an argument is A'-movement to Spec, IP. Since this kind of movement is rather restricted in EP, we find only certain QPs in these contexts, namely, those that are incompatible with CLLD. Moreover, this kind of fronting is not restricted to subjects, as expected. That CLLD yields a marginal result with inflected infinitives embedded under epistemic and declarative verbs is illustrated in the following:

(182)   ??Confesso, essa proposta, não a termos conseguido aprovar ainda.

I-confess that proposal not it to-have-1PL managed to-approve yet

These contrasts in the distribution of topics and quantificational operators are very reminiscent of the Romanian facts discussed in section 2.1.5.3.1. Recall that, in Romanian subjunctives, the complementizer Ca can be omitted when the constituent that precedes the verb bears contrastive focus or is modified by a focus particle. Ca is obligatory in case there is a preverbal subject in the front of să, a sentential adverb, or a dislocated object. This contrast between Focus and CLLDed elements is similar to the contrast noted earlier for Portuguese inflected infinitives. There are two caveats, however. Portuguese inflected infinitives, unlike Romanian *să* subjunctives, are incompatible with *wh*-movement. In addition, Portuguese does not have Focus movement of definite DPs (or of sentential adverbs) unlike the other Romance languages, including Romanian. However, abstracting away from these circumstantial differences, the facts are amenable to a common explanation.

Previously I adopted the suggestion put forward in Boskovič (1996), according to which the absence of the complementizer *ca* in Romanian reflects the absence of a CP projection. In addition, I assumed a general ban on adjunction to an argument. Extending Boskovič's analysis of Romanian to the selected inflected infinitives, I propose that inflected infinitives embedded under epistemics are bare IPs.

(183)   Pensava [$_{IP}$ terem os deputados aprovado essa proposta]

Now consider the contrast between (185a) and (185b):

(184)   a. Pensava só os deputados terem aprovado a proposta.
             I-thought only the deputees to-have-3PL approved the proposal

         b. ??Pensava os deputados terem aprovado a proposta.
             I-thought the deputees to-have-3PL approved the proposal

This contrast can be explained as long as it is assumed that the quantificational operator subject and the nonquantificational operator subject occupy different positions. Example (184a) is analyzed as in (185a) and (184b) as in (185b):

(185)   a. Pensava [$_{IP}$ só os deputados [$_{I'}$ terem aprovado essa proposta]]

         b. ??Pensava [$_{IP}$ os deputados [$_{IP}$ terem pro aprovado esse filme]]

Example (185b) violates the ban against adjunction to an argument, so it has a dubious status. Example (185a) does not involve adjunction, so it is fine. Thus, we conclude that the dislocation hypothesis yields the desired results. If subjects could raise to an A-position in the syntax, it is not at all clear why it is only the expressions that cannot be dislocated that are allowed in this construction. Note, in addition, that the preverbal position is available to any QP argument, not just subjects (cf. 181). This argues against the idea that the preverbal position raises to an A-position.

It has been often claimed in the literature (see Duarte 1987; Raposo and Uriagereka 1996) that dislocation is impossible with inflected infinitives in general. However, inflected infinitives can take overt subjects when they occur in subject position or when they are embedded under factive verbs, as discussed in Raposo (1986), so this appears to be a problem for my proposal:

(186)   a. É melhor eles não falarem com a Maria agora.
             it-is better they not to-talk-3PL with the Maria now

         b. Lamento eles não terem falado com a Maria.
             I regret they not to-have-3PL talked with the Maria

My own intuition is that object CLLD is rare with inflected infinitives, but I would not judge the following sentences as bad:

(187) a. É melhor, à Maria, não dizerem a verdade toda.
       it-is better, to-the Maria, not to-tell-3PL the truth all
       'It is better that they don't tell the whole truth to Maria.'

       b. É pena, a Maria, não a podermos levar agora.
       it-is a pity the Maria not her can-3PL take now
       'It is a pity that we can't take Maria now.'

       c. É pena, à Maria, ninguém poder dizer a verdade.
       it-is a pity, to-the Maria, no one can tell her the truth
       'It is a pity that, to Maria, no one can tell the truth.'

(188) Lamentamos, à Maria, ninguém poder dizer a verdade.
       we-regret to-the Maria, no one can tell the truth
       'We regret it that to Maria no one can tell the truth.'

The examples in (187) and (188) require a heavier intonational break than the examples in (186), which sound perfectly natural without a pause. However, as I have noted, this difference between subjects and objects is observed even in constructions that unambiguously involve dislocation, so the intonational difference is not really a counterargument. Note also that when we consider what happens when a sentential adverb precedes the verb, the intuitions replicate those observed in the case of subjects. Thus, in inflected infinitives embedded under epistemic or declarative verbs a presentential adverb yields a somewhat marginal result; in the other cases, a preverbal sentential adverb is fine:

(189) a. ??O ministro declarou amanhã poderem aprovar a proposta.
       the minister declared tomorrow to-be-able-3PL to-approve the proposal

       b. É pena amanhã não poderes vir.
       it-is a pity tomorrow not to-be-able-2SG to-come
       'It is a pity that you can't come tomorrow.'

       c. Lamento amanhã não poderes vir.
       I-regret tomorrow not to-be-able-2SG to-come

To my ear, (189b and c) differ from (190a) in the same subtle way that (184b) differs from (186a and b). This parallel with sentential adverbs is surprising under the standard view that takes preverbal subjects to sit in an L-related position, although it is in accordance with the predictions of the adjunction hypothesis.

2.2.2 Nonspecific indefinites in preverbal subject position

CLLDed constituents always take wide scope with respect to operators inside the clause, as illustrated by the following for Portuguese (see also Cinque 1991):

(190)   Algumas cartas, ainda não as pude ler.
          'Some letters, I haven´t yet been able to read them.'

Example (190) can be appropriately uttered only in a context in which there is a contextually salient set of letters, and the indefinite is interpreted as a partitive. Thus, my hypothesis makes the very strong prediction that indefinite preverbal "subjects" should always take wide scope.

In effect, this prediction is fulfilled. Consider the following English sentence:

(191)   Look! A flower is growing in every pot!

Example (191) has only one plausible reading, namely, the one in which the indefinite is interpreted with narrow scope with respect to the universal QP. The wide-scope reading of the indefinite is absurd: the same flower cannot grow in several pots at the same time. Now consider the following two possible renderings of (192) in Portuguese:

(192)   a. Olha! Uma flor está a crescer em todos os vasos.
             'Look! A flower is growing in all the pots.'

          b. Olha! Está a crescer uma flor em todos os vasos.
             'Look! is growing a flower in all the pots.'

For me, (192a) only has the absurd reading. Example (192b) is fine. Thus, preverbal subject "indefinites" (that are not quantificational operators in the sense described earlier) have obligatory wide scope with respect to quantifiers inside the clause, and my prediction is confirmed. Under the assumption that preverbal subjects raise to Spec, IP, these facts are harder to accommodate: Why should English differ from Portuguese, given that in both languages the subject would be sitting in the same position?

It has often been noted in the literature that nonspecific indefinite subjects in the NSLs are not felicitous when they appear in preverbal position (Brito and Duarte 1983; Brito 1984; Martins 1994). This restriction against preverbal nonspecific indefinite subjects distinguishes the NSLs from English. It has been claimed that, since subjects can stay in situ in the NSLs, raising to Spec, IP is triggered by topichood (Calabrese 1990; Saccon 1993; Pinto 1994; Adger 1996; Grimshaw and Samek-Lodovici 1995; Costa 1996). By hypothesis, Infl in the NSLs would have a topic feature that needs to be checked. Under this approach, the difference between English and Portuguese would be accounted for. However, it is not the case that all preverbal indefinite subjects are topics. Consider the following contrasts:

(193)   a. ???Um desastre aconteceu na festa.
             a disaster happened at-the party

          b. Aconteceu um desastre na festa.
             happened a disaster at-the party

(194)   Algo aconteceu na festa, mas não me disseram o que foi.
        'Something happened at-the party, but no one told me what it was.'

Example (194) contains a bare indefinite subject (a quantificational operator in the sense discussed earlier) in preverbal position. As discussed, bare indefinites are not topics; yet they can appear in preverbal position.

Note, in addition, that quantificational operators can have narrow scope with respect to a scope taking element inside the clause:

(195)   a.   Ontem algo de estranho aconteceu em todas as festas da cidade.
             'Yesterday something strange happened in all the parties of the city.'

        b.   Apenas uma bactéria cresceu em todos os recipientes.
             'Only one bacteria grew in every recepient.'

In (195a, b) the quantificational operator subject can be interpreted with narrow scope with respect to the universal QP. According to the analysis proposed here, quantificational operators raise to an A'-position, so narrow scope follows from the possibility of reconstruction.

Even though there is general consensus among linguists that nonspecific indefinites resist the preverbal position in the NSLs, there are also arguments against the idea that preverbal subjects are topics precisely on the basis of the distribution of indefinites. Consider the following example, mentioned in Duarte (1987):

(196)   Um médico descobriu uma vacina contra a sida.
        'A doctor discovered a vaccine against AIDS.'

Example (196) is fine, even though the preverbal "subject" is indefinite. However, as Duarte herself notes, (196) is only a problem to the assumption that the indefinite is a topic in theories that assume that the defining property of topic is familiarity (being "old information" or shared knowledge). Reinhart (1981, 1995), however, argues that the familiarity approach to topics is mistaken. In particular, she claims: "It is true that the common way to introduce new entities into the discourse is in focus position, or by use of presentational sentences, but an existing alternative is introducing them as (indefinite) topics." (Reinhart 1995:86).

Here I will not apply Reinhart's (1981) tests for topichood, since they were not designed to detect dislocated topics, which is the construction that concerns me. However, I can use the familiar test for dislocation, recomplementation. To my ear, (197) is fine as a recomplementation sentence:

(197)   Disseram-me que um médico que descobriu a vacina contra a sida.
        they-told-me that a doctor that discovered a vaccine against AIDS

Thus, certain indefinites can be topics doubled by resumptive *pro,* and (196) does not constitute a problem for my hypothesis.

2.2.3 Summary

In this section I have given independent evidence internal to EP in favor of the idea that preverbal subjects do not raise to an A-position. In previous sections, I have shown that this observation extends to Catalan, Spanish, and Romanian, which suggests that this generalization should be regarded as an intrinsic property of the NSLs, as has been independently argued by Solà (1992), Alexiadou and Anagnostopoulou (1996), and Pollock (1996). In the next section I will discuss yet another set of facts that reinforce this view of the null subject property.

2.3 Adnominal en/ne-cliticization

In this section I will show that there are contrasts between French and the NSLs with respect to adnominal ne/en-cliticization from subjects that defy explanation under any theory that assumes that preverbal subjects are A-moved to preverbal position. These facts follow quite naturally once one assumes that preverbal nonquantificational operator subjects are left-dislocated.

French en and Italian ne can pronominalize an adnominal complement of a direct object, as in (198) and (199); the same holds of Catalan, too) see Couquaux 1981; Burzio 1986; Belletti and Rizzi 1990; Pollock 1986, 1997):

Adnominal ne (Italian):
(198)   a. Maria conosce tre libri del questo autore.
           'Mary knows three books by this author.'

        b. Maria ne conosce tre libri.
           Maria cl-of-him knows three books
           'Maria knows three books by him.'

Adnominal en (French):
(199)   a. Luc a cassé le pied de cette table.
           'Luc has broken the foot of this table.'

        b. Luc en a cassé le pied.
           Luc cl-of-it has broken the foot
           'Luc has broken the foot of it.'

When it comes to subjects, there is a split between French, on the one hand, and Catalan and Italian, on the other. Adnominal ne/en can be associated with a preverbal (derived) subject in French, though not in Catalan or Italian.[7] This is illustrated as follows:

French:
(200)   La préface en est trop flatteuse
        the preface cl-of-it is too flattering
        'The preface of it is too flattering.'

Italian:
(201)   a. Ne apparirano molti capitoli.
cl-of-it appeared three books

b. *Molti capitoli ne apparirano
many chapters cl-of-it appeared

Catalan:
(202)   a. En seran editats tres volums.
cl-of-it will-be edited three volumes

b. *Tres volums en seran editats.
three volumes cl-of-it will-be edited

This contrast is a mystery for any theory that claims that preverbal subjects in the NSLs are A-moved to preverbal position, since no relevant *structural* differences are predicted between preverbal subject constructions in French and Italian/Catalan. The adjunction hypothesis, however, states that there are important structural differences between the non-NSLs and the NSLs in subject initial constructions. In French, preverbal subjects are A-moved to Spec, IP. In the NSLs, this configuration never arises. There are only two options: left-dislocation or A'-movement. In particular, this theory predicts that the pattern of adnominal *en/ne* cliticization from preverbal subjects in the NSLs should replicate the pattern observed with left-dislocated objects and focused objects. This prediction is in fact borne out.

When we look at objects, we observe that adnominal *ne* cliticization is compatible with A'- movement (cf. (203)), but incompatible with CLLD (cf. (204)):

Italian:
(203)   a. L' AUTORE ne conoscevo (non l' editore)!
the author cl-of it know-1sg. (not the editor)

b. *Catalan:*
TRES CAPITOLS en vaig llegir (i no pas quatre)!
Three chapters cl-of-it have-read (and not NEG four)

Catalan:
(204)   a. *Aquests capitols els n' he llegit.
those chapters them cl-of-it have read

b. *Italian*
*Quei capitoli, non li-ne /ne-li ho letto/letti.
those chapters them cl-of-it have read

The following Catalan example shows that the impossibility of (204a) is not due to a morphological restriction on the combination of an object clitic with *en:*

Catalan:
(205) (Els llibres) (del Calaix)
(the books) (from the drawer)
ja els n' he tret.
already *them cl-from-there* have taken
(the books) (from the drawer) I have already taken them from there

Under the hypothesis that (nonfocused) preverbal subjects are dislocated in the NSLs, the impossibility of adnominal *ne/en*-cliticization with a preverbal nonfocused subject follows from the incompatibility of adnominal *ne/en*-cliticization with CLLD. Intuitively, CLLD is incompatible with *ne/en*-cliticization because the empty category the clitic is associated with must be maximal, that is, it cannot be modified. In order for (204) to be well-formed, *en* would have to be linked to a modifier of the *ec* associated with the object clitic. However, clitics cannot be "modified." Thus, there is no source for *ne/en* in (204). Likewise, there is no source for *ne* in (206a) if its representation is as in (206b), where *pro* is the real subject, and the lexical DP is a base-generated topic:

(206) a. *molti capitoli ne appariranno

   b. [$_{IP}$ [molti capitoli]$_1$ [$_{IP}$ ne$_2$ apariranno pro$_1$]]

I will now turn to focused subjects. Focus-movement of the object is judged to be compatible with adnominal *ne /en*-cliticization in Italian and Catalan. The Catalan example (207a) illustrates subject focalization and contrasts with the ungrammatical example (207b), where the subject is not focused:

Catalan:
(207) a. TRES volums n' apareixeran.
   three volumes cl-of-it will-appear!
   (i no pas quatre)
   (and not NEG four)
   THREE volumes appeared (not four)!

   b. *Tres volums en seran editats.
   three volumes cl-of-it will-be edited
   'Three volumes of it will be edited.'

The difference between (207a) and (207b) is that the former involves movement (in this case, A'-movement) of *tres volums* 'three volumes,' whereas the latter involves a base-generated topic doubled by an empty category in an A-position. Note that (207a) is parallel to the French example (200). In both cases there is movement to preverbal position, the only difference being in the kind of movement involved: A'-movement versus A-movement.

The contrast in (207), in conjunction with French (200), highlights the relevance of *movement* versus *base-generation* in characterizing the difference between neutral preverbal subject constructions in the NSLs and in the non-NSLs. The standard theory or any variation thereof that assumes A-movement of the subject to a preverbal position has in principle nothing to say about the unacceptablity of (206) and (207b) when compared with French (200).

2.4 Conclusion

To conclude, I have argued that the different patterns of clitic placement in SV constructions in EP follow once one assumes that the preverbal field in EP does not constitute a target for A-movement of subjects. I claimed that the *real A-position* for subjects in EP is to the right of the raised verb:

(208)   [IP [I' V   [VP subject t]]]
         t_____|

SV constructions can be derived in one of two ways. They are instances of either subject CLLD (cf. 209) or A'-movement of the subject (cf. 210)):

(209)   [$_{IP}$ DP$_i$ [$_{IP}$ V ... *pro subject* $_i$ ...]]

(210)   [FP subject [F' V ... t]]
         t_____|

In (209) the adjoined DP is licensed by "rules of predication," in the sense of Chomsky (1977). IP contains an "open" position (*pro*, a pronominal category without independent reference) satisfied by the entity referred to by the topic. Example (209) is barred to expressions that cannot act as discourse "links" (in the sense of Vallduví 1992). These can only be fronted by A'-movement. A'-movement can target Spec, IP, an A'-position, or it can target the specifier of a higher projection (FP).

In line with Rigau (1987), Contreras (1991), Vallduví (1991, 1992), Solà (1992), Alexiadou and Anagnostopoulou (1998), and Pollock (1997), I suggested that this theory of subject positions is a characteristic feature of the NSLs. I argued that it accounts for a wide range of phenomena in the Romance NSLs, including the distribution of preverbal subjects in inflected infinitives in EP; the restrictions on the distribution of the subjunctive complementizer in Romanian (Dobrovie-Sorin 1994); the relative positions of topics and fronted quantificational operators in Catalan (Vallduví 1992; Solà 1992); the restrictions on the interpretation of preverbal indefinites; and certain assymmetries in *ne/en*-cliticization from subjects between French and Italian. It faces the somewhat puzzling conclusion that the real A-position for subjects, the postverbal position, is not the unmarked position as far as its discourse properties are concerned. Inverted subjects tend to be focused in the NSLs. However, this might be caused by the interference of other factors, such as the rule assigning focus in the language. Reinhart (1995) and Zubizarreta (1998) have proposed that there is a relation between stress prominence and focus interpretation, where stress prominence is a function of depth of embedding, as proposed in Cinque (1993). Thus, if the subject remains inside the VP at Spell-Out, it may be assigned focus by this independent rule. Hence, the only way to establish the topic-comment articulation with subjects is by CLLD. The lack of A'-properties of preverbal (nonquantificational) subjects follows from the properties of CLLD: CLLD does not display weak cross-over effects, does not license parasitic gaps, and does not reconstruct (at least not for the purposes of certain syntactic phenomena, like proper binding of the trace of partitive *ne*-cliticization).

This theory of subject positions in the NSLs has the added advantage of accounting for two other well-known properties of these languages: "free inversion" and the fact that subject extraction is from postverbal position. Since the real subject position is to the right of the raised verb, extraction is predicted to take place from this position and no other; the alternations between SV and VS order follow from the processes of constituent fronting independently available in these languages, namely, CLLD and A'-fronting. This allows us to pose new questions about the Null Subject Property, namely, why in NSLs subjects do not raise to an L-related position in the syntax (see Barbosa 1995, Pollock (1997), and Alexiadou and Anagnostopoulou (1998) for theories of the Null Subject property that attempt to answer that question).

Notes

1. See Duarte (1987), Uriagereka (1995), and Raposo (1996) for the differences between this construction and Portuguese topicalization.

2. This pattern of clitic placement is also found in Galician and Asturian Spanish.

3. In this chapter I will concentrate on finite clauses only.

4. According to Halpern (1992a, b), the superficial differences between languages with strict 2P clitics, such as Serbo-Croatian—where clitics need to be adjacent to the verbal string—and Old Romance verbal clitics is that the former are syntactically generated in C, whereas the latter are generated in the vicinity of the verb.

5. There is one particular construction in which an indirect object clitic may occur at the beginning of the utterance:

(i)   Te garanto!
      CL-2SG guarantee-1SG
      'I guarantee you that!'

Example (i) has a particular elocutionary force and a particular intonational pattern. One might explore the possibility that, in this case, the edge of the IntP is not a strong position, due to its intonational pattern. In any case, this example is the only one I can think of where a clitic appears in first position, so it appears to be rather idosyncratic.

6. According to Cinque (1990), CLLD obeys strong islands in Italian. Interestingly, Duarte (1987) and Raposo (1997) show that this observation does not hold for Portuguese. Since the evidence against *wh*-movement in CLLD constructions is overwhelming, I assume that the strong island effect has some other explanation that does not rely on movement of the topic itself from within the clause (see Iatridou 1991 for discussion).

7. Adnominal *en*-cliticization from preverbal subjects is only possible with underlying objects (see Burzio 1986) and Couquaux 1981 for discussion).

References

Adams, M. 1987. "From Old French to the Theory of *pro-drop.*" *NLLT* 5:1–32.

Adger, D. 1996. "Economy and Optionality: Interpretations of Subjects in Italian." *PROBUS* 8: 117–136.

Alexiadou, A., and E. Anagnostopoulou. 1998. "Parametrizing AGR: Word Order, V-Movement and EPP-Checking." *NLLT* 16: 491–539.

Ambar, M. 1988. "Para uma Sintaxe da Inversão Sujeito-Verbo em Português." Ph.D. dissertation, University of Lisbon.

Ambar, M. 1998. "Towards a Definition of CP—Evidence from TopicFocusP and EvaluativeP." Talk presented at Going Romance 1997, Groningen.

Baker, M. 1991. "On Some Subject/Object Non-asymmetries in Mohawk." *Natural Language and Linguistic Theory* 9: 537.

Barbosa, P. 1993. "Clitic Placement in Old Romance and European Portuguese." In *CLS 29: Papers from the Twenty-Ninth Regional Meeting of the Chicago Linguistic Society.* Chicago: University of Chicago.

———. 1995. "Null Subjects." Ph.D. dissertation, MIT.

———. 1996a. "Clitic Placement in European Portuguese and the Position of Subjects. In A. Halpern and A. Zwicky (eds.) *Approaching Second: Second Position Clitics and Related Phenomena.* 1–40. Stanford, Calif.: CSLI Publications.

———. 1996b. "In Defense of Right Adjunction for Head Movement in Romance." In A-M di Sciullio (ed.) *Configurations: Essays on Structure and Its Interpretation,* Somerville, Mass.: Cascadilla Press.

———. 1996c. "A New Look at the Null Subject Parameter." In J. Costa, R. Goedermans, and R. van de Vijver (eds.) *Proceedings of ConSOLE* IV: 375–395. Leiden, The Netherlands.

Belletti, A. 1990. *Generalized Verb Movement.* Turin: Rosenberg and Sellier.

———. 1994. "Verb Positions: Evidence from Italian." D. Lightfoot and N. Hornstein (eds.) *Verb Movement,* 19–40. Cambridge: Cambridge University Press.

Belletti, A., and L. Rizzi, 1981. "The Syntax of *Ne*: Some Theoretical Implications." *The Linguistic Review* 1: 117–154.

Belletti, A., and U. Shlonsky, 1995. "The Order of Verbal Complements: A Comparative Study." *NLLT* 13:489–526.

Benincà, P. 1991. "Complement Clitics in Medieval Romance: The Tobler-Mussafia Law." In H. van Riemsdijk and L. Rizzi (eds.) *Eurotyp Working Papers: Clitics and their Hosts.* Tilburg University.

Benincà, P., and L. Vanelli. 1982. "Apunti di sintassi Veneta." *Guida ai dialetti Veneti* 4. Padua.

Benincà, P., and G. Cinque. 1990. "Su alcune differenze fra enclisis e proclisi. Ms., University of Padua.

Bonet, E. 1990. "Subjects in Catalan." *MIT Working Papers in Linguistics* 13: 1–26.

Borer, H. (ed.) 1986. *The Syntax of Pronominal Clitics.* Syntax and Semantics 19. New York: Academic Press.

Boskovic, Z. 1996. "Selection and the Categorial Status of Infinitival Complements." *NLLT* 14: 269–304.

Brandi, L., and P. Cordin. 1989. "Two Italian Dialects and the Null Subject Parameter." In O. Jaeggli and K. Safir (eds.) *The Null Subject Parameter.* Dordrecht: Kluwer Academic Publishers.

Bresnan, J., and S. Mchombo. 1987. "Topic, Pronoun and Agreement in Chichewa." *Language* 63: 781–782.

Brito, A. 1984. "Sobre as Noções de Sujeito e Argumento Externo: Semelhanças entre a Estrutura de F e a Estrutura do SN em Portuguêa." *Boletim de Filologia* 24: 421–478.

Brito, A., and I. Duarte. 1983. "Condições sobre Posposição do Sujeito em Português." *Boletim de Filologia* 27: 191–254.

Burzio, L. 1986. *Italian Syntax*. Dordrecht: Reidel,

Calabrese, A. 1990. "Some Remarks on Focus and Logical Structures in Italian." *Harvard Working Papers in Linguistics*.

Campos, H. 1994. "Full and Reduced Clitics in Megleno-Romance." Ms., Georgetown University.

————. 1997. "On Subject Extraction and the Antiagreement Effect in Romance." *Linguistic Inquiry* 28: 92–119.

Cardinaletti, A. 1995. "Subject Positions." Ms., Seminario di Linguistica, University of Venice, Venice.

Cardinaletti, A., and G. Giusti. 1991. "Partitive *ne* and the QP Hypothesis: A Case Study." *University of Venice Working Papers in Linguistics*.

Cardinaletti, A., and I. Roberts. 1991. "Clause Structrure and X-Second." Ms., University of Venice and University of Geneva.

Cardinaletti, A., and M. Starke. 1994. "The Typology of Structural Deficiency: On the Three Grammatical classes." Ms., University of Geneva/Max Planck Berlin.

Chomsky, N. 1997." On *wh*-Movement." IN P. Culicover, T. Wasos, and A. Akmajian (eds.) *Formal Syntax*, 71–132. New York: Academic Press.

————. 1986. *Barriers*. Cambridge: MIT Press.

————. 1994. "Bare Phrase Structure." MIT Occasional Papers in Linguistics.

————. 1995. *A Minimalist Program for Linguistic Theory*. Cambridge: MIT Press.

Cinque, G. 1990. *Types of A'-Dependencies*. Cambridge: MIT Press.

————. 1993. "A Null Theory of Phrase and Compound Stress." *Linguistic Inquiry* 24: 239–298.

Contreras, H. 1991. "On the Position of Subjects." In S. Rothstein (ed.) *Perspectives on Phrase Structure: Heads and Licensing*. Syntax and Semantics 25. San Diego: Academic Press.

Costa, J. 1996. "Positions for Subjects in European Portuguese." *Proceedings of WCCFL XV*. Stanford, Calif.: CSLI Publications.

Couquaux, D. 1981. "French Predication and Linguistic Theory." In A. May and J. Koster (eds.) *Levels of Syntactic Representation*. Dordrecht: Foris.

Culicover, P. 1992. "Topicalization, Inversion and Complementizers in English." In D. Delfitto et al (eds.) *Going Romance and Beyond*. Utrecht: OTS Working Papers, University of Utrecht.

Deprez, V. 1990. "Two Ways of Moving the Verb in French." *MIT Working Papers in Linguistics* 13.

Dobrovie-Sorin, C. 1994. *The Syntax of Roumanian: Comparative Studies in Romance*. Dordrecht: Foris.

Dresher, B. 1993. "The Prosodic Basis of the Tiberian Hebrew System of Accents." Ms., University of Toronto, Toronto.

Duarte, I. 1983. "Variação Paramétrica e Ordem dos Clíticos." *Revista da Faculdade de Letras de Lisboa* 50: 158–78.

————. 1987. "A Construção de Topicalização na Gramática do Português: Regência, Ligação e Condições sobre Movimento." Ph.D. Dissertation, Unviersity of Lisbon.

Duarte, L., and G. Matos. 1995. "Romance Clitics and the Minimalist Program." Paper given at the 5th Colloquium on Generative Gramar. Coruña.

Fontana, J. 1993. "Phrase Structure and the Syntax of Clitics in the History of Spanish." Ph.D. dissertation, University of Pennsylvania.

————. 1996. "Phonology and Syntax in the Tobler-Mussafia Law." In A. Halpern and A. Zwicky (eds.) *Approaching Second: Second Position Clitics and Related Phenomena*, 41–85. Stanford: CSLI Publications.

Frota, S. 1994. "Aspectos da Prosódia do Foco no Português Europeu." In L. Bisol (ed.) *Fonologia: Análises não-lineares*. Porto Alegre: Centro de Pesquisas Linguisticas, Letras de Hoje.

————. 1995a. "Acoustic Features of Prosodic Phrases in European Portuguese." Ms., University of Lisbon.

————. 1995b. "Clashes and Prosodic Domains in European Portuguese." *Proceedings* 19, 93–107. Institute of Phonetic Studies, University of Amsterdam.

————. 1996a. "Prosodic Phrases and European Portuguese: In Search of Evidence." *Proceedings from the 3rd Annual Meeting of ConSOLE* 47–69. Leiden: Sole.

————. 1996b. "On the Prosody and Intonation of Focus in European Portuguese," In F. Martinez-Gil and A. Morales-Front (eds.) *Issues in the Phonology and Morphology of the Major Iberian Languages*. Washington D. C.: Georgetown University Press.

Frota, S., and M. Vigário. 1996. "On Weight Effects in European Portuguese." Talk presented at the GLOW Workshop on Weight Effects, Athens.

Giupponi, E. 1988. "Pro-drop Parameter und Restrukturierung in Trentino." Ph.D. dissertation, University of Vienna.

Grimshaw, J., and V. Samek-Lodovici. 1995. "Optimal Subjects." In J. Beckman et al., (eds.) *Papers in Optimality Theory*, UMOP 18.

Hale, K., and E. Selkirk. 1987. "Government and Toanl Phrasing in Papago." *Phonology Yearbook* 4.

Hale, M. 1996. "Deriving Wackernagel's Law: Prosodic and Syntactic Factors Determining Clitic Placement in the Language of the Rigveda." In A. Halpern and A. Zwicky (eds.) *Approaching Second: Second Position Clitics and Related Phenomena*, 165–197. Stanford, Calif.: CSLI Publications.

Halpern. A. 1992a. "Prosody, Syntax and Second Position." Paper presented at the 1992 LSA meeting, Philadelphia.

Halpern, A. 1992b. "Topics in the Placement and Morphology of Clitics." Ph.D. dissertation, Stanford Unviersity.

Halpern, A., and J. Fontana, 1992. "X⁰ and Xmax Clitics." *Proceedings of WCCFL*, 12.

Halpern, A., and A. Zwicky (eds.) 1996. *Approaching Second: Second Position Clitics and Related Phenomena*. Stanford: CSLI Publications.

Hock, H. 1992. "What's a Nice Word Like You Doing in a Place Like This? Syntax versus Phonological Form." *Studies in the Linguistic Sciences* 22(1): 39–87.

Hock, H. 1996. "Who's on First? Toward a Prosodic Account of P2 Clitics." In A. Halpern and A. Zwicky (eds.), *Approaching Second: Second Position Clitics and Related Phenomena*, 166–199. Stanford: CSLI publications.

Iatridou, S. 1991. "Clitics and Island Effects." Ms., MIT.

Inkelas, S. 1989. "Prosodic Constituency in the Lexicon." Ph.D. dissertation, Stanford University.

Inkelas, S., and D. Zec (eds.) 1990. *The Phonology-Syntax Connection*. Chicago: University of Chicago Press.

Jaeggli, O. 1984. "Subject Extraction and the Null Subject Parameter." *NELS* 14: 132–153.

————. 1986. "Three issues in the Theory of Clitics." In H. Borer (ed.) *The Syntax of Pronominal Clitics*. Syntax and Semantics 19. New York: Academic Press.

Jaeggli, O., and K. Safir. (eds.) 1989. *The Null Subject Parameter*. Dordrecht: Kluwer Academic Publishers.

Jelinek, E. 1984. "Empty Categories, Case and Configurationality." *Natural Language and Linguistic Theory* 2: 39–76.

Kanerva, J. 1990. "Focusing on Phonological Prases in Chichewa." In S. Inkelas and D. Zec (eds.) *The Phronology-Syntax Connection*. Chicago: The University of Chicago Press.

Kayne, R. 1975. *French Syntax: The Transformational Cycle*. Cambridge, Mass.: MIT Press.

————. 1984. *Connectedness and Binary Branching*. Dordrecht: Foris.

————. 1989a. "Null Subjects and Clitic Climbing." In O. Jaeggli and K. Safir (eds.) *The Null Subject Parameter*. Dordrecht: Kluwer.

————. 1989b. "Facets of Romance Past Participle Agreement." In P. Benicó (ed.) *Dialect Variation and the Theory of Grammar*. Dordrecht: Foris.

————. 1991. "Romance Clitics, Verb Movement and PRO." *Linguistic Inquiry* 22: 647–686.

————. 1994. *The Antisymmetry of Syntax*. Cambridge: MIT Press.

Kenstowicz, M. 1989. "The Null Subject Parameter in Modern Arabic Dialects." In O. Jaeggli and K. Safir (eds.) *The Null Subject Parameter*. Dordrecht: Kluwer Academic Publishers.

Klima, E. 1964. "Negation in English." In J. Katz and J. Fodor (eds.) *The Structure of Language*. New York: Prentice-Hall.

Laka, I. 1990. "Negation in Syntax: On the Nature of Functional Categories and Projections." Ph.D. Dissertation, MIT.

Lema, J., and M.-L. Rivero. 1989. "Inverted Conjugations and V-second Effects in Romance." *Proceedings of the 19th Linguistic Symposium on Romance Languages*. Amsterdam: John Benjamins.

Lema, J., and M.-L. Rivero. 1990. "Long Head Movement: ECP vs HMC." In J. Carter et al. (eds) *Proceedings of NELS 20*. GLSA, University of Massachusetts, Amherst.

Madeira, A. 1992. "On Clitic Placement in European Portuguese." In H. van de Koot (ed.) *UCL Working Papers in Linguistics*, vol. 4. University College, London.

Manzini, R. 1992. "Second Position Dependencies." Ms., University College, London.

Marantz, A. 1988. "Clitics, Morphological Merger, and the Mapping to Phonological Structure." In M. Hammond and M. Noonan (eds.) *Theoretical Morphology*. New York: Academic Press.

Martins, A. 1994. "Foco e Cliticos no Português Europeu." Ph.D. dissertation, University of Lisbon.

Mateus, M., A. Brito, I. Duarte, and I. H. Faria. 1989. *Gramática da Lingua Portuguesa*. Lisbon: Editorial Caminho.

McCloskey, J. 1996. "On the Scope of Verb Movement in Irish." *NLLT* 14: 47–104.

Montalbetti, M. 1986. "How Pro Is It?" In O. Jaeggli (ed.) *Studies in Romance Linguistics*. Dordrecht: Foris.

Nespor, M., and Vogel. 1986. *Prosodic Phonology*. Dordrecht: Foris.

Ordoñez, F. 1998. "Post-verbal Asymmetries in Spanish." *NLLT* 16: 313–346.

Percus, O. 1993. "The Captious Clitic: Problems in Serbo-Croatian Clitic Placement." Phonology Generals Paper, MIT.

Pinto, M. 1994. "Subjects in Italian: Distribution and Interpretation." In R. Bok-Bennema and C. Cremers (eds.) *Linguistics in the Netherlands*. Amsterdam: John Benjamins.

Poletto, C. 1992. "La Sintassi del Soggetto nei Dialetti Italiani Settentrionali." *Quaderni Patavini di Linguistica,*

————. 1997. *The Higher Functional Field in the Northern Italian Dialects*. Ms., University of Padova.

Pollock, A. 1990. "Verb Movement, Universal Grammar, and the Structure of IP." *Linguistic Inquiry* 20: 365–424.

Pollock, J-Y. 1981. "On Case and Impersonal Constructions." In R. May and J. Koster (eds.) *Levels of Syntactic Representation*. Dordrecht: Foris.

————. 1986. "Sur la Syntaxe de *en* et le Paramètre du Sujet Nul." In D. Couquaux and M. Ronat (eds.) *La Grammaire Modulaire* 211–246. Paris: Editions Minuit.

————. 1997. *Langage et Cognition: Introduction au Programme Minimaliste de la Grammaire Générative*. Paris: Presses Universitaires de France.

Ramsden, H. 1963. *Weak-Pronoun Position in the Early Romance Languages*. Manchester: Manchester University Press.

Raposo, E. 1986. "On the Null Object in European Portuguese." In *Studies in Romance Linguistics*. Dordrecht: Foris.

————. 1987. "Case Theory and Infl-to Comp: The Inflected Infinitive in European Portuguese." *Linguistic Inquiry* 18:85–109.

————. 1994. "Affective Operators and Clausal Structure in European Portuguese and European Spanish." Ms., University of California at Santa Barbara, Calif.

————. 1996. "Towards a Unification of Topic Constructions." Ms., University of California, Santa Barbara.

————. 1997. "Definite/zero Alternations in Portuguese: Towards a Unified Theory of Topic Constructions." Ms., University of California at Santa Barbara, Calif.

Raposo, E., and J. Uriagereka. 1996. "Indefinite SE." *NLLT* 14: 749–810.

Reinhart, T. 1981. "Pragmatics and Linguistics: An Analysis of Sentence Topics." *Philosophica* 27, special issue on Pragmatic Theory.

Reinhart, T. 1995. "Interface Strategies." Ms., Utrecht University.

Rigau, G. 1987. "Sobre el Carácter Cuantificador de los Pronombres Tónicos en Catalán." In V. Demonte and M. Fernández Lagunilla (eds.) *Sintaxis de las lenguas románicas*. Madrid: Textos Universitarios.

Rivas, A. 1977. "A Theory of Clitics." Ph.D. Dissertation, MIT.

Rivero, M.-L. 1986. "Parameters in the Typology of Clitics in Romance and Old Spanish." *Language* 62: 774–807.

————. 1987. "La Teoria de las Barreras y las Completivas del Rumano." In V. Demonte and M. Fernández Lagunilla (eds.) *Sintaxis de las lenguas Románicas*, 329–354. Madrid: Textos Universitarios.

Rizzi, L. 1978. "A Restructuring Rule in Italian Syntax." In S. Keyser (ed.), *Recent Transformational Studies in European Languages*. Cambridge: MIT Press.

————. 1982. "Negation, wh-Movement and the Null Subject Parameter. *Issues in Italian Syntax*. Dordrecht: Kluwer.

————. 1986. "On the Status of Subject Clitics in Romance." In O. Jaeggli, (ed.) *Studies in Romance Linguistics*. Dordrecht: Foris,

————. 1990. *Relativized Minimality*. Cambridge, Mass.: MIT Press.

————. 1997. "The Fine Structure of the Left Periphery." In L. Haegeman (ed.) *Elements of Grammar*. Dordrecht: Kluwer.

Rouveret, A. 1992. "Clitic Placement, Focus and the Wackernagel Position in European Portuguese." Ms., University of Paris.

Saccon, G. 1993. "Post-verbal Subjects: A Study Based on Italian and Its Dialects." Ph.D. dis., Harvard University.

Samek-Lodovici, V. 1994. "Structural Focusing and Subject Inversion in itanian." Paper presented at Linguistics Symposium on Romance Languages, 24, Los Angeles.

Sadock, J. 1991. *Autolexical Syntax: A Theory of Parallel Grammatical Representations*. Chicago: University of Chicago Press.

Schutze, C. 1994. "Serbo-Croatian Second Position Clitic Placement and the phonology-Syntax Interface." In *Papers on Phonology and Morphology*, MIT Working Papers in Linguistics, 21.

Selkirk, E. 1984. *Phonology and Syntax*. Cambridge: MIT Press.

———. 1986. "On Derived Domains in Sentence Phonology." *Phonology Yearbook*, Cambridge University Press.

———. 1993. "The Prosodic Structure of Function Words." Ms., University of Massachusetts, Amherst.

Silva, M-C. 1992. "About V-Movement in Brazilian Portuguese."[Ms., University of Geneva.]

Solà, J. 1992. "Agreement and Subjects." Ph.D. dissertation, University Autonoma of Barcelona.

Sportiche, D. 1992. "Clitic Constructions." [Ms., UCLA.]

Taylor, A. 1996. "A Prosodic Account of Clitic Position in Ancient Greek." In A. Halpern and A. Zwicky (eds.) *Approaching Second: Second Position Clitics and Related Phenomena*, 166–199. Stanford: CSLI Publications.

Tegey, H. 1977. "The Grammar of Clitics: Evidence from Pashto and Other Languages." Ph.D. dissertation, University of Illinois.

Terzi, A. 1992. "*Pro* in Finite Clauses: A Study of the Inflectional Heads of the Balkan Languages." Ph.D. dissertation, City University of New York.

Tobler, Adolf. 1875. Lecture on J. Le Coultre, *De l' Ordre des Mots dans Chrétien de Troyes*. In *Vermischte Beiträge zur Französischen Grammatik* 5: 395–414. Leipzig: Hirzel.

Torrego, E. 1984. "On Inversion in Spanish and Some of Its Effects." *Linguistic Inquiry* 15: 103–129.

Uriagereka, J. 1988. "On Government." Ph.D. dissertation, University of Connecticut.

———. 1995a. "Aspects of the Syntax of Clitic Placement in Western Romance." *Linguistic Inquiry* 26, 79–123.

———. 1995b. "An F Position in Western Romance." In K. Kiss (ed.) *Discourse Configurational Languages*, 153–175. Oxford: Oxford University Press.

Uribe-Etxebarria, M. 1991. "On the Structural Positions of the Subject in Spanish, Their Nature and Their Consequences for Quantification." [Ms., University of Connecticut.]

Vallduví, E. 1990. "The Informational Component." Ph.D. dissertation, University of Pennsylvania.

———. 1992. "A Preverbal Landing Site for Quantificational Operators." In *Catalan Working Papers in Linguistics 1992*: 319–344. Barcelona: University Autònoma of Barcelona.

Zec, D., and S. Inkelas. 1990. "Prosodically Constrained Syntax." In S. Inkelas and D. Zec (eds.) *The Phonology-Syntax Connection*. Chicago: University of Chicago Press.

Zubizarreta, M. L. 1998. "Word Order, Prosody and Focus." Ms., University of Southern California.

3

JOÃO COSTA

Word Order and Discourse-Configurationality in European Portuguese

From the logically possible orderings between SUBJECT, VERB, and OBJECT in (1) only (1f) is ungrammatical in European Portuguese (henceforth EP), as (2) illustrates:

(1)   a. SVO

    b. VSO

    c. VOS

    d. OVS

    e. OSV

    f. *SOV

(2)   a. O Paulo comeu a sopa.
      the Paulo ate the soup

    b. Comeu o Paulo a sopa.

    c. Comeu a sopa o Paulo.

    d. A sopa comeu o Paulo.

    e. A sopa o Paulo comeu.

    f. *O Paulo a sopa comeu.

The purpose of this chapter is to look at the properties of the subjects in each order and try to find out which position each type of subject occupies and why. I will try to account for the optionality explaining what is the source for each order and, ultimately, to capture the basic intuition that EP is an SVO language (cf. Ambar 1992).

In section 3.1, I will identify the positions postverbal DEFINITE and INDEFINITE subjects occupy. In sections 3.2 and 3.3, I will do the same for postverbal subjects in VSO and VOS contexts, respectively. Section 3.5 investigates the contexts in which each word order is felicitous. Finally, in section 3.6 I will elaborate on a theory of MARKEDNESS in order to explain the different positions for subjects and the relation between each position and the respective discourse function.

3.1 Sentence-initial position

Preverbal subjects are traditionally assumed to occupy the Spec, IP position (cf. Duarte 1987; Ambar 1992; Martins 1994). Recent research on subject positions and WORD ORDER has challenged this view, suggesting that, in NULL SUBJECT LANGUAGES, the preverbal position for subjects is derived by LEFT-DISLOCATION of the subject (see, e.g., Barbosa 1995 for Portuguese; Valmala Elguea 1994, Ordoñez and Treviño 1995 for Spanish; and Alexiadou and Anagnostopoulou 1995 for Greek). In this section, I will show that by applying to EP some of the tests these authors use for the other languages, one reaches the conclusion that preverbal subjects in EP occupy the Spec, IP position if they are definite and a left-dislocated position if they are indefinite.

3.1.1 Preverbal definite subjects

Definite subjects in preverbal position appear to be in Spec, IP, as the following tests for detecting whether the position they occupy is of the A or A-BAR type show:

Definite preverbal subjects are A-binders:
(3)   Todos os coelhos$_i$ comem a sua$_i$ cenoura.
      all the rabbits eat poss. carrot

In (3), the QP *todos os coelhos* 'all the rabbits' may bind the possessive pronoun in the object.

No A-bar MINIMALITY effects are induced by extraction
across a preverbal subject:
(4)   Que livro o Paulo leu?
      which book Paulo read

(5)   A sopa, o Paulo comeu.
      the soup the Paulo ate

Neither *wh*-movement nor TOPICALIZATION in (4) and (5), respectively, induces A-bar minimality effects, which might be expected if the subject were left-dislocated.

No complementary distribution between definite preverbal subjects and
other left-dislocated elements:
(6)   a. Com o Pedro, o Paulo falou sobre o Big Bang.
          with the Pedro the Paulo talked about the Big Bang

b. Sobre o Big Bang, o Paulo falou com o Pedro.
   about the Big Bang the Paulo talked with the Pedro

The fact that this complementary distribution would be expected if definite preverbal subjects were right-dislocated is proved by the marginal status of (7) with two left-dislocated PPs:[1]

(7) a. *Sobre o Big Bang, com o Pedro, o Paulo falou.
        about the Big Bang with the Pedro the Paulo talked

     b. *Com o Pedro, sobre o Big Bang, o Paulo falou.

From these tests, I conclude that preverbal definite subjects occupy the Spec, IP position. For the same tests applied to different Null Subject Languages, see Alexiadou and Anagnostopoulou (1995) for Greek; Ordoñez and Treviño (1995), among others, for Spanish; and Barbosa (1995) for a wide range of Romance languages and dialects.

3.1.2 Preverbal indefinite subjects

In this section, I will show that indefinite subjects in EP pattern like the preverbal subjects in other Null Subject Languages in that they are left-dislocated. To obtain a fair comparison, I will use exactly the same tests I did for the definite subjects.

BINDING effects:[2]
(8) a. ??Uma criança$_i$ gosta da sua$_i$ mãe.
        a child likes possessive mother

     b. ??Um homem qualquer$_i$ viu o seu$_i$ filho.
        a men saw possessive child

Unlike definite subjects, preverbal indefinite subjects are not A-binders, which pattern like other cases of left-dislocation:

(9) a. ??A cada realizador$_i$, a Maria deu o seu$_i$ prémio.
        to each director, Maria gave possessive price

     b. ??O seu$_i$ prémio, a Maria deu a cada ralizador$_i$.

A-bar minimality effects:
(10) a. *Que livro um homem leu?
        which book a man read

     b. *Com quem é que umas crianças falaram?
        with whom some children talked

Unlike preverbal definite subjects, indefinite preverbal subjects may not co-occur with *wh*-extraction. This can be explained if preverbal indefinite subjects are left-dislocated, hence A-bar moved, inducing A-bar minimality effects when a *wh*-phrase is extracted.

Complementary distribution with other left-dislocated elements:

(11) a. *A sopa, um cão comeu.
          the soup a dog ate

    b. *Sobre o Big Bang, pessoas falam.
          about the Big Bang people talk

Again, indefinite subjects behave differently from definites in that only the former are in complementary distribution with left-dislocated elements. Interestingly enough, when sentences like (11) may be acceptable (under multiple topicalization reading; cf. n. 1), the left-dislocated element and the preverbal subject appear unordered:

(12) a. ?A sopa, um cão comeu.   (under multiple topic reading)
          the soup a dog ate

    b. ?Um cão, a sopa comeu.
          a dog the soup ate

This optional ordering never exists between left-dislocated elements and definite subjects:

(13) a. A sopa, o cão comeu.
          the soup the dog ate

    b. *O cão a sopa comeu.
          the dog the soup ate

The lack of ordering between left-dislocated elements and indefinite subjects may be interpreted in the following terms: each of them occupies a specifier position at the topic position, so no ordering between these specifiers is established.

Given the tests presented here, I conclude that indefinite preverbal subjects are left-dislocated, meeting the same conclusions reached for preverbal subjects in other Null Subject Languages (cf. earlier references).[3]

3.2 Postverbal subjects in VSO context

In this section, I will present tests to identify the position of postverbal subjects when they are followed by the object. First, I will show that postverbal subjects are not derived by movement of the verb based on similarities between root and embedded contexts. I will further motivate the position of these subjects by relating it to the distribution of adverbs. The conclusion will be that postverbal subjects are in Spec, VP.

Before presenting the arguments for the claim that postverbal subjects occupy the Spec, VP position, I would like to note that in this context there is no difference between definites ot indefinites, as (14) shows:

(14) a. Comeu o Paulo maçãs.
          ate Paulo apples

b. Comeu um homem maçãs.

ate a man apples

In the discussion of this position it will be shown that binding effects provide evidence that both types of subjects occupy the same position.

3.2.1 Why not V-movement?

Ambar (1992) argues that postverbal subjects in EP are the reflex of movement of the verb to a category that is higher than IP (C in Ambar 1992). Martins (1994) claims that postverbal subjects are in the Spec position of a projection lower than the position where the verb moves to, but higher than VP. My claim will be that postverbal subjects are in Spec, VP. There are four main arguments against deriving VS order via verb movement: first, if postverbal subjects were derived by V-movement to C, they should not appear in embedded contexts, since C is occupied by the complementizer. This prediction is not borne out by the data:[4]

(15)   O Paulo disse que comeu a Maria a sopa.

Paulo said that ate Mary the soup

Another piece of evidence against this claim is the fact that, in a more complex construction with an auxiliary and a participle, the subject follows not just the inflected verb but both verbs. In order to assume that the subject in (16a) is in Spec, IP, one has to postulate at least two heads above IP. If more auxiliaries are present, more heads have to be postulated, as (16b) shows, which is not a very appealing solution.

(16)   a. Tinha comido o Paulo maçãs.

had eaten Paulo apples

b. Tem estado comendo o Paulo maçãs.

has been eating Paulo apples

The distribution of adverbs also favors the idea that postverbal subjects do not reflect V-movement to a position higher than IP. In Costa (1997), I argue that the subject-oriented reading for ambiguous adverbs such as *carefully* and *cleverly* is dependent on overt movement of the subject to Spec, AgrSP. Assuming this to be true, and if postverbal subjects were in Spec, IP, I should expect adverbs with a subject-oriented reading to intervene in between the subject and the object, which is not true:

(17)   *Comeu o Paulo inteligentemente maçãs,

ate Paulo cleverly apples

Finally, if the postverbal position was the Spec, IP position, one should not expect to have indefinite subjects in a postverbal context, in compliance with the conclusions reached in the previous section. That this is not true is shown by the data in (14). One could still argue that the verb moves to a position higher than the one for left-dislocated elements, claiming that the indefinite subject in (14b) is not in Spec, IP. However, indefinite postverbal subjects co-occur with fronted constituents, as (18) illustrates, which would not be expected if they were in the left-dislocated position:

(18) Sobre o Big Bang, falou o Paulo com o Pedro.
      about the Big Bang talked Paulo with Pedro

3.2.2 Postverbal subjects are in Spec, VP

In this section, two tests will be presented in favor of the claim that postverbal subjects are in Spec, VP: the distribution of adverbs and binding effects.

3.2.2.1 Ordering with adverbs

To test the position of the subject, I will be using the adverb *bem* 'well'. This is because this adverb, together with most monosyllabic adverbs, has a behavior that makes it reliable enough for marking the left edge of the VP, as I argue in Costa (1996a). Its properties, illustrated for English in the following examples, are that it cannot be right-adjoined, as (19) shows, and that it has a much more restricted distribution than other adverbs (cf. (20)).

(19) a. John looked well at some pictures.

      b. *John looked at some pictures well.[5]

(20) a. John (carefully) has (carefully) looked (carefully) at some pictures (carefully).

      b. John (*well) has (*well) looked (well) at some pictures (*well).

I will now turn to the Portuguese paradigm and see where *bem* may appear when there is a postverbal subject:

(21) a. *Bem* comeu o Paulo maçãs,
         well ate Paulo apples

      b. *Comeu o Paulo *bem* maçãs.

      c. *Comeu o Paulo maçãs *bem*.

      d. Comeu *bem* o Paulo maçãs.

As (21) shows, in a VSO context the only position where the monosyllabic adverb may appear is between the verb and the subject. If it is true that *bem* marks the left edge of VP, the examples in (21) show that the subject is in Spec, VP. That the position occupied by the subject is Spec, VP and not the specifier position of a functional projection below the verb, as is claimed to be the case in Transitive Expletive Constructions in Icelandic (cf. Jonas and Bobaljik 1993), is reinforced by the fact that the adverb *bem* may not intervene between an inflected auxiliary and a participial form:

(22)   O Paulo tinha (*bem) lido (bem) alguns livros.
       Paulo had well read well some books

The fact that it always follows the participles is a further argument in favor of the two claims made earlier: *bem* marks the left edge of VP, and postverbal subjects are in Spec, VP.

3.2.2.2 Binding effects

If postverbal subjects are in Spec, VP (an A-position), one would expect that, independently of their definiteness, they are able to bind anaphors. This is in fact true, as (23) shows:

(23)   a. Leu cada autor $_i$o seu $_i$livro.
           read each author his book

       b. Leu um autor $_i$o seu$_i$ livro.
           read an author his book

These binding effects not only permit identifying the position of these subjects but also provide further evidence against the idea of deriving VSO order by verb movement, since the binding effects should differ with respect to definites and indefinites, as is the case for the preverbal position.

    From these tests I conclude that postverbal subjects in VSO contexts are in Spec, VP.

3.3 Postverbal subjects in VOS contexts

In this section I will argue in favor of an analysis of VOS order as an instance of subject in Spec, VP and scrambling of the object across the subject. Before I present the tests in favor of this analysis, I want to make a distinction between final subjects that are in Spec, VP and subjects in the right-dislocated position. This distinction is important, since these subjects distribute differently in the sentence.

    One first test to distinguish them is to look at the intonation. Right-dislocated subjects are preceded by a pause, whereas subjects in Spec, VP are not:

(24)   a. Comeu a sopa # o Paulo.
           ate the soup Paulo

       b. Comeu a sopa o Paulo.

At first sight, this does not show anything: it could be that both cases are examples of subject right-dislocation, the pause being optionally possible. However, based on the paradigm in (25), when a pronoun is inserted in Spec, IP, the pause is obligatory:

(25) a. Ele comeu a sopa # o Paulo.
          he ate the soup Paulo

      b. *Ele comeu a sopa o Paulo.

Example (26) shows that the pronoun is ungrammatical when subjects remain in Spec, VP, as in the VSO context:

(26) (*Ele) comeu o Paulo a sopa.
       he ate Paulo the soup

One way to interpret these facts is by assuming, with Kayne (1994) and Zubizarreta (1995), that the right-dislocated subjects are clause-external (tags in Zubizarreta 1995; the result of clause reduction for Kayne 1994). Further evidence for this claim comes from the interaction between question tags and subjects. Den Dikken (1995) shows that shifted heavy NPs (traditionally analyzed as right-dislocated) follow question tags:

(27) They have found, haven't they?, the treasure buried in that island one hundred years ago?

The same is true in EP: right-dislocated subjects follow question tags, while subjects in Spec, VP precede it, as the interaction between these orderings and pronoun insertion shows:

(28) a. Comeu a sopa o Paulo, não comeu?
          ate the soup Paulo not ate

      b. *Ele comeu a sopa o Paulo, não comeu?
          he

      c. Comeu a sopa, não comeu?, o Paulo

      d. Ele comeu a sopa, não comeu?, o Paulo.

In the remainder of the chapter, I will ignore the right-dislocated subjects, since they appear to be extrasentential, and concentrate on the ones I claim to be in Spec, VP.

This difference established, I will look at more arguments in favor of the claim that sentence-final subjects are in Spec, VP.

(a) Distribution of adverbs: Pursuing the same test that permitted me to identify the position of subjects in VSO order, I will look at the possible position for the adverb *bem* in VOS context (ignoring the cases of subject right-dislocation, testable with insertion of the pronoun):

(29) a. *Comeu *bem* a sopa o Paulo
          ate well the soup Paulo

      b. *Comeu a sopa o Paulo *bem*.

      c. Comeu a sopa *bem* o Paulo (não comeu?)

From the word order in (29c), one is led to conclude that the object is scrambled outside of the VP[6] and the subject is in Spec, VP, The fact that a question tag may follow the subject in this example confirms this analysis.

(b) Binding effects: Evidence to analyze VOS order as I am doing comes from binding effects. As is well known, A-movement may feed binding, whereas A-bar movement does not. This explains why the QP in (30) binds the possessive only in the passive construction (30b) and not when it is *wh*-extracted (cf. the weak crossover effects in 30c):

(30) a. *O seu$_i$ realizador viu todos os filmes$_i$.
          their director saw all the movies

      b. Todos os filmes$_i$ foram vistos pelo seu realizador$_i$.
          all the movies were seen by their director

      c. *Que filmes$_i$ viu o seu realizador$_i$?
          which movies saw their director

Now consider a case of VSO order in which subject and object behave as expected: if the object is a QP and the subject contains a possessive anaphor, binding is impossible. If object scrambling would be A-movement binding would be acceptable, on a par with (30b), which is not the case, as (31b) illustrates:

(31) a. *Viu o seu$_i$ realizador todos os filmes$_i$.
          saw their director all the movies

      b. *Viu todos os filmes$_i$ o seu$_i$ realizador.
          saw all the movies their director

The impossibility of binding becomes even clearer in cases like (32), which are only acceptable if interpreted as VSO order:

(32) a. *Viu o [Obj o Paulo$_i$] [Subj o seu$_i$ irmão].
          saw Paulo his brother

      b. Viu o [Subj o Paulo$_i$] [Obj o seu$_i$ irmão].

One could argue that these effects do not constitute conclusive evidence in favor of the analysis of VOS order I am advocating, since binding would be impossible anyway if the subject would be moved rightward and adjoined to a position higher than the object, making it impossible for the object to c-command it. However, the following examples prove that this is not true: in the cases I identified as right-dislocated (i.e., those in which a tag may intervene between the object and the subject), binding is possible:[7]

(33) a. Viu o Paulo$_i$, não viu?, o seu$_i$ irmão.
          saw Paulo, not saw, his brother

    b. Viu todos os filmes$_i$, não viu?, cada$_i$ realizador.
       saw all the movies, not saw, each director

(c) No difference between definites and indefinites: if the claim that in VOS context, subjects are in Spec, VP is right, we do not expect to find any difference between definites and indefinites in accordance with the data in (14), which show that in VSO context both definites and indefinites may appear in Spec, VP. This prediction is indeed confirmed by the facts in (34):

(34)   a. Comeu a sopa o Paulo.
       ate the soup Paulo

     b. Comeu a sopa um homem.
       ate the soup a man

From the preceding tests, I conclude that in VOS context, subjects occupy the Spec, VP position. The difference between VSO and VOS is then derived by object scrambling in the latter, in accordance with the evidence I present in Costa (1996b).

3.4 Conclusion

So far, I have shown the following:

1. Preverbal definite subjects occupy the Spec, IP position.
2. Preverbal indefinite subjects are left-dislocated.
3. Postverbal subjects in VSO context are in Spec, VP.
4. Postverbal subjects in VOS context are in Spec, VP.

One question I have not yet asked is what is the source for this word-order variation. One might suppose that the possible orders are in free variation. In the next section, I present arguments showing that this is not true, motivating the position of each subject.

3.5 Felicitous contexts for each word order

In this section I will present the contexts that make each of the possible word orders acceptable, showing that the variation is not discourse-neutral but the reflex of discourse-configurationality (see Kiss 1995 and King 1995 for similar conclusions for other languages). I will provide an appropriate discourse context and check which possible order is an appropriate continuation for each case. I will assume the following tests to identify topics and focus:

1. In a question-answer pair, a focused constituent in the answer replaces the *wh*-word in the question (cf. Dik 1978; Bresnan and Mchombo 1987; Rochemont and Culicover 1990, among others).

2. A TOPIC is information already referred to in the discourse or a subpart of a given referent (see Büring 1995 for discussion and relevant examples).[8]

3.5.1 Context for SVO

3.5.1.1 Definite subjects

The SVO order with definite subjects may be uttered in either of two cases: the subject is familiar to all participants in the discourse but the object is not (35); both subject and object are familiar (36).

(35)   (A and B are checking which languages each person in a given group speaks. They are talking about Paulo)

A: O Paulo sabe que línguas?
'Paulo knows which languages.'

B: *O Paulo sabe francês.*
'Paulo knows French'
#Sabe o Paulo francês,
#Sabe francês o Paulo
#Francês o Paulo sabe.
#Francês sabe o Paulo.

In the given context, the only legitimate order is SVO. All other orders are not felicitous.

(36)   (A and B are checking which persons in a given group speak French. They are talking about Paulo.)

A: O Paulo sabe francês?
'Paulo knows French.'

B: *O Paulo sabe francês.*
#Sabe o Paulo francês,
#Sabe francês o Paulo
Francês o Paulo sabe.
#Francês sabe o Paulo.

Again in this case SVO is legitimate. The only difference with respect to (36) is that OSV is also possible if the object is topicalized.[9] Note that the fact that the subject is old information does not mean that it is a topic (cf. Büring 1995). This is proved by the fact that it is not in complementary distribution with a topicalized constituent, as shown earlier and illustrated again in (37):

(37)   A: Com que é que o Paulo falou sobre o Big Bang?
with whom Paulo talked about the Big Bang

B: Sobre o Big Bang, o Paulo falou com o Pedro.
about the Big Bang, Paulo talked with Pedro

3.5.1.2 Indefinite subjects

SVO order is acceptable with indefinite subjects if they are not new information, as the following context shows (I will skip the discussion of objects, since the results would be the same for definite subjects):

(38)   A: Estão imensos animais neste parque: cães, gatos, galinhas.
'There are a lot of animals in this park: dogs, cats, chickens.'

   B: *Olha: um cão mordeu uma criança.*
'Look: a dog bit a child.'
#Mordeu um cão uma criança.
#Mordeu uma criança um cão.
#??Uma criança um cão mordeu.
#Uma crianca, mordeu um cão.

If the indefinte subject represents new information, the SVO order is not felicitous:

(39)   A: O que é que mordeu o Paulo?
'What bit Paulo?'

   B: #Uma cobra mordeu o Paulo.
'A snake bit Paulo.'

The conclusion from the preceding paradigms is that preverbal subjects must constitute old/accessible information in the discourse.

3.5.2 Contexts for subject in Spec, VP

I will not distinguish between definites and indefinites in this section, since, as I showed earlier both types of subjects occupy the same position in postverbal context.

VSO order is felicitous when both subject and object are new in the discourse:

(40)   A: Nnguém sabe línguas neste grupo.
'No one in this group knows any language.'

   B: *Sabe o Paulo francês.*
knows Paulo French
#O Paulo sabe francês.[10]
#Francês, o Paulo sabe.
#Sabe francês o Paulo.
#Francês sabe o Paulo.

Contrast (40) with (41), in which only the subject constitutes new information. In that case, the only felicitous order is VOS or OVS, derived by object left-dislocation (which is not surprising, since the object is old information):

(41)　A: Nnguém sabe francêsneste grupo.
　　　　'No one in this group knows French.'

　　　　B: #Sabe o Paulo francês,
　　　　knows Paulo French
　　　　#O Paulo sabe francês.
　　　　#Francês, o Paulo sabe.
　　　　Sabe francês o Paulo (não sabe?).
　　　　Francês sabe o Paulo.

3.5.3 Conclusions

The contexts described in the previous section permit drawing the following conclusions:

1. Preverbal definite subjects are old information.
2. Preverbal indefinite subjects are old information.
3. Postverbal subjects must be new information: if they precede the object, the object is also new information. If the object is not new information, the subject follows it.

The main conclusion of this section is that the word-order variation identified in the first part of this chapter is not free. Each order reflects a different discourse function. Very similar conclusions were reached for Italian by Pinto (1994), who to my knowledge was the first to address this issue in a systematic way (see also Adger 1995). What still remains to be explained is the relation between the discourse information and the positions identified in sections 3.1 through 3.4. In the next section, I hope to show how to combine these two aspects.

3.6 The mapping between syntax and discourse

Combining the conclusions reached in the previous sections yields the following descriptive generalizations:

1. Spec, VP is a position for subjects that are new information.
2. Spec, IP is a position for subjects that are old information, but not necessarily topics.
3. The left-dislocated position is for subjects that are new information and indefinites. See Costa (in preparation) for a different perspective.

The question I intend to answer in this section is the following: Why should these relations between positions and discourse information exist? What does each of the identified syntactic positions have to do with the correspondent discursive function?

Throughout this section I will be assuming the following:

1. I will assume that old information has to be either topicalized or defocused, while new information is the FOCUS of a sentence.
2. I will follow Cinque's (1993) proposal that sentential stress falls in the most embedded constituent of a sentence. Thus, in a normal SVO sequence, stress will fall on the object. Assuming with Jackendoff (1972) that the focused element in a sentence is the one that bears the most prominent stress, Cinque's proposal captures the fact that in an SVO sentence with unmarked intonation the object is interpreted as the focus (cf. Lambrecht 1994, who shows that objects tend to be focus).

   Still concerning focus, I will follow Reinhart's (1995) suggestion that any XP in a sentence, which does not get default stress because it is not the most embedded constituent, may be marked as focus by being assigned a heavy stress.
3. I will assume with Zubizarreta (1995) and Reinhart (1995) that some syntactic operations are prosodically motivated.
4. I will assume that the following tendencies hold, as observed by Lambrecht (1994): subjects tend to be topics; objects tend to be foci; definites tend to be old information (topic); indefinites tend to be new information (focus). It is important to emphasize that these are just tendencies and not absolute statements. Optimally, we would be able to derive these tendencies from some structural property of subjects, objects, definites, and indefinites.[11] So far, I have not been able to do so.

I will now return to the issue under investigation in this chapter and see how these assumptions derive the facts described in the previous sections. From the line of inquiry I am pursuing, it is obvious that some new facts have to be added to the paradigms described. More specifically, since I am dealing with the notion of focus and assuming with Cinque (1993), Zubizarreta (1995), and Reinhart (1995) that focus is a prosodic phenomenon (see arguments in favor of interpreting focus as a prosodic phenomenon in EP in Frota 1992), it will become important to see how subjects behave with respect to intonation in each of the positions identified earlier.

3.6.1 Position and intonation

3.6.1.1 In VSO order

In VSO order all subjects have to bear heavy stress (I will use capital letters to mark heavy stress; the starred sentences in the following examples are ungrammatical without heavy stress):

(42) a. Comeu O PAULO maçãs.
          ate Paulo apples

b. Comeram MENINOS maçãs.
ate children apples

c. *Comeu o Paulo maçãs.

d. *Comeram meninos maçãs.

3.6.1.2 In VOS order

In this context there are two possibilities: the subject may receive just the default sentential stress (43a) or may bear heavy stress (43b):[12]

(43)   a. Comeu a sopa o Paulo.
ate the soup Paulo

b. Comeu a sopa O PAULO.

These two possibilities hold for both definites and indefinites:

(44)   a. Comeu a sopa um menino.
ate the soup a child

b. Comeu a sopa UM MENINO.[13]

What is interesting about here is that it is possible to establish a difference between the (a) cases and the (b) cases. As the following interaction with tags shows, heavy stress is impossible when the subject precedes a tag (Spec, VP position), being optional after the tag:

(45)   a. Comeu a sopa o Paulo, não comeu?
ate the soup Paulo, not ate?

b. *Comeu a sopa O PAULO, não comeu?

c. Comeu a sopa, não comeu?, o Paulo.

d. Comeu a sopa, não comeu?, O PAULO.

Thus, the generalization to be drawn for VOS context seems to be that heavy stress is impossible when the subject is in Spec, VP. If it is in the "right-dislocated" position, it is optionally possible.

3.6.1.3 In SVO order

Looking at the intonation effects in SVO order will turn out to be more revealing than one might suppose. At first sight, nothing is really surprising: both indefinites and definites may optionally bear heavy stress:

(46)   a. O PAULO comeu maçãs.
Paulo ate apples

b. O Paulo comeu maçãs.

c. UM MENINO comeu maçãs.
a child ate apples

d. Um menino comeu maçãs.

What is interesting is to follow the spirit of what I have just done for post-object subjects, reviewing the tests I applied to indefinite subjects in section 3.1.2, and check whether the different intonational patterns correspond to the same position identified there. Surprisingly, if an indefinite subject is heavily stressed, it behaves as if it is in an A-position. Compare the following contrasts:

Binding effects:
(47) {??Uma criança$_i$/UMA CRIANÇA$_i$} gosta da sua$_i$ mãe.
a child likes possessive mother

A-bar minimality effects:
(48) Com quem é que {*umas crianças/UMAS CRIANÇAS} falaram?
with whom some children talked

Complementary distribution with other left-dislocated elements:
(49) A sopa, {*um cão/UM CÃO} comeu.
the soup a dog ate

Also, in this case, the lack of order between indefinite subjects and left-dislocated elements ceases to exist:

(50) a. ?A sopa, um cão comeu.   (under multiple topic reading)
the soup a dog ate

b. ?Um cão, a sopa comeu.

c. A sopa, UM CÃO comeu.

d. *UM CÃo, a sopa, comeu.

Summing up, what seems to happen when an indefinite subject bears heavy stress in SVO order is that it remains in Spec, IP, a legitimate conclusion given the disparity of behavior when compared with unstressed indefinites and the similarities with the behavior of definites (cf. 3.1.1).

3.6.2 Topic, focus, markedness, and syntax

Before beginning the analysis, I will review the position of each type of subject and respective intonation and function, integrating the data just found:

Spec, TopP:[14]
Indefinite subjects: old information; normal stress

Spec, IP:

Definite subjects: old or new information; heavy or normal stress

Indefinite subjects: old or new information; heavy stress

Spec, VP:

Definite subjects: new information; heavy stress (VSO), normal stress (VOS)

Indefinite subjects: new information; heavy stress (VSO), normal stress (VOS)

The hypothesis I want to explore to solve this puzzle is the following:

(51)   Markedness (either prosodic or syntactic) comes about every time there is a contradiction of any of the following tendencies:

a. Subjects tend to be topics

b. Objects tend to be focus

c. Definites tend to be topics

d. Indefinites tend to be focus

I assume that operations such as topicalization or focalization yield to marked structures (see Reinhart 1995 for a similar idea). A corollary of the idea of markedness is that there must be unmarked counterparts. I claim that the tendencies in (51) represent the unmarked cases. Discourse factors may intervene to force a speaker to violate the tendencies specified here. Note that these tendencies are certainly derivable from some other notions (e.g., as noted earlier, the tendency for object to be focus follows from Cinque's default stress algorithm). For the present, I will not investigate the source of these tendencies, but I will assume them, since they correspond to factual evidence (see Lambrecht 1994). I will now examine how this proposal accounts for the possible subject positions and respective function.

According to (51), an unmarked subject will be a subject which is both a topic and definite. In that case, no markedness is required; such a subject can stay in the canonical subject position without requiring a special intonation or movement to a topic position. This is indeed what I found for preverbal definite subjects.

If a subject is a topic, but is indefinite, there is a clash in the tendencies specified earlier in this section. On the one hand, it has topic properties; on the other hand, it should be a focus. In this case, markedness is required: the subject has to be moved to a position where it will be unambiguously interpreted as topic (recall that Spec, IP allows a topic interpretation but does not force it). This captures the similarity between preverbal indefinite subjects and topicalized objects (an object that by default ought to be interpreted as focus must move to a topic position if, by discourse reasons, one wants it to be interpeted as topic).

These two possibilities exhaust the options for subjects to be topics.

What happens when subjects are forced to be foci by discourse reasons? Every time this happens, independently of their definiteness, they will have to be marked, since (51a) is violated. According to Frota (1992), who presents several arguments against a focus projection (defended by Uriagereka 1995, among others, for languages like Portuguese), focus marking in EP is a prosodic process. I will assume that this is true and that focus stress may be assigned by two mechanisms: either the most embedded constituent bears the default focus stress (Cinque 1993), or a prominent stress has to be assigned to the focus constituent (Jackendoff 1972; Büring 1995; Truckenbrodt 1995; Reinhart 1995; among others).

I will now address how these two mechanisms account for the data described earlier. The first contrast that follows is the fact that subjects in VOS order do not need to bear a very heavy stress. Since the object scrambles across the subject, the latter will be in the most embedded position and receive the default sentence stress (see also Nash 1995 for a proposal in which prosodic markedness and configurational stress assignment are in complementary distribution). In all the other cases (SVO and VSO), the subject is not in the most embedded position; hence, it must be marked with a heavy stress.

One question that remains is why focused subjects may appear in all orders, unlike topics, which appear only in SVO order. I am assuming, in accordance with Reinhart (1995), that topicalization is a syntactic phenomenon; hence, marked topics will have to be licensed in a specific syntactic position, explaining their strict distribution. Note that the same is true for focused constituents in languages where marked focus is licensed in the syntax (cf. Brody 1990; Horvath 1995). In EP, focalization is a prosodic phenomenon; hence, the distribution of focused constituents is freer and, I would like to suggest, determined by the focus set of constituents (Reinhart 1995) one wants to build. Reinhart proposes that when focalization applies, a focus set is established, which is defined as the most prominent constituent and all the constituents it dominates. That is, in (52a) the focus set would be {ZP, XP, YP}, while in (52b) it would be {XP, YP}:

(52) a. $[[ZP]_F [XP [YP]]]$

b. $[ZP [[XP]_F [YP]]]$

This formulation captures the fact that focused subjects may appear in Spec, IP or Spec, VP. The choice between these two positions will depend on the focus set the speaker intends to construct. The following tests show that this is indeed the case: in (53) the whole sentence is focused, so the only position where the subject may appear focused is in Spec, IP, since this is the only position where it will dominate all the other constituents of the sentence. Example (53B') is infelicitous because it presupposes that it is already known that someone threw something somewhere. In (54), the subject has to be in Spec, VP because the question implies that we already know that someone yelled; hence, the verb must not be a member of the focus set of constituents.

(53) A: O que é que aconteceu?
          what happened?

      B: UM MIUDO atirou a sopa ao chão.
          a kid threw the soup to the floor

      B': #Atirou um miudo a sopa ao chão.

(54) A: Quem é que gritou?
          who yelled

      B: Gritaram três ladrões.
          yelled three thieves

      B': #Três ladrões gritaram.

Summing up, the analysis I proposed claims that indefinite topic subjects have to be marked as topics by left-dislocation; focused subjects have to be marked prosodically, their position depending on the scope the speaker intends to assign to focus; definite topic subjects do not need to be marked and thus may stay in the canonical subject position without further requirements.

3.7 Conclusions

In this chapter I have investigated the possible word-order alternations between subject, verb, and object in EP to find which position is occupied by the subject in each order and why. I conclude from the analysis of different types of subjects that there are three positions for subjects: the left-dislocated position (indefinite topics); Spec, IP (focused subjects, definite topics, unfocused and nontopic definites); and Spec, VP (focused definites and focused indefinites).

Relating these positions with discourse factors, I managed to relate the word-order alternations with different discursive functions and attempted to derive different orders and prosodic facts from a theory of markedness. According to this theory, the unmarked subjects are definite topics, which captures the basic intuition, expressed in Ambar (1992), among others, that EP is an SVO language. This intuition follows from the fact that in a sentence like (55) markedness plays no role, and the subject is optimal in the sense that it is both definite and a topic:

(55) O Paulo come maçãs.
      Paulo eats apples

The conclusions reached here permitted me to make sense out of a pattern in which everything looked possible, explaining optionality in EP as the reflex of discourse configurationality (cf. Kiss 1995), and relate information structure with sentence structure.

Notes

This chapter is a modified and elaborated version of a paper published in *Proceedings of WCCFL XV*, CSLI Stanford, and is also the basis of chapter 2 of Costa (1998). I would like to thank the following people for relevant comments and discussion during the elaboration of this work: Manuela Ambar, Ana Arregui, Hans Bennis, Inês Duarte, Sónia Frota, Richard Kayne, Irene Heim, Teun Hoekstra, Michael Kenstowickz, Sérgio Menuzzi, David Pesetsky, Tanya Reinhart, Johan Rooryck, and audiences at MIT, Rutgers, Amherst, and WCCFL XV. Any errors are my own.

1. Sentences like (7) are marginally acceptable under a multiple topic reading. I will ignore this context for the moment and assume the sentence is ungrammatical.

2. I should note that this test does not work for some speakers. Nevertheless, it is interesting to note that speakers who allow binding by an indefinite subject also find the sentences in (9) acceptable, with reconstruction of the left-dislocated element. An interesting contrast comes about with respect to *wh*-extraction: while subject *wh*-extraction reconstructs, extraction of a nonsubject *wh*-phrase does not (cf. (ii)):

(i)   Que autor$_i$ leu o seu$_i$ livro?
       which author read poss. book

(ii)   ??Que livro$_i$ a Maria deu ao seu$_i$ autor?
       which book Maria gave to poss. author

An explanation for this contrast might be that subject *wh*-phrases are not moved to Spec, CP, as suggested in Grimshaw (forthcoming), among others.

3. An alternative interpretation of these data is explored in Costa (1998). There I consider the hypothesis that all types of subjects are in Spec, IP, but only if they are old information. Since indefinites do not easily express old information, they are not easily preposed. The hypothesis, then, is that the oddness of the data described in this section does not follow from the status of the position where the subjects sit, but rather from the difficulty of preposing indefinite DPs. In this chapter, I decided to adhere to the analysis based on the A-/A-bar status of the position for keeping some parallelism regarding the type of tests applied. An evaluation of the two hypotheses may be found in Costa (1998; in preparation).

4. VS order in an embedded context is possible with all verbs and all types of main verbs, which makes it differ from the contextually dependent embedded V2 phenomena in languages such as Icelandic and Yiddish (see McCloskey 1992 for contexts of CP-recursion).

5. The ungrammaticality is lifted if the adverb is heavily stressed. In flat intonation context, the sentence is bad.

6. The scrambling of the NP outside VP is independently argued for in Costa (1996b). The arguments for this are the similarities between scrambling in EP and Germanic in what concerns specificity effects, parasitic gap licensing, binding effects, and the impossibility for AP and Small Clauses to scramble. A similar hypothesis is argued for Greek in Alexiadou (1995) and for Spanish in Zubizarreta (1995).

7. I am not going to speculate here on the mechanism that renders binding possible in this context. Nevertheless, I would like to note that it is very likely that the object QP is bound not by the right-dislocated subject but by the *pro* in subject position (cf. the possibility of inserting overt pronouns discussed earlier). For an accurate discussion of binding conditions in Portuguese, see Menuzzi (forthcoming).

8. It is important to note that this does not mean that topic is the complement of focus. I will assume with Jäger (1996) and Büring (1995), among others, a tripartite structure for information: topic, focus, and background. These analyses make the right prediction that a sentence may have only a focus, or no topic. See Büring (1995) and references therein for discussion.

9. It can also be shown that in (35) and (36) the objects occupy different positions (the base position, and the scrambled position, respectively). Since the main concern here is the distribution of subjects, I will skip this discussion when it is not relevant, referring the reader to Costa (1996b).

10. It should be noted that SVO order in this context is marginally acceptable if it is shared knowledge that Paulo is a member of the group.

11. Which is done for the case of objects that tend to be focus, if Cinque (1993) is right. Since objects are normally the most embedded constituents, they will bear the default sen-

tence stress; thus, they will be the most prominent element in the sentence, being interpreted as focus.

12. I am grateful to Sónia Frota for pointing out the latter possibility to me.

13. For some speakers (44b) is slightly worse than (43b). For the present discussion, I will ignore this slight difference, since the intuitions of my informants with respect to this difference were not crystal-clear.

14. Assuming with Müller and Sternefeld (1993), that this is the label for the position where topics move to. See Duarte (1987) for similar considerations for EP.

References

Adger, David. 1995. "Optionality and the Syntax/Discourse Interface." Paper presented at the International Conference on Interfaces in Linguistics, November 1995, Oporto.

Alexiadou, Artemis. 1995. "Word Order Alternations in Modern Greek." Paper presented at the Fifth Colloquium on Generative Grammar, Coruña, Spain.

Alexiadou, Artemis, and Elena Anagnostopoulou. 1995. "SVO and EPP in Null Subject Languages and Germanic." *FAS Papers in Linguistics* 4, 1–21, Potsdam.

Ambar, Manuela. 1992. "Para uma Sintaxe da Inversão Sujeito-Verbo em Português." Ph.D. dissertation, University of Lisbon.

Barbosa, Pilar. 1995. "Null Subjects." Ph.D. dissertation, MIT.

Bresnan, Joan, and Sam Mchombo. 1987. "Topic, Pronoun, and Agreement in Chichewa." *Language*, 63:4, 741–782

Brody, Michael. 1990. "Remarks on the Order of Elements in the Hungarian Focus Field." In I. Kenesei (ed.) *Approaches to Hungarian*, vol. 3. Szeged: JATE.

Büring, Daniel. 1995. "The 59th Street Bridge Accent: On the Meaning of Topic and Focus." Ph.D. dissertation, University of Tübingen.

Cinque, Guglielmo. 1993. "A Null Theory of Phrase and Compound Stress." *Linguistic Inquiry* 24: 239–297.

Costa, João. 1996a. "Adverb Positioning and Verb Movement in English: Some More Evidence." *Studia Linguistica* 50: 1–4.

————. 1996b. "Scrambling in European Portuguese." Forthcoming in Proceedings of SCIL 8, *MIT Working Papers in Linguistics*.

————. 1997. "On the Behavior of Adverbs in Sentence-Final Context." *Linguistic Review* 14: 43–68.

————. 1998. "Word Order and Constraint Interaction: A Constraint-Based Approach." Ph.D. dissertation, HIL Leiden University.

————. In preparation. "SVO vs. VSO: Syntactic, Semantic and Prosodic Convergence." Ms. University Nova de Lisboa.

Den Dikken, Marcel. 1995. "Extraposition as Intraposition, and the Syntax of English Tag Questions." Ms., HIL/Free University of Amsterdam.

Dik, Simon C. 1978. *Functional Grammar*. Amsterdam: North-Holland

Duarte, Inês. 1987. "A Construção de Topicalização na Gramática do Português." Ph.D. dissertation, University of Lisbon.

Frota, Sónia. 1992. "Is Focus a Phonological Category in Portuguese?" In M. Schoorlemmer and P. Ackema (eds.) *Console I Proceedings*, Holland Academic Graphics, 1994.

Grimshaw, Jane. Forthcoming. "Projection, Heads and Optimality." *Linguistic Inquiry*.

Horvath, Julia. 1995. "Structural Focus, Structural Case, and the Notion of Feature Assignment." In K. Kiss (ed.) *Discourse Configurational Language*. New York: Oxford University Press.

Jackendoff, Ray. 1972. *Semantic Interpretation in Generative Grammar.* Cambridge, Mass.: MIT Press.

Jäger, Gerard. 1996. "Topic, Scrambling, and Aktionsart." In Laura Brugé et al. (eds.) *Proceedings of Console 3.* Leiden: Leiden University.

Jonas, Diane, and Johnatan Bobaljik. 1993. "Specs for Subjects: The Role of TP in Icelandic." In Johnatan Bobaljik and Chris Collins (eds.) *MIT Working Papers in Linguistics 18: Papers on Case and Agreement.* MIT.

Kayne, Richard. 1994. *The Antisymmetry of Syntax.* Cambridge, Mass.: MIT Press.

King, Tracy H. 1995. *Configuring Topic and Focus in Russian.* Dissertations in Linguistics, Stanford, Calif.: CSLI Publications.

Kiss, Katalin (ed.) 1995. *Discourse Configurational Languages.* New York: Oxford University Press.

Lambrecht, Knud. 1994. *Information Structure and Sentence Form.* Cambridge: Cambridge University Press.

Martins, Ana Maria. 1994. "Os Clíticos na História do Português." Ph.D. dissertation, University of Lisbon.

McCloskey, James. 1992. "Adjunction, Selection and Embedded Verb Second." Ms., University of Santa Cruz.

Menuzzi, Sérgio. forthcoming. Pronominal Anaphora in Brazilian Portuguese: Indexing, Chains and Constraint Interaction. Ph.D. dissertation, HIL/Leiden University of Leiden.

Müller, Gereon, and Wolfgang Sternefeld. 1993. "Improper Movement and Unambiguous Binding." *Linguistic Inquiry* 24: 461–507

Nash, Lea. 1995. "Argument Scope and Case Marking in SOV and in Ergative Languages: The Case of Georgian." Ph.D. dissertation, University of Paris VIII.

Ordóñez, Francisco, and Esthela Treviño. 1995. "Los Sujetos y Objetos Preverbales en Español." Paper presented at the Fifth Colloquium on Generative Grammar, Coruña, Spain.

Pinto, Manuela. 1994. "Subjects in Italian: Distribution and Interpretation." In Reineke Bok-Bennema and Crit Cremers (eds.) *Linguistics in the Netherlands*, 175–187. Amsterdam: John Benjamins.

Reinhart, Tanya. 1995. "Interface Strategies." Ms., OTS University of Utrecht.

Rochemont, Michael, and Peter Culicover. 1990. *English Focus Construction and the Theory of Grammar.* Cambridge: Cambridge University Press

Truckenbrodt, Hubert. 1995. Phonological Phrases: Their Relation to Syntax, Focus and Prominence. Ph.D. dissertation, MIT.

Uriagereka, Juan. 1995. "An F Position in Western Romance." In K. Kiss (ed.) *Discourse Configurational Languages.* New York: Oxford University Press.

Valmala Elguea, Vidal. 1994. "Spanish Word-Order and Checking of Morphological Features." Paper presented at Going Romance 8, Utrecht.

Zubizarreta, Maria Luisa. 1995. "Word Order, Prosody and Focus." Ms., University of Southern California.

4

INÊS DUARTE AND GABRIELA MATOS

Romance Clitics and the Minimalist Program

Since Kayne's pioneering work on French clitic pronouns, two major questions have been asked with respect to the syntax of clitics: (i) What are the properties that force clitics to move differently from full DPs and regular affixes? (ii) Why is it that clitics do not surface at the same positions cross-linguistically and within the same language?

In this chapter we try to provide an answer to both questions, insofar as the central aim is to account for clitic placement in European Portuguese versus other Romance languages, namely, Spanish, Italian, and French. We will try to show that the differences in clitic placement exhibited in these four Romance languages follow from the interaction of properties of Merge/Move and Economy principles and conditions on feature checking with the formal features of clitics and their hybrid status as X°s/XPs (Kayne 1991; Chomsky 1994).

4.1 Patterns of clitic placement in Romance: Proclisis, enclisis, and mesoclisis

In the four contemporary Romance languages considered, clitics display two major order patterns with respect to their V-host (*proclisis* and *enclisis*) and a regressing pattern, occurring in complementary distribution with enclisis in some contexts (*mesoclisis*). As is well known, the triggering elements of these patterns differ across languages. In French, complement clitics are always proclitic, assuming that weak pronouns, not clitic ones, are present in affirmative imperatives (Cardinaletti and Starke 1994):

(1) a. Il *la* voyait chaque jour.

 b. Il veut *la* voir chaque jour.

In Italian and Spanish, proclisis is triggered by finite T, and enclisis occurs in untensed clauses:

(2) a. Lo conosco.

    b. Vorrei conoscerlo.

    c. Non farlo.   (Belletti 1993)

(3) a. Lo oimos.

    b. Para oirlo . . .   (Uriagereka 1995)

In standard European Portuguese (EP), enclisis is the basic pattern in finite and nonfinite clauses (see (4)), and mesoclisis is the alternative pattern to enclisis in clauses with future and conditional verb forms (see (5)):

(4) a. Ele viu-*a*.
    he saw-3sing-CL-accus-3singfem
    'He saw her.'

    b. O João pensa vê-*la* mais tarde.
    João intends see-INF-CL-accus-3singfem later
    'João intends to see her later.'

(5) a. Ele vê-*la*-á.
    he see-INF-CL-accus-3singfem-FUT-3sing
    'He will see her.'

    b. O João vê-*lo*-ia, se quisesse.
    João see-INF-CL-accus-3singmasc-COND-3sing, if he wanted
    'João would have seen him, if he wanted to.'

Mesoclisis is a regressing pattern that tends to be replaced by enclisis:

(6) a. ?"Telefonarei-*te* mais vezes." (12 years, 6th grade)
    I phone-FUT-1sing-CL-dat-2sing more often.
    'I shall call you more often.'

    b. ?"Na conjuntura sócio-económica, poderá-*se* verificar um saldo bastante positivo."
    (written exam to be admitted in the university, after 12th grade)
    in-the socioeconomic situation, may-FUT-3sing-CL-REFL-3sing obtain a very positive balance
    'Given the socioeconomic situation, a very positive balance may well obtain.'

Proclisis is triggered by the presence of so-called operator-like elements ccommanding the verbal host of the clitic: (i) sentential negation operators and negative phrases in preverbal position—see the contrast between (7) and (8); (ii) overt complementizers—see the contrast between (9) and (10); (iii) *wh*-operators—see the contrast between (11) and (12); (iv) quantified NPs in subject position—see the contrast between (13) and (14); (v) fronted contrastive focused elements—see the contrast between (15) and (16); and (vi) certain adverbs in preverbal position—see the contrast between (17) and (18):

(7) a. O João <u>não</u> *o* comprou.
     João not CL-accus-3singmasc bought
     'João didn't buy it.'

   b. O João <u>não</u> *o* comprará.
     João not CL-accus-3singmasc buy-FUT-3sing
     'João will not buy it.'

   c. Ele pensou <u>não</u> *lhe* comprar o livro.
     he thought not CL-dat-3sing buy the book
     'He thought he wouldn't buy him the book.'

   d. <u>Não</u> *lhe* comprando esse livro, ele pensa agradar-lhe.
     not CL-dat-3sing buying that book, he thinks please-INF-CL-dat-3sing
     'Not buying him/her that book, he thinks he will please him/her.'

   e. <u>Ninguém</u> *se* lava sem sabonete.
     nobody CL-refl-3 washes without soap
     'Nobody washes himself without soap.'

(8) a. *O João <u>não</u> comprou-*o*.

   b. *O João <u>não</u> comprá-*lo*-á.

   c. *Ele pensou <u>não</u> comprar-*lhe* o livro.

   d. *<u>Não</u> comprando-*lhe* esse livro, ele pensa agradar-lhe.

   e. *<u>Ninguém</u> lava-*se* sem sabonete.

(9) a. Eles disseram <u>que</u> os amigos *lhes* deram livros.
     they said-3pl that the friends CL-dat-3-pl gave books
     'They said their friends gave them books.'

   b. Eles disseram <u>para</u> nós *lhes* darmos os livros.
     they told-3-pl for we-nom CL-dat-3-pl giveINF-1pl the books
     'They told us to give them the books.'

(10) a. *Eles disseram <u>que</u> os amigos deram-*lhes* livros.

   b. *Eles disseram <u>para</u> nós darmos-*lhes* os livros.

(11) a. As pessoas a <u>quem</u> *o* contámos ficaram surpreendidas.
      the people to whom CL-accus-3singmasc told-1pl were-3pl surprised
      'The people we told it were surprised.'

b. Que mentira *lhe* contaste?
which lie CL-dat-3sing told-2sing?
'Which lie did you tell him/her?.'

c. Pergunto-me que mentira ele *lhe* contou.
ask-1sing-CL-refl-1sing which lie he CL-dat-3sing told-3sing
'I wonder which lie he told him/her.'

(12) a. *As pessoas a quem contámo-*lo* ficaram surpreendidas.

b. *Que mentira contaste-*lhe*?

c. *Pergunto-me que mentira ele contou-*lhe*.

(13) a. Todos os alunos *se* riram.
all the students CL-refl-3 laughed-3pl
'All the students laughed.'

b. Qualquer pessoa *se* engana facilmente.
any person CL-refl-3 mistakes-3sing easily
'Every one makes mistakes easily.'

(14) a. *Todos os alunos riram-*se*.

b. *Qualquer pessoa engana-*se* facilmente.

(15) a. A todos *o* leram (eles).
to all CL-accus-3singmasc read-PAST-3pl (they-nom)
"To everyone did they read it.'

b. Até a ele *lhe* contaram (elas) mentiras.
even to him CL-dat-3sing told-3pl (they-nom-fem) lies
'They told lies even to him.'

(16) a. *A todos leram-*no* (eles).

b. *Até a ele contaram-*lhe* (elas) mentiras.

(17) a. O João já *o* comprou.
João already CL-accus-3sing-masc bought
'João bought it already.'

b. Ele também *o* leu.
he also CL-accus-3singmasc read-PAST-3sing
'He read it also.'

c. Raras vezes *se* vendem livros desse autor.
seldom CL-refl-3 sell-3pl books of- that author
'Books by that author are seldom sold.'

(18) a. *O João já comprou-*o*.

      b. *Ele também leu-*o*.

      c. *Raras vezes vendem-*se* livros desse autor.

The position of the trigger at Spell-Out is crucial. When it is asymmetrically c-commanded by the verbal host of the clitic, enclisis obtains—contrast, for instance, (11b), (15a), and (17b) with (19a, b, c):

(19) a. Contaste-*lhe* que mentira?
        you told-2sing-CL-dat-3sing which lie?
        'You told him/her which lie?'

      b. Eles leram-*no* a todos.
        they read-PAST-3pl-CL-accus-3singmasc to all
        'They read it to everyone.'

      c. Ele leu-*o* também.
        he read-PAST-3sing-CL-accus-3singmasc also
        'He read it also.'

Contemporary EP displays the range of so-called argument and nonargument clitics also found in other Null Subject Languages. As the contrast between the sentences in (20) and (21) shows, nonargument clitics obey the same placement conditions as argument clitics—enclisis is the basic pattern of tensed and untensed sentences, and proclisis obtains under c-command of a so-called operator-like element:

(20) a. Nós rimo-*nos* da Maria.
        we laughed-1pl-CL-inh-1pl of-the Maria
        'We laughed at Maria.'

      b. O gelado derreteu-*se* (com o calor).
        the ice cream melted-3sing-CL-erg-3sing (with the heat)
        'The ice cream melted (with the heat).'

      c. Estes livros vendem-*se* bem.
        these books sell-3pl-CL-middle-3 well
        'These books sell well.'

      d. Venderam-*se* ontem 100 cópias do artigo dela.
        sold-3pl-CL-pass-3 yesterday 100 copies of her paper
        100 copies of the paper of-she were sold yesterday

      e. Diz-*se* que o partido do governo vai perder as eleições.
        says-CL-nom-3 that the party of-the government goes lose-INF the elections
        'People say that the government's party will lose the elections.'

(21) a. <u>Todos</u> nós *nos* rimos da Maria.
      all we-nom CL-inh-1pl laughed of-the Maria
      'We all laughed at Maria.'

   b. O gelado <u>não</u> *se* derreteu (com o calor).
      the ice cream not CL-erg-3 melted-3sing (with the heat)
      'The ice cream did not melt (with the heat).'

   c. Estes livros <u>também</u> *se* vendem bem.
      these books also CL-middle-3 sell-3pl well
      'These books also sell well.'

   d. Sei <u>que</u> *se* venderam ontem 100 cópias do artigo dela.
      know-1sing that CL-pass-3 sold-PAST-3pl yesterday 100 copies of the paper of-she
      'I know that 100 copies of her paper were sold yesterday.'

   e. <u>Raras vezes</u> *se* diz que o partido do governo vai perder as eleições.
      seldom CL-nom-3 says that the party of the government goes lose-INF the elections
      'People seldom say that the government's party will lose the elections.'

Summarizing: the data presented here show that EP behaves differently from other well-known Romance languages with respect to clitic placement; crucially: (i) neither enclisis nor proclisis is sensitive to the tensed/untensed distinction; (ii) enclisis is the neutral pattern, proclisis being triggered by the presence of so-called operator-like elements c-commanding the clitic host.

4.2 Clitic movement and clitic placement

In most Principles and Parameters approaches to Romance clitics, these have been considered either as affix-like elements directly generated under a head (the Affix Hypothesis) or as heads of DPs generated as arguments of some verb and then moved to V or to some functional projection targeted by the verb (the DP Hypothesis).

In this chapter, we will adopt the version of the DP Hypothesis proposed in Corver and Delfitto (1993), according to which clitics are transitive Ds that subcategorize for a *pro* complement:

(22)
$$
\begin{array}{c}
\text{DP} \\
\diagup\diagdown \\
\text{D}_{\text{CL}} \quad \text{NP} \\
| \\
\text{pro}
\end{array}
$$

Assuming Romance clitics are transitive Ds, (i) what is the motivation for clitic movement in Overt Syntax, and (ii) why is it the case that this movement yields different order patterns across Romance and within the same Romance language?

Different answers have been provided for these two questions. In response to the first question, it has been suggested that motivation for clitic movement was to be found in (i) intrinsic formal features of clitics (Kayne 1975; Corver and Delfitto 1993; Uriagereka 1995); (ii) subcategorization properties of clitics (Kayne 1991); (iii) intrinsic formal features of clitics (their affix-like nature) and interaction of their X-bar hybrid status with the LCA (Chomsky 1994).

The answer we will propose in this chapter is very close to Kayne's (1975) and receives support from the diachronic process of Romance cliticization attested in the four languages under consideration. In their change from strong pronouns to clitic pronouns, Romance clitics passed through a stage where they needed a nonspecialized host and moved into a stage where they fixed V as their host. We will implement this idea in the following way: contemporary Romance clitics have a strong formal feature *V-host* that must be checked against a V-head, thus forcing them to move in Overt Syntax.

In other words, adopting additionally the classical idea that Romance clitics (contrary to Semitic ones, for instance), are specified for Case (as in Jaeggli 1982; Borer 1984; Belletti 1993, among others), the relevant and common part of Romance clitics' formal specification is the one presented in (23):

(23)

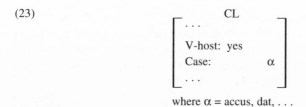

where α = accus, dat, . . .

The hypothesis that Romance clitics move to check strong formal features. (V-host and Case) does not explain why they surface as proclitics versus enclitics/mesoclitics; that is, it does not provide an answer for the second question noted earlier in this section.

In recent literature, the special behavior of EP (and Galician) versus other Romance languages with respect to clitic placement patterns has been attributed to the presence or strength of functional projections above the I-system (CP, WP, ΣP, FP, respectively, in Madeira 1992; Rouveret 1992; Martins 1994; Uriagereka 1995). The outstanding common properties of these analyses can be summarized as:

1. In some cases, at Spell-Out, the clitic and the verb remain in two different functional heads (for Rouveret 1992, this is the case of proclisis in EP tensed subordinate clauses and root *wh*-interrogatives without V-to-C; for Uriagereka 1995, this is the case of proclisis in French; for Martins 1994, this is the case of enclisis in EP). So, in these contexts, cliticization is a morphophonological process.

2. In all these analyses, the derivation of enclisis in tensed clauses resorts to extrastructure and additional overt movements: V-movement forced by strong V-features of the additional functional head and subject NP movement forced by strong N-features of the extra functional head.

3. Clitic movement to the relevant functional projection is not considered a case of Short Movement.

Some of these analyses make empirical predictions for EP.

For Rouveret (1992), clitic constructions in EP crucially involve WP, a functional projection higher than AgrSP and lower than CP, which hosts clitics as well as nonoperator phrases (NP subjects and marked topics). Enclisis, illustrated in (24) and (25), is the result of V-adjunction to W, triggered by strong V or Topic features of W (see (26)):

(24)   a. Li-*o* ontem.
          read-PAST-1sing-CL-accus-3singmasc yesterday
          'I read it yesterday.'

       b. Eu sei que esse livro, o José deu-*lhe* ontem.
          I know-1sing that that book, the José gave-3sing-CL-dat-3sing yesterday
          'I know that that book, José gave him/her yesterday.'

       c. Esse livro, o José deu-*lhe* ontem.
          that book, the José gave-3sing-CL-dat-3sing yesterday
          'That book, José gave him/her yesterday.'

(25)   Ao povo, governa-*o* o rei.
          to the people, rules-CL-accus-3singmasc the king
          'The people, it is the king that rules it.'

(26)   ... [WP XP [W V [W CL]] [AgrSP]]

Proclisis may be the result of two different configurations. In one of them WP is not projected—this is the case of *wh*-interrogatives with V/2 and of sentences with focused phrases in Spec of F(ocus)P, where proclisis derives from left-adjunction of the clitic to V in AgrS and further raising of the clitic-V complex to either C or F (see (27)):

(27)   a. [CP Que [C *lhe* ofereceu]$_i$ [AgrSP o João [AgrS t$_i$] ... ontem]]?
          what CL-dat-3sing gave-3sing the João yesterday?
          'What did João give him/her yesterday?'

       b. [FP Isso [F *lhe* disse]$_i$ [AgrSP eu [AgrS t$_i$]]].
          that CL-dat-3sing told-1sing I-nom.
          'That I told him/her.'

Proclisis may also involve the WP projection, as in subordinate clauses with overt complementizers, root *wh*-interrogatives without V/2, and sentences with interpolation (see (28)); in this case, at Spell-Out, the clitic and the verb are in two different functional heads (W and AgrS, respectively); hence, cliticization is a PF process:

(28)   a. Afirmo [CP [C que] [WP ele [W *o*] [AgrSP leu . . .]]].
say-1sing that he CL-accus-3singmasc read-PAST-3sing
'I say that he read it.'

b. [CP Que livro [WP o João [W *lhe*] [AgrSP ofereceu . . .]]]?
which book the João CL-dat-3sing gave-3sing?
'Which book did João give him/her?'

c. [Se [WP a memória [W *me*] não falha, . . .]]]
if the memory CL-dat-1sing not betrays . . .
'If memory does not betray me . . .'

However, this analysis wrongly predicts the well-formedness of counterparts of (28a, b) where an adverb intervenes between the clitic and the verb:

(29)   a. *Afirmo [CP [C que] [WP ele [W *o*] ontem [AgrSP leu . . .]]].
say-1sing that he CL-accus-3singmasc yesterday read-PAST-3sing
'I say that he read it yesterday.'

b. *[CP Que livro [WP o João [W *lhe*] ontem [AgrSP ofereceu . . .]]]?
which book the João CL-dat-3sing yesterday gave-3sing?
'Which book did João give him/her yesterday?'

Rouveret (1992) argues for his analysis of sentences like (28) on the basis of the possibility of so-called ATB clitic placement in EP, which he illustrates with sentences such as (30):

(30)   Afirmo que ele *me* viu e cumprimentou.
say-1sing that he CL-accus-1sing saw-3sing and saluted-3sing
'I say that he saw me and saluted me.'

According to Rouveret, ATB clitic placement can only be licensed if the clitic and the V are not incorporated at Spell-Out.[1] However, as (31) shows, this prediction is not borne out:

(31)   [CP Quando [C' [C *lhe* telefonou] o João e pediu um livro]]?
when CL-dat-3sing phoned-3sing the João asked-3sing a book?
'When did João call him/her and asked him/her a book?'

Following the claims made in Cardinaletti and Roberts (1991) and Benincà (1991) for Old Romance, other recent approaches to clitic placement in EP have claimed that enclisis in contemporary EP is the result of V-raising to a head external to AgrSP (C, C[+Agr], or F), leaving the clitic stranded in AgrS (see Madeira 1992; Galves 1992; Martins 1994). So, enclitic pronouns are just phonological clitics, since neither at Spell-Out nor at LF do they occur in the same functional head hosting the verb. Thus, these analyses do not provide an explanation for the fact that, apart from residual cases of interpolation with negation, contemporary EP clitics cliticize only onto a V-host and cannot cliticize, for instance, onto adverbs interposed between the verb and the clitic.

In fact, according to these analyses, one would expect that, in paradigms like (32) and (33), the (a) sentences would behave alike (i.e., would both be ungrammatical) and the (b) sentences would also behave alike (i.e., would both be grammatical), contrary to fact. Example (34) shows the relevant part of the derivation of (33):

(32) a. *[CP/FP A quem ontem [C/F deu] [AgrSP o João um livro]]?
         to whom yesterday gave-3sing the João a book?
         'Whom did João give a book to yesterday?'

      b. A quem [C deu] [AgrSP ontem [AgrSP o João um livro]]?
         to whom gave-3sing yesterday the João a book?
         'To whom did yesterday João give a book?'

(33) a. [CP/FP O João ontem [C/F deu] [AgrSP lhe um livro]].
         the João yesterday gave-3sing-CL-dat-3sing a book
         'João yesterday gave him/her a book.'

      b. *O João [C/F deu] [AgrSP ontem [AgrSP lhe um livro]].
         the João gave-3sing yesterday CL-dat-3sing a book
         'João gave yesterday him/her a book.'

(34) [CP/FP DP$_i$ [C/F V$_j$ [AgrSP t$_i$ [AgrS t$_j$ CL] . . .]]

The analysis given in Uriagereka (1995) for Galician also assumes an extra-functional projection above the I-system, F. In his approach, enclisis is derived through raising of the V complex to the left of F (an instance of lexical incorporation), followed by clitic raising to the right of F (an instance of functional incorporation). In this way, enclitic pronouns and verbs are syntactically incorporated in the same functional head, F; consequently, this analysis does not present the problems raised by the previous ones. However, it is grounded on the difference between lexical incorporation (affixation), involving left-adjunction, and functional incorporation (cliticization), requiring right-adjunction, which results in the unprincipled claim that the empty head F counts both as a legitimate host for a clitic, that is, a syntactic word level head, and as a target for lexical incorporation, that is, an affix.

In what concerns proclisis, Uriagereka (1995) assumes that in Galician and contemporary Portuguese the clitic and the V target two different functional heads in Overt Syntax, respectively, F and AgrS. Thus, his analysis faces the same problems as Rouveret's (1992) account of proclisis not involving V/2 (see the earlier discussion of (28) and (29)). Moreover, it faces problems of deriving proclisis in V/2 contexts as well, since it predicts that at least the subject of the clause could intervene between the clitic and the verb, contrary to fact (see the contrast between (35a) and (35b)):

(35) a. *[$_{FP}$ [O que]$_i$ [$_F$ F lhe$_j$] [o João [$_{AgrS}$ deu] t$_i$ t$_j$]]?
the what CL-dat-3sing the João gave-3sing
'What did João give him/her?'

      b. O que lhe deu o João?
the what CL-dat-3sing gave-3sing the João
'What did João give him/her?'

Finally, if taken seriously, Uriagereka's (1995) claim that in Galician and in contemporary EP, F is active and strong, and V has strong F morphological features, which forces overt V-raising to F, combined with the claim that clitics right-adjoin to F and Vs left-adjoin to F, makes it impossible to derive proclisis in these languages (as the author himself remarks, see Uriagereka 1995: note 41). In other words, these claims predict enclisis everywhere in both Galician and contemporary EP.

To summarize, the approaches reviewed here agree in relying on extrastructure, extravert movements, and marked movements (LHM) to account for the syntax of contemporary EP clitics, and they fail to account for relevant empirical properties of clitic placement in EP.

4.3 Clitic placement in EP versus Spanish, Italian, and French

Sticking to Minimalist assumptions, we would like to propose that, in order to account for the syntax of Romance clitics, there is no need to postulate additional functional heads or marked devices. So, our analysis of clitic placement only makes use of the core extended V-projections resulting from the splitting of I (AgrS, T, AgrO).[2] Furthermore, in what concerns X^0 movement in Overt Syntax, we will assume, as usual, that (i) the Minimal Link Condition applies and (ii) excorporation and right-adjunction are not available in Overt Syntax (Kayne 1991, 1994). Finally, we will claim that, in Romance languages, both proclisis and enclisis are always the result of syntactic cliticization; that is, at Spell-Out, the clitic and its V-host occupy a single functional head.

4.3.1 The specificity of EP

Assuming a current idea in functionalist approaches to grammar (see, for instance, Givón 1976), clitics are elements at some stage of a diachronic process that takes free morphemes and turns them into agreement affixes. We claim that clitics in contemporary Romance languages are not all at the same stage of this process. In particular, we will argue that both diachronic and synchronic evidence show that EP clitics are one step farther along in this cycle than those of the other Romance languages considered here; that is, EP clitics are more affix-like than other Romance clitics, and we will show that this is the reason that enclisis is both the neutral and the spreading clitic placement pattern in contemporary EP.

At the same time, we will claim that with respect to the formation of future and conditional forms, the grammar of standard contemporary EP exhibits a conservative feature lost in the other Romance languages we have been considering. To be more precise, both the new synthetic forms, generated fully inflected under the V-node, and a survival of the analytic forms found in Iberian Old Romance coexist. However, as we shall argue, the analytic future and conditional forms still available in standard contemporary EP are already distinct from the old ones.

Strong diachronic evidence for this claim is given by Martins (1994), who shows that in the seventeenth century a catastrophic change occurred in the grammar of EP, with direct effects on clitic placement: proclisis, which was overwhelmingly dominant during the fifteenth and sixteenth centuries, severely regresses afterward, with enclisis becoming the dominant pattern (see Martins 1994:273).[3] However, this change should not be identified with some move backward, in the direction of the conservative pattern of medieval EP. In fact, clitic placement in root sentences and interpolation facts show that the emerging clitic pattern is different from the medieval one.[4] So, for instance, interpolation was an available option until the sixteenth century with a great variety of constituents, but from the seventeenth century on it disappeared in standard EP in every context but *não*, the lexical head of NegP.

Data from language acquisition corroborate this claim. If, as assumed in most analyses, enclisis in EP, contrary to proclisis, resorts to functional projections above I and extravert movements, under Minimalist assumptions we should expect enclisis to be more costly than proclisis. And, even accepting the Continuity Hypothesis, according to which in the early grammar all functional heads are available but become "active" bottom-up, we should expect proclisis to be the first and dominant pattern of clitic placement in children, since enclisis would need the activation of a functional head above the I-system. However, in EP, enclisis is the systematic pattern of clitic placement until around forty-two months, irrespective of the presence of proclisis triggers, as shown in (36):[5]

(36) a. *Não* chama-*se* nada. (M., 20 months)
      not calls-CL-refl-3sing nothing

      'That's not his name at all.'

   b. É que n̲ã̲o̲ estragou-*se*. (J. G., 39 months)
      is that not spoiled-3sing-CL-refl-3sing

      'In fact, it didn't break.'

   c. P̲o̲r̲q̲u̲e̲ é que foste-*me* interromper? (R., 29 months)
      why is that interrupted-2sing-CL-accus-1sing?

      'Why did you interrupt me?'

   d. Foi alguém q̲u̲e̲ meteu-*me* nesta fotografia. (J. G., 39 months)
      was-3sing someone who put-PAST-3sing-CL-dat-1sing in-this photo

      'It was someone who photographed me.'

e. Mas ele já foi-*se* embora. (P., 39 months)
   but he already went-3sing-CL-refl-3sing away
   'But he went away already.'

f. Que(ro) pôr os papeles aqui pa(ra) pa(ra) <u>não</u> rasgar-*se*. (P., 39 months)
   want put-INF the papers here for for not tear-INF-CL-refl-3
   'I want to put the papers here for them not to tear.'

. So, these data strongly argue against the view that enclisis is more costly and less basic than proclisis in EP. On the contrary, they support the claim that children are analyzing EP clitics as affix-like elements.

Data from younger generations and adult speakers provide additional evidence for this claim, since they show that in the grammar of teenagers and young adults enclisis is spreading to contexts with proclisis triggers (see (37)):

(37) a. *Porque não* apercebeu-*se* que . . . (12 year-old-child, written speech)
         because not realized-3sing-CL-refl-3 that . . .

         'Because he didn't realize that . . .'

      b. É uma verdade *que* pode-*se* ver de uma forma muito clara . . . (literate adult, TV debate)
         is a truth that can-PRES-3sing-CL-nom-3sing see-INF of a form very clear

         'It is something that can be easily seen.'

      c. *Porque* ela começou-*o* a tirar . . . (illiterate adult, interview, Portugues Fundamental, 0091)
         because she started-3sing-CL-accus-3singmasc to remove-INF . . .

         'Because she started to remove it . . .'

      d. Correspondem à classe *onde* "só" combina-*se* com SN . . . (university student, written speech)
         correspond-3pl to-the class where "only" combines-CL-refl with NP

         'They correspond to the class where "only" combines with NP.'

To summarize, we take the rise of enclisis starting in the seventeenth century, the preference for enclisis during language acquisition, and the spreading of enclisis to contexts with proclisis triggers in teenagers and young adults to be consequences of the process of reanalysis of EP clitics as affix-like elements.

4.3.2 The derivation of enclisis, economy, and convergence

Assuming that Romance cliticization always involves incorporation before Spell-Out, the resulting derivations must display the required configurations for feature checking.

Elaborating on Rizzi (1993b), we claim that strong feature checking of the clitic or the verb against the relevant functional head requires strict immediate adjunction; on the contrary, weak feature checking does not. These generalizations are summarized in (38):[6]

(38)   Strong feature checking between heads requires immediate adjunction of the checking and target heads. Weak feature checking does not.

Notice that the last clause of (38) is plausible in a framework where weak features are invisible at PF and may procrastinate their checking until LF. Thus, the specificity of our claim crucially reduces to positing that whenever the target head has weak features, checking before Spell-Out is still possible, though not obeying the same strict adjacency requirement as strong feature checking.

Moreover, we will assume that a head intervenes between the checking and the target head only if it has some features to check against the functional target head, that is, only in this case is it visible for the checking process. This claim is summarized in (39):

(39)   In the head-checking process, a head X intervenes between a checking head Y and a target functional head Z iff X and Z have some common feature α.

In the next sections, we will show that the different patterns of clitic placement in EP versus Spanish, Italian, and French derive directly from the interaction of the conditions on feature checking stated in (38) and (39) with the status of clitic pronouns in these languages.

Recall that in EP clitics entered a diachronic process leading to their reanalysis as affix-like elements. So, it is expected that they do not block strong feature checking since they no longer count as regular syntactic $X°$ heads. In the other Romance languages mentioned earlier, clitics still count as regular syntactic heads, thus blocking strong feature checking in the relevant contexts.

4.3.3 Enclisis in EP as Short Movement to AgrO

According to the DP Hypothesis, clitics are originally generated under VP. Because clitics are D-heads, the Minimal Link Condition predicts D_{CL} adjunction to V, at least, for complement clitics:

(40)

```
                VP
              /    \
             V      DP
           /  \    /  \
         Cl_i  V  D_i  pro
```

However, this movement does not produce a convergent derivation, since the next step, CL-V raising to AgrO, would create a configuration violating condition (38) for strong feature checking—Case checking between CL and AgrO, as shown in (41):

(41)

```
              AgrO
             /    \
            V      AgrO
          /  \
        CL_i  V
```

So, (complement) clitics must skip the V-head and raise to AgrOP, the first functional projection above VP.[7]

Being a head, the clitic moves from DP to AgrO, to check its strong Case and agreement features;[8] this movement is allowed, and it obeys Economy. The verb moves next to check AgrO strong V-features (see (42)):

(42)

```
                        AgrO
                     ___/  \___
                  AgrO          VP
               __/  \__      __/  \__
           AgrO      AgrO   V       DP
          _/  \_    _/  \_  |     _/  \_
         V  AgrO  Cl  AgrO  t    D     pro
               (Vstr)          |
               (Natr)          t
```

In a configuration like (42), the requirements for strong feature checking of V cannot be met, since another head—the clitic—intervenes between V and AgrO. We argue that the status of clitics in EP as quasi-verb inflectional affixes allows strong feature checking, making it possible for the verb to check its features against AgrO in spite of the intervening clitic. Furthermore, D_{CL} movement to AgrO renders unnecessary (and thus forbids, under Economy considerations) movement of its *pro* complement to Spec, AgrO, since the clitic heads a chain that is able to identify *pro* through head-complement feature sharing (see Chomsky 1993, 1994).

Notice that the reverse order, that is, V to AgrO first and then clitic to AgrO, would not yield a convergent derivation because the strong N-features of the clitic would not be checked, since V, a word that must check strong features against AgrO, intervenes between the clitic and the target head (see (43)):

(43)

```
                        AgrO
                     ___/  \___
                  AgrO          VP
               __/  \__      __/  \__
           AgrO      AgrO   V       DP
          _/  \_    _/  \_  |     _/  \_
        Cl  AgrO   V  AgrO  t    D     pro
               (Vstr)          |
               (Natr)          t
```

So, the only way for the clitic to check its strong N-features would be movement of the whole DP headed by the clitic to Spec, AgrO, followed by movement of the clitic to T. This derivation is less economical than the previous one, since it involves two overt movements: DP-movement plus CL-movement.

Summarizing, in EP, enclisis corresponds to the most economical derivation, and AgrO is the cliticization site.

4.3.4 The ban on enclisis in Italian, Spanish, and French finite clauses

In Spanish, Italian, and French, enclisis cannot occur in finite clauses, contrary to EP. We claim that this is due to the morphological status of the clitic—in these languages, clitics are at a stage of their diachronic process of reanalysis where they are still analyzed as totally distinct from V-agreement affixes. So enclisis is ruled out because, if the clitic moves to AgrO to check strong N-features, strong V-features of AgrO remain unchecked and the derivation crashes at PF, since the intervening CL adjunct blocks the checking procedure:

(44) *

```
                              AgrO
                      ┌────────────┴───────┐
                    AgrO                   VP
              ┌──────┴──────┐        ┌──────┴────────┐
            AgrO          AgrO       V             DP
          ┌──┴──┐       ┌──┴──┐      │          ┌───┴────┐
         V    AgrO  Cl  AgrO  t      D         pro
                         (Vstr)      │
                         (Natr)      t
```

4.3.5 Enclisis in nonfinite clauses in Portuguese versus Spanish and Italian

EP being a language with generalized V-movement (see, for instance, Raposo 1987; Ambar 1992), there is no reason to suppose, according to our analysis, that in the core cases enclisis in nonfinite clauses is different from enclisis in finite clauses. Let us now look at untensed clauses in Italian and Spanish, where enclisis is the obligatory pattern.

Elaborating on Belletti (1993), we suggest that in these languages AgrO has weak V-features in nonfinite clauses (presumably, a consequence of selectional properties of [- finite] T). Assuming this is the case, weak V-features of AgrO may be present at PF, but the N-strong features of AgrO and of the clitic must be checked before Spell-Out. So the clitic must move overtly.

As V in these languages moves overtly to higher functional positions in untensed clauses, according to Short Movement, it passes through AgrO adjoining to the complex CL-AgrO. By doing so, it checks its weak V-features against AgrO (recall that weak feature checking does not require strict adjacency of the relevant heads). This step of the derivation produces enclisis, as shown in (45):

(45)

```
                         AgrO
                   ┌───────┴──────┐
                 AgrO             VP
            ┌─────┴─────┐    ┌─────┴─────┐
           V          AgrO   V          DP
                    ┌──┴──┐   │       ┌──┴───┐
                   D    AgrO  t   D    NP
                        (Vweak)   │
                        (Nstr)    t
```

According to Rizzi (1993a), the verb must overtly move to AgrS to check strong V-features. Assuming Excorporation is not available in Overt Syntax, the whole V-CL complex raises to AgrS, presumably through T.

The problem now is to explain why a configuration such as (46) is legitimate, since strong V-feature checking requires strict adjacency:

(46)   [AgrS V-CL [AgrS [+Vstrong]]]

Our claim is that the clitic has no N-features to check against AgrS. In these circumstances, the clitic is invisible for checking purposes. Thus, the configuration satisfies strong feature checking requirements.

Recall that at some point of the derivation before Spell-Out the verb and the clitic must target the same functional head, otherwise, the strong feature V-host would remain unchecked and the derivation would crash at PF. Since the step of the derivation represented in (45) yields a convergent derivation and this derivation is more economical than the one producing proclisis (because it spares overt movement of the clitic complement *pro*), it is the only one allowed under Economy considerations.

4.3.6 The ban on enclisis in nonfinite clauses in French

Let us now look at French nonfinite clauses, where proclisis is the only available pattern. Following Rizzi's (1993a) reinterpretation of the data in Pollock (1989), let us assume that in French untensed clauses main verbs may overtly move, although they do not reach the highest functional head, AgrS—more precisely, they cannot move higher than T, as the data with negation show.

If the V-features of AgrO in French are strong in both tensed and untensed clauses, our analysis predicts that the same pattern of clitic placement will obtain in these two types of clauses. It also predicts that in untensed clauses with clitics the nonfinite verb must overtly raise to T, the cliticization site in French (see section 4.3.8.1, which presents an account of proclisis in Spanish, Italian, and French tensed clauses).

4.3.7 Mesoclisis in EP as Short Movement of the V-CL complex

Let us now consider the mesoclisis cases of contemporary EP. Recent proposals analyzed mesoclisis in Old Spanish and EP as the result of Long Head Movement, a strategy available in certain languages in order to obey the Wackernagel Law (clitic elements must occupy the second position in the sentence) or the Tobler-Mussafia Law (clitic elements are banned from sentence initial position; cf. Lema and Rivero 1989, 1991; Rivero 1994; Roberts 1994). According to these proposals, mesoclisis is LHM (V-to-C) of some untensed main verb over an inflected (weak) auxiliary.

We will present two arguments challenging the claim that mesoclisis in contemporary EP is a case of LHM. First, suppose the accounts mentioned earlier are correct in considering that the motivation for LHM of the untensed V is the Tobler-Mussafia Law. In this case, mesoclisis should not occur in sentences with full XPs preceding the untensed V, contrary to fact (see (47)):

(47)   a.   O João telefonar-*te*-á amanhã.
            João phone-INF-CL-dat-2sing-FUT-3sing tomorrow
            'João will call you tomorrow.'

b. Amanhã eu dir-*te*-ei o que fazer.

tomorrow I tell-INF-CL-dat-2sing-FUT-1sing what do-INF

'Tomorrow I will tell you what to do.'

Second, Lema and Rivero (1989, 1991) have shown that all the cases of LHM share the following property: LHM is restricted to root contexts "or to the inferior empty C of a two-layered CP complementing a V of propositional attitude" (Lema and Rivero 1991, p. 250). However, in contemporary EP we find (optionally) meso-clisis in subordinate tensed clauses, not only in contexts where one might argue for a double CP layer—that is, in embedded sentences with overt complementizers and Clitic Left Dislocation (see Rouveret 1992 for the enclisis cases) or "fronted" clauses, as shown in (48), (49)—but also in contexts where a double CP layer analysis is difficult to motivate (see (50)):

(48) a. Acho [CP que ao João, far-*lhe*-ia bem ir à festa].

      think-1sing that to John do-INF-CL-dat-3sing-COND-3sing well go-INF to-the party

      'I think that to John, it would do him good to go to the party.'

   b. Acho [CP que ao João, far-*lhe*-á bem ir à festa].

      think-1sing that to John do-INF-CL-dat-3sing-FUT-3sing well go-INF to-the party

      'I think that to John, it will do him good to go to the party.'

(49) a. Acho [CP que, quando acabarem o trabalho, far-*lhes*-á bem sair].

      think-1sing that when finish-SUBJ-3pl the work do-INF-CL-dat-3sing-FUT-3sing well leave-INF

      'I think that when they finish their work, it will do them well to go out.'

   b. Ele afirmou [CP que, se quisessem saber os resultados, poder-*lhe*-iam telefonar].

      he said-3sing that if wanted-SUBJ-3pl know-INF the results, can-INF-CL-dat-3sing-COND-3pl phone-INF

      'He said that, if they wanted to know the results, they could phone him.'

(50) a. Ele disse [CP que amanhã ir-*te*-á visitar às cinco horas].

      he said that tomorrow go-INF-CL-accus-3singmasc-FUT-3sing visit-INF at-the five hours

      'He said that tomorrow he will visit you at five.'

   b. Ele afirmou [CP que no próximo ano o conselho conceder-*te*-á uma bolsa de estudo para os Estados Unidos].

      he said that the next year the committee grant-INF-CL-dat-2sing-FUT-3sing a scholarship for the USA

      'He said that next year the committee will grant you a scholarship in the USA.'

If, depending on the analysis proposed for Clitic Left Dislocation and "fronted" clauses, it could be maintained that mesoclisis in (48) and (49) is V-to-(empty)C, to satisfy the Wackernagel Law in the minimal CP domain containing the clitic, such a

claim is not extendable to contexts like those in (50), where one would have to assume that time adverbials may be fronted to Spec, TopP, an assumption challenged
by data in Longobardi (1983) and Cinque (1990), who show crucially that (nonfocused) adverbials in IP initial position differ in scope properties and crossover effects from either topicalized or Clitic Left Dislocated phrases.

Since the two arguments presented here argue against an LHM account of mesoclisis in contemporary EP, we would like to suggest an alternative analysis. It is a
well-established fact that, in future and conditional forms, the ancient auxiliary *(h)aver*
entered a diachronic process leading to its reanalysis as an affix. Suppose that, in the
grammar of standard EP, two forms for the future and the conditional coexist: the
"new" synthetic form used in proclisis and in enclisis (see the examples in (6)), which
is inserted fully inflected, and a survival of the analytic form found in Old Romance,
where the ancient auxiliary is interpreted as a "lexicalized" T-affix, generated under
the T head, in a way similar to English support *do* (see Lasnik 1994).

Assuming this to be the case, mesoclisis in contemporary EP is a conservative
pattern but one that is already distinct from LHM in Old Romance (where clitics could
move as XPs and the infinitival form did not incorporate syntactically in the auxiliary verb) and its properties follow directly: mesoclisis has the same distribution of
enclisis (in tensed contexts) because its derivation is exactly the same as the derivation of enclisis (see (51), the step in the derivation where AgrO adjoins to T):

(51) a. Ele lê-*lo*-á.

   b.

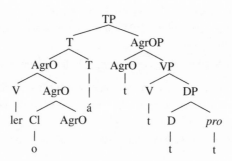

4.3.8 Two derivational strategies of proclisis in Romance

In this section we will try to show that proclisis in Romance corresponds to two different derivational strategies.

4.3.8.1 Proclisis in Spanish, Italian, and French finite clauses

Recall we have claimed that in Spanish, Italian, and French enclisis was forbidden due
to the morphological status of the clitic, a regular X° syntactic head in these languages.

Following Corver and Delfitto (1993), we assume that the first relevant step of
the derivation is movement of the DP headed by the clitic to Spec, AgrO, followed
by V-movement to the immediately dominating functional head (T) and Short Movement of the clitic head to check its V-host feature against V, as shown in (52):

(52)

```
                         TP
              _____/\
             T              AgrOP
        ____/\           __/\____
       D       T        DP       AgrOP
       |      /\       /\       __/\__
       Cl   AgrO  T   D   pro  AgrO   VP
    (V-host)/\    |    |        |    /\
          V  AgrO t    t        t   t  t
```

So, in the three languages considered, proclisis yields the only convergent derivation, and the cliticization site is the first functional node above AgrO, that is, T.

4.3.8.2 Proclisis in EP as Last Resort Movement

Proclisis in contemporary EP has a different derivational source from other Romance languages considered earlier: recall that proclisis is not sensitive to the tensed/untensed distinction, occurs later than enclisis during language acquisition, and is regressing in younger generations (see the data presented in (7), (36) and (37)); recall also that, as many Portuguese and Brazilian grammarians have noticed, proclisis occurs in clauses with a class of so-called operator-like elements (see (7) through (18)), whose common property is "attracting" clitics. That this is an intrinsic property of lexical items is suggested by contrasts like (53) and (54), showing that whereas *raras vezes* 'seldom' triggers proclisis, *muitas vezes* 'often' does not:[9]

(53)   a. *O João <u>raras vezes</u> dá-*me* razão.
         the João rare times gives-CL-dat-1sing reason
         'João seldom agrees with me.'

      b. O João <u>muitas vezes</u> dá-*me* razão.
         the João many times gives-CL-dat-1sing reason
         'João often agrees with me.'

(54)   a. O João <u>raras vezes</u> *me* dá razão.
         the João seldom gives-CL-dat-1sing reason
         'João seldom agrees with me.'

      b. *O João <u>muitas vezes</u> *me* dá razão.
         the João often gives-CL-dat-1sing reason
         'João often agrees with me.'

Since clitic attraction must rely on c-command from the proclisis trigger (see (55)), this lexical property might be seen as a syntactic condition with an LF counterpart:

(55)   a. [<u>Todos</u> os alunos] *o* leram.
         all the students CL-accus-3mascsing read-3sing
         'All the students read it.'

b. [Os pais de <u>todos</u> os alunos] leram-*no*.

the parents of all the students read-3sing-CL-accus-3mascsing

'All the students' parents read it.'

We pursued an explanation along these lines in Duarte and Matos (1995), where we suggested that proclisis triggers must have scope over (extended) V-projections and contain, as part of their lexical entry, a formal specification of the categorial nature of their scope domain. According to this hypothesis, enclisis would prevent a proclisis trigger to meet this requirement, since it would originate a syntactic hybrid complex head.

In Duarte and Matos (1995), we also suggested that proclisis in standard EP was Short Movement of the clitic within the X^0 functional projection that meets the scope requirements of the proclisis trigger. Illustrating this claim with tensed subordinate clauses, enclisis is "undone" in AgrS, through movement of the clitic from the inner AgrO projection in AgrS to the left of the topmost AgrS node (see (56)):

(56)   a. Acho que ele o leu.

think-1sing that he CL.accus-3mascsing read-3sing

'I think that he read it.'

b.

```
                        CP
                      /    \
                    C       AgrSP
                    |      /     \
                  que    DP       AgrSP
                         |       /     \
                        ele    AgrS    ...
                              /    \
                            CL      AgrS
                            |      /    \
                            o     T      AgrS
                                 /   \
                              Agro    T
                             /    \
                           V      AgrO
                           |       |
                          leu      t
```

Thus, proclisis in standard EP was considered a Last Resort movement.

Although we maintain some of the crucial assumptions of the preceding analysis, namely, that proclisis derives from enclitic configurations, we will depart from our earlier analysis (Duarte and Matos 1995) in the precise way to characterize the property common to proclisis triggers, as well as the point of the derivation where enclisis is undone: in Overt Syntax or between Spell-Out and the P-A Interface.

In fact, if the common property of proclisis triggers was a formal specification of the categorial nature of their scope domain, one would predict, contrary to fact, that in sentences where marked topics and parentheticals intervene between the proclisis trigger and the clitic, only one of the clitic placement patterns would be legitimate, since only proclisis would meet the relevant requirement at LF and the derivation with enclisis would crash (see (57) and (58)):

(57) a. Acho que ao João, a Maria *lhe* ofereceu um livro.
think that to-the João, Maria CL-dat-3-sing gave-3-sing a book
'I think that to João, Mary gave him a book.'

b. Acho que, ao João, a Maria ofereceu-*lhe* um livro.
think that to-the João, Maria gave-3-sing-CL-dat-3-sing a book
'I think that to João, Mary gave him a book.'

(58) a. Disseram-me que embora tivesse sido difícil, *lhe* concederam a bolsa.
told-3plu-CL-dat-1-sing that although had been difficult, CL-dat-3-sing gave-3-plu
the grant

'I was told that although it was difficult, they gave her the grant.'

b. Disseram-me que, embora tivesse sido difícil, concederam-*lhe* a bolsa.
told-3plu-CL-dat-1-sing that although had been difficult, gave-3-plu-CL-dat-3-sing
the grant

'I was told that although it was difficult, they gave her the grant.'

On the basis of this kind of data, Frota and Vigário (1996) argued that proclisis in standard EP is driven by phonological weight. They suggest that an enclitic must occur as proclitic whenever a heavy functional word[10] c-commands and precedes it in the same CP. This approach accounts for the well-formedness of (57) and (58), since prosodic phrasing is different in the (a) and (b) sentences: an I(ntonational Phrase)-boundary intervenes between the proclisis trigger and the clitic in the (b) sentences, whereas no such boundary occurs in the (a) sentences.

Assuming this hypothesis, the core cases of proclisis in standard EP are instances of *Move* occurring between Spell-Out and the P-A Interface, an interesting consequence in a framework where *Move* is procrastinated.

Only in those cases where independent LF requirements intervene (e.g., identification of empty categories in ATB contexts, which requires c-command by the clitic) must proclisis occur in Overt Syntax, as a Last Resort operation (see Matos 1998), to ensure that a convergent derivation will obtain in both interface levels:

(59) a. Só o João *o* viu e cumprimentou.
only the João CL-accus-3-singmasc saw-3-sing and greeted
'Only João saw him and greeted him.'

b. *O João viu-*o* e cumprimentou.
only the João saw-3-sing CL-accus-3-singmasc and greeted
'Only João saw him and greeted him.'

4.4 Concluding remarks

We have tried to show that the differences in clitic placement exhibited in the four Romance languages considered follow from the interaction of properties of Merge/

Move and Economy principles with the formal features of clitics. Our account does not resort to extrastructure, extraovert movements or Long Head Movement to account for the syntax of Romance clitics. In fact, sticking to Minimalist assumptions, we made use only of the core extended V-projections, standardly referred to as IP, and claimed that in both proclisis and enclisis the clitic and its V-host are at the same functional head at Spell-Out.

We tried to show that the different patterns of clitic placement in EP versus Spanish, Italian, and French directly derive from the interaction of the conditions on feature checking stated in (38) with the status of clitic pronouns in these languages.

On the basis of diachronic and language acquisition evidence, we claimed that EP clitics are a step ahead in the process of affix reanalysis, which makes enclisis the most economical pattern of clitic placement in this language and, hence, the basic one. At the same time, we claimed that mesoclisis in contemporary EP is a survival of an older stage, where the ancient auxiliary was reanalyzed as an affix generated under T: thus, mesoclisis was shown to be a subcase of enclisis, where the target T-head of the V-CL complex dominates an affix instead of just abstract features.

Finally, we claimed that proclisis in standard EP is derived from enclisis, is driven by the phonological weight of functional words, and consequently, in the core cases, occurs between Spell-Out and the P-A Interface. The claim that proclisis derives from enclisis in EP receives empirical support from the fact that it is systematic only in later stages of language development and that it is regressing in younger generations.

Notes

1. For an alternative view of ATB clitic placement, see Matos 1998.

2. See, for instance, Chomsky (1993); Bobaljik and Jonas (1996); Thráinsson (1996); Guasti (1997).

3. In the texts she studied, proclisis was above 95 percent in the sixteenth century; starting in the seventeenth century, proclisis continuously decreases (below 30 percent in the eighteenth century, below 20 percent in the nineteenth century) and enclisis rises (around 70 percent in the eighteenth century, above 80 percent in the nineteenth century); the rise of enclisis goes with the loss of interpolation for every constituent but *não* (from the seventeenth century on, it is unattested in the texts she studied).

4. An alternative approach takes these facts to follow not from the reanalysis of clitics as affix-like elements but from two different changes in the grammar of EP: the rise of enclisis in root sentences (including nondependent coordinated clauses) is due to the loss of Focus Movement for non-operator-like NP subjects (see Martins 1994), and the virtual disappearance of interpolation is a consequence of the loss of NP Scrambling in contemporary EP (Raposo, personal communication). However, neither of these explanations can account for the ungrammaticality of (i) in contemporary EP:

(i) a. quando *vos* <u>ora</u> *fez* merçee (Martins 1994:165)

　　 b. como *se* <u>nesta carta</u> *contem* (Martins 1994:169)

　　 c. quaes *les* <u>o dito Stevão</u> *mâdar* fazer (Martins 1994:172)

　　 d. assi como *les* <u>a elles</u> *semellava* (Martins 1994:178)

　　 e. dos sobredictos autos que *se* <u>pressente mi tabaliam</u> *pasará* (Martins 1994:178)

　　 f. de quallquer pessoa que *lha* <u>enbargar</u> *quiser* (Martins 1994:177)

In all the sentences of (i) the clitic is in second position in the clause, preceded by elements occupying (presumably) the Spec or the head position of CP and is separated from the verb by adverbs, θ-marked NPs, clitic doubling NPs, clauses, and VPs. So, assuming the clitic was in F/Σ/W, neither loss of Focus Movement for non-operator-like subjects nor loss of NP Scrambling may be invoked to account for the ungrammaticality of such sentences in contemporary EP.

5. Contrary to what happens in other Romance languages. See, for instance, the following data from Italian, from Hyams (1992):

(i)   *L*'ha buttata via a Lila. (25 months)
       'Lila threw it away.'

(ii)   Si, *li* ho visti io (27 months)
       'Yes, I have seen them.'

(iii) *L*'ha portata la tata.
       "The nanny brought it.'

6. A similar (and even stronger) claim is made in Zwart (1993:23–24), concerning checking in a Spec-head configuration.

7. This violation of the Minimal Link Condition is in the spirit of Kayne's (1991) generalization concerning the nature of the targets of clitic movement: only functional heads may host a clitic. Notice that current analysis of sentential negation in Romance (see, for instance, Pollock 1989; Matos 1989; Belletti 1990; Gonçalves 1994; Haegeman 1995) also rely in a Minimal Link Condition violation: in its movement to AgrS, the V-head skips Neg; in the next step of the derivation, the Neg head must adjoin to the V-functional complex in AgrS.

8. As standardly assumed in the literature, we take both AgrS and AgrO to have strong V-features and weak N-features in Null Subject Romance languages. Whenever a complement clitic is present, an AgrO with strong V- and N-features is introduced in the numeration; whenever a nominative clitic is present, the AgrO and AgrS introduced in the numeration have strong V- and N-features. In the last case, the complement *pro* of the nominative clitic is forced to raise to Spec, AgrSP. This last claim is supported by contrasts with expletive subjects as those shown in (i) and (ii):

(i)   a. ?Ele ouve-se boatos a toda a hora.
          (it-expl is heard rumours all the time)
          'Rumours are constantly heard.'

       b. ?Ele diz-se mal de toda a gente.
          (it-expl is spoken ill of everybody)
          'One speakes ill of everybody.'

(ii)   a. *Ele troça-se por tudo e por nada.
          (it-expl one laughs at everybody for no reason at all)
          'One laughs at everybody for no reason at all.'

       b. *Ele chega-se sempre atrasado.
          (it_expl one arrives always late)
          'One always arrives late.'

Whereas in the (i) sentences, with transitive verbs, the expletive subject may marginally occur, since the clitic is identified with a passive one, in the (ii) sentences, with unergative and unaccusative verbs, the presence of the expletive subject yields a stronger degradation, since both the expletive and the complement *pro* of the nominative clitic compete for the same structural position—Spec, AgrSP.

9. In fact, it seems that no common syntactic or semantic property unifies this class. For instance, quantifiers like *poucos* 'few' trigger proclisis, whereas *muitos* 'many' allows proclisis and enclisis (see (i) and (ii)):

(i) a. Muitos alunos leram-no cuidadosamente.
     many students read-3plu-CL-accus-3sing carefully
     'Many students read it carefully.'

    b. Muitos alunos o leram cuidadosamente.
     many students CL-accus-3sing read-3plu carefully
     "Many students read it carefully.'

(ii) a. *Poucos alunos leram-no cuidadosamente.
     few students read read-3plu-CL-accus-3sing carefully
     'Few students read it carefully.'

    b. Poucos alunos o leram cuidadosamente.
     few students CL-accus-3sing read-3plu carefully
     'Few students read it carefully.'

Furthermore, definite specific DPs fronted in so-called Focus Preposing constructions induce proclisis, despite their nonoperator status (see (iii)); in fact, it can be shown that such DPs are neither informational nor quantificational focus (see Duarte 1997):

(iii) Isso lhe disse eu.
     that CL-dat-3-sing told-1sing I
     'That it was I who told him/her.'

10. According to Frota and Vigário (1996), a prosodic constituent is heavy in EP iff it is focused or it branches.

References

Ambar, M. 1992. *Para uma Sintaxe da Inversão Sujeito-Verbo em Português*. Lisbon: Colibri.
Belletti, A. 1990. *Generalized Verb Movement*. Torino: Rosenberg and Sellier.
———. 1993. "Case Checking and Clitic Placement." *GenGenP* 1, no. 2:101–118.
Benincà, P. 1991. "Complement Clitics in Medieval Romance: The Tobler-Mussafia Law." In H. van Reimsdijk and L. Rizzi (eds.) *EFS-Eurotype*, vol. 3.
Bobaljik, J., and D. Jonas. 1996. "Subject Positions and the Role of TP." *Linguistic Inquiry* 27: 195–236.
Borer, H. 1984. *Parametric Syntax: Case Studies in Semitic and Romance Languages*. Dordrecht: Foris.
Cardinaletti, A., and I. Roberts. 1991. "Clause Structure and X-Second." In press. In W. Chao & G. Horrocks (eds.) *Levels of Representation*.
Cardinaletti, A., and M. Starke. 1994. "The Typology of Structural Deficiency. On Three Grammatical Classes." Ms., University of Venice, University of Geneva.
Chomsky, N. 1993. "A Minimalist Program for Linguistic Theory." In K. P. Hale and S. J. Keyser (eds.) *View from Building 20*. Cambridge, Mass: MIT Press.
———. 1994. "Bare Phrase Structure." In G. Webelbuth (ed.) *Government and Binding Theory and the Minimalist Program*. Oxford: Blackwell.

————. 1995. *The Minimalist Program*. Cambridge, Mass.: MIT Press.

Cinque, G. 1990. *Types of A'-Bar Dependencies*. Cambridge, Mass.: MIT Press.

Corver, N., and D. Delfitto. 1993. "Feature Asymmetry and the Nature of Pronoun Movement." Ms., University of Tilburg, University of Utrecht.

Duarte, I. 1997. "Ordem de Palavras: Sintaxe e Estrutura Discursiva." In A. Brito, F. Oliveira, A. Pires de Lima, and R. Martelo (eds.) *Sentido que a Vida Faz. Estudos para Óscar Lopes*. Oporto: Campo das Letras.

Duarte, I., and I. Faria. 1994. "Specificity of European Portuguese Clitics in Romance." In *Studies in the Acquisition of Portuguese*. Lisbon: APP/Colibri.

Duarte, I., and G. Matos. 1995. "Romance Clitics and the Minimalist Program." Paper presented at the Fifth Colloquium on Generative Grammar, Coruña, Spain.

Frota, S., and M. Vigário. 1996. "On Weight Effects in European Portuguese." Paper presented at the Glow Workshop on Weight Effects, Athens.

Galves, C. 1992. "Clitic Placement in European Portuguese: Evidence for a Non-homogeneous Theory of Enclisis." In *Actas do Workshop sobre o Português*. Lisbon: APL.

Givón, T. 1976. "Topic, Pronoun and Grammatical Agreement." In C. Li (ed.) *Subject and Topic*. New York: Academic Press.

Gonçalves, F. 1994. "Negação Frásica em Português. Caracterização Sintáctica com Referência ao Processo de Aquisição." M.A. thesis, University of Lisbon.

Guasti, T. 1997. "Romance Causatives." In L. Haegeman (ed.) *The New Comparative Syntax*. London: Longman.

Haegeman, L. 1995. The *Syntax of Negation*. Cambridge: Cambridge University Press.

Hale, K. P., and S. J. Keyser. 1993. "On Argument Structure and the Lexical Expression of Syntactic Relations." In K. P. Hale and S. J. Keyser (eds.) *The View from Building 20*. Cambridge, Mass: MIT Press.

Hyams, N. 1992. "The Genesis of Clausal Structure." In J. Meisel (ed.) *The Acquisition of Verb Placement: Functional Categories and V2 Phenomena in Language Acquisition*. Dordrecht: Kluwer.

Jaeggli, O. 1982. *Topics in Romance Syntax*. Dordrecht: Foris.

Kayne, R. 1975. *French Syntax. The Transformational Cycle*. Cambridge, Mass.: MIT Press.

————. 1991. "Romance Clitics, Verb Movement and Pro." *Linguistic Inquiry* 22:647–686.

————. 1994. *The Antisymmetry of Syntax*. Cambridge, Mass.: MIT Press.

Lasnik, H. 1994. "Verbal Morphology: *Syntactic Structures* Meets the Minimalist Program." Ms., University of Connecticut.

Lema, J., and Rivero, M. L. 1989. "Inverted Conjugations and V-Second Effects in Romance." To appear in *Proceedings of the XIXth Linguistic Symposium on Romance Languages*. Amsterdam: John Benjamins.

————. 1991. "Types of Verbal Movement in Old Spanish." *Probus* 3, no. 3: 237–278.

Longobardi, G. 1983. "*Connectedness*, Complementi Circostanziali e Soggacenza." *Rivista di Grammatica Generativa* 5: 141–185.

Madeira, A. 1992. "On Clitic Placement in European Portuguese." *University College London Working Papers in Linguistics*, 4.

Martins, A. M. 1994. "Clíticos na História do Português." Vol. 1. Ph.D. dissertation, University of Lisbon.

Matos, G. 1989. "Null VP in Portuguese and English." In *Actas do Workshop sobre Gramática Generativa*. Lisbon: APL, 1990.

————. 1998. "ATB Clitic Placement in Romance Languages." Ms., University of Lisbon.

Meisel, J., ed. 1992. *The Acquisition of Verb Placement: Functional Categories and V2 Phenomena in Language Acquisition*. Dordrecht: Kluwer.

Meisel, J., and N. Müller. 1992. "Finiteness and Verb Placement in Early Child Grammars:

Evidence from Simultaneous Acquisition of Two First Languages. French and German." In J. Meisel (ed.) *The Acquisition of Verb Placement: Functional Categories and V2 Phenomena in Language Acquisition.* Dordrecht: Kluwer.

Pierce, A., and V. Deprez. 1993. "Negation and Functional Projections in Early Child Grammar." *Linguistic Inquiry* 24: 25–67.

Pollock, J.-Y. 1989. "Verb Movement, UG and the Structure of IP." *Linguistic Inquiry* 20: 365–424.

Raposo, E. 1987. "Case Theory and Infl-to-Comp: The Inflected Infinitive in European Portuguese." *Linguistic Inquiry* 18: 85–109.

Rivero, M. L. 1994. "Clause Structure and V-Movement in the Languages of the Balkans." *Natural Language and Linguistic Theory* 12: 63–120.

Rizzi, L. 1990. *Relativized Minimality.* Cambridge, Mass.: MIT Press.

————. 1993a. "The Case of Root Infinitives." *GenGenP* 1, no. 2: 15–25.

————. 1993b. "Some Issues on Cliticization." Ms., University of Geneva.

Roberts, I. 1994. "Two Types of Head Movement in Romance." In D. Lightfoot and N. Hornstein (eds.) *Verb Movement.* Cambridge: Cambridge University Press.

Rouveret, A. 1992. "Clitic Placement, Focus and the Wackernagel Position in European Portuguese." Ms., University of Paris-8.

Sportiche, D. 1992. "Clitic Constructions." Ms., UCLA.

Thráinsson, T. 1996. "On the (Non-)Universality of Functional Categories." In W. Abraham, S. Epstein, H. Thráinsson and J. W. Zwart (eds.) *Minimal Ideas.* Amsterdam: John Benjamins.

Uriagereka, J. 1995. "Aspects of the Syntax of Clitic Placement in Western Romance." *Linguistic Inquiry* 26: 79–123.

Zwart, J.-W. 1993. "Dutch Syntax: A Minimalist Approach." Ph.D. dissertation, University of Groningen.

5

CHARLOTTE GALVES

Agreement, Predication, and Pronouns in the History of Portuguese

The recent history of Portuguese provides an interesting case of change from one grammar, Classical Portuguese (henceforth ClP), to two grammars, Modern European Portuguese and Brazilian Portuguese (henceforth, respectively, EP and BP). This chapter aims to describe and analyze, in the framework of the Minimalist Program (Chomsky 1995b), the basic aspects of this double change, which give interesting evidence of the deep correlation existing in grammars between the licensing of subjects and the licensing of clitics and weak pronouns ("deficient" pronouns in the sense of Cardinaletti and Starke 1994). Although this correlation clearly appears in many analyses of various pronominal systems, it has received little theoretical status. Here I will argue that it derives from the fact that both deficient pronouns licensing and predication relations are dependent on the parametrization of languages with respect to Agr, which will be considered not as a category, in accordance with Chomsky (1995b), but as a feature.

Despite their differences, the three Portuguese grammars considered here share an important syntactic characteristic: they license constructions in which the verb and the subject are not in a Spec-head configuration. This will be argued to derive from the peculiar combination of the V-feature and the Agr-feature in these languages.

In the first section of the chapter, relevant aspects of the syntax of subjects and deficient pronouns in the three grammars will be presented. The second section will discuss the nature of Agr in the Minimalist Program, as well as the categorial nature of deficient pronouns. Finally, the third section will propose a minimalist analysis of the change from ClP to EP and to BP.

5.1 Facts and analyses

5.1.1 Classical Portuguese

The history of European Portuguese is traditionally divided into three periods, Old Portuguese (henceforth OP), ClP, and EP. ClP is generally defined as the period from the sixteenth century to the middle of the nineteenth century. Here the language in focus will be eighteenth-century ClP, since it can be considered the common origin of both EP and BP, but it is worthwhile to recall some relevant aspects of the entire history of the language.

The striking fact about the history of Portuguese is that it did not lose, in its classical period, two syntactic properties that disappeared from other Romance languages at the end of their archaic period.[1] These two properties are V2 order and obligatory enclisis in V1 contexts, in application of the so-called Tobler-Mussafia Law (see, among others, Fontana 1992 for Spanish; Adams 1987 for French; Benincà 1994 for Italian). The following examples, drawn from texts from the sixteenth through nineteenth centuries, illustrate this claim:[2]

V2 order:

(1) Eem quanto faziamos alenha, *faziam* dous carpenteiros huua grande cruz dhuu paao. (16th c.)
while (we) did the-wood, made two carpenters a big cross out of wood

(2) No mesmo homem *descobriram* os homens dois livros sempre abertos e patentes. (17th c.)
in the same man discovered men two books always open and manifest

(3) Com a lingua *faz* o arrieiro a celebre cantiga. (18th c.)
with his tongue does the muleteer the famous song

(4) O outro dia *compus* eu uma modinha para ela. (19th c.)
the other day composed I a song for her

Enclisis in V1 sentences:

(5) veedeo-lhe hua terra de pão com terra de mato (16th c.)
(he) sold-to-him a land of bread with land of forest

(6) Levanta-se este assunto sobre toda a esfera da capacidade humana. (17th c.)
raises-SE this topic about all the sphere of human capacity

(7) Obrigão-me os médicos a tomar vinho quinado em jejum. (18th c.)
oblige-me the doctors to take wine with quina on an empty stomach

(8) Trouxe-me grande tranquilidade a tua carta. (19th c.)
brought-me great quietness your letter

Note that enclisis in V1 contexts is categorical in EP throughout its history, since the first documents of the twelfth century to our time (cf. Martins 1994 and Ribeiro 1995 for the archaic period; Lobo 1992 and Torres-Moraes 1995 for the classical period; and all the works quoted in the next section for EP). Besides differentiating EP from all the modern Romance languages, except Galician, this categorical nature of enclisis in V1 contexts already differentiates OP from other Romance languages, which very soon present exceptions to the law (cf. Fontana 1992, who reports a case of proclisis in this context as early as the thirteenth century, and Benincà 1994 for similar cases in Old French and Old Italian dialects).

Enclisis also appears in non-V1 contexts, in alternation with proclisis.[3] It concerns any construction of the type XP V, with XP a subject, a topic (NP or PP), an adjoined clause, or an adverb.

In eighteenth-century ClP, enclisis and proclisis coexist in non-V1 contexts, with a variation between authors that goes from 0 to 40 percent of enclisis (Torres-Moraes 1995):

(9)   e depois o irei repondo por ser dinheiro dotal
      and afterward (I) it-will return for being dowry money

(10) depois segue-se a sintaxe
      afterward follows-SE the syntax

(11) O nosso amigo Coelho me deu cabal noticia.
      our friend Coelho to-me-gave important news

(12) Filena converteu-se em burro.
      Filena changed-herself into a monkey

This alternation was studied by Salvi (1990), who assigns different structures to proclitic and enclitic constructions. According to him, what crucially differentiates these constructions is the position of the topic or subject preverbal phrase, as represented in (13a and b). Example (13a) corresponds to the proclitic construction, in which the preverbal XP is in the specifier position of the head that hosts the verb. According to Salvi, this head is Comp. Example (13b) corresponds to the enclitic construction, in which the preverbal XP is outside the projection of the head that hosts the verb (i.e., outside CP):

(13) a. $[_{CP}$ XP cl-V $[_{IP}$ . . . $]]$

      b. XP $[_{CP}$ V-cl $[_{IP}$ . . . $]]$

This analysis allows Salvi to formulate the Tobler-Mussafia Law in an abstract framework: enclisis is obligatory whenever the verb is in first position in CP. The same idea is presented by Benincà (1994), who shows that this alternation also exists in Northern Italian Languages, for which the same explanation is available. Note that this analysis makes a strong claim about the relation between the position of the clitic and the type of predication relation instantiated by the clause. In systems allowing alternation between proclisis and enclisis, the former corresponds to a V2-like topicalization and the latter to a structure containing an external topic.

5.1.2 Modern European Portuguese

One of the most described features of EP is clitic placement. I will not propose a new description of it here but will base my argument on the numerous recent works on this matter (cf. Barbosa 1991, 1996; Duarte and Matos, chapter 4, this volume; Galves 1992a, e, b; Madeira 1992; Manzini 1992, 1994; Martins 1993; Raposo 1995; Rouveret 1987, 1992, 1996).

All these works observe that EP makes a crucial difference in main clauses between quantified subjects, which require proclisis, and specific subjects, which force enclisis, as exemplified in the following.

(14)   Alguém me viu.

   *Alguém viu-me.

   'Somebody saw me.'

(15)   O Paulo viu-me.

   *Paulo me viu.

   'Paulo saw me.'

The obligatory enclisis in (15) differentiates EP from ClP, in which proclisis is possible, and even preferred, with specific subjects (cf. sentence 2). The possibility of proclisis is also lost in EP when the first element of the sentence is a topic. This means that sentences like (4) are also ungrammatical. This is the first aspect of the change between ClP and EP.

The second aspect is that EP is no longer a V2 language. Sentences like (1) through (4) are no longer produced by the grammar.[4] In EP, sentences (1) and (4), for instance, would have the following form, with the verb following the subject instead of preceding it:[5]

(16)   Enquanto faziamos a lenha, dois carpenteiros faziam uma grande cruz.

   while (we) did the-wood, two carpenters made a big cross out of wood

(17)   O outro dia eu compus uma modinha para ela.

   'The other day I composed a song for her.'

Salvi (1990) derives the loss of proclisis from the loss of V2, since, according to his analysis, once Spec, CP is no more an available position for subjects and topics, the verb is always in first position in the clause, and the only option is enclisis. The same analysis is proposed by Benincà (1994). The price this attractive analysis has to pay is the odd hypothesis that subjects[6] in EP are always external to CP in main clauses.

Other researchers came to a similar conclusion only on the basis of synchronic properties of EP. Rouveret (1987), for example, argues that the subject is external to S (cf. also Barbosa 1991, 1996). In a more recent framework, allowing more positions for subjects, the idea that the subject is in some sense external in EP has been reformulated in two types of analysis:

1. The subject is not in the specifier position of the category that hosts the verb (Rouveret 1996).

2. The subject and the verb are in a Spec-head agreement configuration, but this configuration involves a functional category higher than Infl (or Agr) (W for Rouveret 1992; Comp for Madeira 1992, Manzini 1994; Sigma for Martins 1993, 1994).

In other words, according to these analyses, either it is only the subject that is external to the rest of the clause, or it is the whole complex subject/verb that is higher than Infl.[7]

The main argument for the first position is that adverbs may always occur between the subject and the verb in EP, even when this subject is a nondislocatable expression. Rouveret quotes Costa (1996), who observes that the grammaticality of the following sentences shows that the subject is not left-dislocated, contrary to what seems to be the case in Italian (Belletti 1990):[8]

(18)   Todos provavelmente errarão.
        all probably will-fail

(19)   Ninguém provavelmente errará.
        nobody probably will-fail

If one makes the hypothesis that adverbs cannot be attached at the X' level, this argument definitively favors the first representation of the externality of the subject over the other one. I will adopt this hypothesis in the third section. Furthermore, it is interesting to point out that (18) and (19) show that even subjects that require proclisis, like *todos* and *niguém*, are external in this sense in EP.

5.1.3 Brazilian Portuguese

Unlike what is sometimes claimed in essays on Portuguese, BP clitic placement in tensed sentences is not simply like Spanish or Italian, nor can it be identified with the French system only because clitics are preverbal in infinitival clauses. It is true that BP has lost enclisis[9] in tensed as well as in infinitival sentences, but its syntax of clitic placement differs crucially from all these languages in two respects:

1. Its paradigm is deficient. Third person accusative clitics *o/a* appear to be acquired at school and used only in written texts and formal contexts. In normal spoken language, even educated people use either the third person tonic pronoun *ele* or the null object, whose distribution is much less constrained than in EP (Farrell 1990; Galves 1997). Furthermore, the third person dative form *lhe* no longer refers to a third person but is used as an equivalent for the second person form *te*, both functioning as the oblique form corresponding to *voce* 'you'.[10] It seems, therefore, that the third person has entirely disappeared from the paradigm.

2. In compound tenses, first and second person clitics are attached not to the auxiliary but to the main verb. As already noticed by Teyssier (1974), the sequence Aux-cl-V does not correspond to the same structure in EP and BP. Adverbs occur

between the clitic and the verb in EP, and between the auxiliary and the clitic in BP. Furthermore, in the latter, but not in the former, the clitic remains in the same position independently of the presence of negation or a conjunction. Examples (20) and (21), respectively, illustrate the BP and the EP paradigm.[11]

(20) a. Tinha me lembrado.
          (I) had me-remembered

      b. agora não tinha me lembrado
          now (I) neg had me-remembered

      c. essas industrias novas que estão se implantando
          those new factories that are SE-installing

      d. Estava sempre te vendo.
          (I) was always you-seeing

      e. me chocou
          (it) me-shocked

(21) a. Tinha-me lembrado.
          (I) had-me remembered

      b. agora não me tinha lembrado
          now (I) neg me-had remembered

      c. essas industrias novas que se estão a implantar
          those new factories that SE-are installing

      d. Estava-te sempre a ver.
          (I) was-you always seeing

      e. chocou-me
          (it) shocked-me

The contrast between (20) and (21) clearly shows that, unlike what happens in EP, BP clitic placement is insensitive to syntactic processes like negation and subordination. Furthermore, (20d) show that in compound tenses, clitics are attached to the past participle, and not to the auxiliary. This strongly distinguishes BP clitic placement from French clitic placement and seems to indicate that clitics are licensed in a very low position in the clause. Furthermore, as already mentioned, BP breaks off the long-standing prohibition of clitic first, which, as we saw earlier, is strongly maintained in EP. I conclude that the BP clitic paradigm instantiates a very strong change with respect to ClP, which, as far as the sentences in example (21) are concerned, behaved exactly like EP.

As for the main predication relation of the sentence, BP is no longer a V2 language but was defined by the pioneer study of Pontes (1981) as a "topic-oriented" language. One kind of construction that leads Pontes to make this claim is illustrated in (22) and (23):

(22) O relógio estragou o ponteiro.
       the clock broke the hand
       'The clock has its hand broken.'

(23) A revista está xerocando.
       the journal is Xeroxing
       'The journal is being Xeroxed.'

In these examples, an internal argument has raised to the subject position without any morphological modification of the verb. In (22) this argument is the genitive complement of the direct object of the verb. In (23) it is the direct object itself. These sentences are completely impossible in EP[12] and in ClP. That the preverbal NP is the subject of the clause is shown by the agreement relation instantiated in (24), which is the plural version of (23):

(24) As revistas estão xerocando.
       'The journals are being Xeroxed.'

Again, this kind of phenomenon raises the question of the position of the subject in (23) and (24). Observe that in this kind of construction, as in V2 constructions, the NP that precedes the subject is not its external argument. But there are some important differences between the two constructions. First, there is overt agreement between the preverbal NP and the verb. Second, the external argument of the verb is not lexically present. The following contrast shows that, contrary to passive sentences, the agent argument is completely inactive in the sentence:

(25) A revista foi xerocada para ganhar tempo.
       the journal was Xeroxed to save time

(26) ??A revista xerocou para ganhar tempo.
       the journal Xeroxed to save time

In (25) the subject of *ganhar tempo* is controlled by the implicit agent of *foi xerocada*. In (26) this interpretation is not available. This indicates that no null external argument is projected in the sentence. Finally, this kind of construction may appear in embedded sentences:

(27) Você sabe se a revista está xerocando?
       you know whether the journal is Xeroxing?

Topic-Oriented Languages are characterized by the possibility for the subject of the sentence not to be the external argument of the verb, without any morphological marking on the verb. In other words, they are languages in which topics are treated as subjects, independently of their argumental status. An interesting case is given by BP sentences (22) through (24).

Inversely, in these languages, argumental subjects are frequently expressed like topics, as will be described later. Figueiredo Silva (1994) argues that there is a topic position lower than Comp in BP. Interestingly, this proposal somehow characterizes BP as the reverse of EP. In the latter, the subject is external to the clause; in the former, it is the topic that is internal to the clause. Notice, however, that the well-formedness of (18) and (19) in BP shows that subjects can be also characterized as external in this language.

The remainder of this chapter will be devoted to a discussion and a unified analysis of these rather unexpected forms of predication in languages and their relation with the corresponding pronominal systems. I will argue that they depend on the peculiar way Agr is associated with functional categories in the languages considered and its interaction with the V-feature of the same categories. I will conduct this discussion in the framework of the last version of the Minimalist Program proposed by Chomsky (1995b).

5.2 The nature of Agr and of the weak pronouns

5.2.1 Agr and φ-features in the Minimalist Program

In his very influential article, Pollock (1989) goes against a long-standing tradition that considered Agr merely as a part of Infl and argues that Agr is an autonomous functional category. At the origin of Pollock's analysis is the necessity of extending the available positions for subjects. The need for more positions is also the main reason for the multiplication of Agr nodes in the sentential domain (Chomsky 1995b; chapter 2 for AgrO; Cardinaletti and Roberts 1991 for Agr1 and Agr2, among others) as well as in nonsentential domains. The first Minimalist model adopts this view of Agr and even reinforces it by assigning Agr a crucial role in Case theory, since, in this model, Case-checking is always mediated by an Agr head.

In the last version of the Minimalist Program, however, Chomsky breaks off this line of thinking and proposes a restrictive theory of functional categories, which makes no place for Agr. His main argument is that Agr, unlike the other functional categories Comp, Tense, and D, consists of [–Interpretable] features only, and hence does not provide any instructions to the interface levels.[13] Therefore, it is "present only for theory internal reasons" (Chomsky 1995b:349). Essentially, as in Pollock's analysis, its only function is to make available different overt positions for DPs and verbs in the clause. In this view, "Agr exists only when it has strong features."

Here I will explore an alternative view that is entirely compatible with Chomsky's argumentation that Agr is not a category but is based on two possible conclusions of this argumentation that he does not draw.

1. Although Agr is not a category, it does have a role in the syntactic computation. Coherently with some proposals in former frameworks, Agr can be considered a formal feature. This was the current analysis before Pollock (1989) and is in the spirit of Rizzi (1990:52), who claims that "Agr can both be an independent head with its own autonomous inflectional projection (AgrP) and be assigned to another head as a feature or a set of feature."

According to this view, which categories are endowed with a feature Agr in languages is a matter of parametrization. The main hypothesis this chapter intends to bring support to is that this feature is responsible for two major differences between languages: the licensing of deficient pronouns and the position of subjects. As for the licensing of deficient pronouns, I generalize the hypothesis put forth by many researchers for particular languages (cf., for instance, Cardinaletti 1994; Haegeman 1994; Zwart 1994) that clitics and weak pronouns are licensed by an Agr head, and rephrase it in terms of a functional head endowed with an Agr feature.

As for subjects, I propose that in grammars Agr plays the role assigned by Chomsky to the D-feature; that is, its presence forces the projection of the specifier of the category that bears it. Besides providing a unitary analysis for clitic placement and subjects licensing, this proposal has the advantage of getting rid of the conceptual problems of the notion of D-feature, in particular, its exact definition. Chomsky (1995b) in effect assumes that it is a "nominal" feature, leaving open the question of whether it is a D- or an N-feature. Furthermore, this feature sometimes seems to be satisfied by a nonnominal phrase, for instance, in English locative constructions where the phrase preceding the verb is a PP. No such problems arise with Agr, which only requires a phrase in its specifier, being neutral with respect to the category that checks it.[14] Since in Chomsky's (1995b) framework, specifiers are projected only in overt syntax, Agr is by definition a strong feature.

2. Although the category that dominates Tense is not Agr, there is such a category. I will propose that this category is Person.[15] Person fulfills the requirements imposed by Chomsky (1995b) on functional categories, since it arguably has [+ Interpretable] features at LF. Furthermore, it is comparable with Tense in its deictic interpretation. Finally, in many languages, it plays a crucial role in syntax. For instance, in many ergative languages, there is a split between ergative-absolutive and nominative-accusative Case-marking, depending on the Person mark on the verb (cf., for instance, Nash 1997).

A further rather natural claim is that the formal features intrinsically associated with Person are ϕ-features. As is the case for all the features associated with functional categories (Chomsky 1995b), they are [–Interpretable] and must therefore be checked. This checking can be performed either by the ϕ-features of some phrase in Spec/Person or by ϕ-features moving to Person. Recall that in the framework developed here, the first option depends on the presence of Agr on Person. I will argue that the latter can be instantiated either by overt movement, when verb movement pied-pipes ϕ-features, or by autonomous covert movement of ϕ-features.

Unlike what he claimed in the first version of the model, Chomsky (1995b) argues that some formal features are interpretable at LF. Interpretable features do not need to be checked, and therefore erased, since they are legitimate objects at the interfaces. With respect to ϕ-features, he makes a distinction between the ϕ-features of nouns, which are interpretable, and those of verbs, which are not.

Some researchers have recently argued that deficient pronouns are ϕ-features. Dobrovie-Sorin (1994) claims that the only difference between agreement morphemes and deficient pronouns is that the former are bound morphemes. The same idea is defended at length by Everett (1996:2), who claims that "pronominal clitics, argument affixes, and pronouns are epiphenomena, produced by the insertion of PHI-FEATURES into different syntactic positions." I will adopt this view here.

In Chomsky's last framework, it is natural to assume that deficient pronouns are interpretable φ-features, and their behavior is therefore not governed by checking theory. I will assume without further discussion that they move for a reason of visibility at LF. Since their interpretation requires some antecedent in discourse, they must occupy a designated position.[16]

To summarize, we now have Agr as a formal feature, Person as the highest functional category of the Infl layer, and deficient pronouns as interpretable φ-features.

5.2.2 Pronouns and predication

This analysis is based on the claim that weak pronouns and bound agreement morphemes are the same element, with the only difference that the latter are inserted in the derivation as a part of a word. Further support for this analysis can be found in the fact that, in some languages, free weak pronouns play an agreement role that is entirely comparable to that of bound morphemes. An example of this occurs in BP, in which subjects generally show up in a dislocated position, with a resumptive pronoun immediately preceding the verb.

(28) Essa competência, ela é de natureza mental.

this competence, it is of nature mental

'This competence is mental in nature.'

Beyond its frequency, it can be shown that this construction has different properties from its equivalent in other Romance languages, including EP. Namely, it can be embedded in subordinated clauses and in relative clauses, as illustrated in the following:

(29) Eu acho que o povo brasileiro ele tem uma grave doenca.   (Duarte 1995)

I think that the Brazilian people he has a serious illness

(30) Um pais que o presidente, ele nao obedece mais as leis não pode ser respeitado pelos outros.   (Kato 1993)

a country that the president, he does not obey the laws, cannot be respected by the others

Cinque (1983) and Benincà (1989), for Italian, and Duarte (1987), for EP, claim that this kind of dislocation, which involves a tonic pronoun either in subject or in another position ("hanging topic construction"), cannot be embedded, in contrast with constructions in which the pronominal element is a clitic ("clitic left dislocation construction"). For Cinque, this is due to the fact that it is not sentence grammar that is responsible for the connection between the NP and the tonic pronoun, but the same principle of discourse grammar that rules the relation between a full NP and a pronoun in two adjacent sentences in discourse. By the same reasoning, the well-formedness of (29) and (30) shows that the relation between *o povo brasileiro* and *o presidente* and the following pronoun is ruled by sentence grammar—in other words, that the tonic pronoun has the same status in BP as the clitic in EP and Italian. This calls for an explanation.

Clitic-left-dislocation sentences are constructions in which the clitic plays a role of morphological agreement between a dislocated phrase and the head of the sentence. It is likely that the licensing of embedded topics depends on this agreement relation, which characterizes the dislocated phrase as the subject of a predication. In contrast, tonic pronouns cannot enter in this kind of relation because they occupy a full DP position. BP sentences in example (28) are therefore unexpected, unless some property of the language enables tonic pronouns to function as clitics, which is what I will propose later.

The last version of Chomsky's theory of movement makes it possible to implement this idea in a very simple way. In effect, after Spell-Out, only features move, and they always adjoin to a head. At LF, the features of a pronoun that occupy an argument position in overt syntax can move for checking reasons to a category endowed with φ-features and act exactly like a clitic (i.e., establish an agreement relation with an external DP that licenses this DP as a subject). Chomsky's theory of feature movement allows us to consider that in (28) through (30) there are hidden clitics that correspond to the features of the tonic pronoun, moved in the covert syntax in order to check the φ-features of Person.

5.2.3 Enclisis

The theory of enclisis developed here is based on the hypothesis made so far that clitics are φ-features, which is far from an uncontroversial claim. Most authors, in effect, argue that they are Determiners (cf. Uriagereka 1995; Corver and Delfitto 1993, among others).

Although it seems attractive, mainly because of the morphological identity of the third person clitic and the article in Romance languages, this hypothesis is problematic. If D is the category that codifies reference, how is it possible to explain the total absence of referential interpretation associated with clitics in the following French constructions, in which the clitic is interpreted not as an argument but as a proposition or an adjective?

(31)   Je le sais.
        I it-know

(32)   Belle, elle ne l'a jamais été.
        pretty, she neg it-has never been
        'Pretty, she never was.'

On the contrary, if we admit that they are φ-features that simply allow a position to be interpreted as anaphoric of a previous argument or predicate, independently of any referential interpretation, their whole behavior becomes coherent. This analysis makes it possible to distinguish proclisis and enclisis in the following way. In proclisis, the φ-features are generated independently, in argumental position, and they must adjoin to the verb for the reasons suggested earlier. Enclisis, instead, is a case of inflectional morphology. In this case, the φ-features are adjoined to the verb as soon as the lexicon. Note that this assumption allows us to formulate, in Minimalist framework, the claim made by Benincà and Cinque (1993) that, in enclitic constructions, the verb and the clitic form a morphological unit. They show how coordination facts clearly distinguish the two types of constructions. Observe the following French examples:

(33)   Il chantera et dansera avec nous.
       he will sing and dance with us

(34)   *Chantera-t-il et dansera avec nous?
       sing-he and dance with us

(35)   Jean le lit et relit sans cesse.
       John it reads and reads again

(36)   *Lis et relis-la!
       read and read-it again

When the pronoun is proclitic, it is licit not to repeat it in the second segment of a coordinate structure. When it is enclitic, this is impossible. Furthermore, in some languages, such as Romanian, two clitics can be coordinated when they are proclitics but not when they are enclitics.[17]

(37)   Îmi si îti scrie.
       CL and CL Verb

(38)   *Dîndu-mi si îi cartea.
       Verb-CL and CL

All these facts show that verb + clitic and clitic + verb are not the same object, and that the clitic and the verb function as an indissociable morphological unit in the former but not in the latter. Obviously, there are different manners of interpreting this fact. In this analysis, clitics are considered as φ-features, that is, of the same nature as inflectional morphemes. The interpretation proposed for the cases in which they appear on the right side of the verb, which is the side of the inflectional morphology in Romance languages, is therefore coherent with the assumption made by Chomsky (1995 a, b) that inflectional morphemes are affixed to the words in the lexicon. Furthermore, it is the only way to morphologically distinguish proclisis and enclisis if we assume that, in both cases, the clitic and the verb are in the same head in the visible syntax.[18] Proclisis is the result of the adjunction of the clitic to the verb. Enclisis corresponds to a word formed in the lexicon.

The last point that requires explanation is the licensing of enclitic structures. Obviously, few modern Romance languages legitimate enclisis in tensed affirmative sentences, and this seems to be a highly restricted option. This has been generally related with the activation of a functional category higher than Infl (or Agr) that attracts the tensed verb. In the Minimalist framework, this amounts to assigning a V-feature to this category. According to the analyses, either the clitic is stranded in Infl (Martins 1994) or it occupies the head of the functional category and attracts the verb (Madeira 1992; Manzini 1994; Rouveret 1992). In both cases, enclisis obtains. In this view, enclisis depends on verb movement.

Here I will argue that it is more accurately described in terms of the interplay between Agr and the V-feature. I will maintain the idea that in Portuguese tensed sentences enclisis is dependent on the properties of Comp, but this is not true for all the cases of enclisis, since Infl is likely to be the licensing category for enclisis in infinitival sentences in languages like Italian and Spanish.

The common property between topicalization and infinitival clauses is that the head that contains the verb and the clitic enters in no Spec-head relation. In infinitival clauses, there is no lexical subject to agree with, and in topicalized constructions, as represented in (15b), the topic is outside CP. This similarity between these two cases of enclisis leads to the generalization that enclisis is incompatible with the existence of a Spec-head relation involving the head that contains the clitic. This incompatibility was already observed by Benincà (1994) for EP and the medieval Romance languages, and by Galves (1996) for ClP and EP.[19]

In the analysis proposed here, this generalization can be formulated in such a way that the complementary distribution of enclisis and proclisis straightforwardly follows. In effect, the incompatibility of enclisis with the existence of a Spec-head relation involving the verb can now be formulated in terms of the association of an Agr-feature with the category hosting this verb. I have assumed, with many other researchers, that proclitic constructions obey the opposite requirement, since clitics must adjoin to a head endowed with Agr. Putting things together, I can formulate the following generalization about clitic placement:

1. Clitics adjoin to the verb in a head endowed with an Agr-feature.
2. Enclisis requires that the verb be at Spell-Out in a head that does not contain Agr.

The distribution of enclisis and proclisis is therefore dependent on the movement of the verb, as in the analyses mentioned earlier, but not only. It is sensitive to the parametrization of the host of the verb with respect to the Agr-feature. In a theory of parameters formulated in terms of the formal features of functional categories, clitic placement derives, therefore, from the combination of two of them: the Agr-feature and the V-feature.[20] I shall now describe how this hypothesis accounts for the differences between ClP, EP, and BP.

5.3 A minimalist approach of the change from ClP to EP and BP

The properties considered in section 5.1 can be summarized in table 5.1.

In this table, "external subjects" refers to the possibility of occurrence of an adverb between a nonreferential subject and the verb, as illustrated in (18) and (19). I

TABLE 5.1 Comparative table of the syntactic properties of ClP, EP, and BP

	ClP	EP	BP
Enclisis	yes	yes	no
V2	yes	no	no
External subjects	no	yes	yes
Embedded dislocation	no	no	yes
Subject topics	no	no	yes

therefore make a distinction between topicalized subjects, on one hand, and "external" subjects, on the other. Although they share the property of not being in a Spec-head relation with the verb, only the latter are internal to CP. It must be noted that the "no" assigned to ClP with respect to this property is more a hypothesis than an attested fact, given the absence of a systematic description of the position of the adverbs in this language. Evidence for this claim, however, can be found in the fact that the V3 orders are very rare in ClP and are always analyzable as V2 constructions in which the adverb occupies Spec, CP, and the subject is in an external to CP topic position.

"Subject topics" refers to the kind of constructions exemplified in (22) through (24), in which a nonexternal argument behaves exactly like a subject. No construction of this type has been reported in ClP.

This table evidences a more drastic change between BP and ClP than between EP and ClP. In fact, ClP and BP can be considered as two opposite realizations, with EP as an intermediate form. EP shares at least one positive property with each of the other languages: enclisis with ClP and external subjects with BP.

In this section, I will show that these differences derive from the following parametrization of the functional categories Comp, Person, and Tense.[21]

ClP:

Comp: +V/–Agr

Person: +V/+Agr

Tense: +V/–Agr

EP:

Comp: –V/+Agr

Person: +V/–Agr

Tense: +V/–Agr

BP:

Comp: –V/–Agr

Person: –V/–Agr

Tense: +V/+Agr

The change from CLP to EP consists of an inversion of the values of the V-feature and the Agr-feature of Comp and Person. From CLP to BP, there is a much more catastrophic change, probably correlated with the weakening of the pronominal system mentioned earlier (cf. Galves 1997). In BP, V-movement is limited to Tense, and Tense is also the category that bears the Agr-feature.[22]

The analyses adopted so far characterize ClP as a V2 language. I will adopt the natural assumption that in V2 languages the verb raises to Comp because of the V-feature of Comp. This movement has the effect of licensing the so-called V2 topicalization, that is, topicalization in the specifier of Comp.[23] This is a case in which a Spec-head relation is forced not by Agr but by a strong operator feature.

According to Salvi's analysis, which I adopted earlier, two different structures are available in ClP when the subject or a topic precedes the verb. These structures are repeated in (39a) and (39b). Example (39c) represents the ungrammaticality of enclisis in a Spec-head configuration, implicit in Salvi's analysis.

(39) a. XP $[_{CP}$ V-cl $[_{IP} \ldots]]$

  b. $[_{CP}$ XP cl-V $[_{IP} \ldots]]$

  c. *$[_{CP}$ XP V-cl $[_{IP} \ldots]]$

Assuming these representations, the analysis proposed here straightforwardly accounts for enclisis in (39a), since by the parametrization here, the verb in Comp is in a position that does not bear Agr. The structures in (39b, and c) however, show that even when there is no Agr, a Spec-head relation involving the verb blocks enclisis.

I conclude that the feature Agr is incompatible with enclisis because it forces a Spec-head configuration. At the CP level, the presence of strong operator features has the same effect when Comp has a V-feature. In this case, proclisis is legitimate because the clitic adjoins to the verb in Person, which bears Agr, and raises with it to Comp. The rule governing enclisis proposed earlier should therefore be reformulated as follows:

Enclisis requires that the verb be at Spell-Out in a head that contains no strong feature (besides the V-feature itself).

Two kinds of strong features appear in derivations: strong operator features and Agr. They are in complementary distribution, and in many languages Agr is limited to the Infl level. However, if the analysis proposed here is right, it is not an exclusive property of this level. I will suggest later that operator features can be associated with categories other than Comp as well.

In the next sections, I will describe how the parametrization proposed earlier accounts for the changes in clitic placement from ClP to, respectively, EP and BP.

5.3.1 From ClP to EP

I will now show that the differences between ClP and EP derive from the inversion of the values of the V-feature and Agr-features of Person and Comp.

EP's relevant properties can be summarized as:

1. It is not a V2 language.
2. Its subject is external.
3. It forces enclisis when the verb is preceded by a topic or a specific subject.

The first property derives from the absence of V-to-Comp raising.[24] The two others derive from the fact that Agr is now associated with Comp.[25] The absence of V-movement to Comp has the effect, already noted by Salvi (1990), that Spec, CP in EP is no more an adequate position for topics, in contrast with ClP. But, according to my assumptions, the presence of Agr makes Spec, CP a subject position, since the subject must raise to the checking domain of Comp in order to check Agr, yielding the structure represented in the following.

(40) $[_{CP}$ DP $[_{\_PersP}$ V]]

Crucially, in this structure, the subject and the verb are not in Spec-head relation, and enclisis is licit.

I am now able to address one of the most intriguing problems of EP: the sensitiveness of clitic placement to the referential nature of the subject. In a structure such as (40), the subject has to be interpreted as a sort of topic, predicated of the projection of Person, in which there are coreferring ϕ-features on the verb.[26] This implies that the subject independently refers. On the contrary, quantified elements cannot corefer with ϕ-features, since they have no reference. This means that (40) is not a well-formed structure when the subject is not referential. But it must be recalled that sentences like (18) and (19), in which a sentential adverb occurs between *alguém/ todos* and the verb, show that quantified subjects are as external as referential subjects. My earlier discussion of the complementary distribution of Agr and operator features suggests that Person in EP matrix sentences may receive operator features, since it is not assigned an Agr feature. I will adopt this hypothesis and propose that Person may optionally be assigned a feature that attracts quantified subjects in its specifier.[27] Because of the Agr feature of Comp, quantified subjects must also raise to Spec, Comp, yielding the following structure:

(41) $[_{CP}$ alguém$_i$ $[_{PersP}$ t$_i$ V]]

In (41), the relation between the subject and the ϕ-features on the verb is mediated by the trace in the specifier of the category hosting the verb. This structure, which licenses quantified subjects, excludes enclisis because it creates a specifier for the category hosting the verb.

5.3.2 From ClP to BP

As shown in table 5.1, BP corresponds to a more drastic change with respect to ClP. Both V2 and enclisis disappear, indicating that Comp is no more associated with

Agr and V-features. Moreover, as noted earlier, constructions in which a topic is treated like a subject or there is a left-dislocation involving a tonic pronoun can be embedded. Thus, these constructions do not display the effects normally observed when a predication relation involves either Comp, as in V2 languages, or a phrase external to Comp, as in the so-called hanging topic constructions. I conclude that, in BP, there is a topic position lower than C.

Instead of calling this category Top, as Figueiredo Silva (1994) does, I propose that it is Person itself, whose special properties are explained by the fact that it is associated with no strong feature at all.

As in other languages that have lost V-to-Person, this can be correlated with a morphological modification of the verbal paradigm. In BP, this modification results from the loss of the second person of the singular, *tu*, which is substituted by a third person form, *você*, with the consequent loss of the second person form in the verbal paradigm and a general confusion between the pronouns of second and third person (cf. Galves 1994, 1997). However, the familiar tests show that V moves out from VP in this language (Galves 1994; Figueiredo Silva 1994). For instance, manner adverbs occur between the verb and the object:

(42)   a.   As crianças acabaram cuidadosamente a sua tarefa.
            the children finished carefully their homework

       b.   ??As crianças cuidadosamente acabaram a sua tarefa.
            the children carefully finished their homework

I will therefore assume that V is in Tense at Spell-Out. I will now suppose that Tense bears Agr as well and attracts the external argument. The structure of the proposition when the derivation reaches Person will be therefore:

(43)   [$_{PersP}$ Pers [$_{TP}$ DP V]]

The ϕ-features of V agree with, and are checked by,[28] the subject DP in Spec, TP. Person, however, must have its ϕ-features checked. Because there is no Agr feature in Person, this cannot be performed under Spec-head agreement. The only option left by UG is feature movement in covert syntax.

I have already noted that covert feature movement can explain the fact that embedded topics are licensed even if they are doubled by a tonic pronoun, in contrast with what happens in other Romance languages. The negative value for the features Agr and V explains this possibility in BP, since neither the verb nor the subject can check the ϕ-features of Person. What sentences like (29) and (30) show is that the pronoun plays this role, acting as a null clitic. In languages in which the ϕ-features of Person are checked by the agreement morphology on the verb, there is no room for such null clitics, and these sentences are ruled out because, in the absence of agreement between the head of the clause and the adjoined DP, only a discursive relationship can be established between this DP and the pronoun, as pointed out by Cinque (1983). But this relationship does not occur inside clauses, since it is the domain of grammatical relations.

The structure underlying "hanging topic" constructions is represented as follows:[29]

(44)   [$_{PersP}$ DP [$_{PersP}$ ϕ_i [$_{-TP}$· . . . ele$_i$ V]]]

Example (44) is subjacent to sentences (28) through (30), in which the tonic pro-noun *ele* plays the role of an agreement element because its features raise to Person after Spell-Out and license the agreement relation of the clause with the external DP.

The consequence of this analysis for the subject is that in sentences in which there is no "hanging topic," there is a pro in the specifier of TP, whose features move to check Person, and the lexical subject occupies the same position as topics (i.e., is adjoined to PersP), as represented in (45):

(45)   [$_{PersP}$ DP [$_{PersP}$ ϕ_i [$_{-TP}$ pro$_i$ . . .]]]

Example (45) provides a representation of the externality of the subject in BP. How-ever, it is not possible to assign this structure to sentences like (19) and (20), in which the subject is not referential. Again, a structure like (45) is interpretable only if the subject is referential, since it implies a coreference relation between the ϕ-features of the null subject and the external DP. That this is impossible is evidenced by the grammaticality in BP of sentences like (46):

(46)   *Ninguém ele veio.
        nobody he came

The grammar of BP therefore shares with the grammar of EP the property of requiring two different structures for referential and nonreferential subjects. The question now is what is the position of the subject in sentences like (19) and (20). Again, my assumption about the complementary distribution of Agr and operator features allows me to suggest that since Person is not assigned an Agr feature in BP, it may receive operator features and attract quantified subjects in its specifier, yield-ing the following structure:

(47)   [$_{PersP}$ DP$_i$ [$_{TP}$ t$_i$ . . .]]]

This analysis predicts that, in the presence of an operator feature, there is no room for a "hanging topic" construction, since the ϕ-features of Person are checked by the quantifier. This prediction is borne out, as shown by the ill-formedness of sentences like (48):

(48)   *Quem o João ele encontrou?
        who John he met
        'Who did John meet?'

So far, I have accounted for two properties of BP: the "externality" of the sub-ject and the possibility for dislocated "hanging topic" constructions to be embedded. The fact that only the former is a shared property with EP derives from the fact that while both grammars generate structures in which the subject is outside the projection of the head that contains the verb, the position of this subject is different. It is in the specifier of C in EP, and is adjoined to Person in BP. This difference accounts for the two peculiar aspects of the pronominal syntax of these languages. In BP, tonic pronouns can play a role of agreement in embedded sentences, since they are clitics on Person at LF. In EP, enclisis is licit, and obligatory in root tensed clauses, if the subject is referential. The other phenomenon that strongly differentiates EP and BP is the existence in the latter of what I have been calling "subject topics," as illustrated in (22) through (24). I have shown that in sentences like (23), which contain a transitive verb, the external argument of the verb is completely inactive.

I will assume that in these constructions this argument is not projected. In the Minimalist framework, such an assumption is possible because there is no Projection Principle that requires all the arguments of a verb to be present in a derivation. The only requirement is that the output of the computation be interpretable by the "Conceptual-Intentional" performance system.

The sentences in (22) through (24) coexist in BP with structures in which the preverbal DP is dislocated and doubled by a resumptive pronoun, as illustrated in (49b), to be compared with (22), repeated here as (49a):

(49)   a. O relogio estragou o ponteiro.
          the clock broke the hand

       b. O relogio, estragou o ponteiro dele.
          the clock broke the hand of it

Example (49b) is a sentence of the type already exemplified in (28) through (30). The interesting question is what is the underlying difference between (49a) and (49b). I will consider their superficial differences:

1. There is a lexical resumptive pronoun in (b) but not in (a).
2. There can be agreement between the verb and the postverbal DP in (b) but not in (a), as illustrated in the following:
   a. *O relogio estragaram os ponteiros.
      the clock broke+pl the hands
   b. O relogio, estragaram os ponteiros dele.
      the clock broke+pl the hands of it
3. There can be agreement between the verb and the preverbal DP in (a) but not in (b), as illustrated in the following:
   a. Os relogios estragaram o ponteiro.
      the clocks broke+pl the hand
   b. *Os relogios, estragaram o ponteiro deles.
      the clocks broke+pl the hand of them

These facts show that there are two ways for the preverbal DP to be licensed, either by coindexation with a pronoun or by agreement with the verb. In the first case, the φ-features of the verb are checked in Spec, TP by an expletive pro. As I argued earlier, the features of the resumptive pronoun check the φ-features of Person in the covert syntax, and the topic adjoins to PersP. The structure of these sentences will be as follows:

(50) $[_{\text{PersP}}$ DP $[_{\text{PersP}}$ ϕi $[_{\text{TP}}$ pro$_{\text{expl}}$ V . . . ele$_i$]]]

The other option of derivation consists in starting from a numeration that contains no resumptive pronoun and no expletive pro. Since I assume that the ϕ-features of the verb are not interpretable in BP, the only way they can be checked in this case is against the ϕ-features of Person to which they raise by covert movement, as represented in (51):

(51) $[_{\text{PersP}}$ DP $[_{\text{PersP}}$ ϕi $[_{\text{TP}}$ V$_i$]]

I will assume that this movement has the effect of characterizing PersP as the extension of TP and consequently putting the DP adjoined to PersP into the checking domain of Tense. This entails that this DP is able to check the Agr feature of Tense.[30] The existence of agreement between the verb and the preverbal DP exemplified in (24) is the morphological effect of this derivation.

There is also a semantic effect. In effect, a further difference between (49a) and (49b) is that only in the former does a semantic restriction exist on the relationship between the preverbal and the postverbal DPs. Observe the contrast between (52) and (53):

(52)   a.   Esta mesa quebrou o pé.
           this table broke the leg

       b.   Esta mesa, quebrou o pé dela.
           this table broke the leg of it
           'This table had its leg broken.'

(53)   a.   *Esta mesa quebrou o pote.
           this table broke the pot

       b.   Esta mesa, quebrou o pote dela.
           this table broke the pot of it
           'The pot which is on this table is broken.'

Both (52b) and (53b) are well-formed, but only (52a) is possible. The ill-formedness of (53a) illustrates the fact that in the absence of a resumptive pronoun, the preverbal DP must be interpretable as the whole of which the postverbal DP is a part. This is the case between the table and its leg, but not between the table and the pot. This difference can be derived from the different grammatical status of the preverbal DP in the two structures. In (50), which underlies (52b) and (53b), it is in a peripheral, A'-position, where it is assigned any interpretation associated to the resumptive pronoun in argumental position. By contrast, in (51) there is no resumptive pronoun, and the preverbal position can be characterized as an A-position, since it is in the checking domain of Agr (cf. Rizzi 1991). The restriction illustrated here therefore derives from the compositional assignment by the VP of a semantic property to the subject, which implies a certain relationship between the two DPs.

Summarizing, all the topic-oriented constructions of BP derive from the lack of movement of the verb to Person, which has the following consequences:

1. φ-features from a pronominal argument covertly raise to Person in order to check it, and license a predication relation with a DP external to PersP.
2. In the absence of the projection of an external argument, the φ-features of V raise to Person in order to be checked. This characterizes Spec/Person as an A-position, with morphological and semantic consequences.

In all these cases, the subject is external in the sense defined here, since it is never in the specifier of the category containing the verb. This explains that an adverb can always show up between the subject and the verb in BP.

5.4 Concluding remarks

The contrastive description of ClP, EP, and BP provided in this chapter brings evidence for a unitary approach to the syntax of subjects and the syntax of pronouns, since it clearly appears that changes in the latter are correlated with changes in the former. Here this correlation was studied in the framework of the Minimalist Program, and I proposed that the feature that is responsible for the variation observed among languages is Agr, understood as a feature parametrically associated with functional categories. This proposal, together with the claim that there is a functional category above Tense that bears φ-features, makes it possible to account in a unitary way for the following aspects of the syntax of Portuguese:

1. The distribution of enclisis and proclisis in ClP and EP tensed sentences
2. The externality of the subject in EP and BP
3. The peculiar syntactic behavior of "hanging topic" constructions in BP
4. The "subject topic" constructions in BP

It also indicates that, despite their divergence, the three Portuguese grammars have an important common property that underlies their syntactic particularities. It is the fact that they all license constructions in which the subject and the verb are not immediately contained in the same maximal projection. This is at the origin of the possibility of enclisis in tensed sentences, as well as of the "subject topic" constructions of BP. The variation in the effects of this property is due to the nature of the functional categories involved and the peculiar interaction between AGR and the V-feature in each language. Note, however, that this analysis leads to a crucial distinction between the subjects that are external to the projection of the verb inside the boundaries of CP and the subjects that are outside CP. Nonreferential subjects can be licensed only in the former case.

Finally, the analysis developed here is based on the conception of deficient pronouns, in particular of clitics, as interpretable φ-features. This allows me to propose an account of enclisis in terms of a morphological affixation of the clitic to the verb in the lexicon, as a case of inflectional morphology. The generalization that emerges from the description of the distribution of enclisis and proclisis in EP, as well as in ClP, is that enclisis is incompatible with the existence of a phrase in the specifier of the head hosting the verb. I leave the exact explanation of this incompatibility for further research.

Notes

1. It must be noted, however, that it lost another common property of archaic languages: the so-called interpolation constructions, in which the verb and the clitic are separated by one or more phrases. In contrast with Barbosa (1996), among others, I assume that the residual interpolation constructions are archaisms not produced by the grammar of EP.

2. Example (1) is quoted in Ribeiro (1995); (3), (4), and (8) in Torres-Moraes (1995); (5) in Martins (1994); (2) and (6) are from Pe Vieira; and (7) from Marquesa de Alorna.

3. One of the most striking facts of the history of clitic placement in Portuguese is that there is a great variation in the relative frequency of the two constructions over the centuries, with two opposite movements. First, there is a gradual evolution from a very high proportion of enclisis in the twelfth century to an almost categorical proclisis in the sixteenth century (cf. Martins 1994; Lobo 1992). From the seventeenth century on, the reverse tendency is observed, with a strong variation between authors (Martins 1994; Torres-Moraes 1995). Finally, enclitic constructions are again dominant at the beginning of the nineteenth century, and are the only option from the second half of the nineteenth century on.

4. This claim does not imply that such sentences cannot be judged as well-formed by some speakers. They can be found in literary texts and are familiar to educated people. In addition, V2 continues to be possible in EP when the preverbal XP is focalized. In certain cases, it is not so easy to differentiate focus and topic in this position.

5. That is not to say that subject inversion is no more available in EP (cf. Ambar 1992), but it is a complex matter that goes beyond the limits of this chapter. If possible, a sentence like (4) in EP cannot have the interpretation in which the whole sequence VSO is the focus of the utterance. Cf. Zubizarreta (1995) for the various interpretations associated with this order.

6. At least, specific subjects, since, as is widely discussed in the works quoted earlier, quantified subjects require proclisis. But see later discussion for an important reason to argue that quantified subjects are as external as specific subjects.

7. Note that another difference between the authors concerns the difference in the position of the subject, and eventually of the verb, between enclitic and proclitic constructions, or between configurations with and without clitics. For Madeira (1992), for instance, subjects are in Spec, CP in enclitic constructions but are in Spec, IP in proclitic constructions.

8. This fact was already noted by me in Galves (1994) for BP. See the next section for the implications for this language.

9. Again, this claim must be qualified. Enclisis appears in BP formal registers, but it can be shown that its distribution is not grammatically but lexically and stylistically governed (cf. Galves 1997).

10. Furthermore, clitic clusters never occur, not even in written language.

11. Sentences (20b, c, and e) are drawn from the Norma Urbana Culta (NURC) corpus.

12. Duarte (1987) claims that a sentence like (22) is quite uninterpretable for a Portuguese speaker, since the only available interpretation is the one in which the clock intentionally broke its hand!

13. This claim has to do, as far as PF is concerned, with the hypothesis that words enter the derivation already inflected so that Agr has no phonetic features.

14. It must be emphasized that the agreement relation associated with this feature is independent of the morphological agreement, which depends on ϕ features checking.

15. Person was already proposed as a category projecting by its own in the context of the splitting of Agr (cf., for instance, Bianchi and Figueiredo Silva 1994).

16. As for why they move overtly, I will suggest that it is due to a constraint of morphological identity on the outputs of the computation that forces PF and LF to be made of the same words. If a clitic adjoined to a verb after Spell-Out, it would form a word with the verb at LF, but not at PF.

17. Benincà and Cinque also observe that in some languages, enclisis yields accentual modifications of the word, but this does not seem to occur with proclisis.

18. This is not an obvious claim (see Kayne 1991). But given the impossibility of inserting something between a clitic and a verb in Modern Romance languages, it seems to me that the burden of proof must be on the hypothesis that they occupy two distinct heads, which implies that there is a maximal projection boundary between them.

19. Benincà (1994:242) says that "in the medieval Romance languages (and in EP) complement clitics are enclitic to the inflected verb iff the specifier of the CP projection is empty." In Galves (1996:236) I formulate the distribution of enclisis and proclisis in the following terms: "(a) Proclisis is obligatory whenever there is an XP in Spec, Comp licensed by a Spec-head relation at PF with an operator in Comp. (b) Enclisis is obligatory whenever (a) does not apply."

20. This analysis accounts for the difference in clitic placement in Italian and French infinitival sentences in the following way. Belletti (1990) argued that verbs move to AgrS in Italian, in contrast with French, in which, as argued by Pollock (1989), the verb remains in a lower functional category, let us say Tense. In my terms, AgrS is Person. If I now assume that it is a common property to French and Italian that in infinitival sentences Agr is not associated with Person but with Tense, the verb adjoins to a head endowed with Agr in French (Tense), yielding proclisis, but it adjoins to a head that does not contain Agr in Italian (Person), yielding enclisis.

21. This parametrization concerns matrix sentences. In embedded sentences, the values +V and +Agr for Comp can be incompatible with properties of these clauses: the presence of a lexical complementizer and subcategorization features. This explains the asymmetries observed in V2 languages as well as in EP.

22. The facts presented here, however, show that clitics are licensed in a lower position. In Galves (1997), I argue that AgrO is strong in BP. In the framework adopted here, this can be expressed in terms of the assignment of an Agr-feature to v. This feature licenses the first and second person clitics, as well as object tonic pronouns and null objects.

23. It must be recalled, however, that ClP is not phenomenologically a V2 language, in the sense that the verb is not obligatorily the second element of the clause. V1 sequences are frequent in texts, either because the subject is null or because the lexical subject follows the verb, without any phrase in the preverbal position. Moreover, as mentioned earlier, even V2 sequences can be analyzed as Verb-first, with the first phrase outside CP. This is arguably a consequence of the fact that ClP is a pro-drop language.

24. It is outside the scope of this chapter to discuss the V2 order optionally found in EP with *wh* and focalized phrases.

25. Zubizarreta (1982) explained the absence of "that-t effects" in EP, which is a language that does not display free inversion, by positing an abstract que >qui rule. Following Rizzi (1990), this rule can be interpreted as the reflex of Agr in Comp. In Galves (1992b), I give further evidence for this analysis on the basis of other aspects of EP syntax.

26. Note that this analysis suggests that the ϕ features of the verb are interpretable in EP, contrary to Chomsky's claim that they never are. I will not address the question of how null subjects are licensed, but it seems natural to admit that in languages in which the licensing of pro is dependent on the verbal morphology, the ϕ-features of the verb are interpretable. In the framework proposed here, in which weak pronouns are interpretable ϕ-features, this amounts to assigning a pronominal nature to the verbal agreement of pro-drop languages; cf. n. 25.

27. I will argue later that the same option is available in BP.

28. In contrast with what I claimed earlier about EP, the assumption here is that the ϕ-features of the verb are noninterpretable in BP. Later I will note that this assumption is crucial to explain another kind of topic-oriented construction. The fact that BP is a Null Subject Language is not contradictory with this claim, since both the impoverishment of the verbal morphology and the constraints on the distribution of null subjects in this language (cf. Figueiredo Silva 1994) suggest that they are not identified by the verbal morphology. The consequences of the analysis proposed here for the licensing of null subjects in BP are beyond the scope of this text.

29. The subscript indices represent the chains formed by movement.

30. This analysis raises complex theoretical issues concerning the status of strong features that I will not address here. It is sufficient to point out that it does not contradict what has been assumed in this chapter about Agr.

References

Adams, M. 1987. "Old French, Null Subjects and Verb Second Phenomena." Ph.D. dissertation, UCLA.

Ambar, M. 1992. *Para uma Sintaxe da Inversão Sujeito/Verbo em Português*. Lisbon: Colibri.

Barbosa, P. 1991. "Clitic Placement in EP." Ms., MIT.

———. 1996. "Clitic Placement in European Portuguese and the Position of Subjects." In A. L. Aalpern and A. M. Zwicky (eds.) *Approaching Second: Second Position Clitics and Related Phenomena*. Stanford, Calif.: CSLI Publications.

Belletti, A. 1990. *Generalized Verb-Movement: Aspects of Verb Movement*. Turin: Rosenberg and Sellier.

Benincà, P. 1989. *Grande Grammatica Italiana di Consultazione*. Bologna: Il Mulino.

———. 1994. *La variazione sintattica*. Studi di Dialettologia Romanza. Bologna: Il Mulino.

Benincà, P., and G. Cinque. 1993. "Su Alcune Differenze fra Enclisi e Proclisi." In *Omaggio a Gianfranco Folena*. Padua: Editoriale Programma.

Bianchi, V., and Maria Cristina Figueiredo Silva. 1994. "On Some Properties of Agreement-Object in Italian and Brazilian Portuguese." In M. Mazzola (ed.) *Issues and Theory in Romance Linguistics: Selected Papers from the Linguistic Symposium on Romance Languages XXIII*. Washington, D.C.: Georgetown University Press.

Cardinaletti, A. 1994. "On Cliticization in Germanic Languages." In H. Van Riemsdijk and L. Rizzi (eds.), *Clitics and Their Hosts*. Tilburg: ESF-Eurotyp, Tilburg University.

Cardinaletti, A., and I. Roberts. 1991. "Clause structure and X-second." In press. In W. Chao and G. Horrocks (eds.) *Levels of Representation*. Berlin: Mouton.

Cardinaletti, A., and M. Starke. 1994. "The Typology of Structural Deficiency, on the Three Grammatical Classes." *Working Papers in Linguistics* 4-2, 41–109, University of Venice.

Chomsky, N. 1995a. "Bare Phrase-Structure." In G. Webelhuth (ed.) *Government and Binding Theory and the Minimalist Program*. Oxford: Blackwell.

———. 1995b. *The Minimalist Program*. Cambridge, Mass.: MIT Press.

Cinque, G. 1983. "'Topic' Constructions in Some European Languages and 'Connectedness.'" In K. Ehlich and H. Van Riemsdijk (eds.) *Connectedness in Sentence, Discourse and Text*. Tilburg Studies in Language and Literature 4.

Corver, N., and D. Delfitto. 1993. "Feature Asymmetry and the Nature of Pronoun Movement." Ms., Tilburg University, University of Utrecht.

Costa, J. 1996. "Adverb Positioning and V-movement in English: Some More Evidence." *Studia Linguistica*: 50(1): 1–14.

Dobrovie-Sorin, C. 1994. "The Typology of Pronouns and the Distinction between Syntax and Morpho-phonology." Ms., University of Paris VII.

Duarte, I. 1987. "A construão de topicalizaão o Na Gramática do Português: Regência, Ligação e Condições Sobre o Movimento." Ph.D. dissertation, University of Lisbon.

Duarte, M. E. 1995. "A Perda do Princípio 'Evite Pronome' no Português Brasileiro." Unpublished Ph.D. thesis, University of Campinas.

Everett, D. 1996. Why There Are No Clitics: An Alternative Perspective on Pronominal Allomorphy. SIL and University of Texas at Arlington, Publications in Linguistics 123.

Farrell, P. 1990. "Null Objects in Brazilian Portuguese." *Natural Language and Linguistic Theory* 8: 325–346.

Figueiredo Silva, M. C. 1994. "La Position Sujet en Portugais Brésilien." Ph.D. dissertation, University of Geneva.

Fontana, J. 1992. "Phrase Structure and the Syntax of Clitics in the History of Spanish." Unpublished Ph.D. thesis, University of Pennsylvania.

Galves, C. 1992a. "Clitic-Placement in European Portuguese: Evidence for a Non-homogeneous Theory of Enclisis." Proceedings of the Workshop on Portuguese, Associação Portuguesa de Linguistica, Lisbon, 61–80.

———. 1992b. "Enclise, Infinitif Fléchi et Extraction du Sujet: Evidences pour Deux Accords en Portugais Européen." Paper presented at Second Colloquium on Generative Grammar, Vitoria, Spain.

———. 1994. "V-movement, Levels of Representation and the Structure of S." Revised version of the communication presented at the Thirteenth GLOW Colloquium, Cambridge 1990. Printed in *Letras de Hoje*, 96, Porto Alegre, 1994, 35–58.

———. 1996. "Clitic-placement and Parametric Changes in Portuguese." *Selected Papers from the 24th Linguistic Symposium on Romance Languages*. Washington, D.C.: Georgetown University Press, 227–239.

———. 1997. "La Syntaxe Pronominale du Portugais Brésilien et la Typologie des Pronoms." In A. Zribi-Hertz (ed.) *Les Pronoms*, 11–34. Saint-Denis; Presses Universitaires de Vincennes.

Haegeman, L. 1994. "The Distribution of Object Pronouns in West Flemish." In H. Van Riemsdijk and L. Rizzi (eds.) *Clitics and Their Hosts*. Tilburg: ESF-Eurotyp, Tilburg University.

Kato, M. 1993. "Recontando a História das Relativas em Uma Perspectiva Paramétrica." In M. Kato and I. Roberts (eds.) *Viagem Diacrônica Pelas Fases do Português Brasileiro*. Campinas: Ed. da UNICAMP.

Kayne, R. 1991. "Romance Clitics, Verb Movement, and PRO." *Linguistic Inquiry* 22: 647–686.

Lobo, T. 1992. "A Colocação do Clíticos em Português: Duas Sincronias em Confronto." Unpublished MA thesis, University of Lisbon.

Madeira, A. M. 1992. "On Clitic Placement in European Portuguese." In H. van de Koot (ed.) *UCL Working Papers in Linguistics* 4. University College, London.

Manzini, R. 1992. "Second Position Dependencies." Paper presented at 8th Workshop on Germanic Syntax, University of Tromso.

Manzini, M. R. 1994. "Triggers for Verb-Second: Germanic and Romance." *Linguistic Review* 11: 299–314.

Martins, A. M. 1993. "Clitic Placement from Old to Modern European Portuguese." Paper presented at the Thirteenth International Conference on Historical Linguistics, Los Angeles.

———. 1994. "Clíticos na História do Português." Ph.D. dissertation, University of Lisbon.

Nash, L. 1997. "La Partition Personnelle dans les Langues Ergatives." In A. Zribi-Hertz (ed.) *Les Pronoms*, 11–34. Saint-Denis: Presses Universitaires de Vincennes.

Pollock, J. Y. 1989. "Verb-Movement, Universal Grammar, and the Structure of IP." *Linguistic Inquiry* 20: 365–425.

Pontes, E. 1981. "Da Importância do Tópico em Português." Anais do Encontro Nacional de Linguística, Rio de Janeiro.

Raposo, E. 1995. "Clitic Position and Verb Movement in European Portuguese." Paper presented at the Fifth Colóquio internacional de Gramática Gerativa, Corunã, Spain.

Ribeiro, I. M. 1995. "A Sintaxe da Ordem no Português Arcaico: O Efeito V2." Ph.D. dissertation, University of Campinas.

Rizzi, L. 1990. *Relativized Minimality*. Cambridge, Mass.: MIT Press.

———. 1991. "Proper Head-Government and the Definition of A-Positions." *GLOW Newsletter*, 26: 46–47.

Rouveret, A. 1987. "Syntaxe des Dépendances Lexicales: Identité et Iidentification dans la Théorie Syntaxique." Ph.D. Paris VII.

———. 1992. " Clitic Placement, Focus and the Wackernagel Position in European Portuguese." Paper presented at the European Science Foundation workshop on clitics, Donostia.

———. 1996. *Clitics, Subjects and Tense in European Portuguese*. Ms., University of Paris.

Salvi, G. 1990. "La Sopravvivenza Della Legge di Wackernagel Nei Dialetti Occidentali Della Peninsola Iberica." *Medioevo Romanzo* 15: 177–210.

Teyssier, P. 1974. *Grammaire de la langue portugaise, Portugal—Brésil*. Paris: Klinksieck.

Torres-Moraes, M. A. 1995. "Do Português Clássico ao Português Moderno: um Estudo da Cliticização e do Movimento do Verbo. Ph.D. dissertation, University of Campinas.

Uriagereka, J. 1995. "Syntax of Clitic Placement in Western Romance." *Linguistic Inquiry* 26: 79–123.

Zubizarreta, Maria Luisa. 1982. "Theoretical Implications of Subject Extraction in Portuguese." *Linguistic Review* 2: 79–96.

———. 1996. Prosody, Focus, and Word Order." Ms., University of Southern California.

Zwart, C. J. W. 1994. "Notes on Clitics in Dutch." In H. Van Riemsdijk and L. Rizzi (eds.) *Clitics and Their Hosts*. Tilburg: ESF-Eurotyp, Tilburg University.

ANA MARIA MARTINS

A Minimalist Approach to Clitic Climbing

In the Minimalist framework (Chomsky 1993, 1994), movement is driven by morphological necessity, that is, movement is possible only for the purposes of morphological feature checking. In Kayne's (1989) account of clitic climbing (CC), languages displaying this phenomenon are showed to have certain properties, induced by the nature of INFL, which make clitic extraction out of an infinitival clause available. A minimalist approach to this subject, however, will have to show that clitics *must* move out of the infinitival clause, not that they *can* move, since the principles of economy would preclude movement if it were not necessary to satisfy morphological requirements. Postulating a restructuring rule (which maps a biclausal structure into a monoclausal one), applying optionally in some languages as in Rizzi's account (1982) and several others, does not hold water on minimalist assumptions either. My goal in this chapter is to show why movement of the clitic out of an infinitival clause is in certain instances needed. I will restrict my attention to Romance.

An object clitic originating in an embedded infinitival clause can be extracted from it and cliticized to the main verb in three types of configurations: Control (usually Subject Control, but see (51)), Exceptional Case Marking (ECM), and Subject Raising configurations. However, not every verb belonging to these syntactic types allows CC; a great deal of synchronic and diachronic variation is observed with respect to the constituency of the relevant set.[1] In general, the verbs that more regularly behave as CC verbs across dialects (and idiolects) have modal, aspectual, or temporal import, although they are not (English-type) syntactic auxiliaries. Relevant examples are given in the following. Sentences (1) to (3)—from Italian, Spanish, and Portuguese, respectively—display the phenomenon of CC with Subject Control verbs. Sentences (4) and (5)—from French and Portuguese, respectively—present CC with ECM (perception and causative) verbs. And sentence (6), from Italian, shows CC with a Subject Raising verb. Object clitics are given in bold type.

(1) Piero **lo** vuole / sta per / comincia a / finisce di leggere.[2]
     P. it wants / is for / begins to / finishes of read-INFN

     'P. wants / is going / is beginning / is finishing to read it.'

(2)   **Te lo** quiero / prefiero / vino a / acabo de dar.
       you it want / prefer / come to / finish of give-INFN
       'I want to give / prefer to give / come to give / have just given it to you.'

(3)   O polícia quer-**me** / pode-**me** / vai-**me** multar por excesso de velocidade.
       the cop wants-me / can-me / go-me fine-INFN for excess of velocity
       'The cop wants / can / is going to fine me for breaking the speed limit.'

(4)   Cette maison, je **l'** ai vu bâtir.
       this house, I it has seen build-INFN
       'This house, I saw building it.'

(5)   Ele mandou-**nos** dizer que não podia vir.
       he send-us tell that not could come
       'He sent to tell us he couldn't come.'

(6)   **Mi** comincerà a / protebbe piovere sulla testa da un momento all' altro.[3]
       me will begin to / might rain on the head from one moment to the other
       'It will begin to / might rain on my head any minute.'

In contrast to other Romance languages, French admits CC only in ECM configurations; the French counterparts of either (1) to (3) or (6) are unacceptable:

(7)   *Je **te le** veux / préfère / viens / viens de donner. (equivalent of (2))

(8)   *Il **me** comencera à / pourrait pleuvoir sur la tête . . . (equivalent of (6))

On the other hand, in the Romance languages where CC is productive (being displayed in Control, ECM, and Subject Raising configurations), the phenomenon is manifested to a smaller extent with Subject Raising than with Control and ECM predicates. So, a prototypical verb of the Subject Raising class such as 'seem' (It. *parere* or *sembrare*; Sp. and Port. *parecer*) is not a CC verb in Spanish and Portuguese, and it appears to be only marginally accepted as a CC verb in Italian. Napoli (1981:883) groups *sembrare* with the verbs that "cause doubts in [her] consultants' minds, or upon which they disagree, sometimes strongly"; Rizzi (1982:2, 32) marks with "*?" sentences with CC having as matrix verbs either *parere* or *sembrare*:

(9)   ***Lo** parece saber poco.   (Spanish; From Luján 1980:390)
       it seems know-INFN little
       'He seems to know it little.'

(10)   *Ele parece-**o** odiar.   (Portuguese; my own judgment)
       he seems-him hate-INFN
       'He seems to hate him.'

(11)   **Lo** sembra capire.   (Italian, from Napoli 1981:864, based on M. Nespor
and some of A. Radford's consultants' judgments)
it seems understand-INFN

'He seems to understand it.'

(12)   *?**Gli** sembra piovere sulla testa.   (Italian, from Rizzi 1982:32)
him-DAT seems rain-INFN on the head

'It seems to rain on him on the head / It seems to rain on his head.'

(13)   *?Angela **lo** pareva avere riaccompagnato a casa.   (from Rizzi 1982:3)
A. him-ACC seemed have-INFN taken to home

'A. seemed to have taken him home.'

In this chapter, I will concentrate on Control and ECM predicates, leaving aside Subject Raising predicates. I nevertheless claim that the hypothesis I will argue for extends to Subject Raising configurations as well.

The account of CC I will propose is built on the assumption that infinitival complements of CC constructions are TPs, and being so, its structure lacks the position where clitics must move, which I take to be AgrS. In this circumstance, clitics are forced to move to the matrix AgrS,[4] in order to check a certain morphological feature. The idea that the infinitival complements of CC constructions have a "reduced" structure is not new; it has been argued for in previous accounts of CC (the VP-complementation analyses of Fresina 1982, Goodall 1984, Strozer 1976, Picallo 1990, and Moore 1994, among others). Nevertheless, there are several avenues for this approach, made available by Pollock's (1989) Split-Infl Hypothesis, as well as by recent research on the licensing of PRO and the structure of infinitives, which have not been explored yet. It is my purpose to take this direction.

6.1 On (clause internal) clitic movement

The questions of why clitics move and where they move to have long been objects of debate. A prominent view has been that Romance object clitics (overtly) move higher than full object DPs and have as a final target a functional projection. Authors disagree, however, over what the trigger for movement is and which functional position the clitics move to. As for the motivation for movement, some authors have proposed an idea that links clitic movement to the "specific" character of clitics (Sportiche 1992; Uriagereka 1992, 1995; Delfitto and Corver 1995; and Martins (1994a, b). This hypothesis has been implemented in different ways depending on whether movement induced by specificity is considered to have a semantic or a morphological trigger and on what the relevant structural position with respect to specificity is (this being the position where clitics are hosted)—'Acc', 'Dat', and so on in Sportiche (1992); 'F' in Uriagereka (1995); 'Σ' in Delfitto and Corver (1995); 'AgrS' in Martins (1994a, b).

In earlier works (Martins 1994a, b), I have assumed that specificity is morphologically encoded, therefore being, under minimalist assumptions, a trigger for movement. In order to check a strong specific feature, clitics move to the AgrS domain, the same domain where nonpronominal "specific" objects move in languages with Object Scrambling (such as some Germanic and Old Romance languages). Clitics differ from full DPs in that the specific feature on clitics is universally strong, and so clitic movement must always take place in the overt syntax. Moreover, unlike full DPs, clitics move like heads, thus being able to adjoin to AgrS. Elaborating on Diesing's Mapping Hypothesis (Diesing 1992), I take TP as the LF border separating nonspecific elements (inside TP) from specific elements (scoped out of TP).[5] The specific character of clitics leads them to incorporate into AgrS, the functional head immediately outside the TP border (assuming Chomsky's 1993 clause structure). In fact, we can think of the specific feature associated to the clitic as being randomly assigned to one of the functional heads outside the TP border. Movement of the clitic higher than AgrS to check this feature, however, would violate the Shortest Movement economy principle (Chomsky 1993:14–18; 1994:24), leading the derivation to crash. As for the assumption that TP is the border for specificity, it can be deduced if we admit that (i) all predicates have a Davidsonian event argument, and this is also true of nouns, even noneventive ones (Higginbotham 1987); (ii) specificity is just an element taking wide scope with respect to the Davidsonian event operator in the sentence; in other terms, a DP is specific iff its event variable is not bound by the event operator, being instead bound by the discourse (Herburger 1994); and (iii) the event operator is located in TP (Herburger 1994 ; Hornstein 1994).[6]

Since clitics move to AgrS, clitic placement will depend on how high the verb moves. Following Laka (1990), I assume that the structure of the clause includes a projection of the functional head Σ, which dominates AgrS. Σ is the *locus* for truth-value operators like 'Negation' and 'Affirmation'.[7] Like T and Agr, Σ is an inflectional head with V-features that may be either strong or weak. In languages where Σ has strong V-features, the verb moves up to Σ in the overt syntax (in order to check features), therefore going past the clitic position. Hence, enclisis is derived as in the following Portuguese sentence:

(14) $[_{\Sigma P} O António_i [_{\Sigma'} [_{\Sigma} viu_j] [_{AgrSP} t_i [_{AgrS'} [_{AgrS} o [_{AgrS} t_j]] [_{TP} \ldots$[8]
        the A. saw him

In languages where Σ has weak V-features, movement for checking purposes is delayed until LF (in satisfaction of the principle of economy Procrastinate—Chomsky 1993:30–31, 34). Thus, the verb does not overtly move higher than AgrS. Therefore, proclisis surfaces as in the following Spanish sentence:

(15) $[_{\Sigma P} Antonio_i [_{\Sigma'} [_{\Sigma}] [_{AgrSP} t_i [_{AgrS'} [_{AgrS} lo [_{AgrS} vio]] [_{TP} \ldots$
        A. him saw

This analysis finds support in the fact that it can thoroughly account for the cross-linguistic correlation found in Romance between enclisis in tensed clauses and the possibility of VP-deletion, if we claim that both phenomena depend upon the strength of the functional category Σ. Romance languages fall into two groups with respect to the nature of Σ: Galician and Portuguese have strong Σ; Spanish, Catalan, French, and Italian have weak Σ. Licensing of VP-deletion depends on Σ having strong V-features. The null VP in the VP-deletion construction is licensed in a Spec-head relation to strong Σ, Σ containing V-features (similarly to the way the null category *pro* is licensed, in a Spec-head relation to AgrS, AgrS containing strong features—see Chomsky 1993:10). Therefore, VP-deletion is allowed in Portuguese and in Galician but is not an option in Spanish, Catalan, French, and Italian (for details and relevant examples, see Martins 1994b). As described earlier, enclisis in tensed clauses is the outcome of verb movement to Σ in the overt syntax, clitics being adjoined to AgrS (see (14) versus (15)); verb movement in the overt syntax takes place only when the V-features of Σ are strong. Therefore, enclisis is found in the same set of languages where VP-deletion is a possibility, that is, Portuguese and Galician, being excluded from Catalan, Spanish, French, and Italian, which instead display proclisis.

Clitic placement in tensed clauses is the same regardless of whether CC is at stake—compare (14) and (15) with examples (1) through (6). Space considerations preclude discussion of clitic placement in infinitival clauses when CC does not take place. I will just note that enclisis in infinitival clauses and enclisis in finite clauses are likely to be independent phenomena, with only the latter having to do with the nature of Σ. Verb movement past the clitic in infinitival clauses is possibly induced by a temporal dependency between the matrix and the embedded verb (see Kayne 1991). That is why it occurs in languages such as Spanish and Italian, which have proclisis in tensed clauses. In French, infinitival V-movement appears to be delayed until LF, and so proclisis occurs in both infinitival and tensed clauses.

6.2 On the structure of infinitival complements

As was shown in examples (1) through (5), both Control predicates and ECM predicates allow for CC. The standard characterization of these constructions in the Principles and Parameters (P&P) framework, however, takes their infinitival complements to be structurally different; under the standard P&P approach, infinitival complements of Control verbs are CPs, while infinitival complements of ECM verbs are IPs. This distinction is assumed in order to account for the contrasting behavior of control and ECM verbs with respect to the subject's nature of their infinitival complements. Sentences (16) to (19) exemplify the contrast to be analyzed:

(16)   Miss Marple tried [PRO to confuse the murderer]

(17)   *Miss Marple tried [the murderer/him to be confused]

(18)   *Miss Marple believed [PRO to confuse the murderer]

(19)   Miss Marple believed [the murderer/him to be confused]

While Control configurations permit PRO as the subject of an infinitive (see (16)) and disallow a lexical subject in such a position (see (17)), ECM configurations show just the reverse behavior (see (18) and (19)). Under the P&P approach, this is accounted for given the different categorial status of the infinitival clauses. The CP complement of Control verbs, like *try*, is a barrier to government of the complement's subject by the main verb. So PRO is not governed and, not having a governing category, can satisfy the contradictory requirements of Conditions A and B of Binding Theory,[9] being therefore admitted in this configuration. To the contrary, the IP complement of ECM predicates, like *believe*, is not a barrier for government; hence, PRO is governed. PRO now having a governing category, either Condition A or Condition B of Binding Theory is violated; thus PRO is excluded from this configuration. On the other hand, a lexical subject is allowed in the complement of *believe* but not in the complement of *try*, because only *believe* can assign Case (accusative) to its complement's subject, Case being assigned under government. Therefore, in (19) the Case Filter[10] is satisfied, whereas it is violated in (17), leading to the observed ungrammaticality.

Chomsky and Lasnik (1993) show that this Binding-theoretic account of the distribution of PRO is unsatisfactory on both theoretical and empirical grounds. Since, according to the Case-theoretic account, PRO appears in non-Case positions, a disjunctive version of the Visibility Condition, instead of a true generalization, is imposed: "A chain is visible for Q-marking if it contains a Case-position (necessarily, its head) or is headed by PRO." Moreover, even with this unsatisfactory formulation, the Visibility Condition leaves unexplained the empirical fact that PRO is like other arguments in that it is forced to move from a non-Case position, and cannot move from a Case-marked position (see Chomsky and Lasnik 1993:560–561).

Given these problems, Chomsky and Lasnik propose a new approach to the phenomena in question. The so-called Case-theoretic account assumes that PRO, like other arguments, has Case, but a Case different from the familiar ones. PRO is now regarded as a "minimal" NP argument, accordingly bearing null Case (which is licensed by certain instances of nonfinite Tense[11]). Being so, it is expected that PRO is permitted to move from a non-Case position to a position where it has Case checked, and is not allowed to move from a Case position.[12] Furthermore, the Visibility Condition can, under the Case-theoretic account, be simplified: "A chain is visible for Q-marking if it contains a Case-position."

This kind of account of the complementary distribution of PRO-subjects and lexical subjects in infinitives can dispense with the notion of government. It suffices that Case be defined as a Spec-head relation (Case checking), not a government one (Case assignment). It thus fits the Minimalist framework, which does not incorporate "government" as a primitive. The Case-theoretic account has been assumed and worked out by different authors in the current Minimalist literature, and further theoretical and empirical arguments have been raised to support it.[13]

It should be noticed now that under the current approach to the syntax of Control and ECM constructions, the CP-complement versus IP-complement stipulation is no longer necessary. There is no need to specify that Control verbs c-select CP infinitival complements, since what licenses PRO in (16) is the ability of the embedded T to check null Case (and not the fact that PRO is not governed). On the other hand, what rules out the lexical NP in (17) is its incompatibility with null Case, which only PRO, the "minimal" argument, can bear. Movement from the position where null Case is checked to the position where accusative Case would be checked (i.e., Spec of AgrO of the main clause) is not allowed because "movement from one Case position to another is excluded even when the former position licenses the 'wrong' Case for the NP" (Lasnik 1993:67).[14]

We can thus assume that both Control and ECM infinitives are IPs. Yet we would be left with the stipulation that whereas the infinitival complements of the relevant verbs are IPs, their finite complements are CPs. Boskovic's (1996) work goes beyond this undesirable state of affairs by showing that c-selection of infinitival clauses can be al together dispensed with, which lends support to Pesetsky's (1982, 1992) claim that c-selection should be eliminated as an independent syntactic mechanism.[15] If c-selection is not at stake, infinitival clauses could in principle freely be either CPs or IPs. Boskovic, however, brings up empirical evidence showing that in certain instances Control infinitives must be IPs.[16] He then derives this fact from a Principle of Economy of Representation borrowed from Law (1991). Boskovic's version is given in the following:

The Minimal Structure Principle (MSP)
Provided that lexical requirements of relevant elements are satisfied, if two representations have the same lexical structure, and serve the same function, then *the* representation that has fewer projections is to be chosen as *the* syntactic representation serving that function.

Given the MSP (whose theoretical and empirical validity both Law and Boskovic establish), we expect that infinitival clauses are CPs only if their CP status is imposed by lexical requirements independent of c-selection, as in the case of infinitival complements that are interpreted as Q(uestions). Take, for example, the verb *wonder*, which s-selects Q, therefore including a *wh-* word in its complement clause. If a verb such as *wonder* takes an IP complement, as in (20), the construction is ruled out because the [+wh] feature of the *wh-* word cannot be checked:

(20)   *I wonder [$_{IP}$ PRO to believe what]

We also expect that certain types of finite complements are IPs. Law (1991) shows it is so with respect to zero null operator relatives (such as *the man [Op$_i$ John saw t$_i$]*); Boskovic makes a similar point, taking into account English zero declarative finite complements (such as *I believe [John likes Mary]*) and finite complements of American Sign Language verbs such as THINK.

To summarize, current work on the categorial status of infinitival complement clauses has shown that, unless lexical requirements (s-selection or l-selection) make it necessary that CP be projected, infinitival clauses are IPs, not CPs. Their IP status is imposed by a Principle of Economy of Representation.

Assuming the Split-Infl Hypothesis (Pollock 1989), the next step is to ask what kind of IPs infinitival clauses are: maximal IPs (i.e., either AgrSPs or ΣPs, depending on the clause structure adopted) or reduced IPs (i.e., TPs). Thráinsson (1994) investigates the structure of Control and modal infinitival complements in Icelandic, comparing them to each other and to finite complements. He hypothesizes that finite complements are CPs, Control complements are AgrSPs, and modal complements are TPs. Since in Romance, contrary to Icelandic, modal predicates do not display a peculiar syntax, behaving instead as regular Control verbs, I will not present Thráinsson's analysis of modal constructions, concentrating instead on Control ones. By assuming that Control infinitival complements have a more reduced structure than finite complements, Thráinsson accounts for a wide range of facts in a straightforward way. I will now look at the proposed structures:

(21) Hann segir [$_{CP}$ aD [$_{AgrSP}$[hún lesi [$_{TP}$ ... [$_{AgrOP}$ bækur ...
      he says that she reads books

(22) Hann lofar [$_{AgrSP}$ aD [$_{TP}$ PRO lesa [$_{AgrOP}$ bækur ...
      he promises to read books

Because the element introducing the Control complement in (22) is homophonous with the complementizer in (21) (in Icelandic and in other Scandinavian languages), many linguists have assumed that they are "the same" element and occupy the same structural position, namely, C. Thráinsson alternatively proposes that aD in (22) is an infinitive marker occupying AgrS (maybe because "AgrS° of control clauses bears a null agreement feature which can be checked off against this default aD-head"). The PRO-subject of the infinitival complement clause moves up to Spec of TP in order to check Case (T bears the null Case feature), and the infinitival verb moves (through AgrO) to T, which has strong V-features.[17]

Arguments supporting Thráinsson's analysis are built on the basis of word order, Topicalization (i.e., Focus movement), and language acquisition facts. Verb/adverbials' relative word order brings evidence for verb movement to T in Control complements in Icelandic but not for additional movement to AgrS. This is in harmony with theory-internal considerations; since the infinitival form of the verb does not include agreement morphology, it is expected that there is no trigger for movement of the verb to AgrS (given that Spec of TP be projected and thus T does not have to move to AgrS in order to check Case—see Jonas and Bobaljik 1993). As for Topicalization, it is permitted in embedded finite clauses in Icelandic, but it is not allowed in Control infinitival clauses; this is exactly what Thráinsson's analysis predicts (given the general consensus that topicalized phrases move to some position to the left of AgrS). If infinitival aD occupied C, just like the finite complementizer, it would be expected that topicalized phrases would occur equally freely in infinitival complements and in finite complements. With respect to language acquisition, the fact that Icelandic children acquire the infinitival marker and the correspondent infinitival complements earlier than the (phonologically identical) complementizer and the correspondent finite complements goes against the hypothesis that finite and infinitival complements have identical structure.[18]

In Romance, contrary to Icelandic, Control infinitivals are in most instances not introduced by an infinitival marker, as the following Portuguese sentence (with a bare infinitive) shows:

(23) Ele prometeu [$_{XP}$ ler livros]
      he promised read-INFN books

Under the hypothesis that Thráinsson's analysis of Control infinitivals is valid across languages, what would be the nature of the XP in (23)? Recall that the Minimal Structure Principle requires that every functional projection be motivated by the satisfaction of lexical requirements; unless a functional projection is "needed," in the MSP terms, it cannot be part of a structure. Putting together Thráinsson's and Boskovic's insights leads us to conclude thus that in (23) XP = TP; since there is no infinitival marker to occupy AgrS, this position is not "needed" and therefore cannot be projected.

In order to account for the distribution of bare and *to* infinitives in English, Nunes (1992) proposes that infinitival complements may be either AgrSPs or TPs, depending on the selection properties of matrix verbs (Nunes refers to c-selection, but his account could be recast in terms of s-selection). Nunes's work relies on theoretical concepts not available in the minimalist framework, particularly the concept of government. Hence, from Nunes's analysis I will retain only the central ideas he argues for, leaving aside the details of the technical implementation. Following Raposo (1986), Nunes takes infinitival clauses to be partially characterized as a projection of a [–V, +N] element, the infinitival morpheme, which, being nominal, needs to satisfy the Case Filter. When a bare infinitive occurs, the relevant Case is licensed by the matrix verb. This is only possible, however, if the matrix verb and the embedded T, which is the *locus* for the infinitival morpheme, are close enough to define a local relation; this is the case when the infinitival clause is a reduced IP, namely, a TP. Otherwise, a *to*-infinitive occurs, *to* being, in Nunes's analysis a (dummy) preposition inserted as a Last Resort device to license Case. This Last Resort strategy is necessary because when the infinitival clause is a maximal IP (an AgrSP in Nunes's terms), the embedded T is too far away from the main verb for the relevant local relation to obtain. *To*-insertion can be avoided in an AgrSP configuration in languages that allow for the embedded T to raise to a position close enough to the matrix verb. Nunes shows that this was the case in Old English; in Modern English, however, this strategy is not available. Nunes's analysis provides a straightforward account of various changes involving infinitival constructions, as well as of the distribution of bare and *to*-infinitives in Modern English.

In this section I have summarized recent research on the categorial status of infinitives, showing that infinitival complements are by and large IPs, and moreover may be either maximal IPs or TPs. This result has been independently reached by different authors and established on a basis unrelated to clitic behavior. I can now proceed to a more detailed presentation of my hypothesis, which crucially relies on that result.

6.3 On clitic climbing

I am hypothesizing that CC results from the clitic having to move out of the infinitival clause in order to have an inherent specific feature checked, a situation that arises whenever the infinitival clause is a TP. Here I give (simplified) structural representations of the sentences in (24) and (25), visualizing the clitic path in CC structures. I take the object clitic to move first as an X^{max} to Spec of AgrO, where it gets Case checked; then the clitic moves as an $X°$ from head to head, at each step being excorporated, until it reaches the matrix AgrS and has its specific feature checked. Proceeding this way, movement of the clitic satisfies the Minimal Link Condition (see Chomsky 1994). In the representation of (25), I ignore the fact that perhaps in French Spec of TP is not projected (see Jonas and Bobaljik 1993); that is irrelevant for the point I am presenting here. It should also be noted that sentence (25) is structurally ambiguous. The structure shown below is the one in which *laisser* enters an English-type ECM configuration, not a French-type causative configuration.[19]

(24)   Ele queria-**te** ver   (Portuguese)
he wanted-you see-INF

'He wanted to see you.'

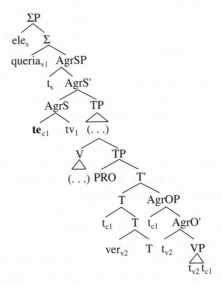

(25)   Je te **les** laisse voir.   (French)
I you them let see-INFN

'I let you see them.'

It is a well-known fact that CC cannot take place when a negative word expressing sentential negation occurs in the infinitival complement clause. This is shown by (27), which is ungrammatical, although French *faire* 'make' marginally allows for a negative infinitival complement.

(26) ??Cela a fait ne pas manger sa soupe à l' enfant. (Kayne 1989:242)
     that has made NEG not eat-INFN his soup to the child

(27) *Cela l' a fait ne pas manger à l' enfant. (Kayne 1989:242)
     that it has made NEG not eat-INFN to the child

Kayne (1989) proposes that Neg, a head of the same general class as C and I, acts as a barrier for clitic movement. In contrast to (27), however, (28), displaying clitic raising of the embedded subject to the matrix clause, is, like (26), marginally acceptable:

(28) ??Cela lui a fait ne pas manger sa soupe. (Kayne 1989:242)
     that him-DAT has made NEG not eat-INFN his soup

To account for the contrast between (27) and (28), Kayne (1989:242) supposes that "*ne* is hierarchically below *à l' enfant* but above *sa soupe*: . . . [ne pas [manger sa soupe]] à l' enfant*," therefore being out of the way of the subject clitic but in the way of the object clitic. This proposal cannot straightforwardly deal with the facts of other Romance languages, however. Take, for example, Portuguese. The sentences in (29) show that CC over a negative head leads to ungrammaticality, whereas (30) shows that raising of the subject clitic is admitted:

(29) *O médico mandou-**lho** não dar. / O médico mandou não **lho** dar.
     the doctor sent-him(DAT)-it not give-INFN/the doctor sent not him-it give
     'The doctor sent to not give it to him.'

(30) O médico mandou-o não beber.
     the doctor sent-him(ACC) not drink-INFN
     'The doctor sent him to not drink.'

In the Portuguese sentence (30), contrary to French (28), there is no VP-movement out of the embedded clause plus Subject dativization (see Kayne 1975:196ff. and Burzio 1986:228ff.). Assuming that *não* 'not' heads ΣP (see Martins 1994b), both the object clitics in (29) and the subject clitic in (30) moved from a position below *não* past the negative head. Thus (30) shows that, contrary to Kayne's claim, the Neg head does not block clitic movement. What does rule out (29), then? The analysis proposed here provides a simple and effective answer. The presence of the negative word implies that Σ (in its Neg instantiation) is projected, and therefore AgrS is also projected, which Σ immediately dominates. Accordingly, because the object clitics can check their specific feature within the infinitival clause, they are not allowed to move out of the infinitival clause (principles of economy preclude that option). Movement of the subject clitic out of the complement clause, on the other hand, is permitted because it is triggered by the necessity of checking (accusative) Case.

So, under minimalist assumptions, extraction of an object clitic out of a complement infinitival clause occurs if and only if the complement clause is a TP. One would thus expect that verbs that do not take TPs as complements (as a result of lexical requirements—recall the MSP) do not allow for CC. Certain epistemic verbs display the relevant properties.

French verbs such as *croire* 'believe' and *penser* 'think' take [-finite] complements whose T licenses null Case, as the PRO subject in (31) shows. At the same time, these verbs allow *wh*-movement from the subject position of their infinitival complement, as exemplified by (32):

(31) Pierre$_i$ croit / pense [PRO$_i$ avoir convaincu son auditoire].   (Boskovic 1996)
      P. believes / thinks (to) have convinced his audience

(32) Paul$_i$, que$_i$ Pierre croit / pense [t$_i$ avoir convaincu son auditoire], . . .
      Paul who Pierre believes / thinks (to) have convinced his audience

The grammaticality of (32) appears to be problematic. Assuming that only PRO can bear null Case and that movement for Case-checking purposes cannot originate from a Case position, how is the infinitival subject in (32) Case-checked? Kayne's (1984) analysis of this type of sentence, as modified in Rizzi (1990) and updated by Boskovic (1996), provides the following answer. Verbs of the *croire*-type 1-select a null complementizer, which can check accusative Case under Spec-head agreement. The infinitival subject can have Case checked in that position, since A'-movement of *que* is motivated by checking of the [+*wh*] feature. Given the Minimize Chain Links Principle (Chomsky and Lasnik 1993), *que* must pass through the embedded Spec of CP on its way to the matrix Spec of CP.[20]

The Portuguese verbs equivalent to French *croire/penser* enter the same configurations, as (33) and (34) attest:

(33) O Pedro crê / pensa ter convencido a audiência.   (same as 31)

(34) O Paulo, que o Pedro crê/pensa ter convencido a audiência.   (same as 32)

Hence these verbs, according to Kayne's analysis, have CP infinitival complements that, given the clause structure I am assuming, necessarily contain an AgrS projection. I therefore predict that they do not allow CC. This prediction is borne out, as (35) and (36) show:

(35) O Paulo crê / pensa tê-**los** convencido.
      the P. believes / thinks (to) have-them convinced
      'P. believes that he convinced them.'

(36) *O Paulo crê-**os** / pensa-**os** ter convencido.
      the P. believes-them / thinks-them (to) have convinced

The analysis I am proposing accounts smoothly for the impossibility of CC out of finite complements of verbs allowing for CC in the context of infinitival clauses, a question raised by Terzi (1995). Finite complements with overt complementizers are CPs; zero finite complements are, according to the MSP, IPs (see earlier discussion); since they include agreement morphology, however, lexical requirements (the need for checking of the agreement features on the verb) force them to necessarily be at least AgrSPs. It is thus expected that embedded object clitics cannot move out of the clause where they can have all their morphological features checked, as in the Spanish sentence in (37):

(37)　Espero **lo** comas rápido / *lo Espero comas rápido.　(Terzi 1995)
　　　hope-IND(1s) it eat-SUB(2s) quickly / it hope eat quickly

　　　'I hope (that) you eat it quickly.'

In Portuguese, infinitival complements with inflected infinitives are like zero finite complements in that they are not introduced by a complementizer but are specified for (overt) Agr features (see Raposo 1987). I thus predict that, contrary to uninflected infinitival clauses, inflected infinitivals preclude CC. This prediction is borne out, as sentences (38) through (40) attest:

(38)　Vi os polícias prender o ladrão / Vi os polícias prenderem o ladrão.
　　　saw the cops arrest-INFN the thief / . . . arrest-INFLECTED-INFN(3pl)

　　　'I saw the cops arrest the thief.'

(39)　Vi-o prender / Vi prendê-**lo**.
　　　saw-him arrest-INFN / saw arrest-INFN-him

　　　I saw [arb.subj.] arrest him—'I saw him being arrested.'

(40)　*Vi-o prenderem / Vi prenderem-**no**.
　　　saw-him arrest-INFL.-INFN(3pl) / saw arrest-INFL.-INFN(3pl)-him

　　　'I saw (them) arrest him.'

Apparently, there are two kinds of counterexamples to the approach taken here. In Italian, CC is marginally acceptable out of a [+wh] infinitival complement—see sentence (41), whose Portuguese and Spanish equivalents are ruled out. In Spanish and Portuguese, infinitival complements of *ter* 'to have' may be introduced by *que* 'that' while allowing for CC—see example (42).

(41)　Non **ti** saprei che dire.　(Rizzi 1982a:36—marginally admitted in the colloquial style)
　　　not you will-know what tell-INFN

　　　'I won't know what to tell you'

(42)　**Lo** tenemos que hacer.　(Spanish; from Luján 1980:384)
　　　it have that do-INFN

　　　'We have to do it.'

In both situations, the complement clauses appear to be CPs, and so the possibility of CC is unexpected. My proposal is that neither the infinitival complement of (41) nor the infinitival complement of (42) is a CP.

In Portuguese, the verb *ter* l-selects either *que* or the preposition *de*, with no semantic distinction resulting from this alternative choice:

(43)   Tenho que vê-**lo**.
       have that see-INFN him
       'I have to see him.'

(44)   Tenho de vê-**lo**.
       have of see-INFN him
       'I have to see him.'

The alternation *de* 'of' / *que* 'that', occurring only in the context of infinitival complements, parallels the more common alternations either between different prepositions or between ø and preposition (l-selected by the same verb), largely attested by traditional grammarians (see Ali 1931:133–137).[21] The fact that *que* in the context of infinitival complements freely alternates with a prepositional element (a situation that usually involves two prepositions) leads me to hypothesize, in the vein of Thráinsson (1993), that *que* in (42) is an infinitive marker that happens to be homophonous with the finite complementizer. I therefore assume that sentences such as (42) through (44) have the structure proposed by Thráinsson for Icelandic Control complements introduced by the infinitival marker *aD*—(see earlier discussion). I furthermore take the "defective" AgrSP (not projecting above AgrS° and not containing V-features), where the infinitival marker is housed, to be unable to check feature any other than the null Agr-feature tentatively proposed by Thráinsson.

As for the Italian sentence in (41), I suggest that the *wh*-phrase *che* is not in Spec of CP but rather in the Spec of a clause internal F(ocus) projection where the [+wh] feature gets checked. (See Uriagereka 1992, 1995 and Martins 1994a for the proposal that in the Romance languages with a syntactic instantiation of F, *wh*-movement can target the Spec of the correspondent projection.) The existence in Italian of a clause internal F position, "located in the VP area," is argued for by Belletti and Shlonsky (1995). I follow the spirit of their proposal, although I do not assume the central aspects of its implementation. Namely, I am not taking this FP to have its Spec on the right, nor to necessarily be projected immediately above VP. (On the matter of clause internal FPs and on the relation between Focus-movement and *wh*-movement, see Sumangala 1992). Whether or not a language displays the relevant property appears to be a matter of parametric variation.

To close this chapter, I will address the issue of the apparent optionality of CC.[22] In the context of CC matrix verbs, embedded object clitics may either move out of the infinitival complement clause or stay inside it:

(45)   a. **Lo** voglio fare.   b. Voglio **farlo**.   (Italian)
          it want do   want do it   'I want to do it.'

(46)   a. **Lo** quiero hacer.   b. Quiero hacer**lo**.   (Spanish)
            it want do   want do it 'I want to do it.'

(47)   a. Quero-o fazer.   b. Quero fazê-**lo**.   (Portuguese)
            want-it do   want do-it 'I want to do it.'

(48)   a. Je te **le** vois faire.   b. Je te vois **le** faire.   (French)
            I you it see do   I you see it do 'I see you to do it.'

Since, under minimalist assumptions, movement cannot be optional, being driven by morphological necessity only, the preceding (a) sentences cannot have the same structure as the (b) sentences (putting aside the difference with respect to clitic placement). According to the hypothesis argued for here, only the infinitival complements in (a) are TPs; I will take the infinitival complements in (b) to be ΣPs. Given this assumption, the "optionality of movement" problem disappears. The apparent "optionality" of clitic climbing derives from the fact that certain verbs can take either a TP complement or a ΣP complement. When a TP is selected, the clitic necessarily climbs; when a ΣP is selected, the clitic does not climb, since the closer checker for its specific feature is the embedded AgrS (hence, moving higher would violate economy). It seems now, however, that I will have to rehabilitate c-selection and put on it the burden of optionality to account for the double categorial status of the infinitival complements of CC verbs. I would like to propose instead that s-selection, not c-selection, is at stake, so I will be able to maintain Pesetsky's theoretically interesting claim that c-selection does not exist as an independent syntactic mechanism. Moreover, it will be clear that some empirical facts fit better into an s-selection approach than into a c-selection approach to the issue under analysis.

Let's then take CC verbs to have the option of either s-selecting for "assertion" or be underspecified for s-selection. In the former situation, a ΣP will have to be projected because an assertion necessarily contains a truth-value operator, either negation or affirmation. If the option for semantic underspecification is taken, on the other hand, the MSP will lead to the generation of a structure as reduced as possible; if in addition the relevant verbs l-select for [-finite], which is a feature of T, the smallest structure that can be successfully generated is a TP. (That selection for features like [+/–finite] is a matter of l-selection is proposed by Pesetsky.) This hypothesis is in accordance with the common claim in the literature that the verbs that allow for CC are semantically weak (see Napoli 1981; Rizzi 1982; Burzio 1986, among others). Translating into my terms, these verbs have the option for underspecified s-selection.

When one observes the body of data relative to the constituency of the CC set of verbs in different languages, two situations occur that are recalcitrant to a formal account. First, there are striking contrasts between verbs of the same class. As an example take the Italian verbs *volere* 'want' and *desiderare* 'wish'; although both are volitional verbs entering Subject Control configurations, *volere* allows for CC whereas *desiderare* rules it out (see (49)). The same contrast holds for Portuguese, where *querer* 'want' is a CC verb but *desejar* 'wish' is not. Second, across Romance languages, some cognate verbs behave differently with respect to CC, even though they answer similarly to other syntactic tests (this kind of variation increases significantly when one takes into account diachronic data). In Spanish, in contrast to Italian and Portuguese, both Subject Control verbs *querer* and *desejar* permit CC (see (50)). Another example of this kind of contrast is given in (51) versus (52): object Control verbs such as 'advise' and 'allow' are CC verbs in Spanish but not in Portuguese. Idiosyncratic properties of (singular) lexical items (intersecting with properties of lexical classes) appear to be at stake. Analyzing the facts under consideration as dependent on s-selection, instead of c-selection, seems to be more consistent with their idiosyncratic lexically governed nature.

(49) **Lo** voglio leggere / *__Lo__ desidero leggere.   (Italian; Burzio 1986:221)
      it want read-INFN / it wish read-INFN
      'I want / wish to read it.'

(50) **La** queria ver / La deseaba ver.   (Spanish; adapted from Luján 1980:385)
      her wanted see / her wished see
      'He/She wanted / wished to see her.'

(51) Me **lo** aconsejó / permitió comprar.   (Spanish; see Luján 1980:386)
      me it advised / allowed buy-INFN
      'He/She advised / allowed me to buy it.'

(52) *Aconselhou-**mo** a / *Permitiu-mo comprar.   (Portuguese)
      advised-me-it to / allowed-me-it buy-INFN
      'He/She advised / allowed me to buy it.'

In an overwhelming majority of contemporary Romance languages (and dialects), all verbs that allow for CC also allow for structures where the object clitic stays inside the infinitival clause.[23] One may wonder why this is so. If idiosyncratic properties of lexical items (related to s-selection) play a significant role with respect to CC, such "uniformity" is quite unexpected. A look at Old Romance provides the clue to understand this.

By and large, Old Romance differs from Modern Romance in two ways: CC is generally attested in Old Romance in instances where it may not take place in Modern Romance; that is, CC appears to be "obligatory" in Old Romance, whereas it appears to be "optional" in Modern Romance. An example from Portuguese is given in (53) versus (54); an identical scenario holds for Spanish, Italian, and French (see Wanner 1986 and the references therein). On the other hand, CC is not possible in Modern Romance with certain matrix verbs that trigger it in Old Romance (see (55)–(56) and Napoli 1981, Roberts 1994, and Wanner 1986, plus the references therein for similar examples in different languages).

(53) sse per uentura **as** quiserem uender . . .   (Old Portuguese; Martins 1994a)
      if by chance them want (to) sell
      'If it happens that you want to sell them (the lands) . . .'

(54)   Se por ventura **as** quiserem vender / quiserem vendê-**las** . . .   (Modern Portuguese)
        if by chance them want (to) sell / want (to) sell-them
        'If it happens that you want to sell them (the lands) . . .'

(55)   Non **se** ousava levantar.   (Old Portuguese; Martins 1994a)
        not himself dare (to) stand-up
        'He didn't dare to stand up.'

(56)   *Não **se** ousava levantar / Não ousava levantar-**se**.   (Modern Portuguese)
        not himself dare (to) stand-up / not dare (to) stand-up-himself
        'He didn't dare to stand up.'

The two types of contrast between Old and Modern Romance are obviously part of
the same change: from s-selection underspecification to s-selection specification, thus
corresponding to a semantic strengthening of CC verbs. Syntactically this translates
into a change from more auxiliary-like verbs to more main-like verbs, and thus is
a process of degrammaticalization (see Roberts 1992). Other signs of this "meta-
morphosis" can be detected, but I will not go into it here.[24] This change develops
in two steps. First, the verbs that in Old Romance are underspecified with respect to
s-selection come to s-select "assertion" while keeping the underspecification option;
second, this option is lost. In Sardinian, the change did not take place and CC is, as
in Old Romance, "obligatory." As for the other Romance languages, the generalized
apparent "optionality" of CC shows that the first step of the change is concluded. As
for its final step, the loss of CC with particular verbs has affected only a few items in
Portuguese, Spanish, and Italian, whereas it has spread heavily in French.[25]

6.4 A Final Remark

The analysis offered here does not correlate CC and null subjects, which may appear
to be a fatal weakness (see Kayne 1989, 1991). The good news is that the diachronic
data do not support the idea that CC and pro-drop are correlated phenomena. The
loss of null subjects occurred in French. Spanish, Portuguese, and Italian did not
undergo such a change. But French, Spanish, Italian, and Portuguese all moved in
the same direction with respect to CC (although French changed more). Being so, it
is not likely that the loss of pro-drop and the narrowing of the set of CC predicates in
French are manifestations of the same grammatical change. Wanner (1986:361) provides an argument supporting this view: the change affecting CC occurred in the
seventeenth century, when the possibility of having null subjects had been lost for at
least one century (see Adams 1987).[26]

Notes

This article originally appeared in *Papers from the Thirty-first Regional Meeting of the Chicago Linguistic Society*, vol. 2, *Parasession on Clitics*, edited by Audra Dainora, Rachel
Hemphill, Barbara Luka, Barbara Need, and Sheri Pargman (Chicago: Chicago Linguistic

Society, 1995), and is published here with minor revisions. I hereby thank the holders of the copyrights for their permission to reprint this material.

1. On this topic see, for example, Napoli (1981:873, 881–884); Rizzi (1982:41, n. 6); Wanner (1986:288ff.); and Roberts (1994:43 n. 1).

2. Example taken from Rizzi (1982:32).

3. Example taken from Rizzi (1982:35).

4. The same line of reasoning is taken by Ian Roberts (1992:247) to account for obligatory "clitic climbing" in Sardinian sentences with "auxiliary verbs" such as *aere* 'to have', *devere* 'must', and *potere* 'can'. It should be noted, however, that the core instances of CC in Romance do not affect auxiliary verbs. As I already mentioned, in the Romance dialects I will be discussing, CC verbs are not auxiliaries (they do not test positively to several of the standard syntactic criteria for auxiliaryhood). On the other hand, Roberts (1994,1997) takes an approach to CC (based on the idea of restructuring) that totally departs from his 1992 analysis of Sardinian "auxiliary + infinitive" constructions.

5. According to Diesing (1992), VP is the relevant border with respect to specificity. There is empirical evidence, however, that this is not correct. Jonas and Bobaljik (1993) show on empirical grounds that transitive postverbal subjects in Icelandic, usually taken as being VP internal, are in fact external to the VP. According to Jonas and Bobaljik, Icelandic postverbal subjects are in Spec of TP, while preverbal subjects are in Spec of AgrS. Relevantly preverbal Icelandic subjects (in the AgrSP domain) semantically contrast with postverbal subjects (in the TP domain) in terms of specificity. An additional argument for reviewing Diesing's proposal comes from the fact that, as Kayne (1994) has pointed out, Object Scrambling (which affects specific DPs) involves movement to a higher position than AgrOP, which is itself external to VP.

6. Herburger (1994) proposes that the event operator appears in INFL, without referring to a particular INFL-type projection. Hornstein (1994) suggests, in footnote 34, that the sentential event position is associated with TP.

7. "I argue here that, similarly to the way in which the head Neg can head its own projection . . . , there is also a X° Aff, which projects an Affirmation Phrase. These two heads (Neg and Aff) are further argued to belong in the same syntactic category, which I will call Σ" (Laka 1990:86).

8. With respect to the subject position, some clarification is due. In languages such as Portuguese and Spanish, preverbal subjects in matrix clauses are interpreted as topics, in contrast to postverbal subjects, which have an existential or focus interpretation. The semantics of preverbal subjects, in these languages coincides with the semantics of subjects overtly marked as topics in languages such as Japanese (see Kuroda 1992). Therefore, I hypothesize that while nontopic subjects (i.e., postverbal subjects, in Spec of TP) are assigned nominative Case, which is checked by T, topic subjects are assigned topic Case, which is checked by Σ (topic Case as well as nominative Case being overt in some languages and covert in others). When the subject is assigned nominative Case, Σ is inert with respect to Case (it is not associated with a Case feature); when the subject is assigned topic Case, T is inert with respect to Case, Σ bearing strong N-features. This issue is addressed in Martins (1994a).

9. PRO as a pronominal anaphor falls under Conditions A and B of Binding Theory, which state, respectively, that an anaphor must be bound in a local domain and a pronoun must be free in a local domain. The local domain, or "governing category," of an element α is, roughly, the minimal clause/XP containing α and a governor of α.

10. The Case Filter states that every phonetically realized NP must be assigned (abstract) Case.

11. This is not exactly the original claim of Chomsky and Lasnik (1993): "Chomsky

and Lasnik actually propose that all instances of non-finite Tense license null Case, but we will see reasons for the narrower characterization presented here" (Lasnik 1993:77).

12. This follows from the Last Resort Condition, which states that an operation is only permissible "if it is a *prerequisite* to the formation of a legitimate LF object; had the operation not taken place, the derivation would not be able to form such an object" (Chomsky and Lasnik 1993:564).

13. See Martin (1992), Lasnik (1993), and Boskovic (1996), among others. Martin (1992) investigates the fact that not every nonfinite INFL has the ability to check null Case and provides a semantic motivation for it with a formal characterization of the two types of nonfinite INFL; Lasnik (1993) brings up some additional syntactic facts in support of Martin's analysis, which is further worked by Boskovic (1996).

14. Raising is possible in (19), since the NP is in a position where no Case is licensed; (18) is ungrammatical because, by hypothesis, PRO cannot bear accusative Case (see Lasnik 1993:66).

15. Also, Grimshaw (1979) and Chomsky (1986) speculate that the lexical entries of predicates need not specify their c-selection properties directly.

16. The arguments presented by Boskovic deal with facts concerning licensing of empty complementizers and scrambling out of Control infinitives.

17. On independent grounds, Bures (1992) and Bobaljik (1992) propose, in the same vein, that AgrS is "defective" in nonfinite clauses in Irish. So even though Agr has strong V-features in Irish, the verb moves only as far as T in infinitival clauses, whereas it moves up to AgrS in finite clauses.

18. While not producing finite embedded clauses, children can perfectly produce finite forms of verbs.

19. French *laisser* 'let', contrary to *faire* 'make', does not necessarily behave as a typical causative, as shown by the contrast between the two verbs with respect to the position and Case marking of the embedded subject (see Kayne 1975:196ff.):

(1) a. Je laisse mon ami partir   Je laisse partir mon ami
       I let my friend leave   I let leave my friend

    b. *Je fais mon ami partir   Je fais partir mon ami
       I make my friend leave   I make leave my friend

(2) a. Je **le** laisse manger les gâteaux   Je **lui** laisse manger les gâteaux
       I him-ACC let eat the cookies   I him-DAT let eat the cookies

    b. *Je **le** fais manger les gâteaux   Je **lui** fais manger les gâteaux
       I him-ACC make eat the cookies   I him-DAT make eat the cookies

20. The Minimize Chain Links Principle requires that every chain link be as short as possible.

21. For example:

(1) começou **a** chover / começou **de** chover   (Old and dialectal Portuguese)
    started to rain-INFN / started of rain-INFN
    'It started raining.'

(2) deve ser bom / deve de ser bom   (Modern Standard Portuguese)
    may be good / may of be good
    'It may be good.'

22. Space considerations force me to leave aside an issue extensively discussed in the literature: the impossibility of having double object clitics split apart, one of them climbing while the other is left behind. This is so in Italian, Spanish, and, with certain qualifications,

also in standard French and Portuguese. Examples from Italian and Spanish are given in the following:

(1) Piero **me lo** voleva dare / Piero voleva dar**melo**   (Rizzi 1982:44)
    P. me it wanted give / P. wanted give-me-it
    'Piero wanted to give it to me.'

(2) *Piero **me** voleva dar**lo** / *Piero **lo** voleva dar**me**   (Rizzi 1982:44)
    P. me wanted give-it / P. it wanted give-me

(3) **Te lo** prefiero dar / Prefiero da**rtelo** / ***Te** prefiero dar**lo**
    you-DAT it-ACC prefer give-INFN / prefer give you it / you prefer give it
    'I prefer to give it to you.'   (Luján 1980:385)

My analysis predicts this fact, since either the infinitival complement clause is a TP and both clitics have to move out of it for feature-checking, or the infinitival complement is a ΣP and both clitics can and therefore have to check features inside it. Problematic for my analysis are the dialects mentioned by Kayne (1989, 1991) that allow for clitic splitting in the relevant configurations. A possible way to account for these facts would be to assume that both object clitics have their specific feature checked inside the infinitival clause, with climbing of one of them having an independent trigger, such as emphatic/focus-movement. This is a complex matter, though, and I will not go into it.

23. An exception is Sardinian, which displays obligatory CC. See Kayne (1989, 1991) for references.

24. One of such signs is the absence of negative operators in the infinitival complements of CC verbs in Old Romance. Moignet (1965) points out that infinitives in Old French could not be (independently) negated. An identical situation presumably arises in the other Old Romance languages (see Martins 1994a and Beardsley 1966 for data on Old Portuguese and Old Spanish, respectively). On this and related issues, see Pearce (1990).

25. Brazilian Portuguese parallels French with respect to the (diachronic) narrowing of the set of CC predicates. Throughout this chapter I deal with European Portuguese only ("Portuguese" thus stands for "European Portuguese").

26. On the other hand, Brazilian Portuguese can license null subjects while displaying the same properties as French with respect to CC.

References

Adams, M. P. 1987. "Old French, Null Subjects, and Verb Second Phenomena." Ph.D. dissertation, UCLA.

Ali, M. Said 1931. *Gramática Histórica da Língua Portuguesa*. São Paulo: Melhoramentos.

Beardsley, W. A. 1966. *Infinitive Constructions in Old Spanish*. New York: Ams Press.

Belletti, A., and U. Shlonsky. 1995. "The Order of Verbal Complements: A Comparative Study." *Natural Language and Linguistic Theory* 13: 489–526.

Bobaljik, J. D. 1992. "Nominally Absolute Is Not Absolutely Nominative." In E. Duncan, D. Farkas, and P. Spaelti (eds.) *The Proceedings of the 12th West Coast Conference on Formal Linguistics*. Stanford, Calif.: CSLI Publications.

Boskovic, Z. 1996. "Selection and the Categorial Status of Infinitival Complements." *Natural Language and Linguistic Theory* 14: 269–304.

Bures, A. 1992. "Re-cycling Expletives and Other Sentences." Ms., MIT.

Burzio, L. 1986. *Italian Syntax*. Dordrecht: Reidel.

Chomsky, N. 1986. *Knowledge of Language: Its Nature, Origin and Use*. New York: Praeger.

————. 1993. "A Minimalist Program for Linguistic Theory." In K. Hale and S. J. Keyser (eds.) *The View from Building 20.* Cambridge, Mass.: MIT Press.

————. 1994. "Bare Phrase Structure." Ms., MIT. Published in Gert Webelhuth (ed.) *Government and Binding Theory and the Minimalist Program.* Oxford: Blackwell, 1995.

Chomsky, N., and H. Lasnik. 1993. "Principles and Parameters Theory.". In J. Jacobs, A. von Stechow, W. Sternfeld, and T. Vennemann (eds.) *Syntax: An International Handbook of Contemporary Research.* Berlin: Walter de Gruyter.

Delfitto, D., and Corver, N. 1995. "Feature Primitives and the Syntax of Specificity." In H.-P. Kolb and G. Müller (eds.) *GLOW Newsletter* 34: 18–19.

Diesing, M. 1992. *Indefinites.* Cambridge, Mass.: MIT Press.

Fresina, C. 1982. "Les Verbes de Mouvement et les Aspectuels en Italien." *Lingvisticae Investigationes* 6: 283–331.

Goodall, G. T. 1984. "Parallel Structures in Syntax." Ph.D. dissertation, University of California at San Diego.

Grimshaw, J. 1979. "Complement Selection and the Lexicon." *Linguistic Inquiry* 10: 279–326.

Herburger, E. 1994. "Focus and the LF of NP Quantification." In *Proceedings of SALT III.* Ithaca, N.Y.: Cornell University Press.

Higginbotham, J. 1987. "Indefiniteness and Predication." In E. Reuland and A. ter Meulen (eds.) *The Representation of (In)definiteness.* Cambridge, Mass.: MIT Press.

Hornstein, N. 1994. "An Argument for Minimalism: The Case of Antecedent-Contained Deletion." *Linguistic Inquiry* 25: 455–480.

Jonas, D., and J. D. Bobaljik. 1993. "Specs for Subjects: The Role of TP in Icelandic." *MIT Working Papers in Linguistics* 18, MIT.

Kayne, R. 1975. *French Syntax. The Transformational Cycle.* Cambridge, Mass.: MIT Press.

————. 1984. *Connectedness and Binary Branching.* Dordrecht: Foris.

————. 1989. "Null Subjects and Clitic Climbing." In O. Jaeggli and K. Safir (eds.) *The Null Subject Parameter.* Dordrecht: Kluwer.

————. 1991. "Romance Clitics, Verb Movement and PRO." *Linguistic Inquiry* 22: 647–686.

————. 1994. *The Antisymmetry of Syntax.* Cambridge, Mass.: MIT Press.

Kuroda, S.-Y. 1992. *Japanese Syntax and Semantics.* Dordrecht: Kluwer.

Laka, I. 1990. "Negation in Syntax: On the Nature of Functional Categories and Projections." Ph.D. dissertation, MIT.

Lasnik, H. 1993. "Lectures on Minimalist Syntax." Ms., University of Connecticut.

Law, P. 1991. "Effects of Head-Movement on Theories of Subjacency and Proper Government." Ph.D. dissertation, MIT.

Luján, M. 1980. "Clitic Promotion and Mood in Spanish Verbal Complements." *Linguistics* 18: 381–484.

Martin, R.1992. On the Distribution and Case Features of PRO. Manuscript. University of Connecticut.

Martins, A. M. 1994a. "Clíticos na História do Português." Ph.D. dissertation, University of Lisbon.

————. 1994b. "Enclisis, VP-deletion and the Nature of Sigma." *Probus* 6: 173–205.

Moignet, G. 1965. "L'Opposition NON/NE en ancien français." *Travaux de Linguistique et de Littérature* 3: 41–65.

Moore, J. 1994. "Romance Cliticization and Relativized Minimality." *Linguistic Inquiry* 25: 335–344.

Napoli, D. J. 1981. "Semantic Interpretation vs. Lexical Governance: Clitic Climbing in Italian." *Language* 57: 841–887.

Nunes, J. 1992. "English Infinitives and Case Theory." In A. Kathol and J. Beckman (eds.) *MIT Working Papers in Linguistics* 16, MIT.

Pearce, E. 1990. *Parameters in Old French Syntax: Infinitival Complements*. Dordrecht: Kluwer.

Pesetsky, D. 1982. "Paths and Categories." Ph.D. dissertation, MIT.

———. 1992. "Zero Syntax." Ms., MIT. Version of D. Pesetsky 1995. *Zero Syntax. Experiencers and Cascades*. Cambridge, Mass.: MIT Press; and D. Pesetsky (in preparation) *Zero Syntax II: An Essay on Infinitives*.

Picallo, M. C. 1990. "Modal Verbs in Catalan." *Natural Language and Linguistic Theory* 8: 285–312.

Pollock, J.-Y. 1989. "Verb Movement, Universal Grammar, and the Structure of IP." *Linguistic Inquiry* 20: 365–424.

Raposo, E. 1986. "Romance Infinitival Clauses and Case Theory." In C. Neidle and R. Cedeño (eds.) *Studies in Romance Languages*. Dordrecht: Foris.

———. 1987. "Case Theory and Infl-to-Comp: The Inflected Infinitive in European Portuguese." *Linguistic Inquiry* 18: 85–109.

Rizzi, L. 1982. *Issues in Italian Syntax*. Foris: Dordrecht.

———. 1990. *Relativized Minimality*. Cambridge, Mass.: MIT Press.

Roberts, I. 1992. "A Formal Account of Grammaticalization in the History of Romance Futures." *Folia Linguistica Historica* 13, nos. 1–2: 219–258.

———. 1994. "Restructuring, Pronoun Movement and Head-Movement in Old French." Ms., University of Wales, Bangor.

———. 1997. "Restructuring, Head Movement, and Locality." *Linguistic Inquiry* 28: 423–460.

Sportiche, D. 1992. "Clitic Constructions." Ms., UCLA.

Strozer, J. 1976. "Clitics in Spanish." Ph.D. dissertation, UCLA.

Sumangala, L. 1992. "Long-Distance Dependencies in Sinhala: The Syntax of Focus and Wh Questions." Ph.D. dissertation, Cornell University.

Terzi, A. 1995. "Two Types of Clitic Climbing from Finite Clauses." Ms., City University of New York, Rutgers University.

Thráinsson, H. 1993. *On the Structure of Infinitival Complements*. Harvard Working Papers in Linguistics 3: 181–213.

———. 1994. "On the Structure of Infinitival Complements." *Harvard Working Papers in Linguistics*. Vol. 3, *Papers in Syntax*. Harvard University.

Uriagereka, J. 1992. "An F Position in Western Romance." Paper presented at GLOW Colloquium, University of Lisbon. In K. Kiss (ed.) *Discourse Configurational Languages*. Oxford: Oxford University Press.

———. 1995. "Aspects of the Syntax of Clitic Placement in Western Romance." *Linguistic Inquiry* 26: 79–123.

Wanner, D. 1986. *The Development of Romance Clitic Pronouns: From Latin to Old Romance*. Berlin: Mouton de Gruyter.

7

SÉRGIO MENUZZI

First Person Plural Anaphora in Brazilian Portuguese

Chains and Constraint Interaction in Binding

The theoretical issue I will be addressing in this chapter is what, if any, conditions are necessary to express the fact that anaphoric dependencies such as those in (1) require AGREEMENT between the associated forms.

(1) a. *Mary*$_i$ likes {*herself*$_i$/**himself*$_i$}
     b. *John*$_i$ thinks Mary likes { **her*$_i$/*him*$_i$}

If an agreement condition on anaphoric dependencies is to be formulated on the basis of Binding Theory (BT), it has to be so with the concepts available in the theory (assuming that we do not want to add to its descriptive power).[1] Thus, different versions of BT allow us to formulate different agreement conditions, and any evidence supporting one over the other conditions also supports the corresponding version of the theory. It is from this perspective that I will look at what I call FIRST PERSON PLURAL ANAPHORA (1PPLA) in Brazilian Portuguese (BP): anaphoric dependencies in which the antecedent is the expression *a gente* (literally, 'the people') in its first person plural interpretation. 1PPLA reveals a pattern of intriguing contrasts, such as the one in (2): *a gente* can be an antecedent of a first person plural pronoun only if the dependency is not "local" in a sense to be made precise:

(2) a. *A gente* viu uma cobra atrás de *nós*.
     the people saw a snake behind of *us*
     'We saw a snake behind us.'

     b. **A gente* já *nos* viu na TV.
     the people already *us* saw on-the TV
     'We already saw ourselves on TV.'

I will argue that this and other facts provide evidence that two agreement-like requirements are needed in BT. One of these, AGREEMENT-ON-CHAINS, is of particular interest: it checks whether an anaphoric form is compatible with its antecedent's grammatical specification, and applies when the dependency fits a chain format. What is particularly interesting about Agreement-on-Chains is that, in order to formulate it, BT has to distinguish anaphoric dependencies that fit the chain format from those that do not. This will then provide us a first argument to pursue Reinhart and Reuland's (R&R) (1993) version of BT, the theory of reflexivity and A-chains, rather than the standard version of BT (with and without the LF-movement analysis of anaphors). This chapter is organized as follows:

In section 7.1 I briefly review the notion of indexing relevant for BT. Indexing may be conceived of as a representation for the assignment of interpretation to NPs and, as such, it is subject to an intrinsic requirement: NPs are not assigned interpretations that are not appropriate to their lexical content. I will also introduce some technical apparatus for a proper characterization of both indexing and its intrinsic requirement, which I formulate as the FEATURE-COMPATIBILITY CONDITION ON INDEXING (FCI).

In section 7.2 I show that, by its own nature, the FCI is an agreement requirement on COINDEXING (or cointerpretation of NPs) and, hence, on anaphoric dependencies. The importance of this point is that, being a condition on indexing rather than on coindexing, the FCI is logically prior to any agreement-like requirement on anaphoric dependencies. This sets a limit for postulation of any further agreement requirement on anaphoric dependencies: such an additional requirement cannot be redundant with the FCI. 1PPLA will, then, provide a case in which agreement effects are not reducible to the FCI's effects.

In section 7.3 I describe some properties of the expression *a gente* in BP and, in particular, the pattern of 1PPLA. In section 7.4 I show that 1PPLA justifies the postulation of an agreement-like requirement on anaphoric dependencies that is independent of the FCI: while the FCI requires an anaphoric form to agree with the antecedent's interpretation, 1PPLA points to the existence of another requirement, according to which an anaphoric form has to agree with the antecedent's grammatical specification. In section 7.5 I show that this additional requirement is best formulated as a condition on anaphoric dependencies that fit the chain format; hence, Agreement-on-Chains.

Section 7.6 closes the chapter with a discussion of some of the theoretical issues that arise when we try to formulate Agreement-on-Chains properly. As will be apparent, while Agreement-on-Chains confirms the relevance of Chain Theory for anaphoric dependencies, it raises difficulties for a literal extension of the notion of chain to anaphoric dependencies. In particular, anaphoric dependencies that fit the chain format appear to satisfy only partially the requirement for feature-nondistinctness on chains (from Rizzi 1990), a problem solved in Menuzzi (in preparation).

7.1 Feature-compatibility on indexing

BT was conceived as a theory of syntactic restrictions on interpretative dependencies: intrasentential anaphoric dependencies. Standard BT, for example, determines in which syntactic domain an NP has to or cannot be bound, and binding itself obtains when NP1 c-commands NP2 and both are coindexed. Coindexing is the mechanism that brings in the interpretative nature of binding relationships: it represents the fact that, when anaphorically related, NPs are intended to have, in some sense, the same interpretation. Thus, when the standard Condition B says that a pronoun cannot be bound (within some domain), what it tries to capture is, for example, the fact that *he* and *him* in (3a) cannot refer to the same person, say, John. The interpretation in which *he* and *him* both refer to the same person (e.g., John) is represented by coindexing *he* and *him*, as in (3b). Example (3b), then, represents an interpretation with which (3a) is unacceptable, according to the standard BT, because it violates Condition B. Inversely, (3a) is fine if *he* and *him* do not refer to the same person, for example, if *he* refers to John, and *him* to Paul. This interpretation is represented by (3c). Example (3c), then, represents an interpretation with which (3a) is acceptable, according to the standard BT, because it does not violate Condition B:

(3) a. He likes him.

   b. *He$_i$ likes him$_i$. (e.g., i = John)

   c. He$_i$ likes him$_j$. (e.g., i = John, j = Paul)

Notice that, for this intuitive use of indices to be appropriate for the purposes of BT, it is necessary have to ensure that (i) (3b) expresses the interpretation in which *he* and *him* are intended to refer to the same person and (ii) (3c) expresses the interpretation in which *he* and *him* are not intended to refer to the same person. If this indexing notation were to allow any other interpretation, it would be useless for BT (cf. Lasnik and Uriagereka 1988:43–48). For example, suppose the indexation in (3c) could also express an interpretation of (3a) in which *he* and *him* refer to the same person, say Paul, as in (3d):

(3) d. *He$_i$ likes him$_j$. (e.g., $i = j$ = Paul)

Sentence (3a) with the interpretation represented by (3d) is, of course, no better than with the one represented by (3b). But, since *he* and *him* are not coindexed in (3d), *he* does not bind *him* in (3d); hence, (3d) cannot be excluded by Condition B. However, the interpretation of (3a) represented in (3d) has to be excluded precisely for the same reason the one represented by (3b) is: *he* and *him* in (4a) cannot refer to the same person. In other words, what has to be prevented by Condition B is not coindexing per se but a situation in which, say, *he* and *him* in (3a) are intended to refer to the same person. And, if coindexing is to be of any use for BT, it cannot lead to representations like (3d).

Thus, as far as binding facts are concerned, coindexing is not a meaningless notation but a means of representing some SEMANTIC notion of IDENTITY: for example, the notion of identity that allows us to say that *he* and *him* may refer to the same person in (3a). From this perspective, INDEXING itself may be taken to represent whatever allows us to pick up an NP's interpretation in the relevant sense. For my purposes, it suffices to assume that NPs' interpretations are identical in the sense relevant to binding in two cases: when COREFERENCE obtains, that is, when two NPs are intended to denote the same discourse referent or individual, as in (4); or when VARI-ABLE binding obtains, that is, when two argument positions are intended to be interpreted as occurrences of the same variable bound by a quantificational NP, as in (5):

(4)   a. *John* thinks Mary likes *him.*
       thinks (John, [likes (Mary, John)])

      b. **John* likes *him.*
       likes (John, John)

(5)   a. *Every boy* thinks Mary likes *him.*
       Every x: [boy (x)] [thinks (x, [likes (Mary, x)])].

      b. **Every boy* likes *him.*
       Every x: [boy (x)] [likes (Mary, x)].

To make proper use of terms like *interpreted as a bound variable* requires a two-stage procedure for interpretation: in one stage the "real" object language L, English in the case of (4) and (5), is translated into some logical language L with quantification (e.g., first order predicate calculus with restricted quantifiers, as usually assumed in GB literature); in the second stage, the logical language L is interpreted (e.g., by a model in model-theoretic semantics). Then, two NPs may be said to be coindexed or to have the same index if and only if they are translated as occurrences of the same term in L, that is, either as two occurrences of the same individual constant, as in (4), or as two occurrences of an individual variable bound by the same operator, as in (5).[2] Let me state this, then:

(6)   Let NP be a noun phrase in a sentence S of L; *NP* an individual term of L (i.e., either an individual constant or variable in L); and I a function such that I translates NP as *NP* when S is translated into S in L. Then:

      a. i is the index of NP in S wrt. S iff $i = I(NP) = NP$.

      b. NP1 and NP2 are coindexed iff $I(NP1) = I(NP2) = NP$.

      c. Indexing (for BT) is the collection of functions I of which (6a) and (6b) are true.

According to (6a), indices of NPs are the individual terms that these NPs get when they are translated into expressions of L, and (6b) says that NPs are coindexed only if they are translated as (occurrences of) the same individual term of L. But recall that what I really want to say is that *John* and *him* in (4a, b), for example, refer to the same individual. This is achieved through (6), however, because occurrences of the same individual constant and occurrences of a variable bound by the same operator are always assigned a unique SEMANTIC VALUE when propositions of L are evaluated for truth. Individual constants are assigned one individual from the domain of discourse once in a model. Individual variables, on the other hand, are assigned one individual possibly several times, each time a different one.[3] Since, according to (6), two NPs are coindexed only if they are translated by the same individual term of L, and individual terms are assigned a unique semantic value, (6) allows us to say that two NPs are coindexed if and only if they receive the same semantic value or are COVALUED (as in Fiengo and May 1994:3–14).

Indexing here, then, is taken to be part of the theory of semantic valuation or ASSIGNMENT of REFERENCE. As defined in (6), it provides BT with a notational device to abbreviate the mapping between NPs and their semantic values: "NP_i" abbreviates "NP (in S) is mapped into (the semantic value of) $i = NP$ by I (with respect to S)," and "$[NP1_i \ldots NP2_i]$" abbreviates "NP1 and NP2 (in S) are mapped into the same (semantic value, that of) $i = NP$ by I (with respect to S)."[4] Hence, when Principle A requires, for example, that an anaphor be bound in its GC, it actually requires the anaphor to be covalued with some other NP in its GC when the sentence is interpreted. Force of habit will often make me say "an NP is assigned an index $i (= \text{John})$," instead of the theory-neutral "an NP is assigned John as its semantic value/reference/interpretation." But I should stress that, technically, both turns of language are to be understood as meaning: "an NP is translated by I as the term i whose the semantic value/reference is John."

Once we make more explicit what the content of indexing is (the representation for the mapping of NPs into their interpretations), it becomes clear that, previous to binding conditions or any other condition on coindexing, an NP's indexing itself must be appropriate: one cannot simply assign an NP a reference that is inappropriate to this NP's "lexical specification:"

(7)   a. *Bill*$_i$ arrived late,
        *if i = John, ok if i = Bill

      b. *He*$_k$ is really stupid,
        *if k = Mary, ok if k = Bill, or John

      c. Indices don't annoy *me*$_j$
        *if j = you (addressee), ok if j = I (speaker)

Sentence (7a) is unacceptable if the NP *Bill* is assigned John as its referent (i.e., if $i = I(Bill) = \text{John}$) because it is part of the "lexical specification" of *Bill* that it applies only to people called *Bill* (and, in the less tedious case, if somebody is John, he is called *John*, and not *Bill*). By the same token, (7b) is unacceptable if *he* is assigned Mary as its referent because it is part of the "lexical specification" of *he* that it applies to entities that are categorized as masculine (and, in the usual case, Marys are females and, hence, categorized as feminine). Finally, (7c) cannot be uttered by a speaker who intends to refer to the addressee, and this is so because it is part of the lexical meaning of *me* that it has to refer to the speaker, that is, to the first person of the discourse. I can describe the generalization behind (7) as:[5]

(8)   *Appropriateness of Indexing:* An NP is not assigned an index that is inappropriate to its lexical specification.

Just as the characterization of what an index is ultimately depends on the theory of assignment of reference one adopts, proper statement of (8) depends on the way this same theory distinguishes the lexical contribution of linguistic forms from the particular interpretation these forms may get whenever they are put to use. Example (8) can be explicitly stated, however, in any theory such that:

(9)   *Required Properties of Assignment of Reference*:

a.   It tells us when an individual is called *Bill* or is a boy; when s/he is the speaker, or whether s/he belongs to the set of females or males, etc.

b.   It tells us that it is part of the lexical specification of the NP *Bill* that it has to be assigned somebody called *Bill* as a value; and of the lexical specification of a feminine pronoun like *she* that (in the normal case) it has to be assigned a value from the set of human females, etc.

For example, model-theoretic semantics qualifies as a theory in which (8) can be stated, since it incorporates statements to the effect of both (9a) and (9b). Statements like those in (9a) follow from structure of the domain D of discourse, necessary to define truth for the propositions of an interpreted language: D, the set of things that can be referred to, is partitioned in subsets because, for any proposition $P(i)$ of an interpreted language L (say, our first order predicate calculus) to be true, there must be a subset P of D and an individual i in D such that P is interpreted as P, i is interpreted as i, and i belongs to P in D. Statements like those in (9b), on the other hand, are incorporated into the notion of intension of an expression. Intensions are functions whose role is to assign NPs all and only those denotations such NPs may have in each possible world; thus, assignments such as those in (7) are simply not possible in model-theoretic semantics, and this as a matter of definition of what the intension of an expression is. In other words, (8) would appear to be a trivial lemma of model-theoretic semantics, rather than some primitive condition.

Instead of adopting model-theoretic terminology, however, I will try to state (8) in terms more familiar to syntactitians. But I should say from the outset that my sole intention is to be able to refer to the generalization in (8) in unambiguous, though uncommitted, terms. In particular, I will not try to determine the status of (8) in the theory of assignment of reference (whether it should be considered a primitive condition, or whether it follows from other assumptions independently necessary), nor will I try to determine which specific theory of assignment of reference is needed, for that matter.

Any theory of language must have means for representing those properties of linguistic expressions that determine their grammatical use and semantic interpretation. For concreteness, let me refer to such properties by the feature specification of linguistic expressions, features taken to be abbreviations for whatever an appropriate representation of those properties would be:

(10)   An expression E is associated with a FEATURE SPECIFICATION, the set $FS_E = \{[\alpha F_1], [\beta F_2],$
    $\ldots, [\gamma F_n]\}$ containing the morphosyntactic and semantic features of E.

For example, the name *Bill* has as its feature specification the set $FS_{Bill} = \{[+N], [+3p],$ [+singular], $\ldots$, [+called-*Bill*]\}. One may also adopt the strategy of using features to abbreviate that part of the assignment of reference embodied in (9a). In other words, it is impossible to express statements like those in (9a) by associating semantic values of NPs or indices with features representing semantic categorizations such as belong to the set of Bill's ([+called-*Bill*]), or to be the speaker ([+first person]), or to belong to the set of (human) females ([+feminine]), and so forth (see also Bouchard 1984; Cornish 1988; Farkas and Zec 1993, among others):

(11)   An index i is associated with a feature specification, the set $FS_i = \{[\alpha F_1], [\beta F_2], \ldots,$ $[\gamma F_n]\}$ containing the features corresponding to the semantic categorizations of i.

The statement in (11), then, is intended to provide an index $i = $ Bill with a feature specification $FS_i = \{[+3p], [+singular], \ldots, [+called-Bill]\}$, for instance. Before I proceed to formulate (8) on the basis of (10) and (11), let me stress two points concerning (11). First, it should be recalled that, though I have been using the phrase "an NP's index" to refer to this NP's semantic value, technically these two things should be distinguished: according to (6), an NP's index is the individual term of L into which that NP is translated, and the NP's semantic value is actually the semantic value assigned to this individual term or index. Thus, technically, (11) should be a statement about semantic values, since only these are semantically categorized: an individual term cannot belong to the set of Bills, since individual terms are expressions of a language, not things in the world; only an individual (denoted by some individual term of L) can belong to the set of Bills. In practice, indices and semantic values can be used interchangeably, however, because indices, that is, individual terms of L, are always assigned a unique semantic value. Thus, as before, I will keep referring to individuals in the domain as indices of NPs.

The second point to keep in mind is that reference to an index's FS in (11) does *not* amount to claiming that the theory of semantic interpretation assigns features to indices. Rather, all that (11) is claiming is as follows: in a semantic theory in which individuals can be categorized as belonging to the set of Bills, and so on (cf. (9a)), one may associate an individual with the set of semantic categorizations this individual has. In other words, features and feature specifications in (11) are meant only as an abbreviation for the proper statement of (9a) in the theory of semantic interpretation adopted (cf. the discussion of note 6). For example, in model-theoretic semantics an individual in the domain D of the discourse can be associated with a set containing all the subsets of D that individual belongs to. That is, if one adopts model-theoretic semantics, an index's FS would actually be the set of subsets of D to which that index (an individual) belongs.

I will now return to generalization (8), which actually is the result of ensuring that the part of the assignment of reference described in (9b) be respected. Given (10) and (11), one can think of (8) as a condition requiring some compatibility between an NP's FS (its lexical specification) and the FS of the index it is assigned (the semantic categorizations of the index). Consider an example such as (7b), repeated here:

(7)   b. *He*$_k$ is really stupid,
            *if $k = $ Mary, ok if $k = $ Bill, or John

The FS of *he* in (7b) has to be compatible with the FS associated with its semantic value. Suppose *he* is assigned John as its value. The FS of *he* is something like {[+3p], [+masculine], [+singular], [–accusative]}. In the usual case, John is an atomic individual who belongs to the set of human males and is called *John*. Following the procedures sketched earlier, this ends up in an FS like {[+3p], [+masculine], [+singular], [+called-*John*]}. If I now compare both FSs, it is apparent that, although they have nonidentical features (e.g., *he* is [–accusative], while the FS associated with John is unspecified for Case), there is no feature for which they are distinct, in the standard sense of feature-distinctness (see (12a). Suppose *he* is assigned Mary as its value in (7b). Mary is an individual belonging to the set of human females called *Mary*, which maps into an FS like {[–masculine], [+singular], [+Mary]}. If I compare the FS of the pronoun *he* with the FS associated with Mary, there is a feature that distinguishes them, namely, [±masculine]. Thus, k = Mary is not compatible with assignment of k to *he* in (7b).

Given (10) and (11), then, the notion of compatibility relevant for cases like (7) may be appropriately expressed by means of the standard notion of FEATURE NONDISTINCTNESS (as defined in Chomsky 1965:81, for example):

(12)   Let the feature specification of a category A be the set $FS_A = \{[\alpha F_1], [\beta F_2], \ldots, [\gamma F_n]\}$ in which each $[XF_i]$ is either $[-F_i]$ or $[+F_i]$. Then:

    a. FS_A is distinct from FS_B (with respect to some $[\alpha F]$) iff $[\alpha F]$ is such that either (i) $[+F] \in FS_A$ and $[-F] \in FS_B$, or (ii) $[-F] \in FS_A$ and $[+F] \in FS_B$. Otherwise, FS_A is NONDISTINCT from FS_B (with respect to $[\alpha F]$).

    b.   A is (FEATURE-)COMPATIBLE with B iff FS_A is nondistinct from FS_B.

Now it is possible to state (8) in more explicit terms. As in (6), let *I* be a function that translates NP in S into the term *NP* of *L* when S is translated into *S* (recall that indexing is the collection of the functions *I*; cf. (6c)). Then:

(13)   *Feature-Compatibility Condition on Indexing* (FCI, first statement):
    I translates NP as *NP* iff FS_{NP} is nondistinct from FS_{NP}.

Adopting the terminology of (6a) and (12b), I can also state the FCI in more familiar terms, now made equivalent to those in (13):

(14)   *Feature-Compatibility Condition on Indexing* (FCI, second statement):
    An index *i* is assigned to an NP iff *i* is compatible with NP.

The FCI is, then, the condition responsible for the exclusion of the inappropriate indexings in (7). To summarize the discussion up to this point, for BT to be a theory of constraints on the distribution of indices, indexing has to be properly interpreted: it represents the assignment of semantic values to NPs on the basis of which the semantic notion of identity relevant for binding can be defined. Being indexing such an assignment, it has to proceed in a way such that NPs get only those values that are compatible with their lexical specification. In order to express this fact, I have formulated a condition that checks whether the interpretation assigned to an NP is compatible with the NP's lexical information: this condition is the FCI in (14).

7.2 Other agreement conditions on binding?

As long as anaphoric dependencies are taken to be the result of (co)indexing in the sense of (6), they will be restricted not only by (whatever the proper formulation of) BT but also by the FCI. In the standard literature on binding it is also assumed (often implicitly) that anaphoric relations are also subject to some requirement for agreement, usually taken to mean "match for person, number, and gender features" (as in Chomsky 1981:193; Lasnik and Uriagereka 1988:47). This looks pretty reasonable at first sight, given the fact that anaphoric elements do appear to agree with their antecedents. Compare the following:

(15)   a. *Mary*$_i$ likes {*herself*$_i$/**himself*$_i$}.

b. *John*$_i$ likes {**herself*$_i$/*himself*$_i$}.

(16)   a. *John*$_i$ thinks Mary likes {**her*$_i$/*him*$_i$}.

b. *Mary*$_i$ thinks John likes {*her*$_i$/**him*$_i$}.

Notice, however, that the FCI itself, being a compatibility condition on the assignment of indices to NPs, derivatively imposes an agreement-like requirement on coindexing: for NP1 and NP2 to be coindexed, both have to get one and the same index i; then, it follows from the FCI that i must be compatible with both NP1 and NP2. For example, if NP1 and NP2 are assigned an index i that is a male, in principle they cannot be [–masculine] according to the FCI (they could be either [+masculine] or unspecified for [±masculine], in either case satisfying nondistinctness). This derivative effect, however, is not equivalent to a requirement that both NPs have to be compatible with each other. For example, consider (17):

(17)   *He*$_i$ thinks Mary likes *him*$_i$. (i = John)
FS$_{he}$ = {[+3p], [-pl], [–acc]}
FS$_{him}$= {[+3p], [-pl], [+acc]}
FS$_i$ = {[+3p], [-pl], [+called-*John*]}

Notice that both *he* and *him* are compatible with i in (17) (in particular, because it is senseless to say that individuals are specified for a feature like [±accusative]). But *he* and *him* are not compatible with each other, since they are distinguished by [±accusative]. That is, the FCI ensures agreement between two NPs insofar as they have to be compatible with the reference they are assigned.[6] Still, this appears to be sufficient for cases like (15) and (16): for example, since i = John and John is a male, i is [+masculine], hence, incompatible with *her* in (16a), *her* being [–masculine]. Since something like the FCI is independently required (for cases like (7), which involve only indexing, and not coindexing), the question is whether any other agreement requirement is necessary, as usually presumed in the standard literature on binding.

In order to show that such an additional agreement requirement is necessary, it is necessary to find some case of agreement between an antecedent and an anaphoric form that could not possibly be assigned to the FCI. Recall that the FCI was conceived of as a condition checking the compatibility of an NP and the interpretation or index it is assigned. Thus, the obvious cases to look at are those in which the antecedent has an interpretation that does not match its grammatical specification. With this type of antecedent, we might expect two types of agreement (the labels are traditional; cf. Corbett 1990:225–226):

(18)   a. *Semantic agreement*: the anaphoric form agrees with the interpretation of the antecedent.

   b. *Grammatical agreement*: the anaphoric form agrees with the grammatical specification of the antecedent.

Semantic agreement is, of course, captured by the FCI. Thus, if one finds only cases of semantic (dis)agreement, no other condition is necessary beyond the FCI. Suppose, however, that one also finds cases of grammatical (dis)agreement; then, this would supply evidence that another condition, independent of the FCI, is not only necessary but also sufficient to license some dependencies: the acceptable form would satisfy grammatical agreement and violate the FCI, while the excluded form would satisfy the FCI and violate grammatical agreement.

I will now consider, then, some of the examples of mismatch between grammatical specification and semantic content, which are abundantly attested in the literature on "pragmatic control" of anaphoric devices (see Cornish 1988; Bosch 1988; Tasmowski and Verluyten 1985, and references cited there). Portuguese, a language in which nouns are grammatically specified for [±feminine], includes nouns like *vítima* 'victim', which is grammatically specified as [+feminine] (cf. adjectival agreement, for example), but whose semantics allows it to refer equally to male and female animates. Thus, a conflict arises when an NP containing this noun is assigned an index i = a male, since such an index will be specified as [−feminine]. Similarly, in Dutch, a language in which nouns are grammatically specified for [±gender], there are nouns like *meisje* 'girl', which is grammatically specified as [−gender] (cf. selection of the definite article) but denotes a subset of human females. A conflict arises in this case because any NP containing this noun has to be assigned an index i = a female, hence a [+gender] index. Thus, in principle sentences like (19) should count as violations of the FCI as formulated in (14):[7]

(19)   a. *A vítima$_i$ tinha sido agredida sem motivo.*   (i = a male)
         The victim(f)$_i$ has been assaulted without motive.

   b. *Het meisje$_j$ is ziek.*   (j = a female)
         The girl(n)$_j$ is sick.

Despite the fact that i and j are compatible with the lexical semantics of *vítima* and *meisje*, respectively, they are not compatible with the grammatical specification of these nouns, and no provision for this mismatch is made if compatibility is defined as overall feature-nondistinctness (cf. (12)). Thus, it appears that, even before checking the properties of NPs like those in (19) as antecedents, one would have to amend the FCI somehow in order to cope with (19). Consideration of other facts, however, throws a different light on (19). As pointed out by Tasmowski and Verluyten (1982, 1985), examples like the ones in (20) show that "pragmatic control" of pronouns is sensitive to the linguistic categorization of the things they refer to, even if such categorization is absent in the linguistic discourse:

(20) a. (John wants his *pants*ᵢ that are on a chair and he says to Mary:)
          Could you hand {*them*/*it*}ᵢ to me, please?

      b. (John is trying to stuff a large tableᵢ—in French, *la table*, feminine—into his car; Mary says:)
          Tu n'arriveras jamais à {*la*/**le*}ᵢ faire entrer dans la voiture.
          'You'll never manage to stuff {*it*(f)/**it*(m)}ᵢ into the car.'

      c. (the same situation, but with a deskᵢ—in French, *le bureau*, masculine:)
          Tu n'arriveras jamais à {**la*/*le*}ᵢ faire entrer dans la voiture.
          'You'll never manage to stuff {**it*(f)/*it*(m)} into the car.'

As T&V put it, "Clearly the real-world object PANTS does not have anything inherently plural in it (in French it would be rendered by a word which is singular [*pantalon*]). . . . Only the grammatical number of the NOUN . . . can explain the occurrence of *them* in (20a). . . . Similarly, the objects TABLE and DESK are neither feminine, nor masculine; only the French nouns *la table* and *le bureau* can explain the respective occurrence of the pronouns *la* and *le*" (T&V 1985:342).

In other words, it appears that the things referred to in discourses like (20) "inherit" the grammatical specification of the noun they are categorized for despite the fact that there is no mention of this noun. In the terminology I have adopted, one may say that, if an index (e.g., an object in D) belongs to a set N of objects (independently of whether this is stated in the linguistic discourse), that index will be associated with the feature specification of the noun N that is interpreted as N. Recall that an index i may be associated with a feature specification FS_i containing features corresponding to the semantic categorization of i (cf. (11)): for example, the index $i =$ Bill has as its $FS_i = \{[+3p], \ldots, [+called\text{-}Bill]\}$. It is necessary to add to this some statement to accommodate cases like (20), as in (21):[8]

(21) An index i is associated with a feature specification, the set $FS_i = \{[\alpha F_1], [\beta F_2], \ldots, [\gamma F_n]\}$ containing:
      a. either features corresponding to the semantic categorization of i;
      b. or the FS of a noun N such that $I(N) = N$, and $N(i)$ is true.

From (21b), it follows that, if i = a table, then FS_i may contain the FS of the French noun *table* in (20b), and similarly for the other examples.

Reconsider now the cases in (19), in which the grammatical specification of an NP conflicts with its lexical semantics. As noted, this might be a problem for the FCI: according to (21a), an index for such an NP would "inherit" the FS associated with this NP's lexical semantics; when assigned to this NP, the index would then be incompatible with the NP's grammatical specification, violating the FCI. Notice, however, that once one assumes something like (21b) to hold, this problem appears to vanish: one may simply assume that, in case the grammatical specification of a noun conflicts with its lexical semantics, (21b) will come into scene and associate the index with a FS compatible with the noun's full FS, instead of assigning an FS corresponding only to its semantic content. In plain terms, the point is: if an individual's categorization for the lexical semantics of some noun is possible, one can refer to such individual by means of (forms compatible with) that noun's grammatical specification (which includes NPs containing that noun itself).[9]

I will now look back, from this point of view, at the question of whether antecedents containing the Portuguese noun *vítima* or the Dutch noun *meisje* trigger semantic or grammatical agreement of an anaphoric form. As seen in (22), it seems that both semantic and grammatical agreement are possible:

(22) a. (i = a male:)
  A vítima$_i$ disse que {ele/ela}$_i$ foi agredid{-o/-a} sem motivo.
  The victim(f)$_i$ said that {he/she}$_i$ was assaulted{-m/-f} without motive.

  b. (i = a female:)
  *Het meisje$_i$ beweert dat {?*het/ze}$_i$ ziek is.*
  The girl(neuter)$_i$ says that {?*it/she}$_i$ sick is.

The Dutch pattern in (22b) might indicate, in principle, that the FCI is at work, excluding the neutral pronoun *het* on the grounds of its incompatibility with the interpretation of *het meisje*, a case of semantic agreement. The Portuguese pattern, on the other hand, might indicate that grammatical agreement is a sufficient condition to license pronouns: the feminine *ela* can be bound by *a vítima* despite its incompatibility with the interpretation assigned to *a vítima* in (22a) (where it refers to a male).[10]

Nevertheless, this understanding of (22) is not warranted if (21) holds. In particular, given (21b), one cannot conclude from the availability of the pronoun *ela* in (22a) that grammatical agreement is a sufficient condition to license bound pronouns. As in (20), it may just as well be the case that the index i in (22a) has simply "inherited" the FS of the noun it was categorized for: in (22a) i is overtly categorized for the noun *vítima*, since "i is a victim" is true if (22a) is true, and *vítima* denotes the set of victims in Portuguese); the noun *vítima* is [+feminine], hence i may "inherit" [+feminine] by (21b); then no violation of the FCI arises if one assigns i to the [+feminine] pronoun *ela* in (22a). In other words, the FCI and (21) together may account for (22a) just as well as an additional grammatical agreement condition would.[11] Since the FCI and (21) are independently motivated, Occam's razor advises us to drop such an additional condition, if its only motivation is cases like (22a).

To sum up the discussion of this section: I started by pointing that, if we want to motivate an additional agreement condition on anaphoric dependencies, we would have to show that this condition has effects distinguishable from those of the FCI, which is a condition independently necessary. To find such cases requires some pattern where an anaphoric form agrees with the grammatical specification of its antecedent rather than with the antecedent's interpretation, since the last case is covered by the FCI. I have presented some cases that might distinguish the FCI from such a grammatical agreement condition, namely, cases involving antecedents whose grammatical specification is in mismatch with its lexical semantics. But independent evidence shows that, if an individual's categorization for the lexical semantics of some noun is possible, that individual appears to "inherit" the grammatical specification of the noun it was categorized for. (Recall that this categorization may not be parasitic on the linguistic environment, and so it is not reducible to linguistic antecedence.) As a consequence, whenever this feature-inheritance is possible, one cannot distinguish the effects of the FCI from those of a potential requirement for grammatical agreement. This, I suggested, might also happen in cases involving nouns whose grammatical specification is in mismatch with their lexical semantics. Therefore, "grammatical agreement" in these cases fails to provide clear support for an independent agreement requirement on anaphoric dependencies. The remaining question is: Isn't there any clear evidence at all for such an independent agreement condition? In the next sections, I turn to the task of showing that 1PPLA is the sort of phenomenon needed to establish the existence of a condition independent of the FCI.

7.3 First person plural anaphora in Brazilian Portuguese

In Brazilian Portuguese (BP) it is possible to use the expression *a gente* (literally, 'the people') to refer to first person plural (1ppl), instead of the forms of the 1ppl pronominal paradigm (actually this use of *a gente* is available in colloquial Portuguese in general, but I will be considering its properties only in BP). The same expression may also have an arbitrary interpretation analogous to the generic use of the English pronoun *one*. The two interpretations of *a gente* can be distinguished because the arbitrary one requires a generic-like environment, as in (23a), and sentences referring to specific events allow only the 1ppl interpretation, as in (23b):

(23)   a. *A gente* sempre vê fantasmas atrás d*a gente.*
      the people always sees ghosts behind of-*the people*

      'One always sees ghosts behind one.'
      'We always see ghosts behind us.'

    b. *A gente* viu uma cobra atrás d*a gente.*
      the people saw a snake behind *the people*

      #'One saw a snake behind one.'
      'We saw a snake behind us.'

Such occurrences of *a gente* have many intriguing properties. The first and most obvious one is that they "borrow" the interpretation of elements that are pronominal in nature: 1ppl pronouns and arbitrary or impersonal subjects can be bound without giving rise to Condition C violations (for examples of these well-known facts, see (41) and (43)). Actually, *a gente* appears to have lost its compositional meaning in colloquial BP, since it does not preserve the lexical meaning of the noun *gente*. This can be seen when one compares NPs containing *gente* with NPs containing nouns with similar properties, such as *pessoa* 'person' and *água* 'water': *gente* and *pessoa* are similar in meaning, *gente* meaning something like 'people, persons'; *água* is like *gente* in being uncountable (cf. **três gentes/águas* 'three people/persons/waters'). As seen in (24) and (25), nouns like *pessoa* and *água* preserve their lexical meaning independently of the determiner they occur with; in particular, with the definite article (cf. (24c) and (25c)). Example (26c), however, shows that the noun *gente* cannot be used with its lexical if accompanied by the definite article; (26a, b), on the other hand, indicate that this is not a property of the noun *gente* itself but of the expression *a gente*:

(24)   a. *Muitas pessoas* chegaram tarde à festa.
'*Many persons* arrived late to the party.'

b. *Poucas pessoas* chegaram tarde à festa.
'*Few persons* arrived late to the party.'

c. *A pessoa de quem falávamos* chegou tarde à festa.
'*The person we spoke of* arrived late to the party.'

(25)   a. *Muita água* havia sido estocada para o verão.
'*A lot of water* had been stored for the summer.'

b. *Pouca água* havia sido estocada para o verão.
'*Little water* had been stored for the summer.'

c. *A água que havia sido estocada para o verão* estava contaminated.'
'*The water that had been stored for the summer* was contamined.

(26)   a. *Muita gente* chegou tarde à festa.
'*A lot of people* arrived late to the party.'

b. *Pouca gente* chegou tarde à festa.
'*Few people* arrived late to the party.'

c. (?)*A gente de quem falávamos* chegou tarde à festa.
'*The people we spoke of* arrived late to the party.'

Another fact corroborates the unavailability of a compositional meaning for *a gente*: despite having the internal structure of a full NP (i.e., [Det N], just like *a menina* 'the girl'), *a gente* cannot be altered by any compositional operation such as adjectival modification, as shown in (27a, b) (the same is true of modification by restrictive relatives, as in (26c)). This is a property that *a gente* shares with pronouns (cf. (27c)), and that distinguishes it from full NPs (see Abney 1986 and references cited there):

(27) a. *[*A gente assustada*] sempre vê fantasma atrás da gente.
[*the people scared*] always sees ghost behind of-the people
*'One scared always sees ghosts behind one.'

b. *[*A gente desatenta*] não percebeu uma cobra atrás da gente.
[*the people inattentive*] not noticed a snake behind the people
*'We inattentive did not see a snake behind us.'

c. *[*Ele desatento*] não percebeu uma cobra atrás dele.
[*he inattentive*] not noticed a snake behind of-him
*'He inattentive did not see a snake behind him.'

Another of the intriguing properties of *a gente* is that its gender specification is un-available to syntax, too (though not its number and person specification, as I will show in the next section). Internal information would suggest *a gente* to be [+femi-nine]: the form of definite article is the feminine *a* 'the(f)', versus *o* 'the(m)'; *gente* itself is obviously a feminine noun in its lexical uses, since it triggers feminine agree-ment on adjectives and determiners (as in *muita gente bonita* 'many(f) people beautiful(f)'). In its arbitrary use, however, *a gente* triggers the default gender speci-fication in BP, namely, masculine, as in (28) (example (28b) is fine if *a gente* is in-terpreted as 1ppl, of course); in its 1ppl use, the gender agreement *a gente* triggers on predicative adjectives depends on whether the 1ppl of the discourse does or does not include a male, as in (29):

(28) a. *A gente* sempre fica surpres-*o* quando se é elogiad-*o* pelo inimigo.
the people always gets surprised-*m* when SE is praised-*m* by-the enemy

b. **A gente* sempre fica surpres-*a* quando se é elogiad-*a* pelo inimigo.
the people always gets surprised-*f* when SE is praised-*f* by-enemy
'One always gets surprised when one is praised by the enemy.'

(29) a. (John speaking of Mary and himself:)
A gente ficou surpres-*o* com aquele elogio.
the people got surprised-*m* with that praise

b. (Susan speaking of Mary and herself:)
A gente ficou surpres-*a* com aquele elogio.
the people got surprised-*f* with that praise
'We got surprised with that praise.'

The fact that *a gente* is compatible with masculine in (28) and (29) shows that it is not specified as [+feminine] for external purposes, unlike NPs containing the noun *gente* in its lexical use. Notice that in an environment like (28) or (29), a lexical NP would trigger grammatical agreement on the predicative adjective in BP independently of its interpretation (recall from section 7.2 that the noun *vítima* 'victim(f)' is compatible with a masculine interpretation):

(30)   (TV news report:)
Um homem₁ foi atacado enquanto caminhava pela rua X esta manhã.
a man₁ was attacked while walking on street X this morning.
a. A vítima₁ foi atingid-a por três tiros.
the victim₁ was hit-f by three shots.

b. *A vítima₁ foi atingid-o por três tiros.
the victim₁ was hit-m by three shots.

Actually, the gender of *a gente* is essentially the same as that of the interpretation it gets: thus, arbitrary interpretation is masculine in BP, as in (31), and 1ppl can be either masculine or feminine, as in (32):[12]

(31)   a. __ sempre *se* fica surpres-*o* quando __ *se* é elogiad-*o*
pro always *SE* gets surprised-*m* when *pro SE* is praised-*m*

b. *__ sempre *se* fica surpres-*a* quando __ *se* é elogiad-*a*
pro always *SE* gets surprised-*f* when *pro SE* is praised-*f*
'One always gets surprised when one is praised.'

(32)   a. (John speaking of Mary and himself:)
nós ficamos surpres-*o*-s com aquele elogio
we got surprised-*m*-pl with that praise

b. (Susan speaking of Mary and herself:)
nós ficamos surpres-*a*-s com aquele elogio
we got surprised-*f*-pl with that praise

Finally, *a gente* also has the external distribution of pronominal elements: as exemplified in (23), repeated here as (33), *a gente* can be bound by itself, like the pronouns in (34a, b), and unlike the lexical NPs in (35a, b):

(33)   a. A *gente* sempre vê fantasmas atrás d*a gente*.
the people always sees ghosts behind of-*the people*
'One always sees ghosts behind one.'

b. A *gente* viu uma cobra atrás d*a gente*.
the people saw a snake behind *the people*
'We saw a snake behind us.'

(34)   a. *Ele* sempre vê fantasmas atrás d*ele*.
he always sees ghosts behind of-*him*
'He always sees ghosts behind him.'

b. *Nós* vimos uma cobra atrás de *nós*.
we saw a snake behind of *us*.
'We saw a snake behind us.'

(35) a. *O Paulo viu uma cobra atrás do Paulo.
          Paulo saw a snake behind of Paulo
          *'Paulo saw a snake behind Paulo.'

      b. *O canalha viu uma cobra atrás do canalha.
          the bastard saw a snake behind of-the bastard
          *'The bastard saw a snake behind the bastard.'

Examples (35a and b) are typical violations of Condition C. The fact that a gente in (33a, b) does not violate this condition shows that it does not count as a lexical NP for the purposes of BT. Moreover, where pronouns trigger Condition B effects, as in (36), a gente triggers them too, in either of its pronominal interpretations, as in (37) and (38):[13]

(36) a. O Paulo viu ele *(mesmo) na TV.
          Paulo saw him *(same) on-the TV
          'Paulo saw {*him/himself} on TV.'

      b. Nós passamos a desconfiar de nós *(mesmos) depois do incidente.
          we started to suspecting of us *(same) after the incident
          'We started suspecting of {*us/ourselves} after the incident.'

(37) a. A gente viu a gente ??(mesmo) na TV.
          the people saw the people ??(same) on-the TV
          'We saw {*us/ourselves} on TV.'

      b. A gente passou a desconfiar da gente (?)*(mesmo) depois do incidente.
          the people started to suspecting of the people (?)*(same) after the incident
          'We started suspecting of {*us/ourselves} after the incident.'

(38) a. A gente sempre quer ver a gente ??(mesmo) na TV.
          the people always wants to see the people ??(same) on-the TV
          'One always wants to see {*one/oneself} on TV.'

      b. A gente sempre desconfia da gente (?)*(mesmo).
          the people always suspects of the people (?)*(same)
          'One always suspects of {*one/oneself}.'

That is, a gente appears to have essentially the binding behavior of a pronoun. To summarize, the expression a gente has the following pronominal-like properties in BP:

(39) Pronominal-like a gente in BP:
      a. pronominal interpretation (either 1ppl or arbitrary interpretation);
      b. absence of compositional meaning (lexical meaning of gente unavailable);
      c. pronominal internal syntax (no modification possible);

d. gender determined by interpretation (not by lexical specification);

e. binding behavior of pronouns (Condition B rather than Condition C effects).

Given the properties in (39), it seems clear that the expression *a gente* does not derive its semantic and grammatical properties compositionally from the properties of its component parts. In particular, unlike other NPs with the structure [Det N], *a gente* inherits neither its gender specification nor its lexical meaning from the noun head *gente*.

As for its binding properties, I have just shown that *a gente* is a pronominal-like expression, incurring Condition B rather than Condition C violations. Having a 1ppl or an arbitrary interpretation, it is not surprising, then, that *a gente* may establish anaphoric dependencies with other expressions with these interpretations: it can be bound and bind 1ppl pronouns, as in (40) and (41), and also can be bound and bind arbitrary subjects, as in (42) and (43):

(40)   a. *Nós* achamos que o Paulo já viu *a gente* na TV.
       we think that Paulo already saw *the people* on-the TV
       'We think Paulo has already seen us on TV.'

       b. *Nós* perguntamos pr'o Paulo quando *a gente* apareceria na TV.
       we asked to Paulo when *the people* would appear on-the TV
       'We asked Paulo when we would appear on TV.'

(41)   a. *A gente* acha que o Paulo já *nos* viu na TV.
       the people think that Paulo already *us* saw on-the TV
       'We think that Paulo has already seen us on TV.'

       b. *A gente* perguntou pr'o Paulo quando *nós* apareceríamos na TV.
       the people asked when *we* would-appear on-the TV
       'We asked when we would appear on TV.'

(42)   a. __ sempre *se* imagina que *a gente* pode escapar do perigo
       pro always *SE* imagines that *the people* can escape from the danger
       'One always thinks that one can escape from the danger.'

       b. __ sempre *se* pensa que os outros conseguem tolerar *a gente*
       pro always *SE* thinks that the others can tolerate *the people*
       'One always thinks that other people can tolerate one.'

(43)   *A gente* sempre imagina que __ *se* pode escapar do perigo.
       the people always imagines that *pro SE* can escape from the danger
       'One always think that one can escape from the danger.'

Since *a gente* both is a pronominal form and enters into anaphoric dependencies with other pronominal forms having the same interpretation, we might expect it to have the same range of anaphoric choices as those forms themselves. This appear to be true with respect to its arbitrary interpretation: where an arbitrary subject takes a third person (3p) anaphor, arbitrary *a gente* can take it too; where an arbitrary subject cannot take a 3p anaphor, arbitrary *a gente* cannot take it either:[14]

(44)   a.   __ sempre *se* deve *se* preparar para o pior
            pro always *SE* must *SE* prepare for the worst

            'One always must prepare oneself for the worst.'

       b.   __ nunca *se* deve confiar demais em {*si (?)(mesmo)*} nestas situações
            pro never *SE* must trust too-much in {*SE (same)*} in-such situations

            'One never must trust too much in oneself in such situations.'

       c.   __ sempre *se* vê fantasmas atrás de {*(?)?si ??(mesmo)*} nestas situações
            pro always *SE* sees ghosts behind of {*SE (same)*} in-such situations

            'One always sees ghosts behind one.'

       d.   *__ sempre *se* imagina que os outros devem confiar em *si*
            pro always *SE* imagines that the others must trust in *SE*

            'One always imagines that the others must trust in one.'

(45)   a.   *A gente* sempre deve *se* preparar para o pior
            the people always must *SE* prepare for the worst

            'One always must prepare oneself for the worst.'

       b.   *A gente* nunca deve confiar demais em {*si (?)(mesmo)*} nestas situações
            the people never must trust too-much in {*SE (same)*} in-such situations

            'One never must trust too much in oneself in such situations.'

       c.   *A gente* sempre vê fantasmas atrás de {*(?)?si ??(mesmo)*} nestas situações
            the people always sees ghosts behind of *SE (same)* in-such situations

            'One always sees ghosts behind one.'

       d.   **A gente* sempre imagina que os outros devem confiar em *si*
            the people always imagines that the others must trust in *SE*

            'One always imagines that the others must trust in one.'

By an analogous reasoning, one might expect that whenever a 1ppl pronoun may bind another 1ppl pronoun, 1ppl *a gente* may too. This appears to be true for many contexts, as we in (46) and (47) ((47c, d) repeated from (41a, b)):

(46)   a.   *Nós* vimos o *nosso* carro ser roubado.
            we saw the *our* car to-be stolen

            'We saw our car to be stolen.'

       b.   *Nós* tínhamos visto uma cobra atrás de *nós*.
            we had seen a snake behind of *us*

            'We have seen a snake behind us.'

    c. *Nós* achamos que o Paulo já *nos* viu na TV.
       we think that Paulo already *us* saw on-the TV
       'We think that Paulo has already seen us on TV.'

    b. *Nós* perguntamos pr'o Paulo quando *nós* apareceríamos na TV.
       we asked to Paulo when *we* would appear on-the TV
       'We asked Paulo when we would appear on TV.'

(47) a. *A gente* viu o *nosso* carro ser roubado.
       the people saw the *our* car to-be stolen
       'We saw our car to be stolen.'

    b. *A gente* tinha visto uma cobra atrás de *nós*.
       the people had seen a snake behind of *us*
       'We have seen a snake behind us.'

    c. *A gente* acha que o Paulo já *nos* viu na TV.
       the people think that Paulo already *us* saw on the TV
       'We think that Paulo has already seen us on TV.'

    b. *A gente* perguntou pr'o Paulo quando (*nós*) apareceríamos na TV.
       the people asked to Paulo when (*we*) would appear on the TV
       'We asked Paulo when we would appear on TV.'

But there is a context where this correspondence with 1ppl pronouns breaks down, namely, in local binding of 1ppl object clitics: in such structures, 1ppl *a gente*, unlike a 1ppl subject pronoun, cannot bind a 1ppl clitic:

(48) a. *Nós* devíamos *nos* preparar para o pior.
       we should *us* prepare for the worst
       'We should prepare ourselves for the worst.'

    b. **A gente* devia *nos* preparar para o pior.
       the people should *us* prepare for the worst
       'We should prepare ourselves for the worst.'

Rather, 1ppl *a gente* requires the 3p anaphor *se*, just as arbitrary *a gente* (cf. (45a)); a 1ppl subject pronoun, however, cannot take the 3p clitic:

(49) a. **Nós* devíamos *se* preparar para o pior.
       we should *SE* prepare for the worst
       'We should prepare ourselves for the worst.'

    b. *A gente* devia *se* preparar para o pior.
       the people should *SE* prepare for the worst
       'We should prepare ourselves for the worst.'

Since 1ppl *a gente* behaves as arbitrary *a gente* in taking the 3p anaphor clitic, one might also expect it to take the 3p anaphor in other environments where arbitrary *a gente* does, too. But this expectation is not fulfilled: with 1ppl *a gente* as an antecedent the 3p anaphor is essentially out *within* PPs in BP, and a 1ppl pronoun appears to be a better choice: compare (50a, b) with (45b, c), respectively:[15]

(50)   a. *A gente* confiou demais em {*(?)*si/?nós*}.
           the people relied too-much on {*(?)?SE/?us*}
           'We relied too much on *us/ourselves.*'

       b. *A gente* viu uma cobra atrás de {**si/nós*}.
           the people already had seen a snake behind of {**SE/us*}
           'We have already seen a snake behind us/??ourselves.'

Thus, while the anaphoric choices of arbitrary *a gente* as an antecedent are hardly surprising—they are essentially those of any antecedent with an arbitrary interpretation—things are more complex with the 1ppl use of this expression: in some contexts it behaves as a 1ppl pronominal antecedent, in others it does not. More specifically:

(51)   *First Person Plural Anaphora in BP* (1PPLA, first statement):
       a. 1ppl *a gente* can bind a 1ppl pronoun, but only if this does not result in local binding of a 1ppl verbal clitic *nos* (in particular, it can bind 1ppl within PPs belonging to the same clause).

       b. 1ppl *a gente* can bind a 3p anaphor, the verbal clitic *se*, if binding is local; but it cannot bind 3p anaphors anywhere else (in particular, it cannot bind 3p anaphors within PPs belonging to the same clause).

To simplify the generalizations in (51), assume that "local binding" in BP means "binding of an object clitic by the subject of the same clause"; that is, local binding is binding within a transitive structure and does not cross PPs. Then, (51) may be restated as (52):

(52)   *First Person Plural Anaphora in BP* (1PPLA, second statement):
       a. 1ppl *a gente* can bind a 1ppl pronoun, but not locally.

       b. 1ppl *a gente* can bind a 3p anaphor, but only locally.

The question I will try to answer in the next sections is: What is behind the pattern described by (52)? Before I turn to this issue, however, it seems advisable to make a few remarks about the generality of the effects summarized in (52): How does one know that this pattern is not an idiosyncrasy concerning the expression *a gente* in BP? I am aware of at least two types of evidence suggesting that (52) is actually the result of deep and systematic principles regulating anaphoric dependencies. First, French has an expression, the so-called impersonal *on*, that appears to have very similar properties as the BP expression, despite their distinct historical sources: *on* is also a pronominal-like element, it may have an arbitrary-like or a 1ppl-like interpretation, and it requires the third person singular form of the verb as well. Not surprisingly, in its 1ppl interpretation *on* shows the same pattern of anaphoric choices as BP *a gente* (judgments provided by Pierre Pica, personal communication):

(53) a. *On { *nous/s'}* est vu à la télé.
           one {us/SE} is seen on the TV
           'We saw ourselves on TV.'

      b. *On* a vu un serpent derriére *{nous/*soi}*.
           one has seen a snake behind *{us/SE}*
           'We saw a snake behind us.'

The second fact confirming the generality of the pattern in (52) is internal to BP and concerns the anaphoric pattern triggered by the second person–like pronoun *você*. This form is one of the second person forms found in Romance that developed out of honorific expressions and, as such, preserved a 3ps grammatical specification, again attested by verbal agreement. In many dialects of BP, *você* has substituted the old (informal) second person form *tu* in subject position, while the rest of the old second person paradigm was preserved to some degree. In these dialects, old second person forms can be bound by *você*. In particular, the old second person clitic *te* can, but again, only if binding is nonlocal; locally, only the 3p anaphor is possible. This is attested by examples like (54) (from Rubem Fonseca's novel *Agosto* [p. 63]; unacceptable *te* was added):

(54) *Você {se/*te}* arrisca por causa de uns vadios. Acha que vão *te* dar alguma medalha por isso?
       You {SE/*you} risk-3ps because of some vagabonds. (*You*) think-3ps that (they) will *to-you* give a medal for this?
       'You risk yourself because of some vagabonds. Do you think that somebody will give you a medal for this?'

Patterns such as (53) and (54) clearly show that 1PPLA is not one of BP's whimsies but a particular instantiation of a larger empirical generalization.

7.4 On the nature of 1PPLA

It is instructive to start by demonstrating that the pattern characteristic of 1PPLA in BP cannot be subsumed under conditions that do not refer to properties of the antecedent. Consider, for example, the relevant principles in the standard BT:

(55) *Condition A:* An anaphor must be bound in its GC.
       Condition B: A pronominal must be free in its GC.

If the fact that an anaphoric form can occur free or not is taken as a diagnostics for its binding type (if it cannot occur free, it is an anaphor; if it can, it is a pronominal), one may assume that the 1ppl clitic *nos* counts as a pronominal, and the 3p clitic *se* as an anaphor for the purposes of (55). Compare (56):

(56)　a.　O João$_i$ tinha *nos*$_j$ visto no cinema ontem.

　　　　　João$_i$ had *us*$_j$ seen in-the cinema yesterday

　　　　　'João saw us in the cinema yesterday.'

　　　b.　O João$_i$ tinha *se*$_{i/*j}$ visto na TV ontem.

　　　　　João$_i$ had *SE*$_{i/*j}$ seen on-the TV yesterday

　　　　　'João$_i$ saw {*him$_j$/himself$_i$} on TV yesterday.'

If *nos* is a pronominal, it should be constrained by Condition B in (55), that is, *nos* should not be able to be bound locally. Assume, for the sake of the argument, that "GC" in (55) means the same as "locally bound" in the sense of (52).[16] Then it would appear that (52a) follows from Condition B: *nos* can be bound by *a gente* only nonlocally, as exemplified in (57a, b) (repeated from (47c) and (42b), respectively):

(57)　a.　*A gente* acha que o Paulo já *nos* viu na TV.

　　　　　the people think that Paulo already *us* saw on the TV

　　　　　'We think that Paulo already saw us on TV.'

　　　b.　*A gente* devia *nos* preparar para o pior.

　　　　　the people should *us* prepare for the worst

　　　　　'We should prepare ourselves for the worst.'

But this explanation for (57b) can be easily dismissed: as is well known, first and second person clitic pronouns can be locally bound in Romance, including BP, as in (58) (repeated from (48a)):[17]

(58)　*Nós* devíamos *nos* preparar para o pior.

　　　we should *us* prepare for the worst

　　　'We should prepare ourselves for the worst.'

Example (58) is exactly like (57b), except that in (58) the local antecedent of the clitic is a 1ppl subject pronoun, while in (57b) the local antecedent is 1ppl *a gente*. Example (58)'s full acceptability clearly shows that *nos* can be locally bound, despite Condition B as formulated in (55). It follows that the unacceptability of (57b) cannot be attributed to Condition B: (57b) is not excluded because *nos* is locally bound; if this were the case, (58) should be excluded, too. Example (57b) has to be excluded, then, because 1ppl *a gente* is the local binder of *nos*, and not a 1ppl pronoun, as in (58).

　　　A similar reasoning shows that a Condition A approach to (52b) is not feasible either. To repeat the facts: 1ppl *a gente* can locally bind a 3p anaphor (cf. (59a)) but not an anaphor within a PP (cf. (59b, c), from (49b) and (50a, b)):

(59) a. *A gente* devia *se* preparar para o pior.
          the people should *SE* prepare for the worst
          'We should prepare ourselves for the worst.'

      b. (?)**A gente* confiou demais em *si*.
          (?)**the people* trusted too-much in *SE*
          'We trusted too much in *us/ourselves.'

      c. **A gente* viu uma cobra atrás de *si*.
          **the people* already saw a snake behind of *SE*
          'We already saw a snake behind us/??ourselves.'

For (59b and c) to be cases of Condition A violations, one would have to assume that the binding domain of anaphors in BP includes transitive structures (cf. (59a)) but does not cross PPs (cf. (59b) and (59c), respectively). But this cannot be correct. Not only the 3p form *si* is an anaphor just like the 3p clitic *se* (cf. (60a); cf. with (56b)), but also *si* can be bound in contexts like (59b, c) if the antecedent is a 3p NP (cf. (60b, c), respectively):[18]

(60) a. (Speaking of *Paulo*:) Eu confiei demais em { **si (mesmo)*}
          (Speaking of *Paulo*:) I trusted too-much in {*SE (same)*}
          (Speaking of Paulo:) 'I trusted too much in him.'

      b. *O Paulo* confiou demais em {*si (mesmo)*}
          Paulo trusted too-much in {*SE (same)*}
          'Paulo trusted too much in himself.'

      c. *O Paulo* viu uma cobra atrás de {*(?)?si ??(mesmo)*}.
          Paulo already saw a snake behind of {*SE (same)*}
          'Paulo already saw a snake behind him.'

Given the relative acceptability of (60b, c) (as compared with (59b, c)), one can conclude that *si* does not violate Condition A in these sentences. In other words, (60b, c) should count as binding within the domain of *si* for the purposes of Condition A as formulated in (55). But, then, (59b, c) cannot count as a violation of Condition A either. Again, one must conclude that the trouble with the anaphoric relations in (59b, c), as opposed to (59a), has nothing to do with binding of the anaphor. Rather, it it has to do with the fact that the anaphor is bound by 1ppl *a gente*: this is possible within transitive structures (cf. (59a)), but not into PPs (cf. (60b, c)).

I have noted, then, that one cannot account for the main descriptive generalizations concerning 1PPLA in (52a, b) by resorting to the standard binding Conditions A and B alone, and this is so for a very specific reason: these conditions are not of the appropriate sort. The standard Conditions A and B are formulated as restrictions on the anaphoric form alone, without referring to the properties of the antecedent. The effects summarized in (52a, b) and reviewed here, however, cannot be the result of a restriction on the anaphoric forms themselves, because there is always some antecedent that makes them fine in the relevant contexts: *nos* is fine locally bound by a 1ppl subject pronoun, and *si* is fine within PPs if bound by a 3p antecedent. Rather,

(52a, b) attest to a restriction on these anaphoric forms when they are bound by 1ppl *a gente*.[19] The point is: to know which sort of restriction applies here, one must first understand which properties of 1ppl *a gente* distinguish it from 1ppl subject pronouns, on the one hand, and from 3p subjects, on the other.

The striking thing about 1ppl *a gente* is, of course, the fact that it can have a 1ppl interpretation despite its morphosyntactic composition, which is that of a lexical NP, more specifically, of a third person singular feminine NP. As presented in section 7.3, agreement with predicative adjectives suggests that 1ppl *a gente* is not specified as feminine but has the gender determined by its interpretation, just like 1ppl pronouns. Things are different with respect to person and number. As a subject, 1ppl *a gente* does not require the same verbal form as a 1ppl pronoun; rather, it requires the 3ps form of the verb, just like other 3ps NPs:

(61)   a. *Nós* já {*vimos/*viu*} a Maria na TV.
           we already {*saw-1ppl/*saw-3ps*} Maria on-the TV
           'We have already seen Maria on TV.'

       b. *O Paulo* já {**vimos/viu*} a Maria na TV.
           Paulo already {**saw-1ppl/saw-3ps*} Maria on-the TV
           'Paulo has already seen Maria on TV.'

       c. *A gente* já {**vimos/viu*} a Maria na TV.
           the people already {**saw-1ppl/saw-3ps*} Maria on-the TV
           'We have already seen Maria on TV.'

Example (61c) shows that, although interpreted as a 1ppl pronoun, 1ppl *a gente* has essentially the same specification as 3ps NPs with respect to person and number. (Recall, however, that 1pp *a gente*, unlike 3ps lexical NPs, does not inherit the gender from its head noun.)

Thus, what 1ppl *a gente* and 1ppl pronouns have in common is their 1ppl interpretation, and what distinguishes them is their grammatical specification (one may ignore gender here, since neither 1ppl pronouns nor 3p anaphors are specified for it): 1ppl *a gente* is grammatically specified as 3ps, and 1ppl pronouns are grammatically specified as 1ppl. On the other hand, 1ppl *a gente* shares its specification for person and number with 3ps NPs, but it is distinct from 3ps NPs with respect to interpretation: 1ppl *a gente* has a 1ppl interpretation, and 3ps NPs do not. In the usual case, 3ps NPs are assigned an interpretation that is singular and does not refer to the speaker or the addressee, that is, 3ps NPs have a 3ps interpretation. This may be summarized as in (62) ("GS" means "grammatical specification"; following the discussion of section 7.1, I use "index" instead of "interpretation assigned"):

(62)

NP Type	GS	Index
1ppl pronouns	1ppl	*1ppl*
1ppl *a gente*	*3ps*	*1ppl*
3ps NPs	*3ps*	3ps

1ppl *a gente* is, then, another case of the phenomenon we discussed in section 7.2, namely, of a mismatch between an NP's grammatical specification and its interpretation. Such cases are crucial if one wants to check whether an anaphoric form agrees with the grammatical specification or with the interpretation of its antecedent. This distinction is obviously undetectable when the grammatical specification and the interpretation of the antecedent are compatible with each other, as with 1ppl pronouns and normal 3p NPs. Moreover, as I suggested in section 7.2, it may also be undetectable if the antecedent's lexical meaning is determined by the head noun, as with NPs containing nouns like *vítima* 'victim' in BP. This is so because in such cases the interpretation or index assigned to the antecedent may "inherit" the grammatical specification of the head noun (which is independently necessary for cases of "pragmatic control," as when a discourse referent belongs to the semantic category described by nouns like *table* 'table' and *bureau* 'desk' in French). These facts were captured by clause (b) of (21), which is repeated here as (63):[20]

(63)   An index i is associated with a feature specification, the set $FS_i = \{[\alpha F_1], [\beta F_2], \ldots,$ $[\gamma F_n]\}$ containing:

   a.   either features corresponding to the semantic categorization of i;

   b.   or the FS of a noun N such that $I(N) = N$, and $N(i)$ is true.

But in this respect 1ppl *a gente* differs from the cases of mismatch seen in section 7.2 and appears to constitute a real case of mismatch in the sense that it really counts as a violation of the FCI. Recall that the FCI, the condition in (14) of section 7.1, repeated here as (64), checks the matching between an NP's lexical specification and the interpretation it is assigned:

(64)   *Feature-Compatibility Condition on Indexing* (FCI):
   An index i is assigned to an NP iff i is compatible with that NP.

Even if 1ppl *a gente* were semantically specified as 1ppl, assignment of a 1ppl index would still be in conflict with *a gente*'s 3ps grammatical specification. We cannot avoid this clash by resorting to clause (b) of (63) and make the 1ppl index "inherit" the grammatical specification of the noun *gente*: as seen in section 7.1 (cf. (39b)), the lexical meaning of *gente* is unavailable in 1ppl *a gente*, and so clause (63b) does not apply (clause (63a) is clearly irrelevant, since the index 1ppl *a gente* gets is a 1ppl one and, hence, it has to be semantically categorized as such). In other words, it appears that 1ppl use of *a gente* is a case in which an FCI's violation has to be tolerated as a result of the intrinsic properties of that expression:

(65)   1ppl use of *a gente* results in a mismatch between this NP's GS and the index it is assigned.

Ideally, one would like to formulate the FCI (or the mechanism in (63)) in such a way as to avoid having to stipulate that 1ppl *a gente* is a violation of the FCI. I am not aware of any solution, however, that will not imply some complication for other of the relevant cases. For example, one might try to formulate the FCI in such a way as to check only the semantic specification of an NP, in which case clause (63b) should be eliminated (since it refers to the grammatical rather than the semantic specification of a noun). That is, the semantic categorization of an NP's index would have to match only the NP's semantic features.[21] In this case, under the assumption that 1ppl *a gente* is semantically specified for a 1ppl interpretation, no clash arises between its semantic specification and a 1ppl index (i.e., the assignment of a 1ppl interpretation in a particular discourse). The problem with this approach comes from cases like (22a), repeated here as (66):

(66) (i = a male:)
    A vítima$_i$ disse que {*ele/ela*}$_i$ foi agredid{-o/-a} sem motivo.
    the victim(f)$_i$ said that {*he/she*}$_i$ was beaten{-m/-f} without motive

In (66) the feminine pronoun *ela* is possible only because the index i may "inherit" the grammatical specification of the noun *vítima* (cf. (63b)). If only semantic features were relevant, then *ela* should be excluded in (66) as a violation of the FCI: supposedly, *ela* is not only grammatically but also semantically specified as feminine and, hence, is incompatible with a masculine interpretation (notice that no problem arises with *vítima* itself, since this noun is semantically compatible with a masculine interpretation). This shows that the FCI has to be sensitive to the grammatical specification of NPs. Therefore, I will assume the stipulation in (65), and keep (63) and the FCI in (64) untouched.[22]

Given (65), however, 1PPLA (i.e., anaphoric dependencies involving 1ppl *a gente*) is the sort of phenomenon we expect to show whether or not we need some condition requiring grammatical agreement for anaphoric dependencies. To check whether it does indeed, I will look back to (52), repeated here as (67):

(67) *First Person Plural Anaphora in BP* (1PPLA, second statement):
    a. 1ppl *a gente* can bind a 1ppl pronoun, but not locally;

    b. 1ppl *a gente* can bind a 3p anaphor, but only locally.

Notice that while 1ppl pronouns are compatible with the interpretation of 1ppl *a gente*, they are not compatible with *a gente*'s grammatical specification; inversely, while the 3p anaphor is compatible with 1ppl *a gente*'s grammatical specification, it is not compatible with a 1ppl interpretation. The obvious generalizations that emerge from (67) together with (62), then, are: if binding is LOCAL, (i) 1ppl *a gente* requires an anaphoric form that agrees with its grammatical specification, namely, the 3p anaphor clitic; and (ii) excludes an anaphoric form that does not agree with its grammatical specification, namely, the 1ppl clitic; if binding is NONLOCAL, then (iii) 1ppl *a gente* requires an anaphoric form that is compatible with its interpretation, namely, a 1ppl pronoun; and (iv) excludes an anaphoric form that is not compatible with a 1ppl interpretation, namely, the 3p anaphor. Shortly:

(68) *First Person Plural Anaphora in BP* (1PPLA, third statement):
   a. Nonlocally, 1ppl *a gente* binds a form compatible with its interpretation.

   b. Locally, it binds a form agreeing with its grammatical specification.

Example (68) makes it clear that 1PPLA effects arise from the inconsistency between 1ppl *a gente*'s grammatical specification and its interpretation. More important, however, (68) also shows that *two* agreement-like conditions are necessary: one checking the matching between an anaphoric form and the antecedent's interpretation in nonlocal domains (cf. (68a)); the other checking the matching between an anaphoric form and the grammatical specification of its antecedent in local domains (cf. (68b)):

(69) *Agreement-Like Conditions on Anaphoric Dependencies:*
   a. A nonlocally bound anaphoric form has to be compatible with its antecedent's interpretation.

   b. A locally bound anaphoric form has to agree with its antecedent's grammatical specification.

Note that anaphoric dependencies are established when the anaphoric form and an antecedent share the same interpretation or are covalued. In other words, (67a) is equivalent to saying that the anaphoric form has to be compatible with the interpretation it is assigned (which happens to be the same as that of its antecedent). But, then, there is an obvious candidate to take over the role of (69a): it is the FCI in (64), the condition that checks the compatibility between an NP's lexical specification and the interpretation it is assigned. That is, 3p anaphors cannot be bound by 1ppl *a gente* nonlocally because they are not compatible with the index they would get in this dependency, namely, the same index as 1ppl *a gente*: (i) 3p anaphors are specified as [3p], and 1ppl *a gente* is assigned a [1ppl] interpretation or index; (ii) [3p] and [1ppl] specifications are distinct for person and, hence, incompatible; therefore, (iii) if a [3p] anaphor is assigned a [1ppl] index, a violation of the FCI ensues; hence, (iv) a [3p] anaphor cannot be assigned the same index as 1ppl *a gente* (nonlocally; I return to local dependencies shortly).

This approach to (68a) is further supported by the behavior of arbitrary *a gente*. As shown in section 7.3, arbitrary *a gente* can bind the 3p anaphor *si* nonlocally, unlike 1ppl *a gente* (cf. (45b, c) with (50a, b) = (59b, c)). But recall that (i) other arbitrary or impersonal subjects can bind *si* nonlocally too (cf. (44)), which suggests that (ii) the 3p anaphor *si* is compatible with an arbitrary interpretation. Moreover, (iii) arbitrary or impersonal subjects and arbitrary *a gente* can bind each other (cf. (43) and (42)), confirming that (iv) arbitrary *a gente* is compatible with arbitrary interpretation, too.[23] Since both [3p] *si* and arbitrary *a gente* are compatible with an arbitrary interpretation, (v) no violation of the FCI ensues if arbitrary *a gente* binds *si*, which should be possible wherever *si* is allowed with arbitrary antecedents. And this is true (cf. (44) and (45)). Hence, the FCI predicts that, unlike 1ppl *a gente*, arbitrary *a gente* can bind *si* nonlocally.

The FCI in (64), however, does not make reference to any domain, whereas (69a) appears to have a sort of "antilocality" effect: it applies only to nonlocally bound forms. It is necessary to consider two aspects of this effect: first, the positive statement that the relevant condition applies everywhere except for local dependencies; second, the negative statement that the condition does not appear to apply to local dependencies. The former statement does follow from the FCI: as long as an NP is assigned an index (i.e., an interpretation), it should be subject to the FCI regardless of its localization with respect to an antecedent. As formulated in (64), the FCI is a condition on the mapping between an NP and the interpretation it gets; it is not sensitive to this NP's belonging to a dependency, nor to this dependency's being local. Precisely for this reason, however, it is puzzling that the FCI appears not to apply to locally bound anaphoric forms. If it did, 1ppl *a gente* would not be able to bind the 3p anaphor *se* locally, just as it cannot bind *si* nonlocally: in either case a 3p anaphor is not compatible with 1ppl *a gente*'s index and, hence, violates the FCI. The question this raises is:

(70)   Why isn't a 3p anaphor excluded by the FCI when binding is local?

As I have noted, the FCI is not a condition on dependencies and, as such, has nothing to say about (70). I will return to this issue in section 7.6.

Setting (70) aside for a moment, one has a condition independently motivated that can fill in the role of (69a), namely, the FCI. But, what about the requirement in (69b), which appears to have the profile of the condition I have been looking for: it requires grammatical agreement between antecedent and anaphoric form, and, hence, it cannot be reduced to the FCI. Moreover, the fact that (69b) requires grammatical agreement in a given local domain indicates that (69b) is syntactic in nature: syntactic conditions are supposed to be sensitive only to morphosyntactic properties, as grammatical features are, and are bound to the domain of a sentence. Is it possible, then, for BT to accommodate (69b)?

7.5 The domain of 1PPLA: Agreement-on-Chains

As I noted earlier (see introduction and section 7.3), for an agreement condition on anaphoric dependencies to be formulated on the basis of BT without adding descriptive power to it, this condition has to be formulated with the concepts already available in the theory. Yet different versions of BT put to use distinct concepts, allowing for different conditions to be defined. This provides us with the following test to compare competing versions of BT: given some empirical motivation for an agreement condition on anaphoric dependencies, which theory gives us the appropriate means to state this condition? Sections 7.1 and 7.2, on the other hand, have shown that this test has to be qualified: there is an independent condition on indexing or the interpretation assigned to NPs, the FCI, which is responsible for some of the agreement effects that might seem to motivate a requirement for agreement in anaphoric dependencies. It is necessary, then, to find anaphoric dependencies in which the effects of the FCI can be clearly isolated. In sections 7.3 and 7.4 I argued that 1PPLA is just the sort of phenomenon I am looking for and that it actually provides evidence for an agreement condition on anaphoric dependencies that is distinct from the FCI. The relevant condition was stated in (69b), repeated here as (71):

(71)   *Agreement of Anaphoric Dependencies:*
A locally bound anaphoric form has to agree with its antecedent's grammatical specification.

It is of (71), then, that one must ask: Which theory gives us the appropriate means to state it? In this section I consider two candidates, the main competing versions of BT: standard BT (with and without the LF-movement analysis of anaphors), and R&R's theory of reflexivity and A-chains.

One may start by trying to limit the space for plausible candidates for (71). For example, (71) is stated as a condition on anaphoric forms in general—that is, on bound forms—and not on any NP type in particular. If this aspect of (71) is correct, it will not do to look at conditions on particular NP types—for example, some agreement requirement on anaphors only, as is often suggested.[24] Recall the motivation for (71) (see discussion of (67) and (68)): it is responsible not only for the acceptability of the 3p anaphor when locally bound by 1ppl *a gente* but also for the unacceptability of a 1ppl pronoun when locally bound by 1ppl *a gente*. Compare the following:

(72)   a.   *A gente* já *se* viu na TV.
            the people already *SE* saw on-the TV
            'We have already seen ourselves on TV.'

       b.   **A gente* já *nos* viu na TV.
            the people already *us* saw on-the TV
            'We have already seen ourselves on TV.'

Moreover, the reverse paradigm also follows from (71): a 1ppl subject pronoun can locally bind only a 1ppl pronoun, not the 3p anaphor:[25]

(73)   a.   **Nós* já *se* vimos na TV.
            we already *SE* saw on-the TV
            'We have already seen ourselves on TV.'

       b.   *Nós* já *nos* viu na TV.
            we already *us* saw on-the TV
            'We have already seen ourselves on TV.'

Thus, it appears to be correct to state (71) as a condition on locally bound anaphoric forms in general.[26] As a consequence, it is possible to dismiss agreement conditions devised to hold of specific NP types from the set of possible candidates for (71). This allows one to reject not only agreement conditions on anaphors but also the possibility that the effects of (71) might be deduced from the local domain created by the anaphor's LF-movement to INFL. Although in itself this does not count as an argument against the LF-movement analysis of anaphors, it does lead to a sort of conceptual oddity: since LF-movement to INFL also results in an agreement requirement on the anaphor (cf. Cole and Sung 1994; R&R 1991), this would be partially redundant with (71), which is independently necessary because of pronouns.

Actually, quite independently of (71), 1PPLA does seem to argue against the LF-movement analysis of anaphors. Recall the basic facts motivating this hypothesis (or, better, its more consensual version, the one claiming that only SE anaphors LF-move): (i) the cross-linguistic generalization according to which long distance–bound anaphors are simplex SE forms (i.e., defective pronominal forms such as Romance reflexives, but not complex forms such as *himself* in English); (ii) the subject orientation of such long distance–bound anaphors. The BP 3p anaphor *si* fits this profile: it is simplex, subject oriented (cf. (74a)), and may be long distance-bound under propitious circumstances (cf. (74b, c)):

(74) a. *O João$_i$ tinha lhe$_j$ falado de si$_{i/*j}$.*
         João$_i$ had *him*(dat)$_j$ spoken of $SE_{i/*j}$
         'João has spoken to him about himself.'

      b. *(?)Ninguém pode dizer que tenha me ouvido falar mal de si.*
         nobody can say that *(he)* has me heard to-speak ill of *SE*
         'Nobody can say that he has heard me speak ill of him.'

      c. *?Ninguém admitiria que o Paulo desconfiasse de si.*
         nobody would-admit that Paulo suspected of *SE*
         'Nobody would admit that Paulo suspected of him.'

Since the BP anaphor satisfies the profile of a long distance–bound SE, it seems reasonable to expect that any account of the latter should take care of it, too. Thus, if LF-movement to INFL accounts for the properties of long distance–bound anaphors, BP *si* is expected to undergo LF-movement to INFL in sentences like (74), too, or (75), for that matter:

(75) a. *O Paulo confiou demais em si.*
         Paulo trusted too-much in *SE*
         'Paulo trusted too much in himself.'

      b. *(?)?O Paulo viu uma cobra atrás de si.*
         Paulo already saw a snake behind of *SE*
         'Paulo already saw a snake behind him.'

But, if this were true, there would be no explanation for the contrast between (76a) and (76b, c) (from (59a, b, c) respectively):

(76) a. *A gente se preparou para o pior.*
         the people SE prepared for the worst
         'We should prepare ourselves for the worst.'

b. (?)*A gente confiou demais em si.
the people trusted too-much in SE
'We trusted too much in ourselves.'

c. *A gente viu uma cobra atrás de si.
the people saw a snake behind of SE
'We saw a snake behind us.'

After LF-movement to INFL, the derived structures of (76a, b, c) would be identical as far as the relation between *a gente* and the anaphor is concerned, cf. (77a, b, c):

(77) a. [$_{IP}$ *A gente*$_i$ [$_{I'}$ [$_I$ *se*$_i$ preparou] para o pior]]

b. [$_{IP}$ *A gente*$_i$ [$_{I'}$ [$_I$ *si*$_i$ confiou] demais em t_i]]

c. [$_{IP}$ *A gente*$_i$ [$_{I'}$ [$_I$ *si*$_i$ viu] uma cobra atrás de t_i]]

Thus, an LF-movement of *si* would actually destroy the differences between (76a) and (76b, c) and, hence, predict they should not contrast. Notice that it would not do to assume that simplex anaphors are licensed only in positions from which movement is possible, and that the anaphors are excluded in (77b, c) because movement is not possible in such structures: anaphors are either fine or comparatively better with 3p antecedents in the same configurations. The conclusion appears to be that anaphors do not LF-move in BP, despite the fact that they can be long distance–bound. This, it seems to me, constitutes a serious problem for the LF-movement analysis of simplex anaphors. If one also takes into account that LF-movement to INFL may have an effect that is redundant with the condition in (71), as well as the other arguments collected against this analysis, the suspicion becomes stronger that LF-movement to INFL is not the best way of capturing LD-binding generalizations.

Back to the pursuit of a candidate for (71), another aspect of this condition that excludes a number of possibilities is that it applies to a "local domain." This means that agreement conditions defined on relations and dependencies that are not local by nature do not constitute good candidates to take over the role of (71). For example, in Chomsky's (1981) remarks on the matter, he appeared to suggest two of the possibilities made available within the standard framework. He says, "We will call a pronoun or PRO 'proximate' when it is COINDEXED with an antecedent and 'obviative' when it is not. . . . When PRO is proximate, it must agree in features with its antecedent, exactly as in the case of pronouns" (p. 61), and, later, "A proximate pronominal BOUND by NP must match NP in gender, number, and person, whether it is PRO or a pronoun" (p. 193; emphases mine).

That is, either coindexing or binding might impose or be subject to an agreement condition of the sort I am investigating (i.e., a condition requiring grammatical agreement between antecedent and anaphoric form).[27] But, since neither coindexing nor binding is itself defined on the basis of some local domain, (71) argues against such an agreement condition. And, again, 1PPLA provides the means to refute both possibilities. Consider a sentence like (78):

(78)   *A gente* acha que o Paulo já *nos* viu na TV.
       the people think that Paulo already *us* saw on the TV
       'We think that Paulo already saw us on TV.'

In (78) *nos* is not only coindexed but also bound by *a gente*, and yet it does not agree
with it. Thus, neither coindexing nor binding is subject to an agreement requirement.
Rather, agreement on anaphoric dependencies not only has to be a condition on bound
forms in general but also has to hold in a local domain, as in (71). I will now consider, then, which local domain this might be (see also Menuzzi 1995 for discussion).

In the standard BT, the local domain of binding is called a *governing category*, or
GC, a notion that has undergone a number of revisions in the literature. In its more popular
versions the notion of GC is intended to put together at least two syntactic environments,
transitive structures and subject binding into complement PPs, and this for obvious reasons: in both cases, anaphors are required and pronouns excluded in English:[28]

(79)   a. *Mary* likes {*herself/*her*}.

       b. *Mary* trusts in {*herself/*her*}.

Suppose, then, that (71) is taken to be a condition requiring agreement if binding
occurs within the GC, as in (80):

(80)   *Agreement of Anaphoric Dependencies* (Standard BT version):
       If bound within its GC, an anaphoric form agrees with its antecedent's grammatical
       specification.

In any of the relevant versions of GC, it follows that an anaphoric form agrees with
its antecedent both within transitive structures (79a) and within complement PPs (79b).
But if this is correct, it is not possible to explain the constrast between (81a) and (81b):

(81)   a. *A gente* {*se/*nos*} preparou para o pior.
          the people {*SE/us*} prepared for the worst
          'We should have prepared ourselves for the worst.'

       b. *A gente* confiou demais em {*(?)*si mesmo/(?)?nós mesmos*}.
          the people trusted too-much in {*SE (same)/us (same)*}
          'We trusted too much in *us/ourselves.'

In both cases the anaphoric form has its antecedent within its GC, so in both the
agreeing form should be chosen, contrary to fact: within complement PPs the nonagreeing 1ppl pronoun is a better choice (but see n. 16). Thus, (80) cannot be correct.
More generally, (81) shows that the local domain of (71) has to distinguish transitive structures from complement PPs at least in BP; therefore, any theory of anaphoric
dependencies that is not able to draw this distinction is bound to failure. This is the
case of standard BT but also of R&R's theory of reflexivity. Recall that this theory
reinterprets Conditions A and B as conditions on the representation of reflexive PREDI-

CATES, both syntactic and semantic (cf. section 7.1).[29] Thus, one might take syntactic or semantic predicates to be the domain for (71), in which case either (82a) or (82b), or both, should hold:

Agreement of Anaphoric Dependencies (Reflexivity Theory version):
(82) a. An anaphoric form agrees with its antecedent's grammatical specification if both are arguments of the same semantic predicate.

   b. An anaphoric form agrees with its antecedent's grammatical specification if both are arguments of the same syntactic predicate.

But the contrast in (82) also refutes these two conditions: in (75a, b) *a gente* and the anaphoric form belong to the same semantic and syntactic predicates, and so there should be no contrast, contrary to fact.

R&R's framework, however, provides another possibility: recall that, to account for some phenomena not covered by their reflexivity conditions, R&R suggested that Chain Theory should be extended to anaphoric dependencies. More specifically, they argued that a revised version of the Chain Condition applies to anaphoric dependencies that satisfy a representational definition of CHAIN (see (95)). This extension of Chain Theory to anaphoric relations allows one, of course, to state the local domain of (71) as being that of a chain, as in (83):

(83) *Agreement of Anaphoric Dependencies* (Chain Theory version):
An anaphoric form agrees with its antecedent if they form a chain.

Unlike all other conditions I investigated earlier, (83) draws the line precisely where I want it to draw: it puts apart anaphoric dependencies that occur within transitive structures and those crossing PPs. As has been well known since Kayne (1981), chains cannot cross PPs in Romance, and this is true of BP as well: thus, while passivization and extraction are fine from an object position, they are impossible from within PPs. Cf. the following.

(84) a. O João viu *o Paulo* na TV.
      João saw *Paulo* on TV

   b. *O Paulo* foi visto *t* na TV.
      Paulo was seen *t* on TV

   c. *Quem* o João viu *t* na TV?
      who João saw *t* on TV?

(85) a. O João confia n*o Paulo.*
      João trusts in *Paulo*

   b. **O Paulo* é confiado em *t.*
      Paulo is trusted in *t*

   c. **Quem* o João confia em *t*?
      who João trusts in *t* ?

Thus, PPs are barriers to chains in BP (unlike what happens in English: see section 7.2 for further discussion). What (83) predicts, then, is that (i) an anaphoric form will obligatorily agree with its antecedent in transitive structures in BP; and (ii) this condition will not hold if binding is into complement PPs. This is the pattern found for 1PPLA, as exemplified in (81), repeated here as (86):

(86) a. *A gente* {*se/*nos*} preparou para o pior.
          the people {*SE/us*} prepared for the worst
          'We should have prepared ourselves for the worst.'

      b. *A gente* confiou demais em {*(?)*si mesmo/(?)?nós mesmos*}.
          the people trusted too-much in {*SE same/us same*}
          'We trusted too much in *us/ourselves.'

In (86a) binding is within a transitive structure, and 1ppl *a gente* can bind only the 3p anaphor, not a 1ppl pronoun. This follows from (83): only the 3p anaphor agrees with *a gente*'s grammatical specification (cf. section 7.1, which also shows that the 3p anaphor does violate the FCI, though, an issue to which I return soon). In (86b) binding is into a complement PP, and 1ppl *a gente* can bind a 1ppl pronoun, but not the 3p anaphor. The former case follows from (83) and the FCI: (83) does not apply to (86b), since the anaphoric dependency is not a chain there; that is, a 1ppl pronoun does not violate (83) in (86b); furthermore, the 1ppl pronoun is compatible with 1ppl *a gente*'s index, so the FCI does not prevent it from being coindexed with 1ppl *a gente* either. Thus, (86b) is predicted to be essentially fine with a 1ppl pronoun. Consider (86b) with the 3p anaphor, however. Again, since there is no chain in (86b), (83) is not relevant; in particular, it does not require the 3p anaphor, as it does in (86a). Moreover, since the 3p anaphor is incompatible with a 1ppl index, the FCI predicts that it should be out in (86b), and this is essentially correct, too.

The joint action of the FCI and (83) thus captures most of the 1PPLA pattern quite naturally, suggesting that (83) is on the right track: the local domain of agreement for anaphoric dependencies is the domain of a chain. Let me refer to the condition in (83) as Agreement-on-Chains from now on. The conclusion that BT has to incorporate Agreement-on-Chains in some way supports a version of BT in which anaphoric dependencies that fit the chain format are distinguished from those that do not, such as in R&R's theory of A-chains and reflexivity. By the same token, Agreement-on-Chains argues against any version of BT that cannot draw that distinction, and so it argues against the standard BT (with or without the LF-movement approach to anaphors; actually, 1PPLA appears to be incompatible with an LF-movement analysis of simplex anaphors; cf. discussion of (74) through (77)). Once one acknowledges the need for Agreement-on-Chains to be incorporated into BT, however, a number of issues arise. Let me close this chapter by discussing some of the more pressing ones.

7.6 Chains, indexing, and feature-compatibility conditions

In the previous section I presented an analysis of 1PPLA in BP, in particular as exemplified by the crucial contrast in (86), based on the FCI and on Agreement-on-Chains, which I repeat here:

(87)   *Feature-Compatibility of Indexing* (FCI):
An index *i* is assigned to an NP iff *i* is compatible with that NP.

(88)   *Agreement of Anaphoric Dependencies* (Agreement-on-Chains):
An anaphoric form agrees with its antecedent if they form a chain.

Summarizing the pattern of 1PPLA in BP and the analysis I provided for it yields the following picture:

Analysis of 1PPLA:
(89)   a.   (i) Generalization: 1ppl *a gente* can bind a 1ppl pronoun nonlocally.
(ii) Analysis: Nonlocally they do not form a chain, and, hence, Agreement-on-Chains does not apply; since the pronoun satisfies the FCI, it is fine.

   b.   (i) Generalization: 1ppl *a gente* cannot bind a 1ppl pronoun locally.
(ii) Analysis: Locally they form a chain, and the pronoun violates Agreement-on-Chains (although it satisfies the FCI).

   c.   (i) Generalization: 1ppl *a gente* can bind a 3p anaphor locally.
(ii) Analysis: Locally they form a chain, and the anaphor satisfies Agreement-on-Chains (although it violates the FCI);

   d.   (i) Generalization: 1ppl *a gente* cannot bind a 3p anaphor nonlocally.
(ii) Analysis: Nonlocally they do not form a chain, and, hence, Agreement-on-Chains does not apply; since the anaphor violates the FCI, it is excluded.

This analysis comes very close to the target, but the parenthetical clause in (89cii) provides a reminder that there is still a gap to be filled: I have not yet answered the question in (90), a rephrased version of question (70):

(90)   Why isn't the anaphor excluded by the FCI when it belongs to a chain?

This question is prompted by the fact that, being [3p], the anaphor is incompatible with a 1ppl index, and this leads to a violation of the FCI, whether or not the anaphor forms a chain with its antecedent: since the FCI is formulated as applying to indexed NPs regardless of whether they belong to a dependency (cf. (87)), a locally bound anaphor should be excluded by the FCI as well. But (89cii) appears to require Agreement-on-Chains to be a sufficient condition: when binding is local, that is, when the anaphoric dependency satisfies the chain format, Agreement-on-Chains overrides the FCI. Moreover, the parenthetical clause in (89bii) requires Agreement-on-Chains to be not only sufficient but also necessary: the fact that a 1ppl pronoun satisfies the FCI does not make it able to avoid Agreement-on-Chains effects. Apparently, what is needed, then, is something with the effect of (91):

(91)   *Interaction FCI/Agreement-on-Chains*:
       If an anaphoric dependency is a chain, (a) the anaphoric form is subject to Agreement-on-Chains, and (b) it is not subject to the FCI.

(Of course, the fact that, otherwise, anaphoric forms are subject to the FCI does not need to be stated.) Together with the FCI in (87) and Agreement-on-Chains in (88), (91) would complete the analysis of 1PPLA, capturing the parenthetic clauses of both (89bii) and (89cii) (and answering the question in (90)). Notice, on the other hand, that the statements in (91) regulate the interaction of a condition on chains (Agreement-on-Chains) and another on indexing (the FCI). As such, (91) should follow either from the formulation of those conditions or from a proper understanding of the interaction between chains and indexing themselves.[30] It is clear, however, that the statements in (91) do not follow either from the FCI as formulated in (87), nor from Agreement-on-Chains as formulated in (88). Perhaps a look at the way Chain Theory interacts with indexing might clarify some aspects of (91).

Consider a more standard case of a chain, that is, of a movement chain, as in (92a), and what the ultimate semantic representation of such a chain might be with respect to the truth conditions of the sentence, as in (92b):

(92)   a.   *John* was seen *t* in the airport

       b.   *was-seen-in-the-airport (John)*

What (92b) makes obvious about movement chains is that they are syntactic objects representing discontinuously two aspects of one single semantic procedure, the filling in of an open slot in a predicate by an appropriate argument: the chain (*John,t*) in (92a) is ultimately interpreted as the individual constant *John*, which fills in the open slot of the predicate *was-in-the-airport* in (92b). This semantic procedure is represented by two different elements in the chain: the element that fills in the open slot (the individual constant *John*) is represented by the NP *John*, the head of the chain; the predicate's open slot is represented by the trace *t* in the tail of the chain. Thus, in an intuitive sense, a chain is an object that allows a syntactic position, the tail of the chain, to receive the interpretation assigned to another syntactic position, the head of the chain. That is, the indexing of chains would be such that the tail of the chain ends up receiving the index of the head of the chain:[31]

(93)   *Chain Indexing*:
       If (α, β) is a chain, then ? is assigned the index of α.

Once a mechanism like Chain Indexing is assumed, a more elegant account becomes available for the fact that an anaphoric form may circumvent the FCI if it belongs to a chain (cf. (91)). Suppose NPs have two alternative ways of being assigned an interpretation or index: either (i) they are assigned one freely, that is, by means of Free

Indexing (cf. n. 4); or (ii) they are assigned an index by belonging to a chain, that is, by means of Chain Indexing as in (93). Suppose further that the FCI checks only indices assigned by Free Indexing: it would check indices assigned to NPs forming single chains, or to heads of nonsingle chains, but not those assigned by Chain Indexing to nonhead positions in a chain. In other words, if an anaphoric form happens to belong to a chain (as a nonhead position), it may be assigned an index not by Free Indexing but rather by Chain Indexing. Not being assigned an index by Free Indexing, by hypothesis it would not be subject to the FCI. I will incorporate this hypothesis into the formulation of the FCI itself, as in (94):

(94)   *Feature-Compatibility of Free Indexing* (FCI, second version):
An index i is assigned to NP by Free Indexing iff i is compatible with NP.

Given Chain Indexing in (93) and the FCI in (94), the statements in (91), which govern the interaction FCI/Agreement-on-Chains, are actually deducible from the FCI and from Agreement-on-Chains themselves: since the FCI is now limited to indices assigned by Free Indexing, it is not necessary to state that forms indexed through Chain Indexing are not subject to it. That is, if an anaphoric form belongs to a chain, it may get its index by Chain Indexing, not by Free Indexing, in which case the FCI in (94) does not apply. Hence, the statement (91b) can be eliminated from (91), which is reduced to (91a) alone. But (91a) is a restatement of Agreement-on-Chains in (88). Thus, (91) can be eliminated altogether.

For the line of reasoning sketched here to work, however, it would be necessary to find a way of identifying chains independently of the indexing of the related forms: what I want to say is, precisely, that an anaphoric form can get its index by belonging to a chain. And this is clearly inconsistent with any definition of chain that requires coindexing; in particular, it is inconsistent with R&R's generalized definition of chain, the very mechanism intended to allow extension of Chain Theory to anaphoric dependencies (cf. section 7.1):[32]

(95) $C = (\alpha_1, \dots, \alpha_n)$ is a chain iff C is the maximal sequence such that: (a) there is an index i such that for all j, $1 \leq j \leq n$, α_j carries i, and (b) for all j, $1 \leq j \leq n$, α_j governs α_{j+1}.

According to clause (a) of (95), coindexing is a definitional, hence necessary, condition for chains. Thus, for an anaphoric dependency to be a chain under (95), the anaphoric form must have the same index as its antecedent, and this in a way that is independent of (95) itself. But if one adopts Chain Indexing in (93) and the FCI in (94) instead of (91), what is needed is precisely the reverse: an anaphoric form has to be able to get its index by virtue of belonging to a chain (cf. (93)). In other words, what is needed is a way of identifying chains that does not require coindexing.

Independently of the preceding discussion, Rizzi (1990) has argued for an approach to chains that would appear to satisfy the needs of Chain Indexing and the new FCI. Rizzi's idea is to "replace the coindexation requirement of the usual definition [of chain] with a global nondistinctness requirement (nondistinctness of indices if the elements are indexed, of category, feature content, etc.) in order to rule out the possibility of forming crazy chains (e.g., of an adjunct trace with a verb or a direct object)" (Rizzi 1990:92). The definition he suggests for chains is:

(96) a. $(\alpha_1, \ldots, \alpha_n)$ is a CHAIN iff for all j, $1{\leq}j{\leq}n$, α_j antecedent-governs α_{j+1}.

 b. α ANTECEDENT-GOVERNS β iff: (i) α and β are nondistinct (for indices and features); (ii) α c-commands β; (iii) no barrier intervenes; (iv) Relativized Minimality is respected (Rizzi 1990:92).

Notice the result of adopting clause (96bi): if a position is not indexed, it can still belong to a chain if it is nondistinct in features from its governing antecedent. That is, nondistinctness makes coindexing unnecessary for a chain to be identified. For this reason, Rizzi's definition of chains allows us to adopt Chain Indexing in (93) and the new FCI in (94) with results almost identical to the previous set of assumptions, which required the statements in (91). In particular, the parenthetic clause in (89cii), which required (91), would be eliminated:

(89c) (i) Generalization: 1ppl *a gente* can bind a 3p anaphor locally.
 (ii) Analysis: Locally they form a chain, and the anaphor satisfies Agreement-on-Chains (~~though it violates the FCI~~).

Let me briefly review the analysis of (89ci) under the new set of assumptions. The basic empirical premise is that *a gente* and a 3p anaphor are nondistinct (which is true except possibly for Case, as I will soon indicate). Thus, a local dependency as in (89ci) satisfies Rizzi's definition of chain in (96); and this allows the anaphor to get its index according to Chain Indexing in (93), instead of resorting to Free Indexing. If the anaphor does not get its index by Free Indexing, it is not checked by the FCI as formulated in (94), in which case it does not violate the FCI, and (89ci) is predicted to be grammatical. Notice that, under this analysis, the parenthetical clause in (89ci) is actually incorrect and has to be erased. It should also be clear that the new set of assumptions does not affect the explanations in (89aii) and (89dii). That is, it captures most of the pattern of 1PPLA ((89a, c, d); I return to (89b) shortly).

 The analysis just sketched for (89ci) appears to have a surprising but revealing consequence: it would render Agreement-on-Chains in (88) redundant in (89cii). Notice first that the anaphor does not violate the FCI in (89ci) because locally it can form a chain with its antecedent and, hence, get its index by Chain Indexing rather than by Free Indexing. But, in order for an anaphor to form a chain in (89ci) according to Rizzi's definition, it has to be nondistinct in features from its antecedent in the first place (cf. (96bi)). For ease of reference, let me single out this clause of Rizzi's definition, calling it FEATURE COMPATIBILITY OF CHAINS (FCC) (since feature-compatibility is nondistinctness of feature specification, cf. (13) of section 7.1):

(97) *Feature-Compatibility of Chains* (FCC, from (97bi)):
 $(\alpha_1, \ldots, \alpha_n)$ is a chain iff for all j, $1{\leq}j{\leq}n$, α_{j+1} is compatible with α_j.

For an anaphoric form to be feature-compatible or nondistinct from its antecedent, it has to be nondistinct from the antecedent for person, number, and gender, too, of course. In other words, the FCC entails that an anaphoric form qualifies as a chain position only if it agrees with the antecedent's grammatical specification. Returning to (89ci), this means that, in order for the anaphor to form a chain and avoid the FCI, it will have to satisfy the FCC agreeing with its antecedent. By satisfying the FCC, the anaphor will satisfy Agreement-on-Chains in (88) as well. But the FCC has logical precedence over Agreement-on-Chains: satisfaction of the FCC is necessary for the anaphor to form a chain, while Agreement-on-Chains applies once a chain is formed. Hence, Agreeement-on-Chains is redundant in (89cii).

Thus, it would appear that assuming Chain Indexing as in (93), the FCI as in (94), and Rizzi's definition of a chain allows us to deduce the effects of Agreement-on-Chains in (88), at least as far as (89c) is concerned. Specifically, the effects of Agreement-on-Chains would follow from the FCC, one of the clauses of Rizzi's definition of chains. It seems to me that this is precisely how things should be: (i) Agreement-on-Chains in (88) *is* a nondistinctness or compatibility condition, namely, on person, number, and gender specification; (ii) its domain *is* the domain of a chain. It is hardly believable that it is necessary to state both Agreement-on-Chains and the FCC when they are almost identical. This shows clearly that one should be reduced to the other. Since the FCC belongs to a more general statement, the definition of chains, it is just sound logic to eliminate Agreement-on-Chains.

To sum up the preceding discussion: I began with an account of 1PPLA (as summarized in (91)) based on the ingredients in (98):

(98) a. R&R's definition of chain, as in (95);

b. the first version of the FCI, as formulated in (87);

c. Agreement-on-Chains, as in (88);

d. the statements on the interaction FCI/Agreement-on-Chains in (91).

R&R's definition of chain and the FCI come without cost, since they are independently motivated. Agreement-on-Chains has to be added to the framework, but it does not require any new concept to be stated, and so it would not be costly by itself (in a framework with R&R's definition of chain; but it becomes somewhat redundant if nondistinctness is incorporated into the definition of chain, as in Rizzi's definition). In order to get things working, however, the additional statements in (91), are also needed. As I pointed out, these seem to indicate that something about the interaction between chains and the assignment of interpretation to NPs is being missed in (98). For this reason, I continued looking for some principled explanation for the statements in (91). The result was that most of the 1PPLA pattern would seem to be captured just as well if I changed (98) to (99):

(99) a. Rizzi's definition of chain as in (95) (which includes the FCC in (97));

b. the introduction of a device for indexing other than Free Indexing, namely, Chain Indexing as in (93);

c. the second version of the FCI, as formulated in (94).

The approach based on (99) has many virtues. It eliminates the need for the statements in (91), which were a source of unclarity, and it does so keeping most of the results of (98). The only additional statement (99) needs is Chain Indexing, which not only is based on the apparatus available in the theory but also appears, at first sight, to be a pretty natural property of chains. Adoption of Rizzi's definition is also welcome, since it is more general and, hence, has a broader application than R&R's; actually, Rizzi's definition properly includes R&R's, and the result of (99) is an integration of R&R's framework for anaphoric dependencies into Rizzi's approach to chains. As for the reformulated version of the FCI, it has the same coverage as the first version; the only difference is that it makes room for nonhead positions of chains to resort to a different means of indexing, namely, Chain Indexing. Finally and crucially, the interaction of Rizzi's definition of chains and Chain Indexing would allow us to reduce the effects of Agreement-on-Chains to the FCC, which I have shown to be, by all means, a desirable consequence.

It seems to me that all these advantages suggest that (99) is really close to a correct generalization. But it does not succeed fully. The first problem it would have to face is though I have captured most of the 1PPLA pattern (namely, (89a, c, d)), one of the crucial generalizations, (89bi), has slipped away. The statement in (89bi) and its analysis (89bii) based on (98) are repeated here, with an example in (100):

(89b)   (i) Generalization: 1ppl *a gente* cannot bind a 1ppl pronoun locally.
        (ii) Analysis: Locally they form a chain, and the pronoun violates Agreement-on-Chains (although it satisfies the FCI).

(100)   *A gente já *nos* viu na TV.
        the people already *us* saw on-the TV
        'We have already seen ourselves on TV.'

The approach based on (99), that is, without Agreement-on-Chains in (88) and the auxiliary statements in (91), would yield have the following result: *a gente* and *nos* in (100) are distinct from each other (with respect to their feature composition), so they do not satisfy Rizzi's definition of chain in (96). For this reason, the pronoun *nos* has to get its index by Free Indexing, being subject to the FCI. But, since it gets a 1ppl index, which is compatible with the feature specification of *nos*, the FCI is satisfied. Hence, none of the conditions in (99) is violated, and (100) is predicted to be fine, contrary to fact. It appears that, to capture (89bi), the result we need is: the dependency in (100) has to count as a chain, but a chain that is ill-formed because it violates the requirement that chain positions must agree with each other. And this is precisely what is achieved by (98), rather than by (99).

Another argument against the reduction of (98) to (99) can be made when one considers more carefully the notion of nondistinctness relevant for the FCC in (97), and the notion of agreement relevant for Agreement-on-Chains in (88). Recall that one of the most appealing results of (99) is that it would allow one to deduce the effects of Agreement-on-Chains from the FCC, the requirement for nondistinctness in the identification of chain positions: this, of course, would explain why the domain of Agreement-on-Chains coincides with the domain of a chain. As indicated in section 7.2, however, the notion of agreement is usually construed as a "match for person, number, and gender." Given the fact that unspecified elements like *se* in BP are also supposed to "match" the features of their antecedents, "match" here actually means "nondistinctness for person, number, and gender." Thus, agreement in the usual sense is to be taken as "nondistinctness for person, number, and gender," rather than "nondistinctness" in general, that is, feature-compatibility. More important, this seems to be necessary, since Agreement-on-Chains effects appear to be insensitive to CASE specification. Consider, for example, an anaphoric dependency like (101a), in which a chain is formed between the subject and the object; as shown in (101b), unlike *me* 'me, myself', *eu* 'I' is incompatible with object Case; and (101c) shows that, unlike *eu*, *me* is incompatible with subject Case:

(101)   a. *Eu* já *me* vi na TV.

       I already *me* saw on-the TV

       'I have already seen myself on TV.'

    b. O Paulo já {*me*} viu { **eu*} na TV.

       Paulo already {*me*} saw { **I*} on-the TV

       'Paulo has already seen me on TV.'

    c. {*Eu*} já { **me*} vi o Paulo na TV.

       {*I*} already { **me*} saw Paulo on-the TV

       'I have already seen myself on TV.'

If I draw the distinction in (101b, c) by means of the feature [±accusative], then, *eu* is [–acc], *me* [+acc], and both are distinct for Case. But now *eu* and *me* are distinct, and so the chain in (101a) would violate Agreement-on-Chains, if this condition were to require overall feature-compatibility or nondistinctness, instead of a "match for person, number, and gender." On the other hand, we cannot exclude Case from a set of the features relevant for nondistinctness of chain positions, or we end up allowing sentences such as the following:

(102)   *$Whom_{[+acc]}$ [$t_{[-acc]}$ arrived late to the party]?

It would appear, then, that the effects of Agreement-on-Chains in (88) cannot be reduced to effects of the FCC in (97). Again, the set of assumptions in (98) looks empirically superior to the one in (99).

    Let me summarize the results of this work briefly. I have shown that the pattern of 1PPLA in BP follows in a version of BT that incorporates the set of assumptions in (98). One of the crucial points behind (98) is that two types of anaphoric relations have to be distinguished: those that qualify as chains, and those that do not. Thus, this chapter supports a framework like R&R's, in which that distinction is drawn. In R&R's framework, binding effects are accounted for by two independent modules: Chain Theory and Reflexivity Theory. If this division of labor is necessary, then, the present chapter constitutes an argument for a BT with the following components:

BT Theory:

(103) a. Theory of Reflexivity of Predicates (Conditions A and B, cf. R&R 1993);

b. Chain Theory (a representational definition of chains, the Chain Condition, and Agreement-on-Chains in (88); cf. R&R 1992, 1993);

c. Theory of Assignment of Reference (the FCI in (87));

d. Statements regulating the interaction FCI/Agreement-on-Chains ((91), cf. above).

Finally, I have identified conceptual and empirical problems emerging from a specific source of obscurity: the interaction between Chain Theory and the Theory of Assignment of Reference or Indexing. From the conceptual side, the problem lies in (103d): it was necessary to stipulate some statements regulating the interaction between the FCI and Agreement-on-Chains, when one expects this to follow either from these conditions themselves or from statements independently required by the theories concerned. Empirically, the trouble lies within the Chain Theory summarized in (103b): although there are reasons to believe that the best definition of chain is one including a requirement for nondistinctness among chain positions (cf. Rizzi 1990), it appears that this requirement cannot play the role of Agreement-on-Chains. But this is certainly an odd state of affairs: as I said earlier, (i) Agreement-on-Chains *is* a nondistinctness condition, namely, on person, number, and gender specification; and (ii) its domain *is* the domain of a chain. It is hardly believable that one must state Agreement-on-Chains when this condition is almost identical to a statement that is independently necessary in the theory. This clearly suggests that some generalization is being missed in (103b).

To address these issues, further research will be necessary. In Menuzzi (unpublished), I investigate binding into PPs in Brazilian Portuguese and English, solving this problem based on the hypothesis that conditions on chains, and in particular the FCC, are violable.

Notes

1. I will adopt the following definitions, based on Menuzzi (in preparation): the term ANAPHORIC RELATION or DEPENDENCY has the limited sense of "intended covaluation of two NPs within a sentence" (what used to be called intrasentential coreference; see also section 7.1 and references cited there). This term is merely descriptive and does *not* imply any theoretical claim regarding the existence of a SYNTACTIC relation between the two NPs. I use the term BINDING THEORY (BT) to refer to the theory of anaphoric relations that fit the preceding description; a VERSION or FORMULATION of BT is any specific theory of constraints on those relations. Further terminology: ANTECEDENT is the "nondependent" NP, and ANAPHORIC ELEMENT is the "dependent" element in an anaphoric dependency, either in the referential sense (i.e., wrt. "semantic content") or in the structural sense (i.e., wrt. structural relations such as c-command or scope).

2. The two-stage procedure is necessary because natural languages, as such, do not possess "bound variables" but rather traces and pronouns; and a model does not possess bound variables either, but procedures to check how many individuals in the domain belong to some set. Variables, properly speaking, are expressions in some types of logical languages, like first order predicate calculus or Montague's intensional logic. Of course, one may use dia-

critics other than individual terms in a logical language to express the fact that two expressions are semantically identical; for example, one may take indices to be part of the syntactic representation, and require semantic rules to be sensitive to indices (then, one may define variables as in GB work). Although this decision has consequences for the way one formulates the overall framework, I am not aware of any substantive issue arising in this connection. See Dowty et al. (1981) for detailed presentation of the translational technique, and Chierchia and McConnel-Ginet (1990) for an interpretation procedure for GB-like S-structures, that is, phrase-markers containing indexed traces and pronouns. In this section I will be drawing on model-theoretic terminology quite freely.

3. The number of assignments a variable has to undergo is determined by the quantificational content of the NP. For example, to satisfy the truth conditions of (5a), it is necessary that: (i) the two occurrences of 'x' in the proposition [**thinks** (x, [**likes** (**Mary**, x)])] be simultaneously assigned one and the same individual from the set of boys; (ii) such an assignment be checked for every and each individual in the set of boys; and (iii) the proposition [**thinks** (x, [**likes** (**Mary**, x)])] come out true for each and every such an assignment. Clauses (ii) and (iii) of this evaluation procedure are determined by the semantics of *every*, the element expressing the quantificational content of *every boy* in (5a).

4. Given (6), free indexing in the sense of Chomsky (1981) is to be understood as "assign any semantic value you want to an NP." Conditions on indices, such as the binding conditions and the FCI in (14) (= (8)), exclude, then, the improper assignments.

It should be noticed that, although Fiengo and May (1994) also assume coindexing to be interpreted as covaluation, indices for them are not merely notational devices to represent (part of) the semantic valuation of NPs: indices belong to the syntactic specification of a category and can express syntactic properties, such as whether this category is an occurrence dependent on some other category (see their chapter 2, in particular). As far as I am aware, nothing of what I will say here is incompatible with, nor requires, Fiengo and May's stronger notion of indexing.

Another point to keep in mind is that the translational approach I adopted is compatible with Fiengo and May's claim that *non*-coindexing does not imply *non*-covaluation: two NPs are non-coindexed if they are translated into two different terms of *L*; this means that non-coindexing does not ensure covaluation, but it does *not* exclude covaluation either, since different terms of *L* may still receive the same semantic value. This allows one to treat "accidental coreference" just as in Fiengo and May (1994:1–14).

5. Lasnik (1976) appears to refer to the generalization in (8) when he says that, in using an NP, the speaker is bound to "a principle of cooperation" according to which he "must provide every reasonable means for his listener to know what he is talking about" (p. 91). From this principle it would follow that the speaker has to comply with the language's conventions, in particular with respect to the intrinsic meaning of expressions. "[*H*]*e*, for example, means 'male human being,' and consequently, that pronoun can be used to refer to any member of that class except under circumstances excluded by [BT]" (p. 95).

6. In other words, the FCI covers the effects of Jackendoff's *Consistency Condition*, according to which two coindexed NPs "must in fact be able to describe the same individual" (Jackendoff 1972:112).

7. Although the morphosyntactic properties of Portuguese and Dutch appear to be better dealt with by means of the distinctions [±feminine] (cf. Harris 1991) and [±gender] (cf. Kerstens 1990), respectively, I will also refer (especially in glosses): to [–feminine] as m(asculine) in Portuguese; to [+gender] forms as m(asculine) or f(eminine), and to [–gender] forms as n(euter) in Dutch.

8. Note that a function *I* is used in (21b) slightly differently from how functions *I* were used in (6). In (6) they are conceived as functions translating NPs into terms of *L*; in (21)

their use is extended to the translation of nouns into predicates of *L*. That is, the set of functions *I* is taken to be the set of functions that translate expressions of L into *L*. Still, *I* in (21) does not count as an indexing rule (cf. (6c)).

9. Categorization of individuals is not free, however, but subject to some restrictions of its own. As a consequence, the process of "feature inheritance" described in (21b) is not free either. One of the relevant restrictions is that, in the absence of previous discourse or more specific context, individuals are not identified randomly but by their "default description" or "basic level category" (cf. Tasmowski and Verluyten 1985:342; Bosch 1988:73; for the notion of "basic level category," see Rosch 1978). For example, in an unmarked context TABLE but not PIECE-OF-FURNITURE is a basic level category of the usual taxonomy for concrete objects (cf. Rosch 1978:32–35). Thus, in the unmarked context (20b), the object taken by John will be categorized as a TABLE, hence, associated with *une table* 'a table(fem)' in French. This explains why the feminine pronoun *la* is available in (20b). But since PIECE-OF-FURNITURE is not a "basic level category," the object taken by John in (20b) will not be categorized as a PIECE-OF-FURNITURE; hence, it will not be associated with *un meuble* 'a (piece of) furniture(masc)' in French. That is why the masculine pronoun *le* is unavailable in (20b).

The restriction described here might also be active in contrasts like the following: in the context (i) that follows, in which the surrounding discourse provides the categorization of the individual *i* as *uma vítima* 'a victim(fem)', the feminine pronoun *ela* can be used to refer to that individual, although he is a male; in an unmarked context like (ii), however, in which the surrounding discourse does not categorize *i* as *uma vítima*, only the masculine pronoun is available, and the feminine pronoun *ela* is unacceptable (examples adapted from T&Vs (1985:367):

(i) (paramedic standing in front of a *male* road-accident victim$_i$:)
O estado d*a vítima*$_i$ agora é satisfatório. Mas {*ele/ela*}$_i$ podia ter entrado em coma.
The condition of-*the victim*(f)$_i$ now is satisfactory. But {*he/she*}$_i$ could have been into coma.

(ii) (paramedic standing in front of a *male* road-accident victim$_i$:)
{*Ele/*Ela*}$_i$ parece ter quebrado a perna.
{*He/*She*}$_i$ seems to-have broken the leg.

The contrast between (i) and (ii) can be explained if MALE/FEMALE, but not VICTIM, are "basic level categories" of the taxonomy of human beings. See also n. 12.

10. Johan Rooryck (personal communication) notes that, although the French equivalent of (21a) is fine, semantic agreement becomes impossible if *la victime* and the pronoun are "too close":

(i) *La victime* a honte d' {*elle/*lui*}.

This fact seems to be a particular case of the more general observation, noted in the literature on "pragmatic control" of pronouns, that the trade-off between semantic and grammatical agreement depends on the distance between the antecedent and the anaphoric form: the more distant they are, the more probable semantic agreement is (cf. Tasmowski and Verluyten 1985:368–369, Corbett 1991:240, 242–243; but see Cornish 1988:251 for qualification).

11. But the Dutch pattern in (22b) argues against (21b), which predicts either the feminine or the neuter pronoun to be possible (just as (21b) allows both pronouns in the Portuguese pattern in (22a)). I have no particular insight into why Dutch strongly disfavors "grammatical agreement" in such cases. It should be clear, however, that this has no bearing for the argument developed in the text against a grammatical condition for agreement: (22b) may argue in favor of restrictions on the availability of "grammatical agreement"–like ef-

fects stronger than those imposed by (21b), but obviously *not* in favor of "grammatical agreement" itself. Perhaps this is the place to point that, cross-linguistically, pronominal anaphora strongly favors semantic over grammatical agreement (cf. Corbett 1991: chapter 8), suggesting that the availability of the strategy in (21b) is marked (see also n. 10 for related discussion). For some discussion, in particular concerning the Dutch contrast in (22b), see T&V (1985:364–365).

12. Like other Romance languages, BP has the arbitrary or impersonal *se* construction. For the morphosyntactic properties of impersonal *se*, see Cinque (1988) and references cited there.

13. Cf. section 7.1, *mesmo* 'same' functions as a reflexive marker, in R&R's terms. Note also that Condition B effects in (36) through (38) are not uniform, an issue which I discuss in Menuzzi (in preparation).

14. An auxiliary verb is necessary in (44a) because in BP impersonal *se* and reflexive *se* are incompatible if string-adjacent, as in: *sempre se se prepara para o pior* 'one always prepare oneself for the worst'. In Italian, co-occurrence of impersonal and reflexive *se* string-adjacent appears to be possible, with the first element in the string changing to *ci: si* ? *ci si* (for Burzio 1988:55 n. 47, 80–81, *si* ? *ci* is a phonological rule; but see Burzio 1992:406 and 412 n.16 for a different analysis). As for the effects on *si* in (44c) and (45c), see n. 19.

15. Note that within complement PPs, as in (44a), the relevant contrast is less clear (the judgments here are my own; see section 7.4 for further discussion of the data). The point to pay attention to is that *si* in (50a) is considerably worse than *se* in (49b); *nós* in (50a) is considerably better than *nos* in (48b). In the remainder of this chapter I idealize these subtleties, assuming that the generalization to be captured is the one stated in the text. I will return to the issue in section 7.4, when I will have means to interpret the differences between (50a) and (50b).

16. This assumption is obviously inaccurate: no definition of GC was ever so strong as to pick up only binding within a transitive structure as "local." See also n. 29.

17. Thus, sentences like (58) constitute a problem for the standard Condition B, as noticed by Bouchard (1984) and Ronat (1982), and also for R&R's Chain Condition and Condition B.

18. Example (60c) shows that within some PPs *si* becomes marked, even marginal for some speakers, although everyone agrees that (59c) is much worse than (60c). I return to the effect in (60c) in Menuzzi (in preparation). Note also that (60c) becomes acceptable if we substitute *O Paulo* by *ninguém* 'nobody', a contrast discussed in Menuzzi (in preparation).

19. Neither R&R's Chain Condition nor their Reflexivity Conditions would be of much help here: these conditions do not refer to properties of the antecedent either. (Actually, the Chain Condition requires the head of a chain to be [+R], a requirement that *a gente* presumably satisfies, since it can head chains, as in (59a).)

20. Recall that: (i) the semantic categorization of an NP's index (i.e., the interpretation it is assigned) is a set of features representing the properties associated to this index in the domain of discourse; and (ii) an expression's FS is the set of grammatical and semantic features of that expression. See discussion of (9) and (10) in section 7.1 again for clarification.

21. Recall that an expression's semantic features are abbreviations for the appropriate representation of this expressions's semantic properties; cf. n. 6.

22. The fact that I am assuming the stipulation in (65) does not imply that (65) itself has no explanation, of course. Actually, it clearly belongs to a more general pattern: pronominal elements with arbitrary or impersonal interpretation may also have a 1ppl interpretation in appropriate contexts. This is true of impersonal *on* in French, arbitrary PRO, and impersonal *se* in Italian (see Cinque 1988:550 ff.; also Burzio 1992:406–407 for discussion). Johan Rooryck (personal communication) suggests that, if *a gente* is an arbitrary expression and if arbitrary

expressions are unspecified for features, then *a gente* would be compatible with a 1ppl interpretation (since, being unspecified for features, *a gente* would not be distinct from 1ppl; see Burzio 1992:406 for a similar suggestion). Although this idea may eventually give the right results if properly worked out, it still is necessary to say that, in some contexts, *a gente* has to be made incompatible with 1ppl features, given the unacceptability of both (ia, b):

(i)   a   *A gente* já *nos* viu na TV.

    b. *Nós* já vimos *a gente (mesmo)* na TV.
      'We have already seen ourselves on TV.'

It is no accident that Cinque (1988:552) had to argue that "[i]f we take the pure $arb = 1$st person plural semantic switch in [the proper] contexts to have no effects on the morphological features of *si*, verbal agreement will follow the standard default procedure." In the absence of an explicit theory for these "pure $arb = 1$st person plural semantic switches," I will keep (65).

23. However, one cannot deduce from a form's being bound by arbitrary *a gente* that that form is compatible with arbitrary interpretation. This is so because, while arbitrary *a gente* can bind a null subject in BP (cf. (ia)), arbitrary or impersonal subjects cannot (cf. (ib)):

(i)   a. *A gente* sempre imagina que __ pode tolerar os outros.
      the people always imagines that (*pro*) can tolerate the others
      'One always imagines that one can tolerate the others.'

    b. *__ sempre *se* imagina que __ pode tolerar os outros
      (*pro*) always *SE* imagines that (*pro*) can tolerate the others
      'One always imagines that one can tolerate the others.'

However, neither arbitrary *a gente* nor impersonal subjects can be bound by a null subject:

(ii)   a. *__ sempre imagina que *a gente* pode tolerar os outros
      (*pro*) always imagines that *the people* can tolerate the others
      'One always imagines that one can tolerate the others.'

    b. *__ sempre imagina que __ *se* pode tolerar os outros
      (*pro*) always imagines that (*pro*) *SE* can tolerate the others
      'One always imagines that one can tolerate the others.'

Recall that arbitrary *a gente* and impersonal subjects can bind each other. It appears, then, that (i) arbitrary *a gente* and impersonal subjects are compatible with each other; (ii) null subjects are compatible with arbitrary *a gente* but not vice versa; (iii) impersonal subjects and null subjects are not compatible with each other.

24. For example, Lasnik and Uriagereka (1988:47) say that, "in addition to binding requirements, ANAPHORS are plausibly subject to an agreement requirement: (62) An anaphor must agree in syntactic features with its antecedent." Similar suggestions appear in statements like: "The requirement that a REFLEXIVE and its antecedent agree with respect to their nominal features follows from the fact that the reflexive depends for its interpretation on the antecedent, i.e., the reflexive and its antecedent share their referent" (Haegeman 1991:207); "English has a set of nominal elements, including REFLEXIVES like *himself*, which are referentially dependent on an antecedent in the same sentence, which they must match in such grammatical features as number and gender" (Harbert 1995:180, emphases mine). These suggestions are in line with the conceptual spirit of the LF-movement analysis of anaphors: anaphors are subject to special constraints because they are defective in some sense.

25. Note that the FCI cannot account for (73a): I know from cases like (72a) that the

FCI can be somehow circumvented by local binding (see discussion of (70) and the next section). By the same token, (71) cannot be responsible for (ia, b), since binding into PPs does not count as "local" in the sense of (71):

(i)   a. *Nós confiamos demais em si (mesmo).
       we trusted too-much in SE (same)
       'We trusted too much in *us/ourselves.'

       b. *Nós vimos uma cobra atrás de si (mesmo).
       we already saw a snake behind of SE (same)
       'We already saw a snake behind us/??ourselves.'

Rather, (ia, b) are excluded on the same grounds as (59b, c), namely, as violations of the FCI (see discussion following (69)). For the contrast between (ia) and (59b) (si within complement PPs is better with 1pp a gente than with a 1pp pronoun), see Menuzzi (in preparation).
    26. One may try to avoid this conclusion by considering, for example, the possibility that first and second person clitics in Romance can be either pronominals if free or anaphors if locally bound, as suggested by Ronat (1982) and Bouchard (1984). But see Burzio (1991) and Pica (1984) for arguments against this and similar solutions.
    27. See Bouchard (1984) for agreement on coindexing; and Burzio (1989, 1991) for agreement on binding.
    28. See, e.g., Chomsky (1981); Hestvik (1991).
    29. I repeat the relevant definitions here, from section 7.1:

(i)   A syntactic predicate is formed of a head P, P's syntactic arguments, and a subject for P.

(ii)   Syntactic arguments of P are the projections assigned θ-role or Case by P.

(iii) A semantic predicate formed of P is P and all its arguments at the semantic representation of predicate-argument relations.

Note that objects of subcategorized prepositions are intended to be both syntactic and semantic arguments of the verb: they are supposed to get a θ-role required by the verb and, hence, belong to the syntactic and semantic predicates define by the verb.
    30. Perhaps it should be recalled once again that the notion of indexing relevant here is that of section 7.1, that is, indexing as a representation for the mapping between NPs and their interpretation. This is so because this is the notion constrained by the FCI.
    31. Note that (93) is not a formal statement yet, and it would have to be shaped in a way compatible with my previous assumptions about indexing. If we took it literally, then the framework of section 7.1 would translate (92a) into (i), rather than into (92b) or (ii) (which results in (92b) by lambda conversion):

(i)   #John [was-seen-in-the-airport (John)]

(ii)   John [λx [was-seen-in-the-airport (x)]]

But, unlike (92b) or (ii), (i) is semantically ill-formed: **was-seen-in-the-airport** is a one-place predicate, not a two-place predicate (in GB terms, (i) is a violation of the θ-Criterion). Thus, technically speaking, movement chains cannot result in coindexing in the sense of (6) in section 7.1, a somewhat surprising, though harmless, consequence given the standard usage of indices.
    32. The reasoning here presumes that, as far as anaphoric dependencies and argument chains are concerned, only one notion of indexing is relevant, namely, (the representation of)

the assignment of an interpretation to an NP. Of course, we might still resort to coindexing to define chains if we introduce some different notion of indexing, perhaps one specific for this purpose. I am not sure that such a notion of indexing would have any substantive properties, however.

References

Abney, S. 1986. "The English NP in Its Sentential Aspect." Ph.D. dissertation, MIT.

Bosch, P. 1988. "Pronouns under Control?" *Journal of Semantics* 5: 63–78.

Bouchard, D. 1984. *On the Content of Empty Categories*. Dordrecht: Foris.

Burzio, L. 1986. *Italian Syntax: A Government-Binding Approach*. Dordrecht: Reidel.

———. 1989. "On the Non-existence of Disjoint Reference Principles." *Rivista di Grammatica Generativa* 14: 3–27.

———. 1991. "The Morphological Basis of Anaphora." *Journal of Linguistics* 27: 81–105.

Chierchia, G., and S. McConnell-Ginet. 1990. *Meaning and Grammar: An Introduction to Semantics*. Cambridge, Mass.: MIT Press.

Burzio, L. 1986. *Italian Syntax: A Government-Binding Approach*. Dordrecht: Reidel.

———. 1992. "The Role of the Antecedent in Anaphoric Relations." Ms., Johns Hopkins University.

Chomsky, N. 1965. *Aspects of the Theory of Syntax*. Cambridge, Mass.: MIT Press.

———. 1981. *Lectures on Government and Binding*. Dordrecht: Foris.

———. 1986. *Knowledge of Language*. New York: Praeger.

Cinque, G. 1988. "On 'Si' Constructions and the Theory of ARB." *Linguistic Inquiry* 19: 521–581.

Cole, P., and L. Sung 1994. "Head-Movement and Long-Distance Reflexives." *Linguistic Inquiry* 25: 355–406.

Corbett, G. G. 1991. *Gender*. Cambridge: Cambridge University Press.

Cornish, F. 1988. "Anaphoric Pronouns: Under Linguistic Control or Signalling Particular Discourse Representations?" *Journal of Semantics* 5: 233–260.

Dowty, D., R. Wall, and S. Peters. 1981. *Introduction to Montague Semantics*. Dordrecht: Reidel.

Farkas, D. F., and D. Zec. 1993. "Agreement and Pronominal Anaphora." LRC 93–01, Linguistic Research Center, University of California at Santa Cruz.

Fiengo, R., and R. May. 1994. *Indices and Identity*. Cambridge Mass.: MIT Press.

Haegeman, L. 1991. *Introduction to Government and Binding Theory*. Oxford: Blackwell.

Harbert, W. 1995. "Binding Theory, Control and Pro." In G. Webelhuth (ed.) *Government and Binding Theory*, 177–240. Oxford: Blackwell.

Harris, J. W. 1991. "The Exponence of Gender in Spanish." *Linguistic Inquiry* 22: 27–62.

Hestvik, A. 1991. "Subjectless Binding Domains." *Natural Language and Linguistic Theory* 9: 455–496.

Jackendoff, R. S. 1972. *Semantic Interpretation in Generative Grammar*. Cambridge, Mass.: MIT Press.

Kerstens, J. 1993. *The Syntax of Number, Person and Gender: A Theory of Phi-Features*. Berlin: Mouton de Gruyter.

Lasnik, H. 1976. "Remarks on Coreference." *Linguistic Analysis* 2: 1–22. Reprinted in Lasnik 1989, 90–109.

———. 1989. "On the Necessity of Binding Conditions." In Lasnik, H., 1989, *Essays on Anaphora*, 149–167. Dordrecht: Kluwer.

Lasnik, H., and J. Uriagereka. 1988. *A Course in GB Syntax*. Cambridge, Mass.: MIT Press.

Menuzzi, S. 1995. "First Person Plural Anaphora in Brazilian Portuguese and Chains." In M. den Dikken and K. Hengeveld (eds.) *Linguistics in the Netherlands 1995*, 151–162. Amsterdam: John Benjamins.

———. In preparation. *Topics in Binding Theory*. Ph.D. dissertation, HIL\Leiden University.

Pica, P. 1984. "Liage et Contiguité." In J. C. Milner (ed.) *Recherches sur l'Anaphore*, 119–164. University of Paris.

Reinhart, T., and E. Reuland. 1991. "Anaphors and Logophors: An Argument Structure Perspective." In E. Reuland and J. Koster (eds.) *Long-Distance Binding*, 283–321. Cambridge: Cambridge University Press.

———. 1993. "Reflexivity." *Linguistic Inquiry* 24: 657–720.

Reuland, E. and T. Reinhart. 1992. "Binding Conditions and Chains." Proceedings of the 10th WCCFL, 399–415.

Rizzi, L. 1990. *Relativized Minimality*, Cambridge, Mass.: MIT Press.

Ronat, M. 1982. "Une Solution pour un Apparent Contre-Exemple a la Théorie du Liage." *Linguisticae Investigationes* 4: 189–196.

Rosch, E. 1978. "Principles of Categorization." In E. Rosch and B. B. Lloyd (eds.) *Cognition and Categorization*, 27–48. Hillsdale, N.J.: Erlbaum.

Tasmowski, L. and S. P. Verluyten. 1985. "Control Mechanisms of Anaphora." *Journal of Semantics* 4: 341–370.

Tasmowski–De Ryck, L., and S. P. Verluyten. 1982. "Linguistic Control of Pronouns." *Journal of Semantics* 1: 323–346.

8

GERTJAN POSTMA

Distributive Universal Quantification and Aspect in Brazilian Portuguese

Since Kayne (1975), Williams (1977), and May (1984), quantification has been the subject of debate in the generative literature. Since scope relations are thought to be established under quantifier movement, quantification has been a testing ground for syntactic principles, such as the Empty Category Principle (ECP), the Binding Theory, Path Containment Condition (PCC), Connectedness, and so forth. The universal quantifier *every* in English has been studied in some detail. However, languages have various other universal quantifiers.

Many languages have a three-way distinction in their system of universal quantification. English, for instance, has *all*, which is construed with a plural noun and gives a collective universal quantification. *Each* is construed with a singular noun, just as *every*. These are considered distributive universal quantifiers, although *every* has collective readings, for example, in *everyone*. Little attention is paid to the properties that separate the two distributive quantifiers of English *every* and *each*. I mention just four of them: the (im)possibility to license Negative Polarity Items, (im)possibility to be construed with negation, (un)combinability with possession, and (im)possibility to be used as a formative component of the reciprocal. The tables in (1) lists these four properties in English, Dutch, and Portuguese.

(1) a.

English	*all*	*every*	*each*
licensing NPI	+	+	−
not X	+	+	−
possessives	+	+	−
reciprocal	−	−	+

b.

Dutch	alle	ieder(e)	elk(e)
licensing NPI	+	+	+
niet + X	+	+	+
possessives	+	–	–
reciprocal	–	–	+

c.

Portuguese	todos/todas	todo/toda	cada
licensing NPI	+	+	–
nem + X	+	+	–
possessives	+	+	+
reciprocal	–	–	–

The table in (1) shows that languages do not behave homogeneously with respect to the three universal quantifiers. The semantic distinction between *every* and *each* is especially difficult to determine in sufficiently abstract terms, since native speakers hardly have semantic judgments on their distinct semantics by direct introspection. This holds even more strongly for Dutch than for English. Native speakers of Dutch can interchange *elk* and *ieder* in virtually any context. Nevertheless, the two lexems are not identical, as can be seen from tendencies in usage (ANS 1985:257–259).

The variety in properties between the three quantifiers raises the question of whether they can be identified cross-linguistically. If not, it remains unclear why languages so often have three types of universal quantifiers. Is there perhaps some structural possibility for these three quantifiers? Does syntax or some other module create this possibility? If they can be identified, why do they not behave equally across languages? Do the differences in behavior originate from interactions with other syntactic properties?

In light of these questions, Brazilian Portuguese is interesting because the differences in properties between *todo*+sg and *cada* +sg are quite salient. I will first provide an overview of the properties and discuss them in relation to the existing literature on universal quantification. Then I will examine the interaction between argumental quantification and aspect. This interaction can be made explicit because of the relatively rich aspectual system in Brazilian Portuguese. The interaction with aspect will supply a clue to why the three types of quantifications behave so differently across languages with distinct aspectual systems.

8.1 Properties of cada and todo

8.1.1 Basic properties

In Brazilian Portuguese,[1] *todo* and *cada* (both meaning 'each'/'every') are distributive universal quantifiers. They cannot be coreferential with NPs that are not c-commanded by them (cf. (2)).

(2) a. Todo estudante estava indignado. *Ele queria protestar/??Eles queriam protestar.
        'Every student was indignant. He/they wanted to protest.'

b. Cada estudante comprou um livro. *Ele tinha dinheiro para isso/??Eles tinham dinheiro para isso.
'Every student bought a different book. He/they had money for this.'

Apart from this similarity, they have different syntactic properties, which will be the subject of my investigations.

Whereas *todo* is a simple distributor without argumental requirements in its scope (3a), *cada* has, in the unmarked cases,[2] an additional requirement of binding an argumental position in object/complement position, as illustrated in (3b, c). Only if *cada* can function as an antecedent to *seu/sua* 'his', the structure is well-formed.

(3)   a. *Todo* aluno ia para a praia.
'Every pupil went to the beach.'

b.* *Cada* aluno ia para a praia.
'Every pupil went to the beach.'

c. *Cada* aluno ia para *sua* (propria) praia.
'Every pupil went to his (own) beach.'

d. *Cada* aluno ia para *uma* praia.
'Every pupil went to a different beach.'

This extra position can be of various types, for example, an anaphoric pronoun that is coreferential with its antecedent (3c), but also an indefinite, that is, a position with a distinct referential index (cf. (3d)).

In the absence of a position to be bound, the structure is ill-formed. It seems that *cada* must be distributive with respect to an additional argument position in its scope. Taking indefinites as open variables in the sense of Heim, I can formulate this provisorily by saying that *cada* must bind two variable positions: a position in its restrictive set (RS), just as *todo* does, *and* a position in its nuclear scope (NS). The two binding relations involve distinct referential indexes. Put differently: *cada* binds two variable position *unselectively*. I will call the latter the scope-binding relation and will indicate the construal of *cada* by italicizing the constituents.

(4)   a. *cada*$_{ik}$ [RS t$_i$ homem] [NS . . . x_k . . .]
t‗‗‗‗⌐

b. todo$_i$ [RS t$_i$ homem] [NS . . .]
t‗‗⌐

The semantic effect of the construal ("unselective binding") of *cada* and an open variable (e.g., an indefinite) is that the construction is distributive not only with respect to the subject but also with respect to the argument bound. For instance, (3d) can only mean that everyone went to a different beach. The word *diferente* 'different' does not need to be expressed, but it is possible. This minimally differs from the use of *todo* + singular noun.

Consider the following minimal pair together with their translations in English:

(5) a. Todo pacote tinha um peso.
     'Every pack had a weight.'   (virtually tautological)

     b. Cada pacote tinha um peso.
     'Every pack had a different weight.'

Whereas (5a) is virtually nonsensical, (5b) has a quite substantial meaning. As the translation indicates, the import of (5b) is that every pack had a different weight. This is so without need to express the disjoint reference of the objects. Another minimal pair is given in (6), where both sentences are informative.

(6) a. Todo aluno tinha uma virtude.
     'Every pupil had one specific (good) quality.'

     b. Cada aluno tinha uma virtude.
     'Every pupil had a different (good) quality.'

Whereas the predicate is held referentially constant in the case of *todo*, it must be disjoint in the case of *cada*. In other words, predicates to *cada N* are obligatorily distributive, whereas the predicates to *todo N* are obligatorily collective in further argumental positions. *Cada* may be called "bidistributive." It seems as if the distributor *cada* induces a similar distributivity in the indefinite. In this respect the interaction between *cada* and the indefinite is comparable to what is known as unselective binding in donkey sentences (Heim 1982). The bidistributivity gives rise to typical list readings. Thus (6b) has a semantic representation as given in (7):

(7) $pupil_1$ has $quality_1$, $pupil_2$ has $quality_2$, $pupil_3$ has $quality_3$, . . .

The obligatory distributivity in a position within the predicate to *cada* implies that *cada* cannot be used in a simple object position.[3]

(8) a. *O Flávio comprou *cada* livro.
     'Flavio bought every book.'

     b. O Flávio comprou *cada* livro *numa loja*
     'Flavio bought everybook in another shop.'

When an indefinite constituent is added, the construction becomes fine (8b).

The obligatory distributivity in a position within the predicate to *cada* shows up in another effect. The fact that it is ungrammatical to lexicalize the overt distributor *outro* in the local scope of *cada* (cf. (9b)).

(9) a. *Cada* aluno ia para *uma* praia.
     'Each pupil went to another beach.'

     b. **Cada* aluno ia para *uma outra* praia.
     'Each pupil went to another beach.'

c. *Cada* aluno ia para *uma* praia diferente.
'Each pupil went to another beach.'

Cada is (locally) in complementary distribution with *outro*. This cannot be attributed to a pragmatic aversion against redundancy, in view of the fact that *diferente* 'different' can be added (9c). There must be a structural reason for why *outro* is ruled out. The obligatory distributivity in the object when *cada* is present is analogous to what happens when the quantifier *um ao outro* (= 'each other') is present, which also makes the sentence distributive in two arguments: itself and its antecedent. Viewed this way, *cada* can be considered a counteranaphor in the sense that it needs a dependent that is c-commanded by it. There is a difference with the reciprocal, however. Whereas the reciprocal construction $[N_1 \ldots$ each other] only imposes a restrictive set within the antecedent, the construction $[cada\ N_1 \ldots uma\ N_2]$ relates two NPs with restrictive sets of their own. It is this difference that gives rise to its particular semantics.

There is still another difference with the reciprocal. The reciprocal *um ao outro* 'each other' must be bound by a local antecedent, but this is not true for the relation between *cada* and its counterantecedent, as exemplified in (10a):

(10) a. *Cada professor* pensou que eu prejudiquei *um aluno.*
       'Every teacher thought that I jeopardized a different student.'

      b. *Um aluno* pensou que eu prejudiquei *o outro.*
       'One pupil thought that I jeopardized the other.'

(11) a. *? *Cada professor* lamentou que eu tivesse prejudicado *um aluno.*
       'Every teacher regretted that I jeopardized a different student.'

      b. *? *Um aluno* lamentou que eu tivesse prejudicado *o outro.*
       'One pupil thought that I jeopardized the other.'

From (10a) we learn that *cada* can be construed with an indefinite that resides in a clause that is c-commanded by it. This can be done outside its local domain. In this respect, the relation between *cada* and *um* is to be compared with the reciprocal construction *um N* . . . *o outro*, which does not observe locality. Nevertheless, there are restrictions. Construal can only take place in the complement of epistemic verbs (the so-called bridge verbs). Construal is ruled out in opaque contexts, for example, factives (11a). In section 8.5.1, I will discuss an additional restriction on the distributive construal of *cada* and the indefinite, which is known as "connectedness."

8.1.2 A marked additional reading of *cada*

Apart from the basic readings of *cada*, discussed in the previous subsection, there is an additional reading of *cada* that is rather marked. A typical context is given in (12):

(12) (We have been in Ouro Preto. It is really incredible . . .)
      Cada rua é bonita.

      '(Really) every street is beautiful.'

It is stylistically marked, and not every native speaker accepts this reading without context. The quantifier constituent receives special stress, and the sentence expresses amazement. It must considered as counterevidential, and it seems wise to exclude these readings from this pilot study.[4]

8.1.3 Conclusion

I conclude that *cada* and *todo* have quite distinct syntactic and semantic properties in Portuguese. Both *cada* and *todo* are distributive quantifiers. In addition to creating a distributive relation between one argument and the predicate, the predicate must also be distributive in an additional open variable. I assumed the distributivity in the indefinite to be induced under unselective binding by *cada*. This construal between *cada* and the indefinite is subject to locality constraints that are similar to negative raising and long-distance interrogatives ("bridge verbs"). The bidistributivity of *cada* constructions gives rise to typical list readings, which I will examine in more detail in the next section.

8.2 Distributive quantification and *wh*

List readings are found in two constructions, which have been studied in some detail in the literature: in multiple interrogations (Jaeggli 1980; Chomsky 1981) and in constructions in which a interrogative and a universal quantifier interact in a peculiar way (Williams 1977; May 1985; Aoun and Li 1993).

8.2.1 Multiple interrogation

I will start with multiple interrogation. Consider (13):

(13)   a. *Who* wrote *what*?

      b. Max wrote the introduction, Sue wrote chapter 1, and Oscar wrote chapter 2, . . .

      c. [What$_2$ [who$_1$ [e$_1$ wrote e$_2$]]]

Such multiple interrogation represents a set of questions, to which answers in the form of lists are felicitous. It is usually assumed that the *wh*-word that is in situ at SS moves to COMP at LF. The two *wh*-words mutually c-command each other at LF, which gives rise to the list reading.

There are intriguing restrictions on the shape of multiple interrogations. Example (14), for instance, is ill-formed. This is the so-called superiority effect (Chomsky 1981).

(14)   a. *What did *who* write?

      b. [$_{CP}$ Who$_1$ [$_{CP}$ What$_2$ did [$_{IP}$ e$_1$ write e$_2$]]]

Chomsky explains it in terms of the ECP, which holds not only at SS but also at LF (Kayne 1981; Rizzi 1982). In the LF-representation (14b), *who* cannot properly govern its trace in Spec, IP. Pesetsky (1982) proposes to rule out (14b) by the PCC, that is, the requirement that A-bar chains must be nested with respect to each other.

8.2.2 Quantifying into *wh*

I now turn to another type of constructions with list readings: sentences that combine an interrogative and a universal quantifier, as in (15a):

(15)   a. *What* did *everyone* buy for Max?   (ambiguous)

     b. Who bought what for Max?

May (1985) notices that the construction in (15a) has two readings. It can be interpreted as a single question, requiring an answer of the type (16a). This is called the collective reading. It can also be interpreted as a multiple interrogation. It is then equivalent to "Who bought what for Max?" and requires a list answer of the sort in (16b).

(16)   a. Everyone bought flowers for Max.   (collective reading)

     b. Peter bought a book for Max, Sue bought wine for Max, . . .   (list reading)

May (1985) and Aoun and Li (1993) interpret these effects in terms of scope. By standard assumptions, these authors assume that the interrogative moves to Spec, CP at SS, whereas the universal quantifier undergoes quantifier raising and adjoins to IP at LF, yielding the structure as given in (17).

(17) $[_{CP}$ What$_2$ $[_{IP}$ everyone$_1$ $[_{IP}$ e$_1$ bought e$_2$ for Max]]]

If universal quantifiers have scope over the interrogative, they may quantify into interrogatives, thus creating a set of questions. In this structure, the interrogative and the quantifier mutually c-command each other (May's analysis) or mutually c-command each other's chains (Aoun and Li's analysis). Therefore, *wh* and the quantifier can take scope over each other, resulting in a construction that is ambiguous between a list reading and a collective reading.

It is worth mentioning that in the approaches propounded by both May (1985) and Aoun and Li (1993), the two readings present in (15a) are not tied to distinct LF-representations. The structure only indicates that it is ambiguous. This feature is at odds with the spirit of LF-representations, being a level of representation where surface structures are disambiguated. I will return to this later.

Now, if the interrogative and the quantifier are interchanged, as in (18a), the list reading is absent. The structure is unambiguous, in contrast to the reverse structure, repeated in (18b).

(18)   a. Who bought everything for Max?   (unambiguous)

     b. What did everyone buy for Max?   (ambiguous)

The reason for the absence of the list reading is that *everything* cannot adjoin to IP, but only to VP, since its LF-representation in (19a) violates the PCC (Pesetsky 1982; May 1985).[5]

(19)   a.*[Who$_1$ [IP everything$_2$ [IP e$_1$ bought e$_2$ for Max]]]

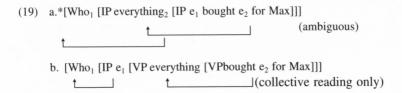

(ambiguous)

   b. [Who$_1$ [IP e$_1$ [VP everything [VPbought e$_2$ for Max]]]

      └____┘   └_____┘(collective reading only)

The LF-representation (19b) cannot have the list reading, since the two quantifiers do not mutually c-command each other (May 1985) or because the two chains do not mutually c-command each other (Aoun and Li 1993).

I will now turn to Portuguese, in which the constructions analogous to the ambiguous English construction in (18b) are given in (20). The construction is grammatical both with *todo* and with *cada*. However, neither of them is ambiguous! The construction with *cada* picks out only the distributive reading (list reading), whereas the construction with *todo* picks out only the collective reading.

(20)   a. Que livro (que) cada aluno lê/?   (distributive/*collective)

   b. Que livro (que) todo aluno lê?   (??distrubutive/collective)
     'What book COMP every student read?'

The judgments with *todo* are somewhat weaker than those with *cada*, which are entirely sharp. It might be that the two are really in complementarity distribution. It is also possible that only *cada* is strictly unambiguous and that, in principle, *todo* has both readings. The distributive use of *todo* might be ruled out by a Gricean maxim to be as accurate as possible: because of the existence of *cada*, the distributive use of *todo* is a least preferred option.

Before addressing the question of why the collective reading is absent with *cada*, it is helpful to inspect the reverse construction, corresponding to English (18b). The construction is grammatical only if the quantifier is *todo*.

(21)   a. *Quem compra *cada* livro?

   b. Quem compra *todo* livro?
     'Who buys every book?'

   c. [Quem [IP cada livro [IP e$_1$ comprou e$_2$]]]

Within May's framework, the ill-formedness of (21a) can be explained by assuming that *cada must* have wide scope, that is, that it *must* adjoin to IP. Since the *wh*-word *quem* moves to Spec, CP, as represented in (21c), the PCC is violated. In English, sentences such as (18b) are saved by adjoining *everyone* to VP instead, giving rise to the collective reading. Apparently, in Portuguese the possibility of adjoining *cada* to VP is not available. I formulate this in (22):

(22)   • [todo N] adjoins to VP
      • [cada N] does not adjoin to VP

   The exclusion of the collective reading in (20a) would follow from (22) as well. This is possible if the collective reading is always a result of VP adjunction of the subject as expressed in (23):

(23)   a. [CP what book$_2$ [IP pro$_1$ [VP everyone$_1$ [VP e$_1$ read e$_2$]]]]   (collective reading)

     b. [CP what book$_2$ [IP everyone$_1$ [IP e$_1$ [VP e$_1$ read e$_2$]]]]   (list reading)

These interpretive rules imply that in the case of *cada* (23a) is not possible, so that *cada* excludes the collective reading.

   The hypothesis in (23) assumes that the quantifier *todo* can remain within the VP domain at LF and therefore must receive nominative case without moving to Spec, IP; that is, it works like a VP-internal nominative construction. These constructions are usually limited to indefinites. At first glance, this seems like an unsurmountable objection. There is, however, evidence that *todo* has indefinite properties in contrast to *cada*, as can be seen from (24):

(24)   Tinha todo/*cada jeito de que ia chover.
     there was every/each chance of that (it) went rain
     'There was every chance that it would rain.'

Similar indefinite (or "open-ended") effects with *every* in Hungarian have been described by Szabolsci (1994). For a detailed discussion of the indefinite use with English *every* (cf. Postma and Rooryck 1995).

8.2.3 Testing May's versus Aoun and Li's Scope Principle

There is one problem with VP-adjunction approach. As Kempson and Cormack (1981) have pointed out, the *every* phrase in (25a) can have wider scope than the *wh*-phrase, in contrast to the simplex (25b). Whereas the simplex construction is unambiguous, the embedded construction is ambiguous.

(25)   a. She told me who inspected every school.   (list /collective)

     b. who inspected every school   (*list/collective)

In Portuguese *cada* construction, one expects an opposition in grammaticality judgments rather than in readings because as the collective reading is absent in the equivalents of (25a and b). So, one would expect the equivalent of (25b) to be ungrammatical and the equivalent of (25a) to be grammatical (unambiguous, list reading only). This is indeed the case, as shown in (26):

(26)   a. Ela me contou quem inspecionou cada escola.   (list/*collective)

       b. *quem inspecionou cada escola   (*list/*collective)

Taking (22) into account (i.e., the fact that *cada* cannot adjoin to VP), I conclude that (27) is its representation.

(27)   [IP cada escola$_2$ [IP ela me contou [CP quem$_1$ [IP e$_1$ inspecionou e$_2$]]]]

Significantly, (26a) has the list reading; that is, the structure in (27) must give rise to a list reading. This implies that the list reading cannot be established by mutual c-command of the operators as is assumed by May (1985) because *cada* cannot make an intermediate adjunction to IP of the embedded clause, which is ruled out by the ECP.

The list reading, however, is predicted if one adopts the Scope Principle as proposed in Aoun and Li (1993). This principle says that quantifier A can have scope over quantifier B if A c-commands a member of the chain of B.[6] Thus, the list reading can come about if two quantifiers mutually c-command each other. In the configuration of (27), such a mutual c-command relation is present, and the list reading is to be expected. In this respect, Aoun and Li's Scope Principle is superior to May's approach.

However, Aoun and Li's Scope Principle as it stands suffers from the same theoretical defect discussed with respect to May's approach: it does not unambiguously project LF-structures on readings. It links a certain LF-configuration to the *possibility* of a reading. Moreover, there is an empirical problem. The Scope Principle would predict for the structure (27) that the other reading is possible as well. Because this prediction does not come true (cf. (26a)) some modification is necessary in Aoun and Li's theory.

This modification is in fact the hypothesis in (22 and 23). These rules show that there is a unique projection between LF-structures and readings.

(28)   *Unambiguous Projection Hypothesis*
       A construction in which two distributive chains mutually c-command each other at LF has a list reading.

This hypothesis has a strong theoretical advantage over and above May's and Aoun and Li's scope principles, which are stated in terms of possible readings. Besides the conceptual appeal, (28) allows interpretive rules like the one in (23) to subsume the typical distributive nature of *cada* to (22). Finally, it ties the LF-configuration of mutual c-command of two quantifiers to the list reading and therefore generalizes over all configurations with list readings: multiple interrogation structures and list readings of distributive quantifiers. In this approach, LF-structures with mutual c-command are uniformly projected on list readings.

It is possible that (28) realizes the more general hypothesis in (29). No ambiguity exists at LF.

(29)   *Unambiguous Projection Hypothesis*
   •LF-representations are unambiguous.

If (29) is defensible, the words *can* or *may* can be removed from Aoun and Li's Scope Principle.

(30)   *Strict Scope Principle*
   A quantifier A has scope over a quantifier **B** if the chain of **A** c-commands a member of the chain of B.

The Scope Principle as formulated in (30) is conceptually more attractive than the original formulation in Aoun and Li (1993) because it takes LF-representation to be unambiguous. The LF-representation *represents* a reading. Moreover, it gives the correct predictions with respect to a language such as Portuguese, which has a specific bidistributive quantifier. Furthermore, it describes the distinction between two types of distributive quantifiers in terms of the VP-adjunction hypothesis (cf.(24)). Finally, it generalizes over list readings in double interrogations, *wh+ each* constructions, as well as *cada* constructions.

8.3 Distributive quantification and aspect

In section 8.1, I showed that Portuguese *cada* imposes argumental requirements on its scope: it must bind an open argumental variable. No such interactions were found with the other distributor *todo*. The question is in what way the distinction between *todo* and *cada* can be stated. Can lexical items have such complex syntactic specifications in the lexicon? Or are *cada* and *todo* not so different? Is the requirement on bidistributivity in the case of *todo* perhaps saturated in another way?
   In order to understand why *todo* lacks an interaction with its predicate, it is worthwhile to widen the perspective somewhat to another syntactic property: aspect. Consider (31), where *cada* and *todo* are inserted with the past tenses *ia* and *foi*, which represent the imperfect and perfect tense of 'went,' respectively.

(31)   a.   *Cada* homem ia/foi para *uma* praia.
          'Every man went to a (different) beach.'

      b.   *Todo* homem *ia*/*foi para a praia.
          'Every man went to the beach.'

Whereas *cada* is insensitive for the verbal aspect, *todo* +sg noun typically occurs only in imperfect tenses. The aspectual effect in (31b) disappears when I add other temporal material, such as *um dia* 'one day', as exemplified in (32b):

(32)   a.   *Todo* homem *ia*/*foi para a praia.

      b.   *todo* homem [foi para a praia] *um dia*

An additional example is given in (33):

(33) a. *Todo* homem foi criança.

  b. *Todo* homem *já* foi criança.

  c. *todo* homem foi criança *um dia*

These data are systematic. They indicate that *todo*, like *cada*, has a requirement of binding an open variable. *Todo* binds an additional indefinite temporal variable outside VP, be it an overt indefinite nominal, such as *um dia* 'one day', or an indefinite tense, such as the past imperfect. If so, imperfect tenses must be considered temporal indefinites, which is quite natural.[7] I summarize:

(34) a. • *Todo* and *cada* are bi-operators, that is, they must bind two open variables.

  b. • *Cada* obligatorily chooses an argumental variable in its nuclear scope.

  c. • *Todo* obligatorily chooses an aspectual variable in its nuclear scope.

  d. • Imperfect tenses are aspectual indefinites.

This simple hypothesis brings distributors such as *todo* and *cada* under one denominator: they are bioperators.

In the next section, I will show that (34a) is also extensible to the plural universal quantifier *todos*. In section 8.5, I will remove the stipulative character of (34b) and will reduce it to a morphological property of *cada*.

8.4 Distributive quantification and number

The aspect sensitivity of *todo* is not inherent to the lexeme *todo* itself, since it is *not* present in the *todo*+plural construction (*todos*, 35a). Nor is it present in the singular when the dummy *mundo* is added (35b):

(35) a. *Todos os* alunos iam/foram para a praia.
      'All pupils went to the beach.'

  b. *Todo mundo* ia/foi para a praia.
      'Every one went to the beach.'

If I take (34a) as a starting point, these data suggest that *todo* can alternatively bind an additional indefinite morpheme with its restrictive set, either a real dummy *mundo*, creating a structure *todo mundo*, (to be compared with 'everyone' in English),[8] or a plural morpheme *todos os alunos*. In these cases, the bi-operatorhood of *todo* is saturated in its restrictive set, and the sensitivity for aspect disappears.

Notice that the similarity of the dummy *mundo* and the plural morpheme is not a mere stipulation. It also shows up in the interaction with another distributor: the reciprocal. The reciprocals *um ao outor* and *each other* are bi-operators as well. Reciprocals, like *cada*, are subject to a double binding relation (Aoun 1985). Significantly, it imposes its subject to be collective: the reciprocal requires a plural morpheme or an additional dummy, such as *mundo* or *one*.

(36) a. Todo {mundo/*aluno} se odeia.

   b. Todos os alunos se odeiam /*todo aluno se odeia.   (reciprocal reading)

(37) a. Every one/*pupil hates each other.

   b. All pupils hate each other.

This parallelism between *cada* and the reciprocal suggests that the reciprocal requires an indefinite (i.e., an open variable) within the antecedent (38):

(38) a. • The reciprocal is a quantifier that is bidistributive, that is, it must bind two open variables.

   b. • It obligatorily chooses a variable in the restrictive set of the antecedent.

   c. • The plural morpheme and dummies like *mundo* are restrictive set indefinites.

This scheme not only captures the effect of the plural morpheme on the aspect sensitivity of *todo* but also covers the "plurality" requirement of the antecedent of the distributor *each other*. Notice that the third assumption is quite natural. It has been noticed that indefinites and plurals share various properties, for example, the licensing of *there* is insertion, and the possibility of unselective binding (Carlson 1977; Lewis 1975; Heim 1982).

There is additional evidence for the characterization of the indefinite nature of the plural morpheme as an indefinite within the restrictive set of a quantifier. The plural not only saturates the bidistributivity of *todo* but also can have similar effects of *cada* as well. It shows that it is the singularity, and not lexeme *cada* itself, that triggers scope binding effects. Consider again the bidistributive requirement of *cada* +sg, repeated in (39):

(39) a. *nas férias, nós vamos *cada dia* para a praia

   b. nas férias, nós vamos *cada dia* para *uma praia*

   c. nas férias, nós vamos *todo dia* para a praia

Now, although *cada* does not take a plural restrictive set, it can subcategorize plural of a particular type, as in (40a):

(40) a. A *cada duas semanas* nós vamos para a praia.   (contrasts with 3b)
      'Every two weeks we go to the beach.'

   b. A *cada duas semanas* nós temos um *outro* professor.   (contrasts with 8b)
      'Every two weeks we have another teacher.'

c. *A *cada duas semanas* nós temos *um* professor.   (contrasts with 5b)
'Every two weeks we have a teacher.'

d. A cada duas semanas nós temos um professor diferente.
'Every two weeks we have a different teacher.'

In combination with a plural NP, there are three effects: (i) No indefinite is necessary anymore within the nuclear scope (40a). (ii) The distributor *outro*, which is in complemetary distribution with *cada*+sg, is not excluded anymore (40b). 3. A simple indefinite gives rise to the nonsensical effect (40c), which was typical of *todo* (cf (5b)).

The table in (41) summarizes my conclusions. Universal quantifiers *cada* and *todo* are bi-operators, that is, they must bind two open variables, under unselective binding. *Cada* is connected with a second variable that resides within the nuclear scope. This gives *cada* a list reading. *Todo* binds a second variable either in its restrictive set (e.g., the plural morpheme (41a) or a dummy *mundo* (41d)) or in a tense-variable (41c).

	pattern		*number of variables*	*consequences*	
(41)	*restrictive set*	*nuclear scope*		*tense sensitivity*	*list reading*
a.	[*todo*] + [PL]		2	no	no
b.	[*cada*].....................	[*um*]..	2	no	yes
c.	[*todo*] aluno	[Tx]...	2	yes	no
d.	[*todo*] + [*mundo*]		2	no	no

The distinction between *cada* and *todo* is not exclusively ruled by the lexicon. Argumental binding and aspect sensitivity are triggered by the syntactic environment, which implies that the characterization of *cada* must be an epiphenomenon. The next section will examine what morphosyntactic property makes *cada* distinct from *todo*.

8.5 Distributivity and connectedness

In the previous sections, I argued that both *cada* and *todo* are bi-operators. Unlike *todo*, *cada* must bind an open variable in its nuclear scope; compare (42):

(42)   a. *Cada aluno* foi para a praia.
'Every pupil went to the beach.'

b. *Cada aluno* foi para *uma praia.*
'Every pupil went to another beach.'

The question then arises: By what mechanism are structures with *cada* able to impose such complex conditions? It cannot be the lexeme itself, since the syntactic environment can remove the requirement. The trigger cannot be the syntactic environment either, since this would not explain the distinction between *cada* and *todo*, which both take a singular. I will show that a morphological property is at work: the lexeme *cada* cannot enter into Spec-head agreement configurations *because it is undeclinable for gender and number*. *Todo*, on the other hand, does enter Spec-head agreement relations, since it declines for gender and number, *todo(s)/toda(s)*, that is, it is morphosyntactically active. Morphological properties must be licensed by specific syntactic structures.

Notice first that if the scope-binding of *cada* is required by syntax, the mechanism must be of a nonlocal nature. One nonlocal mechanism known in syntax is connectedness. In the next section I will review the basic properties of connectedness; in a subsequent section I will apply it to *cada*.

8.5.1 Connectedness

Since Engdahl (1983), the study of parasitic gaps has taken a central position in theoretical linguistics. As is now common knowledge, adjunct clauses can contain an empty slot whose licensing is dependent on another empty category in the sentence. The construction is given in (43). Kayne (1983) shows that multiple interrogation (44) and multiple negation (45) constructions obey the same restrictions.

(43) a. *a person who$_i$ people that talk to t$_i$ is never aggressive

     b. a person who$_i$ people that talk to t$_i$ usually end up fascinated with [*ec*]$_i$ . . . .

(44) a. *We are trying to find out *which man* said that *which woman* was in love with him.

     b. We are trying to find out *which man* said that *which woman* was in love with *which boy*.

(45) a. **Non* pretendo che *nessuno* dica questo.
       'I do not pretend that anyone says this.'

     b. *Non* pretendo che *nessuno* dica *niente*.
       'I do not pretend that anyone says anything.'

In (43) quantificational construal with a variable in a left branch is only possible upon being cointerpreted with a position on a right branch. In (44) and (45) this effect is extendable to quantificational construal. Kayne explains the effect in terms of chains. The ungrammaticality in the a-sentences is due to a lack of connectedness between the head and foot of the chain. Kayne formulates connectedness as the building up of g-projection sets. If the g-projection sets of the syntactic positions under consideration form a connected subtree, the slots can be construed with each other. Typically, g-projection sets project up recursively from a right branch to a dominating node but not from a left branch.[9] This makes subextraction from a left branch or construal into a left branch licit only if it involves a position on a right branch (cf. (40b)) as well. In the cases of multiple interrogation and negation, an analogous mechanism can be formulated. I assume that simultaneous interpretation concerns constituents that are linked through a *formal* index, indicated by α. This formal index is unselective with respect to the extensional indices. Following Lewis (1975), Heim (1982), and Pesetsky (1982), such interpretative relations are called "unselective binding."

8.5.2 *Cada* and connectedness

I will now consider *cada* with the effects of connectedness in mind.

(46)   a. *Cada* professor pensava que ela tinha escrito *um livro*.
          'Every teacher thought that she had written a different book.'

       b. **Cada professor pensava que *uma aluna* tinha escrito este livro bonito.
          'Every teacher thought that a different pupil had written this nice book.'

       c. *Cada* professor pensava que *uma aluna* tinha escrito *um livro*.
          'Every teacher thought that a different pupil had written a book.'

In the paradigm in (46), *cada* can be distributive in an argument that is at a right branch (46a) but not in an argument at a left branch (46b). However, the ungrammaticality disappears upon adding an additional distributivity on a right branch (46c). In the latter case a triple list reading is induced. This shows that construal of *cada* and the open variable to be bound are construed through connectedness.

Why is *cada* construed with a position with the predicate, that is, with a right branch? Consider the basic sentence (47a):

(47)   a. *cada* D aluno foi para *uma praia*

       b. *cada$_i$ [e$_i$ D [aluno]] foi para a praia
          |_____|

If I create a tripartite structure under quantifier raising, I obtain the structure as indicated in (47b). Significantly, such an extraction from a left branch is ruled out by connectedness, since *cada*, which is uninflected for number and gender, is without Spec-head agreement with D^0. Connectedness can be restored if *cada* is interpreted in construal with an open position in a right branch, for example, an indefinite.

       c. cada$_{ik}$ [e$_i$ D [aluno]] foi para [uma praia]$_k$
          |_____|

If the indefinite resides at a right branch with respect to the landing site of the quantifier, the g-projections that are built up from the indefinite with index /k/ and the g-projections of the quantifier trace form a connected subtree. If Spec-head agreement were present, as in the case of *todo/a*, the head D^0 properly governs the trace. As g-projections are built up starting from the governor, connectedness is established.[10]

The impossibility for *cada* to bind an imperfect event implies that events must reside on a left branch.[11] Example (48) presents a structure that gives the correct predictions.

(48)

```
                        IP
                       /\
                  DP      \
                 /\        FP
           cada_i^α D NP   /\
                        Asp  F'
                            /\
                          F   VP
                             /\
                          uma_k^α
```

In (48), Asp_x, whether it is a definite tense (perfect) or an indefinite tense (imperfect), cannot serve for connectedness, although it can serve to saturate the bidistributive nature of universal quantification in *todo* constructions. In the case of *cada*, which has problems with connectedness because of the absence of agreement, this means that there must be another open variable within VP, for example, the indefinite *uma praia*. In section 8.7, I will give independent evidence for this configuration.

Using connectedness, it is possible to hold the absence of agreement in *cada* responsible for the fact that *cada* must find its second binding slot on a right branch, in contrast to *todo*, which has no problems with quantifier extraction. In this view, both *cada* and *todo* are bidistributive, but because of the absence of agreement in *cada*, problems with connectedness arise after quantifier extraction: *cada* therefore must find its second variable at an absolute right branch.

It is probable that *cada*'s inability to combine with *outro* can also be explained as follows: *outro* is prenominal (i.e., at a left branch), whereas *diferente* is postnominal. I will not pursue this issue further here.

(49)   a. **Cada* aluno foi para uma *outra* praia.

     b. *Cada* aluno foi para uma praia *diferente*.
       'Every student went to another/different beach.'

The requirement of *cada* to find a second variable at a right branch rules out construal with indefinite tenses, and indefinites within its restrictive set ("plural morpheme"). The latter two options are available with *todo*: it can be construed with aspect and with a plural. Thus, the following generalization is true: universal quantification always binds two variables.[12]

(50)   Universal quantification involves two variables.

If universal quantifiers seemingly deviate from bi-operatorhood, the requirement is saturated within other domains of syntax, for example, the tense domain (*todo* $+N_{sg}$), where *todo* is construed with an aspectual variable (imperfect), or within the restrictive set (*todo* + N_{pl}), where *todo* is construed with the plural morpheme. *Todo* can circumvent problems with connectedness through agreement. *Cada* cannot. The additional requirement on *cada* to be tied to an open position in a right branch is a result of a syntactic principle: connectedness, in conspiracy with absence of agreement.

8.6 On some differences between Dutch *elk* and Portuguese *cada*

To return to my original question: Why do Dutch *elk* and Portuguese *cada* behave slightly differently? Why is *cada* obligatorily distributive, whereas Dutch *elk* does not need to be, as illustrated in (49)?

(51)   a. Jan kuste elke vrouw.

　　　　b. *João beijou cada mulher.
　　　　'John kissed every woman.'

Are *elk* and *cada* not to be identified with each other? Or is their slightly different behavior due to the properties of their syntactic environment?

Both *elk(e)* and *ieder(e)* are inflected (in a portmanteau way) for gender and number just like any adjective in Dutch. So, if the hypothesis that the nonagreeing behavior of *cada* is the trigger of its scope-binding requirement is correct, one would indeed expect *elk(e)* not to be bidistributive. This is a correct prediction; witness (51).

Interestingly, if *elk* realizes as a floating quantifier, it is uninflected for gender and number, as is exemplified in (52):

(52)   De jongens wilden *elk* een begrijf beginnen.
　　　　the boys wanted each a company begin
　　　　'The boys wanted to start a company of his own.'

Instead of the inflected form *elke*, the floating quantifier realizes as *elk*. This is not just a bare form but an uninflected form. Nouns do require an inflectional -e in Dutch modifiers when they are plural. Only neuter singulars require the bare form (*elk kind*, 'each child'). Therefore, the floating *elk* not only is bare but also is an uninflected form. It is not in agreement with its antecedent *de jongens*.

Looking at the behavior of the floating quantifier *elk*, one observes that it must bind an indefinite in its scope just like Portuguese *cada*. This is illustrated in (53a–c):

(53)   a.*Zij gingen *elk* naar het strand.
　　　　they went each to the beach

　　　　b. Zij gingen *elk* {op *eigen* gelegenheid/met *een ander* hoedje op} naar het strand.
　　　　they went each on own means/ with another hat} to the beach

　　　　c.*Zij gingen elk met hetzelfde boek naar het strand.
　　　　they went each with the same book to the beach

I give an additional minimal pair in (54).

(54)   a. *Elke* student houdt van lezen.
　　　　'Every boy likes reading.'

b. *De studenten hielden *elk* van lezen.
'The students liked each reading.'

c. De studenten hielden *elk* van een *ander* boek
'The students liked each another book.'

I conclude that morphosyntactic properties of quantificational elements determine their semantic behavior rather than that these semantic properties are part of the lexical meaning stated in the lexicon. Morphosyntactic properties result in semantic behavior by means of syntactic interactions such as connectedness.

8.7 Testing the left-branch nature of aspect: Copular drop in Dutch and Portuguese

In section 8.3, I concluded that distributive quantification interacts with the aspectual structure of the clause. The singular use of *todo* can be construed with imperfect tenses but not with perfect tenses; compare (27), repeated here as (55):

(55) a. *Cada* homem ia/foi para *uma* praia.
       every man went to a (different) beach

    b. *Todo* homem *ia/*foi para a praia.
       every man went$_{imperfect/perfect}$ to the beach

Cada, on the other hand, does not exhibit sensitivity to aspect, which leads to the conclusion that aspect resides at a left branch, not visible to the head of the distributive chain via connectedness. This explains the ungrammaticality of (56):

(56)   *Cada \homem ia para a praia.
       cada$_{xy}$ [x homem] ia$_y$ para a praia
       each man went-imperf to the beach

Despite the presence of an indefinite tense *ia* 'went', the bidistributive quantifier *cada* is not licit. The tense variable *ia* is not syntactically visible to *cada*. If the definite *a praia* 'the beach' is replaced by the indefinite *uma praia* 'a beach', the sentence is fine. The structure is repeated in (57):

(57)

This structure accounts for syntactic interactions of *todo* and *cada*. Moreover, it has given a first indication of the configurationality of tense and aspect. Despite these advantageous characteristics, the left-branch nature of Asp is a theoretical innovation. For that reason, I would like to have independent evidence for it.

In order to construe a test, it is worthwhile considering how the aspectual/tensed features in (57) can move to I^0, where they merge with AGR. This possibility is not obvious, since in the structure (57), movement of Asp to I^0 would violate connectedness. If a lexical verb is present, connectedness can be established by the head of VP, as it moves to I^0 as well and merges with agreement. Taking this state of affairs, it is possible to construct a test: when no lexical verb is present (i.e., typically in copula constructions, COP + Adj/N/P), one would expect problems with connectedness. In such cases, no supporting head movement out of a right branch is available. In cases with nominal and adjectival predicates, this might be solved by the predicate's being construed with the subject in gender, number, and other grammatical features. Violation of connectedness only looms in prepositional constructions with a copula. In other words, prepositional copula contexts might be the testing ground for left-branch effects of extraction of the aspectual/tensed features. As will be suggested shortly, a nice test for the structure (57) can be designed in these constructions.

8.7.1 Data

Portuguese and Dutch, like English, make use of a copular verb if no lexical verb is present. However, when two sentences are intimately linked, the copular can be dropped, as shown in (58):

(58)   Eu comprei vários livros. Cada qual (foi) de uma cor.
       I bought various books. Each PRT (was) of a color
       'I bought various books. Each in a different color.'

What strikes one is that the copular verb can be dropped in sentences with *cada qual*.[13]

This phenomenon is not limited to Portuguese. Dutch also can drop the copula in some constructions but not in others; witness the contrast between (59a) and (59b):

(59)   a. Ik kocht verscheidene boeken. *Alle rood.
          'I bought various books. All red.'

       b. Ik kocht verscheidene boeken. *Elk* in een andere kleur.
          'I bought various books. Each in another color.'

It is only the (uninflected!) distributive quantifier *elk* that licenses copula drop. The (inflected!) collective quantifier *alle* does not allow for it (59a). Because of lack of agreement, the distributive quantifier *elk* must be bidistributive in an open variable (cf. (59b) versus (59b). In addition, as a quite marked option, the distributor *ander* can be absent just as in the case of Portuguese *cada*, without loss of the list reading (60c).

(60) a. Ik kocht verscheidene boeken. *Alle in het rood.
         'I bought various books. All in red.'

      b. Ik kocht verscheidene boeken. *Elk in het rood.
         'I bought various books. Each in red.'

      c. Ik kocht verscheidene boeken. (?)Elk in een kleur.
         'I bought various books. Each in a color.'

The necessary bidistributivity in the predicate does not come as a surprise: it correlates with the uninflected nature of Dutch *elk* in these constructions. Apparently, uninflected *elk* has problems with connectedness, unless it is construed with a position in a right branch. Precisely in these bidistributive structures, the copula can be dropped. I list the circumstances of copula drop in (61):

Requirements for copula drop in Dutch

(61) a. There is an intimate construal between an immediately preceding sentence.

      b. There is a distributive quantifier.

      c. The distributive quantifier binds an open variable in VP, just like *cada* does.

      d. The predicate is prepositional.

It is possible to explain the copular drop from the ECP ("connectedness") by adopting the structure in (63), as the next section will show.

8.7.2 Explanation

I will suppose that cases of copula drop in Dutch and Portuguese is a type of topic drop. This seems plausible in view of its discourse sensitivity. Drop of ordinary topic pronouns occurs under movement to the sentence peripheral position, as illustrated by Dutch.[14]

(62) a. Jan is naar huis. - weet ik.
         John went home that/pro know I

      b. Jan is naar huis. *Ik weet -
         John went home I know pro

The V2 effect makes movement of the empty object visible in Dutch. Using crossover effects and opacity constraints, Raposo (1986) argues that topic drop in Portuguese involves movement of the empty topic at SS or LF.

If I now apply the movement analysis to copula drop in Dutch and Portuguese,[15] it is possible to explain the facts if the empty copula is extracted out of a left branch. Only then one would expect that this will be illicit on behalf of connectedness unless there is a construal with a variable in the predicate. Because a *cada* chain typically forces such chain, it can rescue the extraction chain of the copula. This explains that copular drop is impossible unless a subject-predicate construal by *cada* is present. This is evidence that the copula resides in a left branch.

Now, unless lexical verbs, the imperfect and perfect forms of BE do not have any lexical part in common (cf. Port. *era* and *foi*, respectively). The copula represents aspect in pure form, leading to the conclusion that aspect resides in a left branch.

8.8 Conclusions

Universal quantifiers *cada* and *todo* are bi-operators, that is, they must bind two open variables, under unselective binding. Because of morphological restrictions (no agreement), *cada* be connected with the second variable, that is, a distributive variable must reside within the nuclear scope of *cada*. This gives *cada* a list reading. *Todo* has no problems with connectedness because of its agreeing nature. It can have the second variable either in its restrictive set (e.g., the plural morpheme or a dummy *mundo*) or in a tense-variable.

The distinction between the four universal quantifier constructions is not inherent to lexemes but originates from morphosyntax. One would therefore expect the four construals to be present in every language. Portuguese is only special in that it, accidentally, spells out (55a) versus (55b) in a different way. Moreover, Portuguese specifies indefinite and definite aspect in an overt way in the past tense ("perfectum"/"imperfectum"). This makes Portuguese an appropriate research object for tracing syntactic interactions.

Notes

This chapter is a result of a contrastive study of *cada* and *todo* in Brazilian and European Portuguese and Spanish. I am grateful for discussions with and data from Aguinaldo Franco de Bastos (Brazilian Portuguese), Sérgio Menuzzi (Brazilian Portuguese), Cecilia Nussenzveig (Brazilian Portuguese), João Costa (European Portuguese), and Arantzazu Elordieta (Spanish). All data included are Brazilian Portuguese shared by the three Brazilian informants.

1. For the sake of brevity, I will henceforth simply use the label "Portuguese," despite the fact that European Portuguese differs considerably from the patterns discussed here. Modern European Portuguese seems to have lost the *todo* + sg construction in the sense of 'every'. It kept the construction *todo o dia* in the sense of 'whole' To express 'whole'. Brazilian Portuguese usually uses the reverse order: *o dia todo* 'the whole day'.

2. Marked constructions with *cada* expressing amazement are discussed in section 8.1.2.

3. I ignore the exclamative reading of *cada*.

(i)   O Flávio comprou cada livro!
      'Flavio bought such remarkable books!'

Notice that this construction is morphologically singular but semantically plural.

4. Its marked status might follow from its failure to comply with the requirements overtly. Perhaps an empty variable slot is created or is supported by the special stress pattern.

5. Or the Minimal Binding Requirement (MBR; cf. Aoun and Li, 1993).

6. The Scope Principle has a precursor in Kayne's analysis of L-*tous* (Kayne 1984) and Doetjes (1992). Kayne analyzes *tous* as binding the trace of the clitic, turning it into a variable.

(i)   Je les$_i$ ai vus tous t$_i$.

7. In this respect, *todo* + N$_{sg}$ is similar to English free-choice *any*, both in meaning and in syntactic requirements. *Todo* + N$_{sg}$ quantifies, just as *any*, over an infinite set rather than over a defined and limited set. Syntactically, free choice *any* is usually combined with a modal, which has stative, imperfect aspect.

(i)   a. Any student *can* make that exam.

b. Todo estudante *pode* fazer este exame.

8. The structure *todo mundo* is limited to Brazilian Portuguese. European Portuguese has *todo o mondo*, a partitive universal quantifier.

9. Kayne's original formulation distinguishes between right and left governing languages. This distinction is not relevant here and has become obsolete in view of his later work on antisymmetry (Kayne 1994).

10. The Portuguese *cada* construction has semantic and syntactic similarities with the so-called binominal constructions in (i), which are analyzed by Safir and Stowell (1986) as in (ii):

(i)   The men saw two women each.

(ii)   [the men]$_1$ [[each e$_1$]$_2$ [t$_1$ saw [[two women] t$_2$]

The structure in (ii) is very similar to my construction in (47c). In (ii), [the men] must be linked with e$_1$, a left-branch "extraction," which is usually not possible. It must be noticed that this constituent is linked to a right-branch position, indicated with the 2–index.

11. It is essential that there is no Spec-head agreement in FP. If there were, the index would percolate up via the head F^0.

12. This formulation is quite conventional. For a theoretically more advanced formulation of this result, see Postma (1995), in which quantificational elements like *cada* and *todo* are not considered the operators themselves but as open variables. The quantification is always abstract.

13. In a more formal register, it also occurs with *qual* 'what, which'.

(i)   qual (é) a cor de seus olhos
       which (is) the color of your eyes

14. Topic pro also moves in Portuguese (cf. Raposo 1986); for a different position, see Galves (1992).

15. The copular is a pronoun in Chinese (Li and Thompson 1977). In the Semitic languages it is a pronoun in the present tense (Berman and Grosu 1976). In the European languages the copular root -es- has, etymologically, a pronominal origin (Shields 1978). Synchronically, even in the modern European languages, the copular retains pronominal properties (Postma 1993).

References

ANS. [1985.] Algmene Nederlandse Spraakkunst. Groningen: Wolters-Noordhoff.

Aoun, Joseph. 1985. *A Grammar of Anaphora*. Cambridge, Mass.: MIT Press.

Aoun, Joseph, and Yen-hui Audrey, Li. 1993. *Syntax of Scope*. Cambridge, Mass.: MIT Press.

Beghelli, Filippo. 1995. "The Phrase Structure of quantifier Scope." Ph.D. dissertation, UCLA.

Beghelli, Filippo, and Tim Stowell. Forthcoming. "Distributivity and Negation." In Anna Szabolsci (ed.), *Ways of Scope-Taking*. Dordrecht: Kluwer.

Berman, R., Grosu, Alexander 1976. "Aspects of the Copula in Modern Hebrew." In P. Cole (ed.) *Studies in Hebrew Syntax and Semantics*, 265–285. New York: Elsevier.

Burzio, Luigi. 1986. *Italian Syntax*. Dordrecht: Reidel.

Carlson, G. 1977. "Reference to Kinds in English," Ph.D. dissertation, University of Massachusetts, Amherst.

Chomsky, Noam. 1977. "On WH-Movement." In P. W. Culicover, T. Wasow, and A. Akmajian (eds.) *Formal Linguistics*. New York: Academic Press.

————. 1981. *Lectures on Government and Binding*. Dordrecht: Foris.

————. 1982. *Some Concepts and Consequences of the Theory of Government and Binding*. Cambridge, Mass.: MIT Press.

Doetjes, Jenny. 1992. "Rightward Floating Quantifiers Float to the Left." *Linguistic Review* 9: 313–332.

Dowty, David. 1986. "Collective Predicates, Distributive Predicates, and 'all.'" *ESCOL* 3: 97–115.

Engdahl, Elizabeth. 1982. "Parasitic Gaps." *Linguistics and philosophy* 6:5–34.

Galves, C. 1992. "Clitic Placement in European Portuguese: Evidence for a Non-homogeneous Theory of Enclisis." In *Proceedings of the Workshop on Portuguese*, 61–80. Lisbon: APL.

Gillon, Brendan. 1987. "The Readings of Plural Noun Phrases in English." *Lingistics and Philosophy* 10: 199–219.

Heim, Irene. 1982. "The Semantics of Definite and Indefinite Noun Phrases." Ph.D. dissertation, University of Massachusetts at Amherst.

Jaeggli, Osvaldo. 1980. "On Some Phonologically-Null Elements in Syntax," PH.D. dissertation, MIT.

Junker, Marie-Odile. 1991. "Distributivité en Sémantique Conceptuelle: Le Cas des Quantifieurs Flottants." Ph.D. dissertation, University of Sherbrooke.

Kayne, R. S 1975. *French Syntax*. Cambridge, Mass.: MIT Press.

————. 1981. "ECP Extensions." *Linguistic Inquiry* 12: 223–249.

————. 1983. "Connectedness." *Linguistic Inquiry* 14: 223–249.

————. 1984. *Connectedness and Binary Branching*. Dordrecht: Foris.

————. 1994. *The Antisymmetry of Syntax*. Cambridge, Mass.: MIT Press.

Kempson, R., and A. Cormack. 1981. "Ambiguity and Quantification." *Linguistics and Philosophy* 4: 259–309.

Krifka, Manfred. 1992. "Definite NPs Aren't quantifiers." *Linguistic Inquiry* 23: 156–164.

Lakoff, George. 1972. "Linguistics and Natural Logic." In Donald Davidson and Gilbert Harman (eds.) *Semantics of Natural Language*, 545–665. Dordrecht: Reidel.

Li, C. H., and S. Thompson. 1977. "A Mechanism for the Development of Copula Morphemes." In C. N. Li (ed.) *Mechanisms of Syntactic Change,* 419–444. Austin: University of Texas Press.

Lewis, David. 1975. "Adverbs of Quantification." In E. Keenan (ed.) *Formal Semantics of Natural Language*, 3–15. Cambridge: Cambridge University Press.

May, Robert. 1984. Logical Form. Cambridge, Mass.: MIT Press.

————. 1985. *Logical Form*. Cambridge, Mass.: MIT Press.

————. 1988. "Ambiguities of Quantification and WH: A reply to Williams." *Linguistic Inquiry* 19: 118–135.

Pesetsky, David. 1982. *"Paths and Categories."* Ph.D. dissertation, MIT.

Postma, Gertjan. 1993. "The Syntax of the Morphological Defectivity of BE." HIL Manuscripts 3: 31–67.

————. 1995. Zero Semantics: A Study of the Syntactic Conception of Quantificational Meaning." Ph.D. dissertation, University of Leiden.

Postma, Gertjan, and Johan Rooryck. 1995. "Modality and Possession in NPs." *Proceedings of Nels* 1996.

Pritchett, Bradley. 1990. "A Note on Scope Interaction with Definite Plural NPs." *Linguistic Inquiry* 21: 646–654.

Raposo, Eduardo. 1986. "On the Null Object in European Portuguese." In H. Borer (ed.) *The Syntax of Pronominal Clitics*, 373–390. Dordrecht: Foris.

Rizzi, Luigi. 1982. *Issues in Italian Syntax.* Dordrecht: Foris.

Safir, Ken, and Tim Stowell. 1986. "Binomial Each." *Proceedings of NELS* 18, GLSA, University of Massachusetts.

Shields, K. 1978. "Speculations Concerning the I.E. Root *es-." *Archivum Linguisticum* IX(9: 73–78.

Szabolsci, A. 1994. "The Noun Phrase." In S. Kiefer and É. Kiss (eds.) *Syntax and Semantics 27: Syntactic Structure of Hungarian.* Orlando, Fla.: Academic Press.

Verkuyl, Henk. 1988. "Aspectual Asymmetry and Quantification." In Veronika Ehrich and Heinz Vater (eds.) Temporal-semantik, 220–259. Tübingen: Niemeyer.

Williams, Edwin. 1977. "Discourse and Logical Form." *Linguistic Inquiry* 8:101–139.

———. 1988. "Is LF Distinct from S-Structure? A Reply to May." In *Linguistic Inquiry* 19: 135–146.

Wyngaerd, Guido Vanden. 1992. "Een Reviewer zal elk Abstract Nalezen." *TABU* 22: 65–74.

9

EDUARDO RAPOSO

Clitic Positions and Verb Movement

The current literature on clitics reveals a gap between the level of descriptive adequacy and the level of explanatory adequacy, which is much harder to achieve. Whereas the biological UG probably converges on a single analysis for clitics, the model UGs proposed by linguists still leave too much room for descriptive options. This is true even within the very restrictive theories available today (and sometimes precisely as a consequence of achieving restrictiveness in other areas of the grammar). In (1) through (9) I list a variety of descriptive devices/analyses that have been postulated in this area:

(1) The behavior of clitics falls within the domain of (i) phonological/prosodical theory; (ii) syntactic theory; (iii) both.

(2) Clitics are syntactically categorized as (i) Determiners; (ii) Nouns; (iii) a combination of both (Raposo to appear b)

(3) (i) Clitics move from an underlying Q-position (Kayne 1975, 1991); (ii) clitics are based-generated in some designated site in association with an overt or covert argument in a Q-position, which may itself move (Jaeggli 1986; Sportiche 1992).

(4) (i) Clitics head a maximal projection of category DP with internal structure, as in (5);[1] (ii) clitics are the single terminal of a minimal/maximal D projection, as in (6) (Chomsky 1995a, b):

(5)

$$
\begin{array}{c}
\text{DP} \\
\diagup \diagdown \\
\text{spec} \quad \text{D}' \\
\diagup \diagdown \\
\text{D}^0 \quad \text{pro} \\
| \\
\text{clitic}
\end{array}
$$

(6) $$DP = D^0$$
$$|$$
clitic

(7)   In the analysis advocating clitic movement, this is (i) head movement (Kayne 1991); (ii) XP-movement (Rivero 1986); (iii) a combination of both (Kayne 1989).

(8)   XP-movement of the clitic may be (i) A-movement (Kayne 1989); (ii) A'-movement (Rivero 1986; Barbosa 1996).

(9)   If adjunction to a head, this can be left-adjunction (Kayne 1991) or right-adjunction (Uriagereka (1995b).

(10)   When the clitic moves as a head, its target may be one of a number of different functional categories (Agr$_S$, Agr$_O$, Infl, T, F, . . .).

(11)   Since the verb also moves up in the functional skeleton, the final position of the clitic with respect to the verb is also determined by verb movement and its extent.

Even if some of these options necessarily cluster by virtue of UG principles, it seems that research on clitics is still pursuing descriptive adequacy. This clearly sets a double agenda for researchers working on clitics: on the one hand, to seek improvement on the descriptive side (and there is still plenty of room for improvement); on the other hand, to ground their analyses on independently motivated principles of UG. I would like my contribution here to be part of such a research program.

The central issue addressed in this chapter is that of enclisis in European Portuguese (henceforth EP). In section 9.1, I present my own assumptions about clitics and the clausal structure of EP; in section 9.2, I give a brief summary of the main lines of the analysis of proclisis and enclisis that I propose; in section 9.3, I argue that in configurations of proclisis, the verb and the clitic are adjoined to *the same* functional category, contrary to what is claimed in two recent prominent analyses of cliticization in EP (Martins 1994; Uriagereka 1995b); in section 9.4, I discuss the issue of what functional categories may be independently targeted by clitics; in section 9.5, I discuss enclisis and in section 9.6, mesoclisis; in section 9.7, I show, first, that the proposed analysis of enclisis follows from economy considerations in the sense of Chomsky (1995a, b) and, second, that it does not violate the Minimal Link Condition of Chomsky (1993, 1995a, b), although it violates the Head Movement Constraint; in section 9.8, I propose a universal principle that considerably constrains the possible analyses for (pronominal) clitics in human languages, thus contributing to the explanatory problem discussed at the outset; finally, in section 9.9, I offer some concluding remarks.

9.1 General assumptions

9.1.1 Assumptions about clitics

I will now sketch some of my own assumptions about clitics. I assume one particular cluster of the preceding options, given in (12):

(12) (i)   Clitics are Ds heading maximal projections as in (5) (see the references of n. 1).

    (ii) Clitics move as heads, and they adjoin to a functional category.

    (iii) (Clitic) adjunction is invariably to the left.

I am well aware that some of these assumptions would require a good deal of elaboration; for discussion, see Raposo (to appear a). Within the limits of this chapter, I have a more modest goal: to apply these assumptions to several descriptive problems facing the analysis of clitics in EP, to see if it is possible to achieve some degree of explanatory adequacy.

9.1.2 Assumptions about clause structure

A considerable amount of work done in the 1990s has converged on the importance of an extra functional category between C and I for a proper understanding of the syntax of clitics, and especially the phenomenon of enclisis in EP and other contemporary or Old Romance dialects (see, among others, Cardinaletti and Roberts to appear; Martins 1994; Raposo and Uriagereka 1996; Rouveret 1992; Uriagereka 1995a, b). My own implementation of this idea will be Uriagereka's (1995b) "F," with the properties that he ascribes to it in the Western Iberian dialects (see also Raposo and Uriagereka 1996:782). I also assume that there is a peripheral position for dislocated subjects and left-dislocated elements (so-called topics) above CP. For concreteness, I adopt the implementation of Benincà (1995), who has a Topic projection as the highest functional projection, whose Spec is the landing site for such elements. I thus assume the following clausal structure:[2]

(13)

```
            TopP
           /    \
        spec    Top'
               /    \
              T      CP
                    /   \
                 spec    C'
                        /   \
                       C     FP
                            /   \
                         spec    F'
                                /   \
                               F     IP
                                    /   \
                                 spec    I'
                                        /   \
                                       I     VP
```

9.2 A summary of the analysis of proclisis and enclisis

Consider the following paradigms of enclisis-proclisis in EP:

(14) a. (nós) *demos-lhe* muito vinho!
      (we) (we)-gave-him-dat too much wine

b. *(nós) *lhe demos* muito vinho.
(we) him-dat (we)-gave too much wine

(15) a. (nós,) muito vinho *lhe demos*!
(we,) too much wine (emph.) him-dat (we)-gave

b. *(nós,) muito vinho *demos-lhe*!
(we,) too much wine (we)-gave-him-dat

In (15), an affected phrase, *muito vinho* 'too much wine', has moved to [Spec, F] (see Raposo and Uriagereka 1996). The basic generalization concerning proclisis/ enclisis that seems to emerge from these data is that, independently of the presence of an overt preverbal subject, when [Spec, F] is filled by an operator, the resulting pattern is that of *proclisis*;[3] if [Spec, F] is empty, the resulting pattern is that of *enclisis*. A succinct statement of this generalization is given in (16):

(16) (i) [spec, F] filled → proclisis

(ii) [spec, F] empty → enclisis

In terms of (13), (16) implies that the preverbal overt subject in (14) and (15) occupies [Spec, Top]; although this is more visible in (15) than in (14), since the subject in (15) occurs to the left of the affective phrase, I will assume it as well for (14).[4]
One of the goals of this chapter is to challenge the second half of generalization (16). I will claim that [Spec, F] is always obligatorily filled in EP—whether there is proclisis or enclisis. Concerning enclisis in particular, I propose that it is the result of the verb moving across the clitic to *the specifier* of F, as shown abstractly in (17):[5]

(17)   . . . FP   (*t* the trace of Infl containing V)
                         ╱╲
                       I   F'
                     ╱╲   ╱╲
                   V   I F   IP
                   | ╱╲   ╱╲
                demos cl   F   I'
                      | ╱╲
                     lhe   t   . . .
                        (muito vinho)

In section 9.7, I show how this analysis is permitted, and also forced by UG, given reasonable assumptions on phrase structure in general and the nature of the FP projection in particular.

9.3 Verb movement and configurations of proclisis

9.3.1 Martins (1994) and Uriagereka (1995b)

I start by reviewing work by Martins (1994) and Uriagereka (1995b), both of whom propose that enclisis is a consequence of Infl-to-F movement, where Infl contains the verb.[6] For Martins, clitics are canonically left-adjoined to Infl. The derivation of (14a), for example, is the following. The clitic left-adjoins to Infl, then the segment of Infl that contains the verb excorporates to F, stranding the clitic in (the remaining segment of) Infl:[7]

(18)

```
                FP      (t is the trace of the segment of Infl containing V)
              /  \
           spec   F'
                /  \
               F    IP
             /  \   /  \
            I    F I    I'
           / \     / \
          V   I   I   VP
          |      / \
        demos  lhe  t
```

For Uriagereka, clitics are canonically right-adjoined to F by what he calls functional incorporation (see Uriagereka 1995b, 99ff.). Illustrating again with (14a), first Infl (with the verb already adjoined) raises to F (by his lexical incorporation, which involves "standard" left-adjunction); then the clitic right-adjoins to F:

(19)

```
              FP
            /  \
         spec   F'        t the trace of Infl containing V
              /  \
             F    IP
           /  \   /  \
          F   lhe I'
        /  \      /  \
       I    F    t    VP
      /  \
   demos  I
```

In both Martins's and Uriagereka's analyses, movement of the verb is necessary to license F, which has morphological properties that require a special licensing in the Western Iberian dialects (Uriagereka (1995a, b). F may be licensed by Spec-head agreement, as in (15a), where an operator occupies its Spec position; in that case, verb raising is not required and, by economy principles, will not apply; the result is proclisis, with the clitic alone in F, as in (20) (Uriagereka 1995b), or with the clitic and the verb both left-adjoined to Infl, as in (21) (Martins 1994).

(20)

```
                    FP
                  /  \
         muito vinho   F'
                      /  \
                     F    IP
                   /  \    /  \
                  F   lhe  I'
                          /  \
                         I    VP
                             /  \
                            V    I
                            |
                          demos
```

(21)

```
                        FP
                      /    \
              muito vinho    F'
                           /   \
                          F     IP
                              /    \
                             I'
                            /  \
                           I    VP
                         /  \
                       lhe    I
                            /   \
                           V     I
                           |
                         demos
```

In sum, both authors claim that in configurations of proclisis (with F licensed by an operator), the verb is in Infl and never in F. Only when there is enclisis is the verb raised to F. This is a result that I want to challenge. To do so, I must discuss some aspects of subject inversion in EP when the FP projection is "activated" by an operator.

9.3.2 Subject inversion in EP and its relevance to proclisis

In structures where [Spec, F] is filled by an operator, subject inversion is optional:

(22)   a. Muito whisky *o capitão* me tem servido!
          too much whisky the captain to-me has served!

       b. Muito whisky me tem *o capitão* servido!
          too much whisky to-me has the captain served!

Consider first (22a). In terms of (13), the phrase *muito whisky* 'too much whisky' is in [Spec, F]; if the verb (the finite auxiliary *tem* 'has') is raised all the way to Infl, then the subject *o capitão* 'the captain' must be in [Spec, I] and the clitic must be (left-adjoined) in Infl, since it is linearly to the right of the subject. This is shown in (23):

(23)

```
                        FP
                      /    \
              muito whk.    F'
                          /   \
                         F     IP
                             /    \
                         o cap.    I'
                                 /   \
                                I     VP
                              /  \
                            me    I
                                /   \
                               V     I
                               tem
```

I thus agree with Martins (1994), contra Uriagereka (1995b), that clitics in EP may target Infl by left-adjunction.

Now consider (22b), where the main issues concern the structural positions of the auxiliary finite verb and the subject. In terms of (13), the auxiliary verb *tem* 'has' may be in F and the subject *o capitão* 'the captain' in [Spec, I]—this is represented in (24), abstracting away momentarily from the clitic:

(24)

```
                    FP
                  /    \
          muito whk.    F'
                      /    \
                     F      IP
                   /  \    /  \
                  I    F  o cap.  I'
                /  \          /   \
               V    I        t     VP
               |
              tem
```

Alternatively, the auxiliary verb may be in Infl, and the subject *o capitão* in a Spec position lower than [Spec, I]. This could be the Spec of some intermediate functional category resulting from Pollock's (1989) split Infl hypothesis ([Spec, Agr$_s$P] for concreteness), as in (25), with IP now = TP:

(25)

```
                    FP
                  /    \
          muito whk.    F'
                      /    \
                     F      TP
                          /    \
                         T'
                       /    \
                      T      Agr_sP
                    /  \    /    \
                 Agr_s  T  o cap.  Agr_s'
                /  \           /   \
               V   Agr_s      t     VP
              Tem
```

In a model without Agr nodes such as that of Chomsky (1995b, 4.10), the subject might be in [Spec, V], as in (26):

(26)

```
                    FP
                  /    \
          muito whk.    F'
                      /    \
                     F      IP
                          /    \
                         I'
                       /    \
                      I      VP
                    /  \    /   \
                   V    I  o cap.  V'
                  tem
```

The important point raised by (25) and (26) is the following: if the auxiliary verb is in Infl (or T) and the subject lower than [Spec, I] or [Spec, T], *the clitic may be in Infl (or T)*, together with the verb; however, if the subject is in [Spec, I] and the verb is higher in F, as in (24), then *the clitic can only be in F with the verb*, since it occurs between the operator in [Spec, F] and the verb in F. But (22b) exhibits *proclisis*, not enclisis. It follows that if (24) is the correct structure for (22b), verb raising to F is not incompatible with proclisis, contrary to Martins's and Uriagereka's analyses.

I would like to suggest that the correct structure for (22b) is (24), where both the verb and the clitic are within the FP projection in a relation of proclisis.

9.3.3 An argument based on indefinite SE structures

The argument in favor of (24) presented here is based on Raposo and Uriagereka's (1996) analysis of the structural position of the agreeing, preverbal "subject" of indefinite SE clauses:

(27) Esses manuscritos mostraram-se ao papa.
      those manuscripts SE showed-3pl to the pope

      'Those manuscripts were shown to the pope.'

Raposo and Uriagereka argue that the DP *esses manuscritos* 'those manuscripts' occupies [Spec, Top] of (13), reaching that position *without moving through [Spec, I]*, which contains the argument associated with the clitic *se*. Under this analysis, a partial structure of (27) is given in (28):[8]

(28)

TopP   *t* the trace of *eses mans.*

eses mans.   Top'

Top   FP

F'

F   IP

SE   I'

I   VP

V   I   t

mostraram

This analysis predicts that the agreeing DP of the SE construction will not occur between an operator in [Spec, F] and the verb in Infl, since in order for this to be possible the DP would have to occupy [Spec, I], a position that is not available to it (see n. 8). This prediction is confirmed, as shown in (29):[9]

(29) a. *A que papa os manuscritos se tinham mostrado?
          to which pope the manuscripts SE had-3pl showed?

      b. *A muita gente os manuscritos se tinham mostrado!
          to a lot of people the manuscripts SE had-3pl showed

The agreeing DP either precedes the operator, as in (30), or follows the past participle, as in (31):

(30) a. Os manuscritos, a que papa se tinham mostrado?
          the manuscripts to which pope SE had-3pl showed

      b. Os manuscritos a muita gente se tinham mostrado!
          the manuscripts to a lot of people SE had-3pl showed

(31) a. A que papa se tinham mostrado os manuscritos?
          to which pope SE had-3pl showed the manuscripts?

      b. A muita gente se tinham mostrado os manuscritos!
          to a lot of people SE had-3pl showed the manuscripts

In (30), the agreeing DP is in [Spec, Top]—to the left of [Spec, F]; and in (31), I will assume that it is in its initial position inside VP.[10]

Canonical grammatical subjects, in contrast, move to [Spec, I] (see n. 4). One would thus expect that they are able to occur between an operator in [Spec, F] and the finite verb in Infl. This is confirmed by (32); compare with the ungrammatical (29) (I illustrate with reflexive clauses, which, being identical in form to indefinite SE clauses, form a very clear minimal pair with them regarding the properties that concern us here):[11]

(32) a. A que papa os peregrinos se tinham apresentado?
          to which pope the pilgrims SE had introduced?

      b. A muita gente os peregrinos se tinham apresentado!
          to a lot of people the pilgrims SE had introduced

The grammaticality of (33) shows that the DP subject may subsequently move to [Spec, Top] (cf. with (30); in (33) *t* is the trace of *os peregrinos* in [Spec, I]):

(33) a. Os peregrinos a que papa *t* se tinham apresentado?
          the pilgrims to which pope SE had introduced?

      b. Os peregrinos a muita gente *t* se tinham apresentado!
          the pilgrims to a lot of people SE had introduced

Consider now the paradigm in which the agreeing DP of an SE construction occurs *in between* the finite auxiliary *ter* 'to have' and the past participle (see n. 9):

(34) a. *A que papa se tinham *os manuscritos* mostrado?
          to which pope SE had-3pl the manuscripts showed?

      b. *A muita gente se tinham *os manuscritos* mostrado!
          to a lot of people (emph.) SE had-3pl the manuscripts showed

This paradigm, like (29), is ungrammatical. In contrast, the subject of a reflexive clause may occur unproblematically in this position:

(35) a. A que papa se tinham *os peregrinos* apresentado?
         to which pope SE had the pilgrims introduced?

      b. A muita gente se tinham *os peregrinos* apresentado!
         to a lot of people SE had the pilgrims introduced

This strongly suggests that the position of the DPs in italic in (34) and (35) is the same that they occupy in (29) and (32), respectively—that is, [Spec, I]. Since this is precluded for the agreeing DP of the indefinite SE construction, both (29) and (34) are ruled out; since, on the other hand, that position is legitimate for the subject of a reflexive clause, both (32) and (35) are grammatical.

A similar argument involves expressions that are ambiguous between a reflexive/reciprocal reading and an indefinite one, such as (36), which can mean either (37i) or (37ii):

(36) Os especialistas tinham-se consultado só depois da operação.
      the specialists SE had consulted only after the operation

(37) (i) 'The specialists had consulted each other only after the operation.'

      (ii) 'Someone had consulted the specialists only after the operation.'

Consider, however, (38), where the phrase *só depois da operação* 'only after the operation' is moved to [Spec, F], and the DP *os especialistas* 'the specialists' is to its immediate right in [Spec, I]:

(38) Só depois da operação os especialistas se tinham consultado.
      only after the operation the specialists SE had consulted

In (38), only the reciprocal reading survives, and the indefinite one is lost, which is consistent with the idea that the agreeing DP of indefinite SE clauses cannot occupy [Spec, I]. The same happens when the DP occurs between the auxiliary and the past participle, as in (39):

(39) Só depois da operação se tinham os especialistas consultado.
      only after the operation SE had the specialists consulted

This again militates in favor of taking the linear position between the finite verb and the past participle to be [Spec, I]. If one does so, the loss of the indefinite reading in (38) and (39) stems from a single cause: the DP is in [Spec, I].

I thus conclude that the *XP* position in the linear formula (40) is [Spec, I]:

(40) . . . finite Aux [XP] past participle . . .

In turn, this conclusion implies that sentences with that linear order have the finite auxiliary (or Infl containing Aux) in F.[12]

9.3.4 Conclusion: Configurations of proclisis

The conclusion of the preceding section implies that the correct representation of (22b), repeated here as (41), is that of (24), repeated in (42) with a slight retouch to take into account the position of the clitic:

(41)   Muito whisky me tem *o capitão* servido!
       too much whisky to-me has the captain served!

(42)

FP
muito whk.   F'
        F   IP
    me   F   *o cap.*   I'
        I   F   t   VP
         V   I
         |
        tem

Given (22a), repeated here as (43), with representation (23), also repeated here as (44), the conclusions in (45) follow:

(43)   Muito whisky *o capitão* me tem servido!
       too much whisky the captain to-me has served!

(44)

FP
muito whk.   F'
        F   IP
          o cap.   I'
              I   VP
           V   I
           |
          tem

(45)   (i)   In (finite root clauses of) EP, clitics may target either Infl or F.[13]

       (ii)   Whether in Infl or in F, the finite verb and the clitic are in a configuration of proclisis.

       (iii) Enclisis cannot be an automatic consequence of verb (or Infl) raising to F.

9.4 Is F independently targeted by the clitic?

One could ask at this point if the structure of (41) is really (42), with the clitic left-adjoined to F, rather than (46), where the sequence *clitic-verb* is the result of the following series of steps: first the clitic adjoins to Infl (with the verb already adjoined); second, Infl (pied-piping the clitic and the verb) raises to F:

(46)

```
                        FP
                      /    \
              muito whk.    F'
                          /    \
                         F      IP
                       /  \    /  \
                      I    F  o cap.  I'
                    /  \      /  \
                  me    I    t    VP
                 /  \
                V    I
                |
               tem
```

This is the question of whether clitics can target F independently of Infl raising. The phenomenon of *interpolation*, attested in some Old Romance dialects (including Portuguese) and in some contemporary Western Iberian dialects, suggests a positive answer to this question.

Interpolation, which is particularly well studied in Martins (1994), consists in the occurrence of overt material between the clitic and the verb. In the Old Iberian dialects, any constituent could occur in this position, including subjects (as in (47a)), adverbs (as in (47b), and a variety of verbal complements, both direct and prepositional (as in (47c), which illustrates interpolation with a direct object; examples from Martins 1994; I italicize the relevant material; see also Rivero 1986):

(47)   a. E a minha cabeça já *a ele tem* metida na sua boca.
        and my head already *it he has* put in his mouth

       b. Aquellas que *o melhor forem.*
        those that *it better will be*

       c. Poys que *lhe ysto ouve* dito.
        because that *to-him this had* said

In my terms, a straightforward analysis of interpolation has the clitic in F and the verb in Infl (this is also the analysis of Martins 1994 and Uriagereka 1995b). The fact that material other than the subject appears between these two elements is due to the possibility of "scrambling" in Old Iberian Romance (see Rivero 1986; Lema and Rivero 1991), which (following these authors and Barbosa 1996), I construe as adjunction to IP.

Barbosa (1996), however, has a different analysis of interpolation. In the spirit of Rivero (1986), she suggests that clitics target IP as maximal projections, in particular that they left-adjoin to IP. Since scrambling is adjunction to IP, this means that at the relevant level one may derive a structure with a series of elements left-adjoined to IP, including clitics and, crucially, the subject, which she claims may scramble itself. She gives the example in (48) (from Martins), which has the subject, an adverb, and the direct object occurring between the clitic and the verb:

(48)   Se *me Deus enton a morte* non deu.
        if to-me God then the death not gave

Barbosa then claims that the phenomenon of interpolation is a consequence of the fact that adjunction does not impose ordering constraints. Thus, the clitic, is (just another) adjunct to IP, and does not have to occur in a fixed position with respect to the other scrambled elements. Note, however, that the order between the clitic and the other scrambled elements does not appear to be as free as Barbosa claims. To the best of my knowledge, Martins's (1994) corpus does not contain examples where the clitic appears *in the middle* of a sequence of scrambled constituents; the clitic either initiates the sequence, as in (48), or ends it, as in (49) (which is, of course, a case of noninterpolation):[14]

(49)   Se *Deus enton a morte* non me deu.
        if God then the death not to-me gave

I thus speculate that neither of the examples in (50) would be possible:

(50)   a. *Se Deus me enton a morte non deu.
            if God to-me then the death not gave

        b. *Se Deus enton me a morte non deu.
            if God then to-me the death not gave

This suggests that the clitic in (48) occupies a position independent from that of the scrambled elements. This position, in terms of (13), must be F, which is therefore independently targeted by the clitic (Infl with the verb does not raise in this case).

The phenomenon of interpolation is not altogether absent from contemporary EP. Barbosa (1996:18) gives the following example, with an adverb and negation between the clitic and the verb:[15]

(51)   o Carlos disse que *me já não podia* ir buscar
        the Carlos said that me already not could go fetch

        'Carlos said that it was no longer possible for him to fetch me.'

Consider also (52), where the clitic has "scope" over both conjuncts but is not part of the conjoined material (see Rouveret 1992 and Barbosa 1996 for discussion of such examples):

(52)   Só mais tarde o [tirei da biblioteca e trouxe para casa].
        only later it took out of the library and brought home

        'I took it from the library and brought it home only later.'

Under the assumption that only categorially identical phrases can be conjoined, (52) is a case of IP (or I') adjunction, with the verb in Infl. But since the clitic is left out, it cannot obviously be adjoined to Infl. It must then be adjoined to F, independently of the verb.[16]

I thus conclude that clitics in EP can target F independently of the verb and that, in particular, (42) rather than (46) is the correct analysis of (41). I return to this issue from a UG perspective in section 9.8.[17]

One intriguing aspect of interpolation is that there are no attested cases where the clitic is separated from the verb but with the positions of (48) reversed, that is, with the verb in F *higher* than the clitic in Infl, as shown by the contrast in (53):[18]

(53) a. Muita felicidade lhe Deus trouxe!
      much happiness to-him God brought

    b. *Muita felicidade trouxe Deus lhe!
       much happiness brought God to-him

To the extent that this pattern in the interpolation data constitutes a genuine generalization, one would like it to follow from some deeper principle or principles. What is necessary, thus, is to rule out the sequence *verb-X-clitic*, while allowing *clitic-X-verb*.

Under the assumption that in (53b) the clitic is adjoined to Infl, there are two possible ways to derive this example: either the verb targets F directly, skipping Infl; or the verb first adjoins to Infl and then excorporates to F, stranding the clitic in Infl. This is shown schematically in (54a and b), respectively:

(54) a. $[_F \text{ V-F}] \ldots [_I \text{ cl-I}]$

       |_____|
                *

    b. $[_F [_I \text{ V-I}]\text{-F}] \ldots [_I \text{ cl-}t]$

       |_____|
              *

The absence of "reverse" interpolation from the relevant dialects is thus a strong argument that these operations are not available. To exclude (54a), one may assume that the verb in (all dialects of) Romance raises to Infl (see Pollock 1989); in the terms of Chomsky (1995b), Infl has a strong affixal [V-] feature, attracting the verb overtly. As a consequence, even if the ultimate target is F, Infl cannot be skipped by the verb.[19] This reduces the problem to (54b), which is one instantiation of the phenomenon of *excorporation*. Following Baker (1988) and Kayne (1991), I will simply assume that excorporation is a process not permitted by UG (pace Roberts 1991).

9.5 Enclisis

9.5.1 V movement to [Spec, F]

Since Kayne (1991), the standard analyses that have been proposed for enclisis all involve verb movement past a clitic left-adjoined to a given functional category.[20] These analyses, in turn, can be implemented in two ways: either the verb skips the functional category containing the clitic (Cardinaletti and Roberts to appear), or the verb excorporates from that functional category, leaving the clitic stranded (Martins 1994). Note, however, that under the parsimonious assumption that the functional categories involved in structures with clitics are F and Infl, these operations were just ruled out (cf. the discussion of (54a, b)). In other words, within the assumptions of this work, enclisis cannot be the result either of the verb skipping Infl (which contains the clitic) or of verb excorporation (from any functional category), leaving the clitic stranded in that category.[21]

There is, however, one possible operation not yet entertained that is compatible with Kayne's (1991) assumption that enclisis is the result of verb movement across the clitic. This is illustrated schematically in (55):

(55) $[_{FP} [_I \text{V-I}] [_F \text{cl-F}] [_{IP} [_I t] \ldots$

In (55), Infl containing the verb moves to [Spec, F], while the clitic is at the left edge of F. This is shown in tree form in (17), repeated here as (56):

(56)

Notice that verb movement is explicitly construed as *skipping F*, and neither as excorporation from F nor as skipping Infl, avoiding the problems discussed earlier. Still, it is necessary to answer what allows the verb to skip F, in violation of the "descriptive" principle HMC (see n. 19). Another problematic point is that this movement is not "structure-preserving," in the terms of Chomsky (1995a, b), since a head (Infl) is raising to a specifier position. I will put these problems aside until section 9.7, assuming for now that the analysis of (55) and (56) is compatible with (known) UG principles.

9.5.2 The clitic nature of F

Verb movement to [Spec, F] is a Last Resort operation that applies to satisfy PF properties of the functional category F; furthermore, this operation is *independent* of the presence of a clitic in F. However, when a clitic happens to be present, the output of that movement yields enclisis. Thus, enclisis, as such, is simply an epiphenomenon of a distinct grammatical interplay.

Recall the paradigms given in (14) and (15) and the basic generalization (16) for clitic placement (all repeated here) as (56), (58), and (59):

(57) a. (nós) *demos-lhe* muito vinho!
        (we) (we)-gave-him-dat too much wine

     b. *(nós) *lhe demos* muito vinho.
        (we) him-dat (we)-gave too much wine

(58)   a. (nós,) muito vinho *lhe demos*!
           (we,) too much wine (emph.) him-dat (we)-gave

       b. *(nós,) muito vinho *demos-lhe*!
           (we,) too much wine (we)-gave-him-dat

(59)   (i) [Spec, F] filled → proclisis
       (ii) [Spec, F] empty → enclisis

From a simple distributionalist perspective, the verb in (57a) is filling the gap in [Spec, F] left by the absence of an operator (cf. with (58a)). This suggests that [Spec, F] must be filled by overt material in EP and that, when there is no operator of the relevant sort, the verb itself (Infl containing the verb) fulfills that role (see Benincà 1989 for a similar proposal).[22]

Within the Romance languages that project F in the syntax, Uriagereka (1995a) sets the Western Iberian dialects apart (EP, Galician, and remaining pockets of Asturian and Leonese). He argues that in these dialects, F has an abstract morphological matrix and is always projected whether or not it is also specified with an operator feature (see Raposo and Uriagereka 1996 for further discussion). It is this morphological "heaviness" of F that I want to exploit here. I suggest simply that morphological F in the relevant Western Iberian dialects is itself a clitic, and that its direction of attachment is right-to-left; in other words, it is an *enclitic*.[23] This has an immediate consequence, given in (60):

(60)   As an enclitic, F cannot be sentence initial.

The statement in (60) is, of course, reminiscent of the Wackernagel Law and the Tobler-Moussafia Law (Wanner 1991; Benincà 1995), but applied to F itself rather than to unstressed "independent" pronouns. The reason that a clitic cannot be in initial position in FP, left-adjoined to F (whether or not the verb is also in F), is simply an *epiphenomenon* of (60). In order to see this more explicitly, consider the structure of (61), given in (62):

(61)   *O li.
       it I-read
       'I read it.'

(62)

```
                        F'
                       /\
                      F   IP
                     /\   ...
                    o  F
                      /\
                     I  F
                    /\
                   li  I
```

I will adopt May's (1985) hypothesis about adjunction structures whereby the target of adjunction is a complex category consisting of multiple segments. In (62), there is

will then be unnecessary for the verb to raise. However, if the constraint on F is purely a PF one, one does not expect an abstract operator to have any effect in licensing F (despite coindexation), which is the correct result. In other words, when an operator in [Spec, F] satisfies (60) (as in (58a)) it is because of its overt presence, not because it triggers "Spec-head coindexation." Note that this analysis forces the conclusion that the abstract operator in (65a) (if there is any) enters the checking domain of F not in [Spec, F] (since this contains Infl with the verb) but presumably by adjunction to F itself.

To summarize, in this section I propose that in the old and contemporary Romance dialects with enclisis, the element that falls under the Wackernagel Law and the Tobler-Moussafia Law is F itself, not the clitic pronouns. Under this view, the difference between Castilian and the Western Iberian dialects is *not* that the clitic pronouns themselves underwent some change in Castilian (sometime in the Classical Period) that enabled them to violate these laws (i.e., to occur in initial position); rather, the change was in the morphological properties of F. Presumably as a consequence of losing its morphological "heaviness," F in Spanish ceased to fall under (60), thereby permitting clitic-initial sequences such as *lo vi* 'I saw it' as an epiphenomenon. Such a change, as is well known, did not occur in the Western Iberian dialects.

9.6 Some remarks on mesoclisis

Contemporary EP and Galician, as well as Old Iberian dialects, display the so-called phenomenon of *mesoclisis*, where a clitic appears to break up the verbal unit in the future and conditional indicative tenses. This is illustrated in (66), where in the left column I give a simple example of the verb in that tense and in the right column an example of the same form with a clitic:

(66) *beijarás* 'you will kiss' *beijá-lo-ás* 'you will kiss him'
      darias 'you would give' *dar-lhe-ias* 'you would give him'

It is well known that the future and conditional indicative endings of the current synthetic forms in a variety of Romance dialects derive historically from a periphrastic future/conditional, consisting of the auxiliary *(h)aver* 'to have' (in the present and the imperfect, respectively) followed by the main verb in the infinitive (see Lema and Rivero 1991). This was achieved through a process of incorporation of the infinitive to the auxiliary, as illustrated in (67):

(67) a. Penso que ele há cantar.
         I think that he fut.aux sing
         'I think that he will sing.'

      b. Penso que ele [cantar há] t.
         I think that he sing+fut.aux
         'I think that he will sing.'

This process was then progressively "grammaticalized" in dialects such as Spanish and French; that is, the auxiliary was completely reanalyzed as a normal tense/agreement verbal inflection. This grammaticalization, however, was never completed in EP and Galician, where the endings of these "tenses" are still analyzed as an auxiliary verb. In the Old dialects and in Western Iberian, incorporation of the infinitive verb may be due to Case reasons of the sort I have discussed elsewhere (Raposo 1987). That is, the infinitival verb needs Case, but (for some reason) the auxiliary *haver* is not a Case assigner; the infinitival then incorporates to the auxiliary as a means of satisfying the Case Filter (see Baker 1988). This is suggested by the fact that a structure such as (67a) could (and still can) be salvaged by the introduction of the Dummy Case-Marker *de* 'of', exactly like the infinitives discussed in Raposo (1987):

(68)   Penso que ele há de cantar.
        I think that he fut.aux of sing

If a clitic is added to the structure, there is mesoclisis in those contexts in which there would be enclisis with a different tense form, that is, in contexts with no operator in [Spec, F]:

(69)   a. *Dar-lhe-emos* muito vinho.
           (we) to-give-to-him-fut much wine
           'We will give him much wine.'

        b. *Lhe daremos* muito vinho.
           to-him (we)-to-give-fut much wine

        c. (*)*Daremos-lhe* muito vinho.
           (we-)to-give-fut-to-him much wine

The asterisk in (69c) applies to my own dialect of EP. However, expressions like (69c) were attested in the Old Iberian dialects (although being less frequent than mesoclisis, according to Lema and Rivero 1991). They are also attested in some Northern varieties of EP and Galician, although in my dialect (which has productive mesoclisis) they are completely impossible. Duarte and Matos (chapter 4, this volume) also report "younger" dialects (or idiolects) of EP where (69c) is grammatical. I return to (69c) later, after providing an account of (69a).

When [Spec, F] is filled with an operator, only proclisis is possible, as in (70):

(70)   a. Muito vinho *lhe daremos*.
           much wine to-him (we)-to-give-fut
           'Much wine we will give to him.'

        b. *Muito vinho *dar-lhe-emos*.
           much wine (we) to-give-to-him-fut

        c. *Muito vinho *daremos-lhe*.
           much wine (we-)to-give-fut-to-him

This suggests that in contexts of mesocliticization, the infinitival form is moving all by itself to [Spec, F], while the auxiliary verb *haver* is in F with the clitic, in a configuration of proclisis. That is, (69a) has the structure illustrated in (71):[27]

(71)

```
              FP        (t the trace of-emos raised to F)
             /  \
          dar    F'
                /  \
               F    IP
              / \   / \
           lhe   F I'
                / \  / \
            emos   F  t   ...
```

This analysis thus invokes for mesoclisis the same mechanisms involved in enclisis and proclisis. As in enclisis, there is a verbal form (the infinitive) that moves to [Spec, F]; as in proclisis, there is a verbal form (the finite auxiliary) in F with the clitic left-adjoined to it.

Consistent with section 9.5, I analyze simple cases without a clitic, such as (72), as in (71), modulo the clitic in F:

(72)   Daremos muito vinho ao João.
       (we)-will give much wine to John

(73)

```
              FP        (t the trace of-emos raised to F)
             /  \
          dar    F'
                /  \
               F    IP
              / \   / \
          emos   F  I'
                    / \
                   t   ...
```

Again, under this analysis, the movement of the infinitive to [Spec, F] cannot be due to any constraint against initial clitics, but rather to condition (60).[28]

I will now return to the status of (69c), which appears to be derivable without problem in this framework, given my assumptions. This derivation proceeds in the following way:

(74)   a. [$_{I'}$ emos [$_{VP}$ dar [$_{DP}$ lhe]]]
          fut-3pl to-see him-dat

       b. [$_{I'}$ dar+emos [$_{VP}$ t_V [$_{DP}$ lhe]]]

       c. [$_{FP}$ [$_F$ lhe+F] [$_{I'}$ dar+emos [$_{VP}$ t_V t_{cl}]]]

       d. [$_{FP}$ dar+emos [$_F$ lhe+F] [$_{I'}$ t_I [$_{VP}$ t_V t_{cl}]]]

In (74b), the infinitival form incorporates to the auxiliary in Infl, satisfying its Case-requirements. The clitic subsequently left-adjoins to F in (74c), followed by movement of the verbal complex *infinitive+aux* to [Spec, F] in (74d).

That (74) is a permissible derivation is a good result, since there are dialects (idiolects) that accept (69c), as noted earlier. Apparently, the "younger" dialects reported by Duarte and Matos (chapter 4, this volume) lack mesoclisis altogether, meaning that (74) is the only derivation available. In my view (although not theirs), this means that the form *(h)aver* of the future/conditional is in those dialects completely reanalyzed as a normal tense affix, as in Spanish. These considerations also suggest that the dialects for which (69c) is unacceptable have some language-particular property that rules out one or more of the steps of (74).

Although I am far from having a full explanation for the facts, I would like to relate them to the idiosyncratic behavior of the old auxiliary *haver* in EP. Needless to say, the remarks that follow are merely suggestive (I develop a more elaborate account in work in preparation; see also Sola 1997, in preparation).

During the eighteenth century, a nonoperator subject in EP could raise to [Spec, F], determining a configuration with proclisis (as was common in many of the Old Romance dialects that otherwise manifest enclisis, such as Old French):

(75)   A Joana o viu ontem.

       Jane him saw yesterday

By the nineteenth century, however, proclisis became impossible in root clauses with a preverbal subject such as (75) (see Torres-Moraes 1995 for discussion). Interestingly, this change seems to correlate historically with the progressive disappearance of the old auxiliary verb *haver* 'to have', which was fully replaced in standard EP by the possessive form *ter* 'to have, to possess', also around the turn of the century.

Presumably at this time there was a change in the FP system from a full-fledged "A-projection" to an "Operator-projection," such that a canonical subject was no longer eligible to occupy [Spec, F].[29] In all those expressions that did not have an operator-phrase, it is now the verb (Infl containing the verb) that steps in to fulfill the role of licenser of F, therefore raising to [Spec, F]. As a result, the sheer number of E-expressions where condition (60) is satisfied by Infl (with the verb) in [Spec, F] increased enormously.

Consider now the following. While the auxiliary *haver* is no longer in use in Standard EP, some speakers still have (passive) intuitions about its use. One striking contrast that obtains (for speakers like me) is shown in (76):

(76)   a. Muita coisa *lhe hei dado.*

       many things him-dat has I given

    b. ?**Hei-lhe* dado muita coisa.*

       I-have him-dat given many things

That is, *haver* cannot occur in contexts of enclisis. In terms of the analysis proposed here, *haver* cannot move into [Spec, F]. This, in turn, may be due to its phonological "weakness," which would render it unable to provide a phonological support to F.

By relating this to the change mentioned earlier (i.e., the change of FP from an A-projection to an A-bar projection and especially the increased number of

(E)-expressions with the verb raising to [Spec, F]), it can be conjectured that *haver*, not being able to fulfill the role of licenser of F because of its own phonological weakness, was eventually forced out of the language as an auxiliary, being replaced by the "heavier" *ter* 'to have'.

Notice now that (74) involves a step (in (74d)) where -*emos* (a form of *haver*) raises to [Spec, F]. Thus, for those dialects in which this form is still analyzed as an auxiliary, that is ruled out in the same way as (72b) (that is, *haver* is too weak to satisfy the phonological property of F). In the dialects discussed by Duarte and Matos (chapter 4, this volume), on the other hand, the future/conditional endings are reanalyzed as affixes. This implies that future/conditional forms are no different from any other tense form; in particular, they satisfy the properties of F on their own, just like any other finite verbal form.

To sum up, I have shown that mesoclisis (for those dialects that still have it) is simultaneously a case of enclisis (in that a verbal form is in [Spec, F]) and a case of proclisis (in that a second verbal form is in F, with the clitic left-adjoined to it). The reason that (in the relevant dialects) only the infinitive, rather than the complex auxiliary+infinitive, raises to [Spec, F] was tentatively traced to a lack of phonological heaviness of the old auxiliary *haver*, which precludes it from satisfying the phonological requirements of F by itself.

9.7 Structure preservation and the HMC

I will now address directly the two main problems standing in the way of the analysis of enclisis embodied in (56), with Infl movement (containing the verb) to [Spec, F]. The problems are the following:

(77) (i) Movement of Infl to [Spec, F] is non-structure-preserving (a head moves to a specifier position).

(ii) Movement of Infl to [Spec, F] violates HMC (Infl skips F).

9.7.1 Structure preservation

My solution to problem (77i), the non-structure-preserving nature of the movement, is based on proposals of Nunes (1995, 1998) concerning the targets of movement for feature checking, in particular how these are determined by economy conditions.

In the framework of Chomsky (1995b), movement of a minimal nonmaximal projection to a Spec position is blocked by his Uniformity Condition (Chomsky 1995b:253):

(78) A chain is uniform with regard to phrase structure.

How does (78) prevent Infl from moving to a Spec. Before moving, Infl is a minimal nonmaximal projection. But after movement (and assuming that the target of movement projects, say F), Infl is a minimal maximal projection, in violation of (78).

However, as pointed out by Nunes, the Uniformity Condition has certain undesirable effects that require ad hoc stipulations in Chomsky's (1995b) framework. For example, it rules out unmarked instances of head movement adjoining to another head, since the moving head is nonmaximal in its base position but maximal in the target position.[30] This is an odd state of affairs, since, as Nunes points out, adjunction to a head H (rather than substitution into [Spec, H]) is the unmarked configuration for feature checking, since the checking relation is established with features of H, not with the projection H' formed by H and its complement.

Nunes goes on to propose that considerations of economy should decide what the target of movement is. The most economical (and natural) movement is adjunction to a head H: not only the checking relation is with the features of H, but it also involves a shorter link than movement to [Spec, H]. Thus, covert movement and overt movement that pied-pipes a minimal nonmaximal category always take the optimal option. Maximal projections, however, cannot adjoin to a head H, under plausible assumptions about morphology: such a derivation crashes. Therefore, in order to obtain convergence, a maximal projection is allowed to take the less economical path, that of substitution into [Spec, H]. In sum, "movement to a head" is taken to be an "economy condition," which can be violated in order to obtain convergence (presumably always PF convergence).

In light of this, consider again the proposal that F is an enclitic (a morphophonological property) that must satisfy (60), repeated here as (79):

(79)   As an enclitic, F cannot be sentence initial.

Suppose that the derivation of a sentence with F does not include an "affective operator" that moves as a maximal projection to [Spec, F] (or an adverb that adjoins to F', see n. 26). This is the case of a simple sentence such as (80) (see section 9.5):

(80)   li o livro
       (I) read the book

Suppose now that Infl moves to F by adjunction, which is the optimal option. The relevant structure is given in (81):

(81)
```
                    F'
                   / \
                  F   IP
                 / \  ...
                I   F
               / \
              V   I
```

This structure, however, crashes at PF because (79) is not satisfied. Since "movement to a head" is an economy condition, a less optimal option can be taken, and Infl is allowed to move to [Spec, F], yielding (82), which satisfies (79):[31]

(82)

```
              FP
            ⁀
        I      F'
       ⁀      ⁀
      V  I  F    IP
```

9.7.2 HMC

I will now turn to (77ii). In the Minimalist framework, it is assumed that the HMC is not a valid principle of UG but rather reduces to a primitive locality condition (see n. 19). That condition is the Minimal Link Condition (MLC) of Chomsky (1993, 1995a, b). For concreteness, I assume here the version of Chomsky (1993) (the Shortest Movement Condition), incorporating the notion of *equidistance*, as follows (Chomsky 1995b:184):

(83) If α, β are in the same minimal domain, they are equidistant from γ.

Quoting from Chomsky (1995b:185), "In particular, two targets of movement are equidistant if they are in the same minimal domain." Under this interpretation of the MLC, both the head F and its Spec are equidistant from Infl, since they are in the same minimal domain, that of F (which includes its Spec). Movement of Infl to [Spec, F] skipping F is thus permitted under the MLC, which is the relevant principle of UG, rather than the HMC.

9.8 Toward a UG theory of (pronominal) clitics

I have suggested in section 9.4 that when both the clitic and the verb occur in F, the clitic targets F independently of Infl, rather than first attaching to Infl and being subsequently pied-piped to F within Infl. That is, I suggested that the structure of a sentence such as (41) is (42) rather (46) (all repeated here) as (84), (85), and (86):

(84) Muito whisky me tem *o capitão* servido!
      too much whisky to-me has the captain served!

(85)

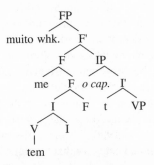

(86)

```
                        FP
                       /\
              muito whk.  F'
                         /\
                        F   IP
                       /\   /\
                      I  F o cap. I'
                     /\        /\
                   me  I      t  VP
                      /\
                     V   I
                     |
                    tem
```

In (85), Infl raises first to F, and the clitic subsequently left-adjoins to F containing Infl; in (86), V raises to Infl, then the clitic left-adjoins to Infl, and Infl (now containing V and the clitic) raises to F. I suggest not only that (85) is the right analysis for (84) on descriptive grounds but also that it is in fact the only possible one. More specifically, I propose that a structure like (86) is barred by a principle of UG. I will present here only a sketch of how to achieve this result.[32]

I will start by proposing the following descriptive statement:

(87)   Once a pronominal clitic adjoins to a head H, H is frozen, both "externally" and "internally."

Statement (87) has several consequences. First, if the clitic moves as a minimal nonmaximal category, as I assume here, this movement consists in a single step, (i.e., the clitic cannot excorporate and move farther up);[33] second, if both a clitic and the verb are adjoined to H, the verb cannot excorporate from H and move farther up (this is essentially Kayne's 1991 prohibition of adjoining the clitic to a trace); and third, the whole unit itself cannot move farther up, carrying the clitic along.

As a descriptive statement, (87) considerably restricts the options for analyzing clitics, and is thus welcome from the point of view of UG. However, as such, it is just that: a descriptive statement. One should thus pursue the goal of reducing (87) to more elementary theoretical primitives that could plausibly be assigned to UG. The rest of this chapter offers some tentative remarks in this direction.

Concerning excorporation, I do not have much to say here. I will simply assume, contra Roberts (1991), that such a process is not permitted, perhaps due to a prohibition against word-internal traces such as proposed by Baker (1988) (see also Kayne 1991, and the end of section 9.4). The thrust of my remarks here will be on how to rule out pied-piping of the clitic within another category, as in (86).

From a morphological point of view, pronominal clitics have a degree of freedom between that of independent words and that of bound morphemes, such as affixes (for relevant discussion see Zwicky and Pullum 1983; Zwicky 1985). Intuitively, they are bound morphemes, but less bound than affixes. This idea could be captured by requiring clitics to always attach to the outer layer of any given functional category that contains them, that is, to be dominated by the highest segment of that category (I call this segment the "edge" of a category, in a well-defined sense of this term in Graph Theory; see Reese 1996). From a different perspective, clitics cannot appear embedded in a functional category that contains them. This is explicitly formulated in the following principle, which I take to be a primitive of the morphological component of UG:[34]

(88)   *The Edge Principle*
A clitic occurs at the structural edge of a head H that contains it.

The principle in (88) has several consequences. First, a clitic is always the last element to adjoin to a functional category; otherwise it does not attach to the edge of that category. To see this, consider a simple case of adjunction of both V and a clitic to Infl. If the clitic attaches first, followed by the verb, there is a configuration that violates the Edge Principle:

(89)

$$
\begin{array}{c}
\text{I} \\
\diagup\diagdown \\
\text{cl} \quad \text{I}
\end{array}
\Rightarrow
\begin{array}{c}
\text{I} \\
\diagup\diagdown \\
\text{V} \quad \text{I} \\
\quad\ \diagup\diagdown \\
\quad\ \text{cl} \quad \text{I}
\end{array}
$$

The Edge Principle thus forces the verb to attach first, followed by the clitic, yielding (90):

(90)

$$
\begin{array}{c}
\text{I} \\
\diagup\diagdown \\
\text{V} \quad \text{I}
\end{array}
\Rightarrow
\begin{array}{c}
\text{I} \\
\diagup\diagdown \\
\text{cl} \quad \text{I} \\
\quad\ \diagup\diagdown \\
\quad\ \text{V} \quad \text{I}
\end{array}
$$

Thus, the Edge Principle, coupled with universal left-adjunction (see Kayne 1994), derives universal proclisis under heads, a result that was always stipulated in the literature on clitics (as it is in Kayne 1991).

Second, a derivation such as (86), with Infl pied-piping the clitic, is ruled out as well because the clitic, while contained in F, is not in its edge, violating (88). More generally, (88) will block further movement of a functional category that already contains a clitic, carrying along that clitic, because the clitic will not end up attached at the edge of the functional category that is the target of movement.

Third, there cannot be more than one clitic per functional category. Consider the structure derived by adjunction of two clitics to a functional head H, shown in (91):

(91)

$$
\begin{array}{c}
\text{H} \\
\diagup\diagdown \\
\text{cl} \quad \text{H} \\
\quad\ \diagup\diagdown \\
\quad\ \text{cl2} \quad \text{H}
\end{array}
$$

In (91), *cl2* violates (88). This means that sequences of clitics (in Romance and elsewhere) such as Sp. *no se lo daré* or Port. *não lho darei* 'I will not give it to him' cannot be analyzed as having the two clitics attached to the same functional head. I leave a discussion of this issue for future work.

The Edge Principle should be either a primitive of UG or made to follow from some still deeper principle. In any case, its place in the overall model appears to be at the interface of syntax and morphology. If correct, it considerably constrains the "space" of possible analysis for clitics, thus contributing toward the goal set at the outset of this chapter.

9.9 Conclusion

The central result of this chapter is that enclisis in EP and other Romance dialects (contemporary or Old) is a side effect of the movement of Infl containing the verb to [Spec, F], with the clitic itself left-adjoined to F. This is due to the fact that in these dialects F itself is clitic-like and needs to be licensed by an element in its Spec position. Movement of Infl to [Spec, F], although skipping F (and thus in violation of the descriptive HMC), is not in violation of the MLC of Chomsky (1993, 1995a, b) because the target of movement is in the same minimal domain as the head F. Movement of Infl to [Spec, F] is also permitted under the bare phrase structure theory of Chomsky (1995a, b), once one conceives of "adjunction to a head" as the optimal movement in terms of economy, thus violable, if necessary for PF convergence (Nunes 1995).

I also proposed a universal principle (the Edge Principle) that severely restricts the movement possibilities of heads containing clitics. Finally, the proposals in this chapter open up the possibility that enclisis in Romance (and perhaps elsewhere) is always the result of movement of the verb to the Spec position of the projection whose head contains the clitic. One other obvious case test is that of enclisis with infinitives. I leave this for future work.

Notes

An earlier and much shorter version of this chapter was presented at the Fifth Coloquio de Gramática Xenerativa, Universidade de A Coruña. I thank that audience for suggestions. I would also like to thank Juan Uriagereka for his comments on an earlier version and for many discussions we had on this topic. Any errors are mine.

1. Following a tradition initiated by Postal (1966) and first proposed for Romance in Raposo (1973). See also Corver and Delfitto (1993), Uriagereka (1995b) and Raposo (to appear b).

2. In main and independent clauses, the role of C under the "F" hypothesis is quite inactive, at least in the overt syntax. Since in this work I restrict myself to these clauses, I will often omit the CP layer from my structural representations. Concerning the representation of topics, see also Duarte (1987) and Raposo (1996).

3. In Contemporary Portuguese, only operators can target the FP projection (see Raposo 1994; Raposo and Uriagereka 1996). Besides wh-phrases, these are "emphatic" phrases such as muito vinho 'much wine' in (15); "emphatic" adverbs such as também 'also', já 'already', and sempre 'always'; "focus phrases" with an overt operator like só 'only', as in Só a Maria o João viu 'Only Mary did John see; and negative phrases. In Raposo and Uriagereka (1996), these are collectively called "Affective operators," adopting a term proposed in Klima (1964) for the first time. For related discussion, see Rouveret (1992), Martins (1994), and Barbosa (1996).

4. There is by now a substantial body of work reaching a similar conclusion (i.e., that preverbal subjects in pro-drop Romance languages occupy a left-peripheral topic position); see Belletti (1990), Barbosa (1995, 1996), and Raposo and Uriagereka (1996), among many others. Note that I am *not* claiming that a subject may not occupy [Spec, IP] in certain contexts (when it occurs to the right of an affective phrase); see my analysis of (22). In fact, the results of Raposo and Uriagereka (1996) entail that canonical preverbal subjects move to [Spec, I] before being topicalized (alternatively, if topics are base-generated, there is a *pro* subject in [Spec, I] coindexed with the topic; see Barbosa 1995, 1996, for a similar though not identical approach).

5. This analysis was first proposed in Benincà (1989).

6. Following Laka (1990), Martins calls the relevant head Σ, keeping the label "F" for Σ with a particular feature specification. This is irrelevant for my discussion here.

7. I give only the relevant part of the structure.

8. I abstract away from the final positions of *se* and the verb with respect to each other. What is important for the argument is that [Spec, I] contains either *se* or its trace, and is thus unavailable for another argument.

9. From a "performance" point of view, the judgment concerning (29) is sometimes felt as an odd semantic interpretation, as if *os manuscritos* 'the manuscripts' were the subject of a reflexive clause, thus resulting in a paradoxical reading. As will be seen later, reflexive subjects occur unproblematically in [Spec, I].

10. The agreeing DP of the SE construction may also be an operator in [Spec, F], as in (i):

(i) Muitos manuscritos se tinham mostrado ao Papa!
     many manuscripts SE had shown to the Pope

This is irrelevant for the purposes of this chapter. See Raposo and Uriagereka (1996) for discussion.

11. This implies that subjects of reflexive (and reciprocal) clauses are canonical; see Raposo and Uriagereka (1996, appendix 1) for discussion.

12. For a detailed discussion of inversion phenomena in EP, see Ambar (1992), who reaches conclusions similar to mine, modulo my FP versus her CP. Under the Minimalist framework, this conclusion raises a host of questions. For example, what forces the raising of the verb, why is it apparently optional (as in, e.g., (38) versus (39)), and so forth. I will not attempt to deal with these issues here.

13. Again this raises a host of questions from a Minimalist perspective: Why can clitics target both functional categories? In what circumstances do they target each of them? I will not attempt to deal with these questions here other than noting that in contemporary EP the clitic adjoins to the functional category where the verb ends up. This is not the case in older stages of the language (Martins 1994), nor in contemporary non-Standard dialects of EP (Barbosa 1996).

14. The sequence "initiated" by the clitic occurs immediately to the right of the licenser of the FP projection, which may be either a complementizer in C (as in (48)) or an element in [Spec, F]. See Martins (1994) for detailed discussion. There is only one exception to the claim that the clitic does not occur in the middle of a sequence of more than one scrambled elements, which involves the negative morpheme *não* 'not'. But interpolation with negation, as Martins shows, is of a "special" type, which very likely does not assimilate completely to the other cases.

15. The relevant material is underlined. Barbosa claims that such examples are grammatical in (nonstandard) northern dialects of EP. The example is somewhat acceptable (in a passive sense) in the standard dialect, although it would be judged "formal."

16. Note that the FP projection is clearly "activated" in (52), with an affective operator in its Spec (see n. 3). For me, (52) has the same degree of formal acceptability as (51), indi-

cating that their structures are similar in the relevant respects; the "unmarked" expression is (i), where the clitic is part of the conjunction:

(i)   só mais tarde o tirei da biblioteca e o trouxe para casa
      only later it took out of the library and it brought home

In (i) there is either F' or IP adjunction, with the clitic together with the verb in F or in Infl.

17. I thus disagree with Martins (1994), who claims that F (her Σ) has lost the capacity for being a landing site for clitics in EP. From my perspective, the reason that interpolation is (marginally) restricted to adverbs and negation in EP must await further research.

18. The sentence in (53a) is an idealized, constructed example, not an attested one.

19. In the framework of Principles and Parameters, this would be one case of the Head Movement Constraint (HMC); but see Chomsky (1995b) for the conclusion that the HMC is not a general principle of UG, and derives (where it applies) from more basic principles. Thus, movement of the clitic past Infl, targeting F, must be permitted, otherwise normal cases of interpolation are ruled out. This can be achieved under Chomsky's (1995b:297) Attract Principle if in the relevant cases the features that attract the clitic are instantiated in F, not in Infl. I will leave this issue aside here, hoping to pursue it in future work.

20. But see Uriagereka (1995b) and Barbosa (1996) for a different approach involving right-adjunction of the clitic to the functional category containing the verb (which is itself left-adjoined). In line with Kayne (1994), I assume that adjunction is universally leftward.

21. Cardinaletti and Roberts (to appear) invoke the category C for their account of enclisis, with the verb skipping past their Agr_1 (which would be somewhat equivalent to F in this framework) and targeting the higher C. Assuming that Agr_1 (or F) does not have a strong [V-] feature, this would be permitted. But under the "F" hypothesis, there is no apparent active role for C in main clauses of EP, and it is not clear how one could reduce movement of the verb to C in enclisis to a Last Resort operation triggered by some (morphological) property of the target (i.e., C) that would come into play precisely when F or Agr_1 (another category) does not have a filled Spec (cf. (16i)).

22. See n. 3. Note that in clauses without an affective phrase, the verb is itself focused. Given the nature of FP as an Operator projection in Contemporary Portuguese, this may explain why the verb is allowed to raise to [Spec, F].

23. One might conjecture that this is due to the fact that although being morphological, F lacks a phonological matrix.

24. In this respect, if the present view of F is on the right track, the analysis proposed in Barbosa (1996) or Uriagereka (1995b) for enclisis (with the verb left-adjoined and the clitic right-adjoined to the host functional projection) is not available here.

25. Neither topics nor preverbal subjects satisfy the licensing requirement for F, since there is enclisis in both cases:

(i)   a. esse livro, dei-*o* ao João.
         that book, (I) gave-it to John

      b. *esse livro, o dei ao João

(ii) a. o rapaz encontrou-a
         the boy met-her'

      b. *o rapaz a encontrou

Following Barbosa (1996), I assume that morpho-phonological constraints are satisfied within Intonational Phrases, and that major category boundaries map into Intonational Phrases. Since (preverbal) subjects and topics in EP are in a projection higher than FP (see n. 4), these phrases do not satisfy the enclitic property of F. Consequently, the verb has to move to [Spec, F], yielding enclisis when a clitic is present. For additional evidence that clitic properties are satisfied within categorial boundaries, see Raposo (to appear a).

26. Another possible way to satisfy (60) is by adjunction to F', since an element so adjoined will precede all segments of F as well. This may be the case in (i), if adverbs adjoin to X':

(i)   já (lhe) lemos esse livro
      already (to-him) we-read that book

27. Unlike Lema and Rivero (1991), I do not analyze movement of the infinitive as being to a higher C (which is presumably not even activated in this case), avoiding the problems they have with the HMC (see n. 21).

28. One question concerns the source of Case for the infinitive in (73), if it moves for Case reasons, as suggested in the text. One possibility is that [Spec, F] is a Case-position, that is, that F is a Case assigner (see Raposo and Uriagereka 1996; Cardinalletti and Roberts to appear, for discussion of this point).

29. But the FP system of EP still retains some remnants of this A-status in being able to assign nominative Case (see Raposo and Uriagereka 1996 for discussion).

30. Requiring Chomsky to propose a principle stipulating that at LF these configurations are ignored by the computational system and submitted to independent principles of word interpretation. Nunes also mentions that (78) rules out adjunction of formal features (FF) to a head, if the notion of projection is extended to FF.

31. This approach to the "non-structure-preserving" nature of Infl movement does not preclude adjunction of Infl to F' (see n. 26). Everything in this work is compatible with that option, if it is independently permitted by UG (see Chomsky 1995b, section 4.7.3, for discussion).

32. I address this issue in more detail in work in preparation. Also, the following account is intended for pronominal clitics. I have nothing to say about other types of clitics.

33. This has consequences for the analysis of clitic climbing, which I will not pursue. If the clitic moves as a maximal projection (Rivero 1986; Barbosa 1996) but has a last movement as an X^0 element, only this last step will "trigger" (79).

34. The principle in (80) can be seen as the structural "mirror-image" of the UG principle that constrains the occurrence of bound agreement morphemes at the rightmost edge of words.

References

Ambar, Manuela. 1992. *Para uma Sintaxe da Inversão Sujeito-Verbo em Português*. Lisbon: Colibri.

Baker, Mark. 1988. *Incorporation: A Theory of Grammatical Function Changing*. Chicago: University of Chicago Press.

Barbosa, Pilar. 1995. "Null Subjects." Ph.D. dissertation, MIT.

———. 1996. "Clitic Placement in European Portuguese and the Position of Subjects." In A. Halpern and A. Zwicky (eds.) *Second Position Clitics and Related Phenomena*. Chicago: University of Chicago Press.

Belletti, Adriana. 1990. *Generalized Verb Movement: Aspects of Verb Syntax*. Turin: Rosenberg and Sellier.

Benincà, P. 1989. "L'Ordine delle Parole nelle Lingue Romanze Medievali." Paper presented at the XIX Congreso Internacional de Linguística e Filoloxia Romanicas, Santiago de Compostela.

———. 1995. "Complement Clitics in Medieval Romance: The Tobler-Mussafia Law." In A. Battye and I. Roberts (eds.) *Clause Structure and Language Change* 325–344. Oxford: Oxford University Press.

Cardinaletti, Ana, and I. Roberts. To appear. "Clause-structure and X-second." In W. Chao, and G. Horrocks (eds.) *Levels of Representation*. Dordrecht: Foris.

Chomsky, Noam. 1993. "A Minimalist Program for Linguistic Theory." In K. Hale and S. J. Keyser (eds.) *The View from Building 20: Essays in Linguistics in Honor of Sylvain Bromberger*. Cambridge, Mass.: MIT Press. Reprinted in Chomsky 1995b.

————. 1995a. "Bare Phrase Structure." In Gert Webelhuth (ed.) *Government and Binding Theory and the Minimalist Program*, 383–439. Blackwell, Oxford and Cambridge.

————. 1995b. *The Minimalist Program*. Cambridge, Mass.: MIT Press.

Corver, Norbert, and Denis Delfitto. 1993. "Feature Asymmetry and the Nature of Pronoun Movement." OTS Publications, University of Utrecht.

Duarte, Maria Inês. 1987. "A Construção de Topicalização na Gramática do Português: Regência, Ligação e Condições sobre Movimento." Ph.D. dissertation, University of Lisbon.

Jaeggli, Osvaldo. 1986. "Three Issues in the Theory of Clitics." In H. Borer (ed.) *The Syntax of Pronominal Clitics*. New York: Academic Press.

Kayne, Richard. 1975. *French Syntax*. Cambridge, Mass.: MIT Press.

————. 1989. "Facets of Romance Past Participle Agreement." In P. Benincà (ed.) *Dialect Variation and the Theory of Grammar*. Dordrecht: Foris.

————. 1991. "Romance Clitics, Verb Movement, and PRO." *Linguistic Inquiry* 22: 647–686.

————. 1994. *The Antisymmetry of Syntax*. Cambridge, Mass.: MIT Press.

Klima, Edward. 1964. "Negation in English." In J. A. Fodor, and J. J. Katz (eds.) *The Structure of Language: Readings in the Philosophy of Language*. Englewood Cliffs, N.J.: Prentice Hall.

Laka, Itziar. 1990. "Negation in Syntax: On the Nature of Functional Categories and Projections." Ph.D. dissertation, MIT.

Lema, José, and Maria-Luisa Rivero. 1991. "Types of Verbal Movement in Old Spanish: Modals, Futures and Perfects." *Probus* 3: 237–278.

Martins, Ana-Maria. 1994. "Clíticos na História do Português." Ph.D. dissertation, University of Lisbon.

May, Robert. 1985. *Logical Form*. Cambridge, Mass.: MIT Press.

Nunes, Jairo. 1995. "The Copy Theory of Movement and Linearization of Chains in the Minimalist Program." Ph.D. dissertation, University of Maryland.

————. 1998. "Bare X'-Theory and Structures Formed by Movement." *Linguistic Inquiry* 27: 1.

Pollock, Jean-Yves. 1989. "Verb Movement, Universal Grammar and the Structure of IP." *Linguistic Inquiry* 20: 365–424.

Postal, Paul. 1966. "On So-Called 'Pronouns' in English." In F. Dinneen (ed.) *The Nineteenth Monograph on Languages and Linguistics*. Washington, D.C.: Georgetown University Press. Reprinted in D. A. Reibel and S. A. Schane (eds.) *Modern Studies in English: Readings in Transformational Grammar*. Englewood Cliffs, N.J.: Prentice-Hall, 1969.

Raposo, Eduardo. 1973. "Sobre a Forma *o* em Português." *Boletim de Filologia* 22: 361–415.

————. 1987. "Romance Infinitival Clauses and Case Theory." In Carol Neidle and R. A. Nuñez Cedeño (eds.) *Studies in Romance Languages*. 237–249. Dordrecht: Foris.

————. 1994. "Affective Operators and Clausal Structure in European Portuguese and European Spanish." Paper presented at the Twenty-fourth Linguistic Symposium on Romance Languages, UCLA/University of Southern California.

————. 1996. "Towards a Unification of Topic Constructions." Ms. University of California, Santa Barbara.

————. To appear a. "Directionality of Cliticization in European Portuguese: Left or Right?" In J. Franco, A. Landa, and J. Martín (eds.) *Grammatical Analyses in Basque and Romance Linguistics*. Amsterdam: John Benjamins.

————. To appear b. "Some Observations on the Pronominal System of Portuguese." In Z. Borras and J. Sola (eds.) *Catalan Working Papers in Linguistics*.

Raposo, Eduardo, and Juan Uriagereka. 1996. "Indefinite SE." *Natural Language and Linguistic Theory* 14: 749–810

Reese, Michael S. 1996. "Essential Mathematics for the Romance Linguist." M.A. thesis, University of California, Santa Barbara.

Rivero, Maria-Luisa. 1986. "Parameters in the Typology of Clitics in Romance and Old Spanish." *Language* 62: 774–807.

Roberts, Ian. 1991. Excorporation and Minimality. *Linguistic Inquiry* 22: 209–218.

Rouveret, Alain. 1992. "Clitic Placement, Focus and the Wackernagel Position in European Portuguese." Ms., Université de Paris-8.

Sola, Dino. 1997. "A Mudança de TER e HAVER + Particípio Passado na História da Língua Portuguesa." M.A. thesis, University of California, Santa Barbara.

————. In preparation. Ph.D. dissertation, UCSB.

Sportiche, D. 1992. "Clitic Constructions." Ms., UCLA.

Torres-Moraes, Maria-Aparecida. 1995. "Do Português Clássico ao Português Europeu Moderno:Um estudo da Cliticização e do Movimento do Verbo." Ph.D. dissertation, Unicamp.

Uriagereka, Juan. 1995a. "An F Position in Western Romance." In K. Kiss (ed.) *Discourse Configurational Languages*. New York: Oxford University Press.

————. 1995b. "Aspects of the Syntax of Clitic Placement in Western Romance." *Linguistic Inquiry* 26: 79–123.

Wanner, Dieter. 1991. "The Tobler-Moussafia Law in Old Spanish." In Héctor Campos and Fernando Martínez-Gil (eds.) *Current Studies in Spanish Linguistics*. Washington, D.C.: Georgetown University Press.

Zwicky, Arnold M. 1985. "Clitics and Particles." *Language* 61: 283–305.

Zwicky, Arnold, and Geoffrey K. Pullum. 1983. "Cliticization vs. Inflection: English *N'T*." *Language* 59: 502–513.

Index

302   INDEX